WILSON
PHILOLOGICAL LECTURES
ON
SANSKRIT AND THE DERIVED LANGUAGES
DELIVERED IN 1877

WILSON PHILOLOGICAL LECTURES

ON

SANSKRIT AND THE DERIVED LANGUAGES

DELIVERED IN 1877

BY

SIR R. G. BHANDARKAR, K.C.I.E. LL.D., Ph. D.,

MEMBER OF THE FRENCH INSTITUTE, & C., &.C

CARRIED THOUGH THE PRESS

BY

SHRIDHAR R. BHANDARKAR, M.A.,

Professor of Sanskrit, Elphinstone College

GYAN

Published by

GYAN

Gyan Publishing House
5, Ansari Road
Daryaganj, New Delhi-110002
Phone: 011-47034999, 9811692060
E-mail: books@gyanbooks.com

Distribution Network
gyanbooks.com
India, USA, Canada, UK, Australia, France

ISBN : 978-81-212-4224-0 (HB)
First Published, 1914

2nd Impression 2020

Printed at: Gyan Press, Delhi.

Wilson Philological Lectures on
Sanskrit and the Derived Languages
Delivered in 1877
Author: R. G. Bhandarkar

Wilson Philological Lectures

ON

SANSKRIT AND THE DERIVED LANGUAGES

DELIVERED IN 1877

BY

Sir R. G. BHANDARKAR, K.C.I.E., LL.D., Ph. D.,

Member of the French Institute, &c., &c

CARRIED THROUGH THE PRESS

BY

SHRIDHAR R. BHANDARKAR, M.A.,

Professor of Sanskrit, Elphinstone College.

BOMBAY:

Mrs. RADHABAI ATMARAM SAGOON.

1914,

PREFACE.

I was appointed Wilson Philological Lecturer in 1877 and was thus the first lecturer under the Endowment. My subject was the Sanskrit and the Prâkṛit Languages derived from it. I understood the word Prâkṛit in a comprehensive sense, so as to include modern Vernaculars of Northern India also; and thus delivered a course of seven lectures on Sanskrit in its several forms, the Pâli and the Dialects of the period, the Prâkṛits and the Apabhraṃs'a, Phonology of the Vernaculars, Remnants of the older Grammatical Forms in the Vernaculars, New Grammatical Formations to supply the place of the forms that had disappeared and General Questions as to the relation between these several languages. The method I followed is strictly historical, tracing the modern vernaculars from the original Sanskrit through all the different stages of development of which we have evidence and assigning the different transformations to their causes, natural or physical, racial, and historical. These lectures, with the exception of the fifth and the sixth, were thoroughly revised afterwards and the first two and the seventh were published in Vol. XVI of the Journal, B. B. R. A. S., between the years 1883 and 1885; while the third and the fourth were published between 1887 and 1889. The other two lectures remained in manuscript for a long time, until I finished in 1911 my book on "Vaiṣṇavism, Śaivism etc." which was written for the series of Encyclopedia of Indo-Aryan Research, which is being published at Strassburg by Karl J. Trübner. These have now been revised and I publish them for the first time along with a reprint of the other five lectures in the present volume. The delay in the publication has been due to my having had to attend to more urgent work, such as the preparation of a translation of the Vâyu Purâṇa for the "Sacred Books of the East," which had afterwards to be given up, the preparation of my Early History of the Dekkan and the search for Sanskrit Manuscripts and writing my several reports on them.

As, since 1908, my eye-sight has been greatly impaired and I am unable to read matter printed in ordinary type or an ordinary manuscript, I have had to depend on Readers and Amanuenses. The work on "Vaiṣṇavism, Śaivism, etc." was written under these conditions, but the publication of the present volume was undertaken by my eldest son, Professor Shridhar Ramkrishṇa Bhandarkar, who has been associated with me in a good deal of my literary work. The lectures were all carried through the press by him at the sacrifice of a good deal of time and trouble.

I regret to find some misprints in the present volume, but one-half of them occur in the fifth and the sixth lectures, which had to be set up from manuscript. There are comparatively few instances in the reprints of the other five lectures.

Sangam, Poona,
22nd June 1914.

R. G. BHANDARKAR.

ABBREVIATIONS.

Abl.=Ablative.
Absol.=Absolutive.
Acc.=Accusative.
Ait.=Aitareya.
Ap., Apabhr., Apbhr., Apbr. =Apabhraṃśa.
Ath. Pr.=Âtharvaṇ-Prâtiśâkhya.
Âtm.=Âtmanepada.
B.=Bangâlî.
Brâhm.=Brâhmaṇa.
Chit.=Chitpâvnî.
Corp. Insc. Ind.=Corpus Inscriptionum Indicarum.
Dat.=Dative.
Dh.=Dhauli.
Dial.=Dialect.
Fem.=Feminine.
G., Guj.=Gujarâtî.
Gen.=Genitive.
Goan.=Goanese.
H.=Hindî.
Imper.=Imperative.
Ind. St.=Indische Studien.
Instr.=Instrumental.
Intr.=Intransitive.
Jñân.=Jñâneśvarî.
Karh.=Karhâḍâ.
Kh.=Khalsi.
Loc.=Locative.
M., Mar.=Marâṭhî.
Mah., Mahr.=Mahârâshṭrî.
Mâl.=Mâlvaṇî.
Masc.=Masculine.
Mod.=Modern.
Neut.=Neuter.
Nom.=Nominative.
O.=Oriyâ.
Obl.=Oblique.
P.=Panjâbî.
Pâṇ.=Pâṇini.
Parasm.=Parasmaipada.
Part.=Participle.
Per., Pers.=Person.
Pl.=Plural.
Pot.=Potential.
P. p. p.=Past Passive Participle.
Pr.=Prâkṛit.
Pres.=Present.
PÛRVA.=Pûrvapakshin.
Rv.=Rigveda.
S.=Sindhî.
Saṃh.=Saṃhitâ.
Śat.=Śatapatha.
Śaur.=Śaurasenî.
SID.=Siddhântin.
Sing.=Singular.
Sk.=Sanskrit.
St.=Standard.
Tad.=Tadbhava.
Tait.=Taittirîya.
Term.=Termination.
Tr.=Transitive.
Tulasi.=Tulasidâs.
Vâj. Pr.=Vâjasaneyi Prâtiśâkhya.
Voc.=Vocative.

Errata.

Page.	Line.	Incorrect.	Correct.
18	2 from bottom	अंतिक्रामाम:	अतिक्रामाम:
32	7 from bottom	वुत्त	वुत्ता
69	14	तनाप	मनाप
74	2 from bottom	नह नख	नह or नख
136	19	कुच्छा	कुच्छी
,,	23	कुठें	कुठ
139	2	*til*	*til̤*
145	4 from bottom	पुत्तवह	पुत्तवहु
148	21	M.	H.
151	10	पतोहू	पतोहु
153	17	बहुक्खा	बुहुक्खा
,,	18	बभुक्षा	बुभुक्षा
157	7 from bottom	नइ or ,	नइ or नय,
170	6	संकोक	संकोच
174	15	शामलक	श्यामलक
195	4	वत	वत्स
207	6	हो	हौं
209	11	आम्हचिया काजाचे निपाडें	आम्हचिया काजाचेनि पाडें.
213	10	G	O
,,	13	करा कसेत	करो करोत
214	17	अवघ	अवघ
223	4	ज्ञानोदर्यी	ज्ञानोदयीं

Page.	Line.	Incorrect.	Correct.
226	13 from bottom	कारण्यें	कारुण्यें
"	1 from bottom		After "performed" add "where there are the six philosophies"
230	19	me, and by	me, by
233	12 from bottom	Me.	M.
237	18	माणसाने	माणसोनें
240	1	of	Oh
242	2	इ.	ई
"	18	इ	ई
"	19	ई	इ or ई
246	10	एखावे, सेखावे	एखानें, सेखानें
250	19	obl.	abl.
253	8	उन्हाळेनि तापे	उन्हाळेनि जो न तापे
"	10	वासि ग्रे	वासि पे
258	12 from bottom	मोहिक है	मोहि कहै
260	10	Râmayan	Râmainî
"	14 from bottom	क	कअ
276	12	घ्	छ्
285	14 from bottom	Barùs	Barús

LECTURE I.

General Laws guiding the Development of Language; the different Stages in the Development of Sanskrit.

THE occasion that brings us here together to-day is the first of its kind in the history of this University. Hitherto the University of Bombay has been merely an Examining Board. But this day witnesses the beginning of an attempt to discharge another and a more important function of such an institution. The main idea of a University is that it is a body of men devoted to learning, and engaged in acquiring knowledge and disseminating it. A country that has no such bodies of men occupies but a low position in the intellectual scale of the world, and contributes little to the general advancement of mankind in knowledge. But a devotion to learning implies sacrifice of worldly interests, and the poverty of learned men has become proverbial. To enable persons, therefore, to apply themselves to the pursuit of knowledge with undivided attention, there exist in connection with such institutions certain appointments tenable for life called professorships or fellowships, endowed by the enlightened liberality of private individuals or of the goverment of the country.

India and the Bombay University are no exception to the general rule. In other times learning flourished in the country under the fostering care of its innumerable princes and chiefs, as well as rich merchants. Though in the words of the poet, Śrî and Sarasvatî are, in a sense, constantly hostile to each other, it is Śrî alone at all times and in all countries that can support Sarasvatî, and enable her to live and grow. Hence it is impossible that the Bombay University should rise to the dignity of a seat of learning without such a provision as is found necessary in more advanced countries. India cannot take her place among the intellectual nations of the West, and compete with them in the advancement of knowledge unless her Universities discharge their proper function, unless we have professorships in connection with them for the cultivation of science, philosophy, history and philology.

But we may be told that an Indian does not care for knowledge for its own sake, and it is only as a means of worldly advancement that he enters the University at all, and, as soon as he takes his degree, flings away his books, and no more troubles himself with the several branches of knowledge to which he was introduced while within the walls of his college. The reproach is true, as well as untrue. It is true if it is meant that since the first school or college was opened by our Government we have had very few or none among us who have devoted themselves to the pursuit of knowledge. But if what it is intended to assert is that a love of knowledge or learning and an unselfish devotion to it are foreign to the nature of a Hindu, it is altogether untrue. Those ponderous tomes which adorn the library of the Sanskrit student and those innumerable *pustakas* in the Sarasvatî Bhâṇḍâras scattered throughout the country tell a different tale. But in this, as in other matters, the circumstances in which our virtues have grown up and are exercised are not the circumstances in which we are expected to display them, and fail to do so. Love of learning is ingrained in the very nature of the Hindu, but the legitimate object of this feeling is Sanskrit literature. A knowledge of English and of English literature and philosophy is, in the first instance, sought for only for its practical benefits. A Hindu would not send his son to an English School if he could help it. A very powerful motive for the pursuit of learning, the respect of the society in which one lives, is also wanting in the case of the so-called educated Indian. A Shâstrî or Pandit is esteemed and treated with respect and consideration by his countrymen; the English-knowing Indian may be feared if he holds some Government appointment, but if none, he enjoys no consideration. The very word *vidvân* or 'learned' is grudged him by the orthodox Hindu. In one branch of learning, however, *viz.* Sanskrit, an English-knowing Indian may meet with appreciation and esteem at the hands of the learned in Europe. That is a subject in which he may successfully compete with his European brother, and in which he has peculiar advantages which the latter does not possess. Among his own countrymen he will find sympathy only if he has studied Sanskrit exactly in the old way, but even in this case his heterodoxy, which is the result of his English education, would stand in the way. But there are indications that a more sympathising and appreciating body of men is growing about us, and the circle will go on widening as education advances. In this, as in other matters, there are hopes that our countrymen will, in the course of time, chiefly through the agency of Government education, adapt themselves to their altered circumstances; and the Hindu's inherent love of learning will gradually extend and engraft itself on the branches of knowledge to which he has been newly introduced by the European.

But encouragement and support are essentially needed; and, taught by our ancient tradition, we naturally look up for these, in the first instance, to our Government. Hitherto it has confined its endeavours to the education of its subjects, a thing which was never before done by any Indian prince, and for which it has the strongest claims on the gratitude of the Indians. But what Indian princes have all along done, *viz.*, the extension of support and patronage to men of learning, and thus enabling them to prosecute their studies, has not yet attracted the attention of our Government, probably because they thought the time had not come for it. Next, it is the duty of those of our countrymen, who enjoy princely fortunes, to encourage the growth and advancement of learning among their countrymen. Now the best and most effectual way, in which learning can thus be encouraged and patronized by all who have the means, is by founding University professorships to be held for life. A beginning, however, has been made, and for it we are indebted to the friends of the late Rev. Dr. Wilson, and to the good old Doctor himself. For, when his friends raised up the sum and expressed to him their intention to present it to him, he declined to receive it unconditionally, and, contenting himself with only a life interest in it, proposed that they should hand it over to the University, and found a philological lectureship. It is in virtue of the advice he thus gave that we meet here to-day. I only regret that the Syndicate was not able to secure the services of an abler man, and that the duty of inaugurating the Wilson Lectureship, and, I may say, the new phase on which the University is entering, has devolved on me.

The subject on which the lectures are to be delivered this year is the Sanskrit, and the Prâkṛit languages derived from it. Sanskrit is the language of the religion, law, philosophy, and poetry of the Hindus; and all their ancient and most revered books on these subjects are written in that language. Even at the present day the language we use in our daily prayers and in the performance of our various religious rites is Sanskrit; learned men carry on their disputations in Sanskrit, and now and then we meet with new poems written in that language. Prâkṛit is a general name given to certain dialects in which we find some old books written; and in ordinary Hindu usage the term is extended to the vernaculars we speak. Marâṭhî, Gujarâtî, and the various other idioms spoken in Northern India are Prâkṛits. The wording of the subject as laid down in the calendar implies that Sanskrit is the more primitive of these, and that the Prâkṛits are derived from it. Our business, therefore, is to trace the history of

Sanskrit, to observe how from the very earliest form in which it is presented to us in the existing literature of the language, it gradually developed or was corrupted into the modern vernaculars. The Sanskrit which we know of as such is not now the spoken language of any part of India or of the world. It is simply preserved in books, and is used by the learned. But if the Marâṭhî, Gujarâtî, and the rest show unmistakable signs of having been derived from this language, it must have been at one time spoken generally by our ancestors; and in being handed down from generation to generation it has undergone various modifications and changes, until we have now come to speak it as we do. But of this more hereafter.

India may justly claim to be the original home of scientific philology. In one of the most ancient Sanskrit books, the Saṃhitâ of the Black Yajurveda, there are distinct indications of the dawn of linguistic study.[1] The Brâhmaṇas of the Vedas, which rank next to the Saṃhitâs, and even the Taittirîya Saṃhitâ itself, the composition of which differs in no particular from its Brâhmaṇa, are full of etymological explanations of words, though often they are fanciful.[2] One Áchârya followed another, and they all carefully observed the facts of their language, and laid down the laws they could discover. They studied and compared the significations and forms of words, observed what was common to them, separated the constant element from that which was variable, noticed the several changes that words undergo in different circumstances, and by such a process of philological analysis completed a system of grammar and etymology. In the Nirukta, Yâska, whose exact date we do not know, but who must have flourished several centuries before Christ, lays down correct principles of the derivation of words. The last of the grammarian Áchâryas were Pâṇini, Kâtyâyana, and Patañjali. The Prâkṛit dialects which

---

1. वाग्वै पराच्यव्याकृतावदत्ते देवा इन्द्रमब्रुवन्निमां नो वाचं व्याकुर्विति सोऽब्रवीद्वरं वृणै मह्यं चैवैष वायवे च सह गृह्याता इति तस्मादैन्द्रवायवः सह गृह्यते तामिन्द्रो मध्यतोऽवक्रम्य व्याकरोत्तस्मादियं व्याकृता वागुद्यते. Speech was once inarticulate and undistinguished (into its parts). Then the gods said to Indra, 'Distinguish our speech into parts.' He said, 'I will ask a gift of you, let Soma be poured into one cup for me and Vâyu together.' Hence Soma is poured into one cup for Indra and Vâyu together. Then Indra going into its midst distinguished it. Hence distinct speech is now spoken. Tait. Saṃh., VI. 4, 7.

2. The Ait. Brâhm. gives the etymology of प्रैष (III. 9), of मानुष (III. 23), of जाया (VII. 13); the Tait. Saṃh., of रुद्र (I. 5. 1), of वृत्र (II. 4, 1, and II. 5, 2); the Tait. Brâhm., of अश्व (I. 1, 5), of नक्षत्र (II. 7, 18), &c., &c.

sprang from Sanskrit were next made the subject of observation and analysis. The laws of phonetic change or decay in accordance with which Sanskrit words become Prâkṛit were discovered and laid down. The Sanskrit and non-Sanskrit elements in those languages were distinguished from each other. This branch of philology also was worked up by a number of men, though the writings of one or two only have come down to us.

In this condition Sanskrit philology passed into the hands of Europeans. The discovery of Sanskrit and the Indian grammatical system at the close of the last* century led to a total revolution in the philological ideas of Europeans. Before this time there was hardly a scientific treatment of linguistic facts, etymological analysis was scarcely known, and philological speculation had not emancipated itself from the trammels of religion. The Jews were the chosen people of God, and hence their language, the Hebrew, was the most original of all languages, and all others were derived from it. This was the belief of European scholars, as that of the orthodox Pandit at the present day is that Sanskrit is the primitive language, and all others are corruptions of it; though, however, the Pandit has an excuse in the fact that the languages he generally hears spoken about him have really sprung from Sanskrit. But several circumstances had about this time prepared Europe for independent thought in philology, and Sanskrit supplied the principles upon which it should be conducted and determined the current in which it should run. The languages of Europe, ancient and modern, were compared with Sanskrit and with each other. This led to comparative philology and the classification of languages, and a comparison of the words and forms in the different languages led scholars into the secrets of the growth of human speech, and the science of language was added to the list of existing branches of knowledge. The progress made within about fifty years is marvellous, and affords a striking instance of the intellectual activity of the Europeans. In the cultivation of philology and the elaboration of this new science the Germans, of all other nations, have been most prominent, and have done by far the greater portion of the work. The more limited field of Prâkṛit philology with which we are here concerned has not been left uncultivated. Pâli, the earliest of the Prâkṛit dialects, is almost as much studied in Europe as Sanskrit. We have editions of Pâli texts by Turnour, a

*18th.

Ceylon Civilian, and a Danish scholar, Fausböll; and of a Native Grammar by Kachchâyana, by M. Senart, a Frenchman; an original treatise on this subject by Clough, and a very useful Dictionary by the late lamented Professor Childers.[3] The derivation of the language from Sanskrit forms the subject of an essay by the great French scholar, M. Burnouf, and the equally great German scholar, Professor Lassen. There are notices of the Prâkṛit dialects in one of Colebrooke's essays and in the preface to Professor Wilson's Hindu Theatre. Lassen also wrote a book entitled Institutiones Linguæ Pracraticæ, based upon the grammatical works of native writers, and upon the Prâkṛit passages occurring in the Sanskrit dramatic plays. Professor Weber, whose industry and comprehensive grasp are admirable, has published an elaborate analysis of the language and contents of a Jaina religious work in Prâkṛit entitled the Bhagavatî, and of the language of a collection of Prâkṛit songs by Hâla, together with an edition and translation of the work. Dr. Cowell has brought out a nice edition of the Prâkṛita-Prakâs'a by Vararuchi; and Dr. Muir, whose works are so valuable to the student, devotes a large portion of his second volume of the "Sanskrit Texts" to Prâkṛit philology, in which he gives his own views and a summary of those of other scholars. In Ceylon, Mr. D'Alwis has published a work on the Pâli, and in India an edition of the Prâkṛit Grammar of Kramadîs'vara has been published in the Bibliotheca Indica, and of that of Hemachandra in Bombay by a Jaina priest with the assistance of a Śâstrî[4]. The modern vernaculars have not yet succeeded in attracting the attention of the learned in Europe. Essays on some points of vernacular philology by Professor Hoernle, of Jayanarayan's College, Benares, have appeared in the Journal of the Bengal Asiatic Society. But the most important work on this subject that has yet appeared is Mr. Beames's Comparative Grammar of the Modern Aryan Languages. Two volumes have been published, and the third and last is expected.[5] Mr. Beames has brought his subject down to the pronoun; and the forthcoming volume will treat of the verb. Dr. Trump in his valuable Grammar of the Sindhî language compares the grammatical forms

3. This lecture was written in 1877 and revised in 1878. It will be necessary for the reader to remember this in going over this short sketch. Many and valuable additions to Pâli publications have been made since then, especially by the Pâli Text Society.

4. Since this was written Dr. Pischel's edition of Hemachandra's Prakrit Grammar and his elaborate contribution to the Grundriss der Arischen Philologie have been published, besides several other minor works.

5. Since published.

existing in the several vernaculars, and recent grammarians of Gujarâtî and Marâṭhî have made attempts in some cases to trace the grammar of these languages from the Sanskrit through the Prâkṛit. A Gujarâtî Śâstrî, named Vrajalâl, has written a useful little tract on the history of his vernacular.[6] But upon the whole, it must be acknowledged that vernacular philology is still in a state of infancy, and a great deal of what has been written is unsatisfactory.

Before I proceed to the subject in hand, it is necessary that I should trace some of the laws of the development and growth of language, as I shall have occasion to refer to them frequently in the course of these lectures. Suppose a person wishes to express the idea *in a village*, and the only means at his command are the roots and independent words in a language such as the Sanskrit. Now the word which expresses *a village* is ग्राम, and another which signifies the *interior* is मध्य. By joining the two together in such an expression as ग्राममध्य he conveys the idea the *interior of*, or *in, a village*. Now this word मध्य is pronounced मज्झ or मद्ध by persons who have either not been taught to pronounce it properly or are not sufficiently careful to do so. This again is reduced to माझ or माध and thence to माह or मह, and ultimately to मा or मे. In this manner ग्राममध्य becomes गाममा or गाममे, which, as you know, are the forms of the Gujarâtî, Sindhî, and Hindî locative. In this condition its origin is forgotten by the speakers, and becomes simply a termination signifying *in the interior*. Again, if a man wants to speak of *one who makes a pot* and has not got a word to express the idea, he naturally puts together the words कुम्भ *pot* and कार *maker*, and uses the compound कुम्भकार. After a time, by faulty pronunciation, the क् goes out and the word is reduced to कुम्भार. In the same way, as before, the persons who use the word कुम्भार have no consciousness that they are putting together two words, one of which means a *pot* and the other *maker*; but the syllable आर becomes with them a simple termination which signifies the doer of the thing expressed by the base. We thus see that these two very general terminations were originally independent words, and that in the course of time they lost that character. If you examine those forms which constitute the declensions and conjugations of any language you may happen to know you will find that these also have originated in the same way. When, our remote ancestors wished to say *I now do*, they put together कृ *do*, नु

6. Hoernle's Comparative Grammar of the Gaudian Languages, Kellogg's Hindi Grammar, Grierson's Linguistic Survey of India have, among others, been published since then.

now, and मि *I*, and said कृनुमि, afterwards changed for the sake of euphony to कृणोमि. In the same way कृणोति means *do now he* कृणुतस् *do now he* (and) *thou*, स् being a corruption of सि a pronoun signifying *thou*, and कृणोषि *do now thou*. Or they expressed present time by using a pronoun equivalent to *here* or *this* and said बोधति *know here he*, the अ being the same as that we find in the forms अनेन, अस्मै, अस्मात्, &c. and signifying something that is near. In this manner we are able to trace the original signification of a good many of these forms, but since after their invention, they are more or less corrupted, it becomes a difficult matter to do so in all cases. Still, we know enough to be able to lay it down as certain that this is the mode in which all our grammatical forms have originated. When a language is in that condition in which grammatical relation is expressed by such compounds consciously formed, and both parts of the compound can be used independently, it is said to be in the analytic stage. The change of मह्य to मा or मे, or of कार to आर, or of तसि to तस् or तः is what is called phonetic decay. Though this is usually spoken of in censure as corruption, it is the means by which a language leaves the analytic stage and develops. The words forming the compound grow together, both being altered in the process, and the original sense of the latter is forgotten. It is this circumstance that renders phonetic change possible, for, if those who speak the language always used the two *words* in the compound with a conscious desire to express their joint sense, such a corruption would not take place. Phonetic decay reduces the latter portion to a mere termination, and thus a language arrives at what is called the synthetic stage. All the dead Aryan languages, and most of the living ones also, are in the synthetic condition, while the Chinese is said to be in the analytic stage.

Phonetic decay or corruption is a process that is constantly going on in a living language. At some stages of its history it is very rapid and at others slow. It sometimes wholly transforms words. Its causes are deeply ingrained in human nature itself. Language is not the end and aim of human life; it is simply an instrument of communicating thought, and the matter of thought is always more important than the expression. The utterance of a word implies an effort. We have to force the breath through the windpipe, check or compress it at different points in its passage through the mouth, and then let it off. The *glottis* or the opening of the windpipe, and the tongue and the various parts of the mouth are our organs of speech, and an innumerable variety of sounds may be produced by their means. In pronouncing certain letters the glottis must be stretched or expanded, while in the case of others it is contracted, which is its more natural condition. The breath which comes out when it is expanded is called *s'vâsa* or simple unintonated breath by the old Indian Philologists, but when the glottis is contracted and the breath is intonated by the vibration of the vocal chords, it becomes what is called *nâda, i. e.,* tone or intonated breath. Simple breath is the material cause of the hard consonants, and the intonated breath of the soft, and of the vowels. When *nâda* is forced out and allowed to pass away without being obstructed we pronounce vowels, and when both *s'vâsa* and *nâda* are obstructed at different parts of the mouth, the sounds that are formed are consonantal. Hence a consonant cannot be pronounced by itself; it is only when the touching organs are separated and the air allowed to pass through any one of the vowel positions, that the sound is produced. When the intonated breath is let off through the rounded lips, it forms उ, and with the lower lip a little further off, ओ; while if the lips completely touch each other, and the breath is thus obstructed in its passage, we have ब् which, with a greater force of respiration becomes भ्, and when it is partly sent into the nose, it assumes the form of म्. If the *s'vâsa* is in the same condition as *nâda* when it forms ब् and भ् we have प् and फ्. When these two kinds of breath are shut up by the tip of the tongue forming a complete contact with the root of the upper teeth, we have त्, थ्, द्, ध्, and न्. When the contact is effected higher up and the forepart of the tongue is made into a curve, we have ट्, ठ्, ड्, ढ्, and ण्. If the middle of the tongue is brought near the palate, *nâda* passing through the intervening space forms the vowel इ; and when the tongue is a little further off and the mouth more open, we have ए; while if there is complete contact, the two kinds of breath give us च्, छ्, ज्, झ्, and ञ् as before. When the root of the tongue touches the lower skirt of the palate, we have similarly क्, ख्, ग्, घ्, and ङ्. If the intonated breath is allowed to pass away when the mouth is in its natural position with the lips open we have the vowel अ, and with greater force of breath, the aspirate ह्. The vowel portion of ऋ and ऌ differs from अ in the whole lower part of the mouth being brought closer to the upper in pronouncing it, while in pronouncing आ the two parts of the mouth are more widely apart; so that the vowel sound involved in ऋ is the closest, आ, the most open. The diphthongs ऐ and औ are अ+इ and अ+उ pronounced hastily. In pronouncing the semi-vowels the organs are brought very close to each other, but do not form a complete contact; so that the breath is compressed and not shut up. Still, like the mutes, they cannot be pronounced without separating the organs. We pronounce व् when we bring the two lips and the ends of the upper teeth into close proximity, and it thus corresponds to the vowel उ; for य् the position is the same as that for इ, the proximity only being greater; while ल् is formed a little above the dental position by emitting the breath by the sides of the tip of the tongue, and र् a little below the cerebral. The sibilants श्, ष्, and स् are continuous sounds made by letting off the *s'vâsa* or simple breath with the same force as in the case of the hard aspirates and through the space between the middle of the tongue and the palatal, cerebral, and dental or dento-palatal positions brought as near to each other as in pronouncing vowels.

You will thus see how minute and laborious these operations are. The difficulty is increased when we have to pronounce two or more consonants together. We have first to put the organs of speech into one position, and immediately afterwards into another, without leaving the first. Accurate pronunciation therefore requires great effort, and since, according to an observation of Locke, labour for labour's sake is against nature, the tendency always exists of making as little effort as is consistent with the necessity of making oneself understood. Hence मुख is transformed to मुह *i. e.* only the quantity of breath necessary to pronounce ख is let off, and the effort of forming a complete and close contact is saved; कदलकम् become कअलअम्, and thence केळं and केळें, where also you will see that the contact is avoided; अर्पं becomes अप्प, in which case we find that the effort involved in the change from one position of the vocal organs to another is economized, though the pressure which the organs exert upon each other in the pronunciation of a conjunct continues the same, *i. e.* we have a conjunct as before, but the two members are assimilated. This is further changed to आप in which the pressure is avoided, but the shortening of the time which this would involve is obviated by lengthening the preceding vowel. This tendency to phonetic decay is so powerful that if not counteracted it would in the short space of a few generations render a language entirely unintelligible to its former speakers. Children, in their first essays at speech, often mispronounce words, and if they were left to themselves, the language of a country would undergo very great transformation in a short time. But at home and in schools they are taught to speak the language of their parents correctly, and this result is averted. Education, therefore, is an agency which arrests the progress of decay. Another check is afforded by the necessity of making oneself intelligible. If a man is careless about his language he will not be understood. He has therefore necessarily to endeavour to speak as other people do. The feeling of society is also arrayed against the corruption of a language. The speech which does not approach the received standard is branded as vulgar. The tendency to corruption is greatly diminished when a language comes to have a literature. Some races are very careful about their speech, and preserve it in a comparatively pure condition; there are others which corrupt it greatly. But even in the case of the former, accidents in its history may transform the idiom considerably. If one race comes in contact with another, and gives it its language, it is sure to be greatly corrupted. The alien race cannot catch the pronunciation properly, or its vocal organs may be naturally so constituted or its previous vocal habits may be of such a nature as to render the sounds of the language difficult or impossible to be imitated. If there were no schools and colleges for teaching English to us, we should corrupt the language of our rulers so greatly as to render ourselves perfectly unintelligible to them. The native sentry's challenge हुकुम् डर् for "who comes there" would be a puzzle to the scientific philologist.

The grammatical terminations which are oftener used than any particular words suffer the most by this process of decay, and after a time they are confused with each other or dropped away. When a language is reduced to this condition, it has to fall back upon the expedient with which it started, and tack on certain words or particles to its nouns and verbs to express the relations which the old terminations denoted, and thus the analytic state returns. But the old process goes on again, and these words in their turn assume the character of terminations. Sometimes along with a case-form there exists in the language another expression conveying the same sense. When the former goes out of use the latter takes its place, or sometimes the latter drives out the former. The modern vernaculars have had to resort to this process of reconstruction in a great measure, and, as in the older languages, it has already become difficult in several cases to trace the origin of the forms. For instance, in Sanskrit the termination which expresses future time is स्य, and when it is applied to the root दा *to give*, we have दास्यति *he will give*. This स्य is very likely a compound of the root अस् *to be* and या *to go*, so that the contrivance the early Áryans had recourse to to express futurity, was to attach to a root two others expressive of *going to be*; दास्यति therefore originally meant he *goes to be giving*, *i. e.* he *does* not give, but *will* give since he goes to do it. Now this दास्यति in the derived dialects becomes first दास्सति, then दास्सदि, दास्सइ, दासइ, दाहइ, दाइ and दे in order. Phonetic corruption has thus reduced this form to दाइ or दे, and that for the present tense *I give* has also assumed the same appearance. There is thus no distinction between them; wherefore to express future time our languages have had recourse to a variety of expedients which I shall endeavour to explain in their proper place. The Hindî, however, has hit upon the same that was used by our early ancestors, and distinguished futurity by adding to this shrunken form the past participle of गम् *to go*, which is गआ, changed to गा by combining the vowels, and thus देगा the form of the future, signifies literally, *gone that he (may) give.*

Another phenomenon constantly observable in the history of the growth of a language is the use of false analogies. Thus in Sanskrit the root श्रु *to hear* takes the augment नु in the Present and three other tenses or moods, and the Sanskrit of *he hears* is शृणोति. Now in the course of time people forgot that this termination was used in these tenses alone, and extended it to the Future, the past participle, and other derivatives, so that in the Pâli and the Prâkṛits the root itself became सुण=शृण instead of श्रु. This root has descended to most of the modern dialects in this same form. In the same way क्री *to buy* became किण, ज्ञा *to know*, जाण, बुध् *to know*, बुज्झ and so on. All these exist in the vernaculars so augmented. In the same way, though कृ is conjugated in Sanskrit by adding उ to the base according to the rule of the eighth conjugation, and forms करोति, कुर्वन्ति &c., in Prâkṛit it is conjugated according to the rule of the first or the tenth which are generalised, and has करइ or करेइ. This arises from the same sort of mistake that children commit, when, for instance, from the analogy of धरलें from धर, पडलें from पड &c., they use करलें from कर, though the correct Marâṭhî form is केलें and you may remember such expressions as "I knowed" and "you was" that Dickens puts into the mouth of his lower characters. The Pâli and the Prâkṛits are full of such formations. This law may be called the law of false analogies or of the generalisation of grammatical forms, or formal generalisation, and the effect of it is to do away with anomalies and introduce simplicity in a language. It springs from the same causes as phonetic decay, *viz.* the economization of effort, and its operation is restricted also by the same causes as those which arrest the progress of phonetic corruption.

Hitherto we have been considering the growth or decay of the grammar of a language. But the names of objects constitute a very important part of human speech. These are not arbitrary or simply conventional. The possibility of mere conventional names can exist only under a supposition of men meeting and agreeing that they should call such a thing by such a name. But this implies a condition of high social and political development, which in an early state of society does not exist, and, in the absence of language, cannot exist. The process is very artificial, and would hardly be worthy of the intellectual nature of man; and though even in a high state of civilisation a language grows, and new names spring up, this is not the way in which they do so. The names of objects are always expressive of some attribute possessed by those objects. पृथ्वी *the earth* is that which is broad, भानु *the sun*, that which shines, उदन्वत् *the sea*, that which has water, पितृ *father*, one who protects, दुहितृ *daughter*, one who milks cows. But you will see that these names are not logical definitions, for they have the defect of *ativyâpti*, *i. e.* are too wide. It is not the earth alone that is broad, nor the sun alone that shines, nor the sea alone that has water. But still these things possess these attributes pre-eminently, and hence the terms become restricted to them. What is general is thus rendered particular, and the sense of words is, so to say, specialized. This process goes on continually in a living language, not only in the invention of new names, but often it works in a manner to narrow the sense of existing words. Thus, वेदना etymologically signifies 'a feeling,' 'a sensation,' thence it is restricted in Sanskrit to a particular sensation, that of severe pain; but the pre-eminent pain is that experienced in child birth, hence वेण the Prâkṛitised form of the word signifies in Marâṭhî that special pain. So, गर्भिणी in Sanskrit denotes 'a female that is pregnant,' but गाभण the Marâṭhî form of the word is restricted to lower animals; ताप in Sanskrit means 'heat' generally, but in Marâṭhî, and in Gujarâtî in the form of ताव, it signifies a particular kind of heat, *viz.* 'fever' though the word has not lost its general sense; हृदय denotes originally 'the heart,' in modern Marâṭhî in the form of हिय्या it signifies 'courage,' which is a quality of the heart, though in old Marâṭhi it preserves its original sense; पिण्ड in Sanskrit means 'a ball' generally, but in Panjâbî and Gujarâtî in the form of पण्ड it is restricted to this ball of flesh and bones, 'the body'; चेटक in Sanskrit signifies 'an attendant', but in the form of चेला it denotes in the Hindî 'a pupil or disciple', who, according to Indian custom, is his master's close attendant, and in Bangâlî and the Goanese Marâṭhî, in the forms of चेटे and चलो 'a boy' or *son*, who is constantly about his parents. Opposed to this is a process which may be called generalisation of the sense. Thus the root गवेष् originally signified 'looking or searching for a cow'; it was then extended to any kind of 'searching', and lastly in the form of गवसणें it signifies in Marâṭhî 'to find'; इन्द्र originally 'the lord of the gods,' is in Sanskrit used to signify 'the lord' of any class of beings, such expressions as मानवेन्द्र, गजेन्द्र &c. being every common; and a notable example of this process is afforded by the word राजा which in Sanskrit means 'a king', but, in the forms of राय or राव, is in the modern languages used as a title of distinction, and in Marâthî, any respectable gentleman not following the priestly occupation, and not a man of learning may be called a *râv*. Sometimes, when by means of phonetic corruption a word is reduced to two forms, each of the two acquires a distinct sense. Thus, Sanskrit वृद्ध is in the modern languages corrupted to बुड्ढा H., बुढो S., बुड B., and in this form it means 'an old man.' It is also corrupted to बडा H., वडो S., बड B., वडो G., and व्हड Goan. M. in which form it signifies 'great,' 'large,' or 'more advanced in age'. In this last sense, the termination ल or र is appended to it (M. वडिल, S. वडेरो). The Sanskrit word क्षण becomes छण in the sense of 'a festival,' in Pâli and the Prâkṛits, but खण in the sense of 'a moment.' In Marâthî छण is further transformed to सण, and खण in the form of खिण also occurs in the old literature and in one of its dialects. The Sanskrit उज्ज्वल in the form of उजळ M., उजल H., उजलु S., उजळु G., उज्जल P. means *bright*, *clear*, *pure*, but in the form of उजाड M., H., G., P., S., B., it means *desolate* or *waste*. This sense it acquired by the first process explained above, since a desolate land is cleared, purified of its tenants or appurtenances. खुजा means in Marâṭhî *a dwarf* and कुबडा *humpbacked*. This last word exists in the other languages also, and both are derived from the Sanskrit कुब्ज.

The last phenomenon in the growth of a language which I shall notice is the gradual disappearance of words. As men advance in knowledge and civilisation new ideas and modes of thinking arise, and the old ones fall into disuse. And since words are the representatives of ideas, new words always come in, and the old go out. The changes that the Marâṭhî language, for instance, has undergone in this respect since the time of Jñânes'vara, or the Hindî since the time of Chanda, render the older books unintelligible to modern readers. There are also various other causes. Sometimes, when another language rises into importance on account of political circumstances, or when it is admired and esteemed by a nation, as Sanskrit is by Hindus, a great many words are borrowed from it, and necessarily the older ones go out to make room for them, or disappear because they are regarded as vulgar. The opening of an intercourse with a foreign nation brings about the same result. These causes account in a great measure for the fact that so many words in our languages have become obsolete. Jñânes'vara's Prâkṛit पसाय had to make room for the Sanskrit प्रसाद, गहिर for गंभीर and नाह for नाथ; and the word जमीन has well-nigh supplanted the old भुई, as हुकुम has done आज्ञा which itself must once have driven out such a word as आणा or आयस, the Prâkṛit forms of आज्ञा and आदेश.

The languages of the civilised nations of the world have been divided into three families, the Áryan or Indo-European, the Semitic, and the Turanian. The first comprises the Indian branch, consisting of Sanskrit, Pâli and the Prâkṛits, and the modern Vernaculars of Northern India and of Ceylon; the Iranic branch consisting of Zend, the sacred language of the Parsis, the Pehlevî and the other cognate dialects; the Hellenic or the Greek branch, comprising the languages of Ancient Greece and its modern representatives; the Italic branch, consisting of the Latin and the cognate ancient languages of Italy and the dialects derived from Latin, the Italian, the French and the old Provençal, the Spanish, the Portuguese, and the Wallachian; the Keltic or the language of those Kelts or Gauls that so often figure in Roman history, and distinguished into two varieties, the Kymric, now spoken in Wales and in the Province of Brittany in France, and the Gaelic, spoken in the Isle of Man, the Highlands of Scotland, and Ireland; the Lithuanian and Slavonic, comprising the languages of Lithuania, Russia, Bulgaria, and of the Slavonic races generally; and the Teutonic branch, consisting of the Scandinavian group, *i.e.* the languages of Sweden, Norway, Iceland, and Denmark, of the High German *i. e.* the old and the present language of Germany, and of the Low German, which comprised the old Anglo-Saxon and the other languages spoken on the coasts of Germany, the modern representatives of which are the English, and the dialects spoken in Holland, Friesland, and the North of Germany. The second family comprises the Hebrew, the Arabic, the Chaldee, the Syriac, the Carthaginian, and the cognate and derived languages; and the third, the Turkish and the languages of the Mongolian tribes. To this last family the dialects spoken in Southern India are also to be referred. The Zend approaches Sanskrit the most, but the affinities of this latter with

Greek and Latin are also very striking, and such as to convince even a determined sceptic. Sanskrit has preserved a greater number of ancient forms than any of these languages, hence it is indispensable for purposes of comparative philology.

The literature of Sanskrit presents, as ordinarily considered, two varieties of the language; but a third may also, as I shall presently endeavour to show, be clearly distinguished. Of these the most ancient is that found in the hymns of the Rigveda Saṃhitâ. These were composed at different times and by different Rishis, and were transmitted from father to son in certain families. Thus the third of the ten collections, which make up the Saṃhitâ, bears the name of Vis'vâmitra, and the hymns contained in it were composed by the great patriarch and his descendants. The seventh is ascribed to Vasishṭha and his family. The composition of these hymns therefore, extended over a long period, the language is not the same throughout, and while some of them present a variety so close to the later Sanskrit that there is little difficulty in understanding them, the style of others is so antiquated that they defy all efforts at interpretation, and their sense was not understood even by the Rishis who flourished in the very next literary period, that of the Brâhmaṇas. Still for our purposes we may neglect these differences and consider the Vedic variety of Sanskrit as one.

The chief characteristics of the Vedic language are these:—It contains a large number of words that have become obsolete or changed their sense in the later or classical Sanskrit. There is a greater variety of verbal derivatives, such as दर्शत in the sense of दर्शनीय 'worthy to be seen, or handsome', जीत्रम्, अवम् &c. abstract nouns from the roots जीत्र्, अव् &c., जनुस् 'something that is produced', पपि, बभ्रि, जग्नि &c., nouns of agency having a past sense (Pâṇ. III. 2,171), which govern an accusative, दृशीक signifying 'handsome' or मृळीक 'favour,' &c. The nominative plural termination of nouns ending in अ is असस् (Pâṇ. VII. 1, 50), as विश्वेदेवासः, as well as अस्, as यज्ञेन यज्ञमयजन्त देवाः; and the instrumental plural is देवेभिः or देवैः (Pâṇ. VII. 1, 10). The vowel cases of nouns in उ are often formed by joining the vowels by the usual Saṃdhi rules; as तन्वम् or तनुवम् accusative singular of तनु; मध्वः and वस्वः genitive singulars of मधु and वसु. The instrumental singular is made up by affixing आ, या, or इया, instead of ना, as मध्वा, उरुया, उर्विया, धृष्णुया, &c. (Pâṇ. VII. 1, 39); sometimes of other nouns also, as स्वपया, नावया &c. The nominative and vocative dual of masculine and the plural of neuter nouns in अ often end in आ; as येनेमा विश्वा

च्यवना कृतानि Rv. II. 12, 4, अश्विना पुरुदंससा नरा Rv. I. 3, 2; and the instrumental singular of feminine nouns in इ is optionally formed by simply lengthening the vowel (Pâṇ. VII. 1, 39), as नविष्ठया मती Rv. I. 82, 2. The locative singular termination is often dropped, as in परमे व्योमन्; or its औ changed to आ, as in नाभा for नाभौ (Pâṇ. VII. 1, 39). The Parasmaipada first person plural termination of verbs is मसि (Pâṇ. VII. 1, 46), as नमो भरन्त एमसि Rv. I. 1, 7, and that of the third person plural is often रे or रते, as दुह्रे or दुह्रते. Other forms also admit of this इ, as अदृश्रमस्य. The त of the Átmanepada terminations is often dropped (Pâṇ. VII. 1, 41), as वस्व ईशे Rv. I. 71, 9. There are eight different forms of mood called लेट् by Pâṇini, which has a conditional or subjunctive sense; सुपथा करत्। प्र ण आयूंषि तारिषत्, Rv. I. 25, 12, स देवानेह वक्षति Rv. I. 1, 2. This is lost in classical Sanskrit. The several conjugations or ways of forming the special tenses do exist, but the roots are not restricted to any particular way, being conjugated sometimes according to one mode and sometimes according to another; as श्रुधी हवम्. There are some instances in which some other than the special tenses also admit of the conjugational sign, as विशृण्विरे perfect. Sometimes guṇa is substituted before the त of the second person plural imperative, though it is a weak termination, as शृणोत.

The infinitive is formed by adding to roots the terminations से, ध्यै, अध्यै, तवै and तवे (Pâṇ. III. 4, 9), as वक्षे, जीवसे, पिबध्यै, दातवै, हन्तवे. These are etymologically the forms of the dative singular of such nouns as वक्ष्, जीवस्, पिबधि &c. A few other datives are similarly used, as दृशे, रोहिष्यै &c. (Pâṇ. III. 4, 10, 11). The accusatives of some nouns are also used as infinitives when governed by शक् (Pâṇ. III. 4, 12), as न ये शेकुर्यज्ञियां नावमारुहम् Rv. X. 44, 6; also in other places, चिकितुषो विपृच्छम् Rv. VII. 86, 3. The infinitive in classical Sanskrit ends in तुम्, as कर्तुम्, which is the accusative form of such a noun as कर्तु, the dative of which, कर्तवे, is one of the forms of the Vedic infinitive. The potential participles are often formed by adding तवे, ए, एन्य and त्व (Pâṇ. III. 4, 14), as नैषा गव्यूतिरपभर्तवा उ Rv. X. 14, 2, न तेन देव आदिशे Rv. VI. 56, 1, दिदृक्षेण्यः, कर्त्वम्. The first two, however, ought properly to be considered as infinitives. The absolutive is sometimes formed by the addition of त्वाय ; as गत्वाय. There is such a form as इष्ट्वीनम् for इष्ट्वा ; and such others as हत्वी and पीत्वी for हत्वा and पीत्वा occur often. These last, as also the usual or classical absolutives, are forms of the instrumental singular of the same nouns, the dative and accusative of which are used as infinitives; त्वाय appears also to be an instrumental. There are a great many other peculiarities which are noticed by Pâṇini, and which you will find collected in the Siddhânta-Kaumudî. One thing, however, should be borne in mind, that notwithstanding there is in these respects a very great difference between the Vedic and the classical Sanskrit, they are in the same phonetic stage, *i. e.* the vocal elements of words and letters remain the same. There are a few such instances, as सध for सह, and गृभ् for गृह्, in which the mute has disappeared, leaving only the aspirate element, and to these may be added the terminations मसि and असस् for मस् and अस्; but both the original and corrupt forms exist in the Vedas, and no general conclusion can be based on these few instances. You will hereafter see that the other dialects I shall speak of differ greatly from the classical Sanskrit in these respects. The following specimen will give you an idea of Vedic Sanskrit:—

१. यच्चिद्धि ते विशो यथा प्र देव वरुण व्रतम् । मिनीमसि द्यविद्यवि ॥
२. मा नो वधाय हत्नवे जिहीळानस्य रीरधः । मा हृणानस्य मन्यवे ॥
५. कदा क्षत्रश्रियं नरमा वरुणं करामहे । मृळीकायोरुचक्षसम् ॥
७. वेदा यो वीनां पदमन्तरिक्षेण पतताम् । वेद नावः समुद्रियः ॥
१०. नि षसाद धृतव्रतो वरुणः पस्त्यास्वा । साम्राज्याय सुक्रतुः ॥
११. अतो विश्वान्यद्भुता चिकित्वाँ अभि पश्यति । कृतानि या च कर्त्वा ॥
१२. स नो विश्वाहा सुक्रतुरादित्यः सुपथा करत् । प्र ण आयूंषि तारिषत् ॥
१९. इमं मे वरुण श्रुधी हवमद्या च मृळय । त्वामवस्युरा चके ॥

These eight verses contain 72 different *padas* or grammatical forms, not counting the prepositions as separate *padas*. Of these 19 have become altogether obsolete in classical Sanskrit, and 12 have changed their significations. This, however, is a specimen of one of the more intelligible hymns, but there are a great many which contain a much larger proportion of words that have gone out of use. It is these obsolete words that constitute the chief difficulty of understanding the Vedic hymns.

1. The use of चित् after यत् is unknown to the later dialect that particle being found joined only to the pronoun किम्. The preposition प्र though connected with मिनीमसि is separated from it by three words. Though the root of this verb is given in the Dhâtupâṭha or Pâṇini's list of roots, it has gone out of use. In modern Sanskrit we should use अतिक्रामामः instead. व्रत is not now used in the sense in which it occurs here; though it is connected with it. We should use शासन

instead. द्यविद्यवि means here 'day by day'; in classical Sanskrit the word द्यो means 'heaven' only. The verse may be translated:— "Though we who are like subjects break thy law, day after day, O divine Varuṇa!" Varuṇa is spoken of frequently as a *rājan*, or king, and men are his subjects, with reference to that attribute of his.

2. वध means 'killing', or 'execution', in classical Sanskrit, but, since हत्नु 'killing' qualifies it here, it must mean some such thing as a weapon or a blow.

हत्नु is obsolete. जिहीळान is a participle of the Perfect of हेड् or हीड्. The form is obsolete; and a verbal form of the root is not ordinarily met with, though a word derived from it does occur. हृणान also is obsolete.

"Do not subject us to the killing blow of the spiteful, nor to the wrath of the angry," *i.e.*, do not kill us out of spite or wrath.

5. क्षत्र signifies in later Sanskrit the order of the Kshatriyas or the warrior caste. Here it is used in the primitive sense of 'valour', 'prowess'. नर does not mean 'man' here, but is used in its original sense of *manly*. आ and करामहे are separated by a word. मृळीक 'favour' is obsolete. चक्षस् 'the reach of sight', 'visual power', has also gone out of use.

"When shall we call the brave, manly, and far-seeing Varuṇa hither to favour us?"

7. समुद्रिय: This form of the derived adjective is unknown to later Sanskrit. The genitive singular is formed by changing ई to इय्.

"Who knows the path of the birds flying in the air and of the boat on the waters."

10. "Enforcing his laws, the powerful Varuṇa sits down in his abode to exercise universal sovereignty."

11. अद्भुता The termination of the accusative plural is here dropped; कर्त्वं is Vedic for कर्तव्य; here also नि is dropped.

"From this place the knowing one sees all secret deeds done or to be done."

12. करत् and तारिषत् are forms of लेट् or the Vedic subjunctive.

"May the powerful God make things easy for us all our days and prolong our lives."

19. श्रुधी. Conjugated as a root of the second class, with धि as the termination of the imperative singular, lengthened for phonetic purposes.

"O Varuṇa, hear this my invocation, and now be propitious. I call on thee, desirous of protection."

The next form of the language is presented to us in the Brâhmaṇas of the Vedas, such as the Aitareya of the Rigveda and the Śatapatha of the White Yajush. A great many of those peculiar words which we meet with in the hymns, and which are so unintelligible have disappeared, the declensions have approached the standard of classical Sanskrit, the nominative plural in असस् for instance, and the instrumental plural in एभि: having gone out of use. The roots have arranged themselves definitely under certain conjugations. The subjunctive has mostly become obsolete, though such forms as निष्पद्याते (Śat. I. 4, 1, 10), and असत् (Ait. II. 11.) are sometimes met with. The roots take those forms of the Aorist that Pâṇini assigns to them, and this tense is scrupulously used in the sense mentioned by that grammarian. Such terminations as मसि and the various modes of forming the infinitive have disappeared, the ordinary one in तुम् being mostly used (Ait. IV. 8, VIII. 23). The language is in most respects the same as that usually called classical Sanskrit. It is rich in verbal forms of all tenses and moods. There are however a few peculiarities and archaisms. There are some antiquated words such as वर्स 'an extremity' (Ait. II. 2), अनीक 'a shaft,' मन्थावल 'a bat' (Ait. III. 26); निशाव 'ultimate referee', अववदितृ 'one who pronounces a decree', भगवम् 'prosperous', तत for तात (Ait. V. 14), इरा 'food' (Ait. VIII. 7), शुष्मिण 'powerful' (Ait. VIII. 8, 23), मेनि 'a destructive instrument, flame' (Ait. VIII. 24), &c. The dative of feminine nouns is often used for the genitive, as पृथिव्यै राजा स्या: (Ait. VIII. 23); सर्वस्यै वाच:.......... परिगृहीत्यै; the त of the third person singular of the Átmanepada is sometimes dropped as in the old dialect, as सविता वै प्रसवानामीशे (Ait. VII. 16); a few roots form their Aorist in another manner than that mentioned by Pâṇini, as अज्ञत वा अस्य दन्ता: (Ait. VII. 14), where अज्ञत stands for अजनिपत, अद्रुक्षो वै म आत इदं (Ait. VIII. 23) where अद्रुक्ष: is for अद्रुह:; the form of the infinitive governed by the word ईश्वर is that which ends in तोस्; as ईश्वरो ह तु पुरायुष: प्रैतो: (Ait. VIII. 7); and ग्रह् appears in the form of ग्रभ् (Ait. III. 26). In the seventh and eighth Pañchikâs of the Aitareya Brâhmaṇa some Gâthâs or songs are quoted, the language of which is more antiquated than that of the body of the work. Notwithstanding these irregularities, these Brâhmaṇas are the best representatives extant of the verbal portion of that language of which Pâṇini writes the grammar, though he did not mean these when he spoke of the Bhâshâ. But nearly the whole of that literature which Pâṇini drew from, if he did so at all, has perished, or to speak more correctly there is no portion of the extant Sanskrit literature that accurately represents Pâṇini's Sanskrit as regards the verb and the Taddhitas or nominal derivatives. Probably the spoken language of his time formed the basis of his grammar.

The next stage of Sanskrit is presented to us by the work of Yâska, whose language appears to be more ancient than that of the rest of the non-Vedic literature. We find a good many archaic words and expressions in the Nirukta, such as उपजन 'proximity,' उपेक्षितव्य in the sense of 'finding' or 'observing', कर्मन् 'signification,' यथो in the sense of 'as to', बिल्म 'variety,' उपदेशाय ग्लायन्त: 'unable to teach', शिशिक्ष राज्येन 'invested with sovereignty', नैचण्टुक 'subordinate', अनिर्वाह 'celibacy', &c. There are also some technical terms which we do not meet with in later works, such as निवृत्तिस्थान 'weak terminations', उपजन or उपबन्ध 'augment', नामकरण 'a nominal termination', &c. After the time of Yâska, Sanskrit underwent a peculiar change, for the proper understanding of which it is necessary for a time to consider the styles in which a man may speak or write. There is what may be considered as the fluent or flowing style of speech, in which the speaker looks at the actions of men in progress, actions in the course of being done or suffered. A man speaking or writing in this style will use a verb on every occasion. But a verb may always be analysed into an attribute of the subject and the connecting link or copula. When one's attention is directed more to the attribute than to the progress or course of an action, he will use verbal nouns or adjectives. Thus instead of अश्वमारुक्षत् a man may say अश्वमारूढः, of सोऽवोचत्, उक्तं तेन, of अयं मांसं भक्षयति, मांसभक्षकोयम्, of मालामग्रथ्नात्, मालां ग्रथितवान् &c. In the same way a verb may be divided into a noun or adjective denoting the special action it involves, and a verb signifying action generally, as पचति, may be analysed into पाकं करोति or पक्तं करोति and पच्यते into पक्वो भवति. The later Sanskrit and the modern Vernaculars are full of such formations. The case forms may also be similarly analysed into attributive expressions; as राज्ञः पुरुषः into राजसंबन्धी पुरुषः or रामेण कृतः कटः into रामकर्तृकः कटः. The mode of thought which gives birth to such forms of expression leads also to a freer use of compound nouns by means of which a whole sentence may be compressed into a small attribute. In argumentation the ablative of an abstract noun saves a long periphrasis. This may be considered a petrified form of speech, and as distinguished from the verbal style it may be called the nominal style. In the earliest literature of Sanskrit the fluent or verbal style prevailed. Since this rarely admits of attributive or nominal expressions, the sentences are short, and the construction easy. Thus, in such books as the Aitareya and Śatapatha Brâhmaṇas, we find short sentences, and abundance of verbal forms. Even in the time of Yâskà this style prevailed to a large extent, and notwithstanding that his book is on a scientific subject, his language often reminds one of that of the earlier works, though he must have written several centuries afterwards. In the time of Pâṇini also verbal forms were in general use, as I shall presently attempt to show. Some time after, however, the petrified or nominal style began to supplant the other. Somehow it commended itself to the genius of the Indian Aryas of the times, and the very richness and flexibility of Sanskrit which allows of a root or noun being twisted in a variety of ways to suit any sort of construction greatly facilitated the change. The Itihâsas, the Purâṇas, and the metrical Smṛitis are written in this style. But here it is not carried to such an extravagant extent as is done in later writings, in some of which verbal forms are rare and in others long and bewildering compounds are frequently met with, and the construction is complicated and involved. This is the general character of the Sanskrit in which the subsequent poetic and dramatic literature is written; and if the language of a certain author is graceful and easy, and not dull and involved, if he does not use long compounds, and writes in a more natural style, it is either because his taste is superior to that of his contemporaries, or because he belongs to an earlier period.

But it was in the field of philosophy, dialectics, and exegesis, scriptural or grammatical, that this nominal style was greatly cultivated and developed. The earliest work of the kind we know of is Patañjali's Mahâbhâshya on Kâtyâyana's Vârtikas or notes on Pâṇini's Sûtras. Nearly the whole of the philosophical literature of the Sanskrit is written more or less in the style of disputation. An Indian author does not lead his readers into the processes his own mind has gone through in arriving at the doctrines he lays down; in other words, he does not tell us how he has come by the opinions he holds, but lays down these doctrines and sets forth those opinions and conceives objections that may be raised and answers them. Or before actually stating the true doctrine or *siddhânta*, certain others, more or less opposed are stated, and reasons given in support of them (*pûrvapaksha*) which are, of course, refuted. The Mahâbhâshya is written in this manner, but it differs in a good many respects from later works of the kind. Unlike the latter, it gives the very words that an opponent, speaking in his own person, may be expected to use. It therefore really consists of a series of dialogues, often smart, between one who maintains the *pûrvapaksha*, and another who lays down the *siddhânta*. Hence, the language is plain and simple, and the sentences are short, and such as a man may naturally use in ordinary conversation or oral disputation. The nominal style, however, as I have ventured to call it, in contradistinction to that of the Brâhmaṇas and also of Yâska, is observable; but it has of course not yet degenerated into the long compounds and algebraic expressions of modern times, and is perfectly natural. In this respect it keeps pace with the language of the Itihâsas and Smṛitis. Vâtsyâyana's Bhâshya on Gotama's Nyâya Sûtra, and Śabarasvâmin's on that of Jaimini, as well as the Bhâshyas on some of the sacrificial Sûtras, are written in the same sort of simple and lively style, though however they present a further stage in the downward progress. But gradually this manner of writing ceased to be used, and the philosophical style went on progressing until it has come to be what it is now. Śaṃkarâchârya's Bhâshya presents it in a middle stage. The sentences are much longer than those of the earlier writers, the construction is more involved, there is a freer use of attributive adjuncts, and the form is that of an essay or a lecture, instead of an oral disputation. But the great Âchârya's style is perspicuous throughout, fluent and charming, and not solidified or petrified, as that of later writers is. These latter hardly ever use a verb, and of the cases only a few are to be met with in their works. The nominative and ablative singular prevail, and long compounds are constantly employed. All our ideas are thrown into the form of nouns, mostly abstract, and even the participles have become rare. This style is the style of formulas rather than of discourse. It has reached its climax in the works of recent *Naiyâyikas*, but it has been more or less used by modern writers in all the Śâstras. The movement which began with a less frequent use of verbal forms and the employment of attributive expressions has thus ended in making Sanskrit a language of abstract nouns and compound words.

I have used the word style in describing this movement, to show what important changes in the structure of a language may originate from what is in the beginning but a style or mode of speaking or writing. If everybody thought and spoke about all matters as the

Naiyâyika does in his own subject our language would be just like his. It would almost have no verbs, no participles, and no cases except one or two. But it is not so. The movement could not be carried so far in other subjects. Hence the real classical Sanskrit is the Sanskrit of the Epics, the Purâṇas, the metrical law-books, the better or earlier specimens of Kâvyas or poems and dramatic plays, and of the early philosophical or exegetical works. And if we examine this literature we shall find that the greater use of attributive or nominal forms of expression gradually drove out a large portion of the Sanskrit verb, and gave a new character to the language, which may be thus described :—Very few verbal forms are used besides those of such tenses as the Present and Future ; participles are frequently met with; the verbal forms of some roots, especially of those belonging to the less comprehensive classes, have gone out of use, and in their place we often have a noun expressive of the special action and a verb expressive of action generally ; compound words are somewhat freely employed ; and a good many of the Taddhita forms or nominal derivatives have disappeared, and in their stead we have periphrastic expressions. If the treatises of Pâṇini and others had perished, and we had to construct a grammar of the Sanskrit from the classical literature I have above indicated, our Verb and the Taddhita portion would be very meagre. Professor Benfey attributes the condition which the language thus assumed to the influence of the Prâkṛits or the spoken vernaculars. But the process appears to me perfectly natural, and no such influence need be supposed. The change may in some respects be likened to that which rendered the Vedic subjunctive and other grammatical forms obsolete in the later stage of the language. The Prâkṛits may have given some words to the Sanskrit, but that they should in this manner have influenced its grammatical structure is very unlikely. It is more natural to suppose that it was the Sanskrit from which the Prâkṛits evidently sprang which gave to these latter their peculiar character. I shall endeavour to determine the exact relation between the Sanskrit and these dialects in the concluding lecture.

We have thus observed and determined the change that came over Sanskrit after the period that elapsed between the Brâhmaṇas and Yâska from an examination of the literature itself. But the fact is borne witness to by Kâtyâyana, who observed it in his time and made it the subject of a few *vârtikas*. Patañjali discusses the points raised in the following manner. An objector or *Pûrvapakshin* is introduced, who says :—

PÛRV. अस्त्यप्रयुक्तः। There exist (some) words which are not used; for instance, ऊष, तेर, चक्र, पेच. (These are forms of the second person plural of the Perfect.)

The *Siddhântin*, or the principal teacher, who advocates the doctrine that is finally laid down asks:—

SID. What if they are not used?

PÛRV. You determine the grammatical correctness of words from their being used. Those then that are not now used are not grammatically correct.

SID. What you say is, in the first place, inconsistent, *viz.*, that words exist which are not used. If they exist they cannot be not used; if not used, they cannot exist. To say that they exist and are not used is inconsistent. You yourself use them (utter them) and say (in the very breath) there are words which are not used. What other worthy like yourself would you have to use them in order that they might be considered correct (lit. What other person like yourself is correct or is an authority in the use of words)?

PÛRV.—This is not inconsistent. I say they exist, since those who know the Śâstra teach their formation by [laying down] rules, and I say they are not used, because they are not used by people. Now with regard to [your remark] "What other worthy, &c." [when I say they are not used] I do not mean that they are not used by me.

SID.—What then?

PÛRV.—Not used by people.

SID.—Verily, you also are one amongst the people.

PÛRV.—Yes, I am *one*, but am not *the people*.

SID.—(Vârt. अस्त्यप्रयुक्त इति चेन्नार्थे शब्दप्रयोगात्). If you object that they are not used, it will not do (the objection is not valid).

PÛRV. Why not?

SID.—Because words are used to designate things. The things do exist which these words are used to designate. (Therefore the words must be used by somebody. If the things exist, the words that denote them must exist).

PÛRV.—(Vârt. अप्रयोगः प्रयोगान्यत्वात्). (It does not follow.) Their non-use is what one can reasonably infer.

SID.—Why?

PÛRV.—Because they (people) use other words to designate the things expressed by these words; for instance, क्व यूयमुषिता: in the sense of ऊष; क्व यूयं तीर्णा: in the sense of तेर; क्व यूयं कृतवन्त: in the sense of चक्र; क्व यूयं पक्वन्त: in the sense of पेच. (We here see that participles had come to be used for verbs of the Perfect Tense.)

SID.—(Vârt. अप्रयुक्ते दीर्घसत्रवत्) Even if these words are not used, they should be essentially taught by rules just as long sacrificial sessions are. It is in this way. Long sacrificial sessions are such as last for a hundred years and for a thousand years. In modern times none whatever holds them, but the writers on sacrifices teach them by rules, simply because [to learn] what has been handed down by tradition from the Rishis is religiously meritorious. And moreover (Vârt. सर्वे देशान्तरे) all these words are used in other places.

PURV.—They are not found used.

SID.—An endeavour should be made to find them. Wide indeed is the range over which words are used; the earth with its seven continents, the three worlds, the four Vedas with their angas or dependent treatises and the mystic portions, in their various recensions, the one hundred branches of the Adhvaryu (Yajur-Veda), the Sâma-Veda with its thousand modes, the Bâhvṛichya with its twenty-one varieties, and the Âtharvaṇa Veda with nine, Vâkovâkya, the Epics, the Purâṇas and Medicine. This is the extent over which words are used. Without searching this extent of the use of words, to say that words are not used is simple rashness. In this wide extent of the use of words, certain words appear restricted to certain senses in certain places. Thus, शवति is used in the sense of motion among the Kambojas; the Âryas use it in the derived form of शव; हम्मति is used among the Surâshṭras, रंहति among the eastern and central people, but the Âryas use only गम; दाति is used in the sense of 'cutting' among the easterns, दात्र among the northerners. And those words which you think are not used are also seen used.

PURV.—Where?

SID.—In the Veda. Thus, सप्तास्ये रेवती रेवदूष। यद्वो रेवती रेवत्यां तमूष। यन्मे नरः श्रुत्यं ब्रह्म चक्र। यत्रा नश्चक्रा जरसं तनूनाम्।

We here see that the objector says that certain words or forms are not used by people, and therefore they should not be taught or learnt. The instances that he gives are forms of the perfect of some roots and he observes that the sense of these forms is expressed by using other words which are perfect participles of these roots. These statements are not denied by the Siddhântin, but he does not allow that the forms should not be taught on that account. Though not used, they should be taught and learnt for the sake of the religious merit consequent thereon, just as the ceremonial of long sacrificial sessions, which are never held, is. Then the objector is told that though not used by people, the words may be current in some other country, continent, or world, or they must have been used somewhere in the vast literature of the language. As regards the particular instances, two of them are shown to be used in the Vedas.

It thus follows that in the time of Kâtyâyana and Patañjali, such verbal forms had become obsolete, and participles were used in their place. But it must have been far otherwise in the time of Pâṇini. He gives minute rules for constructing the innumerable forms of the Sanskrit verb. Our grammarians proceeded upon a strictly scientific basis. Nothing is more clear from several observations scattered throughout the work of Patañjali, besides those contained in the above passage, than this, that the Indian Grammarians do not give us the inventions of their own brains as they are supposed by some scholars to do. The very perfection of their observation and analysis has rendered them liable to this reproach. But notwithstanding all that, there can be *no doubt whatever* that they scrupulously adhered to usage. If so, the verbal forms taught by Pâṇini must have been current in the language at some time. We do meet with them in the Brâhmaṇas, but our grammarian does not include these forms among the peculiarities he has given of the Vedic or Chhandas and Brâhmaṇa dialect, and thus does not restrict them to those works. They must therefore be understood as having been in use in the Bhâshâ or current language, the grammar of which he teaches in his Sûtras. And the Bhâshâ that he means must be that which was current in his time. In Pâṇini's time, therefore, the fluent or verbal style of speech was in use, as I have observed before. But it may be argued that though he refers these forms to the Bhâshâ, the Bhâshâ he means may not be that which prevailed when he lived, but another current before his time and preserved in its literature, on which Pâṇini based his rules. It matters very little even if we make this supposition. The only effect is that the period when the non-Vedic Sanskrit was rich in verbal forms is placed before Pâṇini ; but the fact itself that there was such a period is undeniable. The supposition, however, is unreasonable. For it is not at all likely that he should neglect the language prevalent in his time and teach that which was current before him, and speak of it as the Bhâshâ, which word literally signifies the "spoken language" or vernacular. And the occurrence in the Sûtras of words that became obsolete in later Sanskrit confirms this view. The following are such words :—अन्ववसर्ग 'allowing one his own way,' निरवसित 'excommunicated,' प्रत्यवसान 'eating', अभिविधि 'including', स्वकरण 'marrying', उत्सञ्जन 'throwing up', अभ्रेष 'equitableness'. You will have seen that the Vârtika of Kâtyâyana which starts the discussion I have translated, and Patañjali's comment on it speak of words generally as having ceased to be used though the examples given consist of certain verbal forms only. It is, therefore, to be understood that the observation is applicable to other forms and expressions also taught by Pâṇini which we do not meet with in the later literature. Among such may be noticed उपाजेकृ and अन्वाजेकृ 'to strengthen', निवचनेकृ 'to be silent,' कणेहन्, and मनोहन् 'to fulfil one's longing'[7], &c. कणेहन् occurs in Yâska also. Most of the verbal derivatives ending in the technical termination णमुल् must also be so considered, such as ब्राह्मणवेदं भोजयति 'feeds every Brâhmaṇa that he finds', चेलक्नोपं वृष्टः 'rained till the clothes were wet', स्वपोषं पुष्णाति 'supports by his own means,' ऊर्ध्वशोषं शुष्यति 'withers standing', &c. A good many Taddhita forms taught in Pâṇini's Sûtras must also, I think, be put in the same category.

And there is another circumstance which shows that Pâṇini's Sanskrit was more ancient than Kâtyâyana's. Kâtyâyana's Vârtikas on Pâṇini, which I have already spoken to you of, touch on various points concerning grammar and the system of Pâṇini. The purpose of a great many of them is the proper interpretation of the Sûtras, and there are some which supply the links that are wanting in the system, also a good many which teach forms not taught by Pâṇini, or give the correct forms, when by the strict application of Pâṇini's rules we arrive at such as are incorrect. Now, this strict application of Pâṇini's rules is often in the manner of a quibbling logician, and consequently it was probably never meant by Pâṇini himself. Again, it may also be allowed that some forms existing in the language may have escaped Pâṇini's notice. But even after making allowance for all these considerations, a good many forms taught by Kâtyâyana are

---

7. Professor Goldstücker has used the argument based on the occurrence of obsolete words in the Sûtras and that set forth in the next paragraph, to prove the archaic character of the language as it existed in Pâṇini's time, and some of the instances quoted in the text are the same as his.

left which it is impossible to believe Pâṇini did not observe or know, if they existed in the language in his time. Though not infallible, Pâṇini was not an indifferent grammarian. He justly deserves the reputation he has all along enjoyed of being the pre-eminent teacher of grammar. He has noticed even stray facts about the language. If so, the only reasonable supposition is that these forms did not exist in the language at the period when he lived. For instance, according to Pâṇini's rules the vocative singular of neuter nouns ending in अन् such as ब्रह्मन् and नामन् is ब्रह्मन् and नामन्, but Kâtyâyana in a Vârtika on VIII. 2, 8 tells us it is ब्रह्मन् or ब्रह्म and नामन् or नाम. Pâṇini teaches that the forms of the dative, ablative, genitive, and locative singular of the feminine of द्वितीय and तृतीय are optionally like those of the corresponding pronouns, *i.e.* we have either द्वितीयायै or द्वितीयस्यै, द्वितीयायाः or द्वितीयस्याः &c., but Kâtyâyana in a Vârtika on I. 1, 36 extends this option to the masculine also, and according to him we have द्वितीयाय or द्वितीयस्मै, द्वितीयात् or द्वितीयस्मात् &c., while Pâṇini gives us only the first. Pâṇini's rule IV. 1, 49 allows of मातुलानी only as the feminine of मातुल, but Kâtyâyana gives मातुली also; उपाध्यायानी is not noticed by Pâṇini while Kâtyâyana lays down that as well as उपाध्यायी in the sense of 'wife of the उपाध्याय'. So also आर्या and क्षत्रिया are according to Pâṇini, 'a female Ârya' and 'a female Kshatriya', but Kâtyâyana gives आर्याणी and क्षत्रियाणी as well as आर्या and क्षत्रिया. A good many more instances of a similar nature may be given from other parts of Sanskrit Grammar. Are we then to suppose that the forms ब्रह्म, नाम, कर्म &c. of the vocative singular, द्वितीयस्मै of the dative of द्वितीय &c. मातुली उपाध्यायानी, आर्याणी, क्षत्रियाणी and many more such, escaped the observation of such a grammarian as Pâṇini, or that he did not know them? Is the supposition that they did not exist in the language in his time not more reasonable? It therefore appears clear to me that the language in Pâṇini's time was in a different condition from that in which it was in Kâtyâyana's. The chief differences, to point out which has been the object of this discussion, may be thus stated:—In Pâṇini's time a good many words and expressions were current which afterwards became obsolete; verbal forms were commonly used which ceased to be used in Kâtyâyana's time, and some grammatical forms were developed in the time of the latter which did not exist in Pâṇini's.

Pâṇini's Sanskrit must, therefore, be identified with that which preceded the Epics, and he must be referred to the literary period between the Brâhmaṇas and Yâska. Hence it is that the Brâhmaṇas, as observed before, are the best existing representatives of the language of which Pâṇini writes the grammar. Kâtyâyana, on the other hand, wrote when the language arrived at that stage which we have called cassical. Thus then, we have been able to trace three distinct periods in the development of Sanskrit. First, we have the Vedic period, to which the Rigvedâ Saṃhitâ, the Mantra portion of the Yajurveda, and the more antiquated part of the Atharva-Saṃhitâ are to be referred. Then commences another period, at the threshold of which we find the Brâhmaṇas, which, so to say, look backwards to the preceding, that is, present the Vedic language in the last stage of its progress towards Pâṇini's Bhâshâ; and later on, we have Yâska and Pâṇini. This may be called the period of Middle Sanskrit. And last of all, there is the classical period to which belong the Epics, the earliest specimens of Kâvyas and dramatic plays, the metrical Smṛitis, and the grammatical work of Kâtyâyana. Pâṇini's work contains the grammar of Middle Sanskrit, while Kâtyâyana's that of classical Sanskrit, though he gives his sanction to the archaic forms of the former on the principle, as he himself has stated, on which the authors of the sacrificial Sûtras teach the ritual of long sacrificial sessions, though they had ceased to be held in their time. Patañjali gives but few forms which differ from Kâtyâyana's, and in no way do they indicate a different stage in the growth of the language; hence his work is to be referred to the same period. The form which the language assumed at this time became the standard for later writers to follow, and Kâtyâyana and Patañjali are now the generally acknowledged authorities on all points concerning the correctnesss of Sanskrit speech. We shall hereafter see that the last two stages have left distinct traces on the Prâkṛits or the derived languages.

LECTURE II.

Pâli and the Dialects of the Period.

In the last lecture we traced the development of the Sanskrit language until it assumed the form in which it is usually called classical Sanskrit. This form it acquired several centuries before Christ, as I shall hereafter endeavour to show, but it has since preserved it unaltered. The reason is that the number of people using it has been growing smaller and smaller, and now for a considerable period it has remained confined to a few learned men who devote long time to its study and use it only for religious and philosophical purposes. But in so far as it has been used for these purposes it has not been free from change, as was pointed out on the last occasion. The style and modes of expression used by Gadâdhara Bhaṭṭâchârya, the great Naiyâyika of modern times, are not the same as those of Kaṇâda, Gotama, and Vâtsyâyana, nor those used by Nâgojibhaṭṭa, the same as those of Kâtyâyana and Patañjali. Bnt all these changes have followed one direction. The efforts of our modern writers have been mostly, if not altogether, directed to systematizing and reducing to an accurate and definite shape the conceptions of those ancient sages, and no new ideas or methods of thought have arisen. They have thus elaborated a highly artificial style, abounding in abstract terms. In other branches of the literature also, we may discover some peculiarities and corruptions of diction and manner. But still, making due allowance for all this the generally received standard of good and correct Sanskrit is the same as it was many centuries ago. There are certain models which modern writers and speakers have to conform to. When, however, a language is living, that is, is used by people generally and in matters of every-day life, it must undergo very great changes. Men will not waste time and trouble in accurately ascertaining and imitating the pronunciation of their fathers, or reproducing exactly the several grammatical forms used by their predecessors. All that is necessary is that they should make themselves understood. Old modes of thinking give place to new ones, and new ideas spring up; and both must be represented in the language that is used. Sometimes accidents in the history of a race, such as its coming in contact or being incorporated with another race, serve to transform its language within a short time. But the alterations that occur from these and other causes obey certain laws; and hence the possibility of a Science of Language. Now, by the operation of influences such as these, Sanskrit was, in very remote times, corrupted, and new dialects arose from it. We should have known nothing of these if they had not been preserved in their literatures. Of these dialects that which approaches Sanskrit the most is the Pâli. This is the sacred language of the Buddhists of Ceylon, Siam, and Burmah, and possesses an extensive literature. I will introduce my remarks on this dialect by placing before you a specimen:—

सावत्थियं किर अदिण्णपुब्बको नाम ब्राह्मणो अहोसि। तेन कस्सचि किंचिद्‌-दिण्णपुब्बं तेन तं अदिण्णपुब्बको त्वेव सं जानिंसु। तस्सेकपुत्तको अहोसि पियो मनापो। ....तस्स सोळसवस्सकाले पण्डुरोगो उदपादि। माता पुत्तं ओलोकेत्वा ब्राह्मण पुत्तस्स ते रोगो उप्पन्नो तिकिच्छापेहि नन्ति आह। भोति सचे वेज्जं आनेस्सामि भत्तवेतनं दातब्बं भविस्सति। त्वं मम धनच्छेदनं न ओलोकेसीति। अथ किं करिस्ससि ब्राह्मणा ति। यथा मे धनच्छेदो न होति तथा करिस्सामीति। सो वेज्जानं सन्तिकं गन्त्वा असूकरोगस्स नाम तुह्मे किं भेसज्जं करोथाति पुच्छि। अथस्स ते यं वा तं वा रुक्खतच्चादिं आचिक्खन्ति। सो तं आहरित्वा पुत्तस्स भेसज्जं करोति। तं करोन्तस्सेवस्स रोगो वलवा अहोसि।

This is from the Aṭṭhakathâ or commentary by Buddhaghosha on the Dhammapada. It was written in the fifth century after Christ, long after Pâli had ceased to be a vernacular. The following is from the Dhammapada itself, which we have reason to believe is much more ancient:—

129. सब्बे तसन्ति दण्डस्स सब्बे भायन्ति मच्चुनो।
अत्तानं उपमं कत्वा न हनेय्या न घातये॥

131. सुखकामानि भूतानि यो दण्डेन विहिंसति।
अत्तनो सुखमेसानो पेच्च सो न लभते सुखं॥

133. मा वोच फरुसं कञ्चि वुत्ता पटिवदेय्यु तं।
दुक्खा हि सारम्भकथा पटिदण्डा फुसेय्यु तं॥

134. सचे नेरेसि अत्तानं कंसो उपहतो यथा।
एस पत्तोसि निब्बानं सारम्भो ते न विज्जति॥

The Sanskrit of these passages is as follows:—

श्रावस्त्यां किलादत्तपूर्वको नाम ब्राह्मणोभूत्। तेन कस्मैचित्किंचिददत्तपूर्वं तेन तमदत्तपूर्वकस्त्वेव समज्ञासत। तस्यैकपुत्रकोभूत्प्रियो मनोज्ञः। तस्य षोडशवर्ष-

काले पाण्डुरोग उदपादि। माता पुत्रमवलोक्य ब्राह्मण पुत्रस्य ते रोग उत्पन्नश्चिकित्सयैनमित्याह। भवति स चेद्वैद्यमानेष्यामि भक्तवेतनं दातव्यं भविष्यति। त्वं मम धनच्छेदनं नावलोकयसि। अथ किं करिष्यसि ब्राह्मणेति। यथा मे धनच्छेदो न भवति तथा करिष्यामीति। स वैद्यानामन्तिकं गत्वामुकरोगस्य नाम यूयं किं भैषज्यं कुरुथेत्यप्राक्षीत्। अथास्य ते यद्वा तद्वा वृक्षत्वगाद्याचक्षते। स तदाहृत्य पुत्रस्य भैषज्यं करोति। तत्कुर्वत एवास्य रोगो बलवानभूत्।

129. सर्वे त्रसन्ति दण्डस्य सर्वे बिभ्यति मृत्योः।
आत्मानमुपमां कृत्वा न हन्यान्न घातयेत्॥
131. सुखकामानि भूतानि यो दण्डेन विहिनस्ति।
आत्मनः सुखमिच्छन्प्रेत्य स न लभते सुखम्॥
133. मा वोचः परुषं कंचिदुक्ताः प्रतिवदेयुस्त्वाम्।
दुःखा हि संरम्भकथा प्रतिदण्डाः स्पृशेयुस्त्वाम्॥
134. स चेन्नेरयस्यात्मानं कांस्यमुपहतं यथा।
एष प्राप्तोसि निर्वाणं संरम्भस्ते न विद्यते॥

"In Śrâvastî there was a Brahman of the name of Adattapûrvaka ('who had not given away anything before'). He never gave anything to anybody, whence they called him Adattapûrvaka. A son was born to him, pleasing and delightful. When he was sixteen years old, he got jaundice. Seeing the son thus, the mother said, "O Brahman, your son has got a disease, put him under medical treatment." "Lady, if I get a physician, food and salary will have to be given to him. You do not see that this will entail expense" (lit. lessen my money). "What then will you do, Brahman?" "I will do what will not involve expense" (lessen my money). He then went to physicians and asked, "What medicine do you use against such and such a disease?" They spoke to him at random of the bark of some tree. He brought it and gave it as a medicine to his son. As he went on doing so, the disease was aggravated."

129. "All are afraid of being hurt, all fear death. Taking one's own self as a model, one should not kill and cause to be killed."

131. "He, who looking to his own happiness, inflicts injury upon creatures that equally desire their happiness, does not obtain felicity after death."

133. "Do not speak harshly to anybody; they may speak to you in return. For angry altercation is painful, and revenge will overtake you."

5

134. "If then, like a bottom of a shattered Matallic vessel, you will not stir yourself (utter), then you have reached Nirvâṇa, and you will have no angry altercation."

Here you will see a great many instances of the laws we laid down in the last lecture. And first, as regards phonetic corruption, we have in these passages त्त for त्र as in पुत्त for पुत्र, for क्त as in भत्त for भक्त, and for प्त as in पत्त for प्राप्त, and प्प for त्प as in उप्पन्न for उत्पन्न. This change is usually called assimilation of consonants. In pronouncing a conjunct, one has to pass from one position of the vocal organs to another without letting off the breath checked or compressed in the first, an operation of great difficulty. The sound of the first member is indistinct, but when the second is a weak consonant such as a nasal or a semi-vowel, it glides into the first almost as a vowel does, and thus the sound of the first acquires greater prominence. In the first position, the vocal organs strike and press against each other strongly, and the momentum necessary for this effort is acquired by uttering forcibly and with a jerk the vowel that precedes the conjunct, *i. e.* अ for instance in the word भक्त, just as a man previous to striking and pressing anything with his fist moves the hand with force through some distance. The previous forcible vowel breath and the subsequent strong contact and pressure form the characteristic of a conjunct consonantal sound. This is the only way of rendering the two members at all distinct, for the first is thus uttered with the preceding vowel and the second with the following. Thus, भक्त if pronounced in the manner I have described becomes भक्-त, but, if the previous vowel sound is weak, it becomes भ-क्त, in which case, in consequence of the absence of momentum, the pressure cannot be strong, and the conjunct character is not fully brought out. What we find in the Pâli, therefore, is that the passage from one vocal position to another is avoided, and the more distinct sound only, whether of the first member or the second, is pronounced with this forcible previous vowel breath and the succeeding strong contact and pressure; that is we have a conjunct as before, but it is made up not of two different letters, but of two of the same kind. Hence the instances noted above and also धम्म for धर्म, जम्म for जन्म, यञ्ञ for यज्ञ, सद्द for शब्द, दुद्ध for दुग्ध, खग्ग for खड्ग, मुग्ग for मुद्ग, अब्भुत for अद्भुत, लद्ध for लब्ध, उक्का for उल्का, अप्प for अल्प, तप्पन for तर्पण, अय्य for आर्य &c. But an attempt is made to pronounce the other sound also, and such of its elements as can go in with that which is uttered without involving change of position are transferred to it, that is, in effect the Pâli speaker treated a conjunct consonant as one sound possessing the characteristics of both. Thus the heavy *s'vâsa* or simple breath of स्, श्, and ष् in the conjuncts स्क्, ष्क्, श्च्, ष्ट्, स्त्, स्प् and ष्प् is combined with the distinct sounds क्, च्, ट्, त्, and प् and we have ख्, छ्, ठ्, थ्, and फ् for those conjuncts; but when preceded by a vowel and pronounced with the usual conjunctal characteristic, they become क्ख्, च्छ्, ट्ठ्, त्थ्, and प्फ्; as in सावत्थियं for श्रावस्त्याम् and फुसेय्यु for स्पृशेयुः in the above, and in खन्ध for स्कन्ध, पोक्खर for पुष्कर, पच्छा for पश्चात्, अच्छरिय for आश्चर्य, दिट्ठ for दिष्ट, पुट्ठ for पुष्ट, मत्थक for मस्तक, वत्थु for वस्तु, फन्दन for स्पन्दन, and पुप्फ for पुष्प. In स्न, श्न, ष्ण, स्म, श्म, and ष्म the consonantal portion of the distinct sounds, being made up of *nâda* or intonated breath, the heavy *s'vâsa* or simple breath of the sibilant is first made heavy *nâda*, that is, the sibilant is changed to the aspirate ह् and we have न्ह्, ण्ह् or म्ह् for these conjuncts; as in पण्ह for प्रश्न, उण्ह for उष्ण, अम्हि for अस्मि, अम्ह for अश्म, and गिम्ह for ग्रीष्म. These correspond to the ख्, छ् &c., in the above instances, and must like them be considered as simple sounds, and in our modern languages they are pronounced as such in certain places; but when preceded by a vowel they must have, as in other cases, the characteristic of conjunctal sounds, and be pronounced as न्न्ह, ण्ण्ह or म्म्ह though they are not so written.

I have already observed that when a following semi-vowel or nasal glides into the sound of the first consonant, this latter acquires prominence. But there are cases in which the semi-vowel य् does not so merge into the preceding; and this takes place when it is preceded by a dental mute. The palatal य् and the labial व् have since remote times been often pronounced in two ways, one in which the organs approach each other so closely that it is difficult to distinguish them from ज् and ब्; and another in which they are kept more distant. Hence the confusion between य् and ज् and व् and ब् that we find so often in modern pronunciation and in the modern languages. The Bengali invariably makes ब् of the Sanskrit व् and in most cases ज् of य् and the people of Northern India follow him to a great extent. In the Hindî we have many such forms as जमुना for यमुना, बांस for वंश, बांझ for वन्ध्या.

The heavy or close pronunciation of य्, is favoured by a preceding dental. In pronouncing letters of this class the tongue is nearly horizontal. Consequently, when after the formation of the dental mute it is moved upwards to form य्, the force with which it separates from the teeth carries it nearer to the palate than it should be. In the cerebral position, in which the tongue forms a curve with the concave side inwards, the force with which its tip separates acts downwards; hence if a य् has to be pronounced afterwards, the effort is in no way aided, but, if possible, hindered. In this case, therefore, the य् is always light; and for a similar reason it is so when preceded by a guttural. It is also light when preceded by the dental न्, since a large portion of the obstructed breath passes through the nose, and the tongue is not separated from the teeth with any force. Thus in the word वैद्य in the passage I have placed before you, and in अद्य, पद्य, &c., the य् being heavy does not glide or merge into द्, and, being the latter of two successive consonantal sounds, acquires greater distinctness; and the preceding sound must in virtue of the laws we have heen examining communicate all its elements to it, except of course the organic position. The element that is communicated in this case is the complete contact, wherefore the heavy य् becomes a complete ज्, and this, when pronounced like a conjunct, becomes ज्ज्. In such words as मध्य, वध्य, उपाध्याय &c., the preceding has got its heaviness of *nâda* or tone to communicate besides the complete contact, and thus the ज् becomes झ् and thence ज्झ्; and so we have मज्झ, वज्झ, उपज्झाय &c. In मृत्यु, प्रेत्य, सत्य &c., to the ज् formed as above must be added the hardness or *s'vâsa* of त्, *i. e.* the letter ज् must be pronounced not with the glottis contracted but stretched, wherefore we have च् and, with the conjunctal characteristic, च्च्. Those words therefore become मच्चु, पेच्च, and सच्च. If थ precedes instead of त्, the heavy *s'vâsa* required for its pronunciation is transferred to ज्, and so it becomes छ्, and thence च्छ्; as in रच्छा for रथ्या, नेपच्छ for नेपथ्य &c. The semi-vowel व् is also heavily pronounced when it forms a conjunct with another semi-vowel, and thus we have पुब्ब for पूर्व, सब्ब for सर्व, &c. There are also instances of this pronunciation when व् is preceded by a dental mute as in उब्बेग for उद्वेग, सब्भि for सद्भिः &c. In ऊर्ध्व the preceding ध्, as in मध्य, transfers its heavy *nâda* or tone to व्, and makes it भ्, and so we have उब्भ; but ऊर्ध्व is changed to उद्ध also.

The conjunct क्ष् or क्ष् must in some cases have been pronounced in ancient times like क्श्, as it is invariably so pronounced by the lower classes of the Marâṭhî people at the present day. This latter sound is easier to be made than क्ष्, first because the passage from the guttural position of क् to the palatal which is nearest to it is more natural than that to the more distant cerebral position of ष्, and also because in the latter case, after the guttural contact the tongue has to be rounded and the tip brought near the cerebral position. Thus, the whole weight of that organ has to be supported; while in the case of क्श् when its middle approaches the palatal position in pronouncing श्, the forepart falls into a natural position, and no effort is required to hold it there. Now in this क्श्, the sound of श्, being the latter of the two, is by the general rule more distinct than the other; and the complete contact of क् being transferred to it, it becomes छ्, because sibilants are produced by heavy *s'vâsa* as the hard aspirates are, and thence च्छ्; as in तच्छक for तक्षक, छण for क्षण in the sense of 'a festival', छुर for क्षुद्र, &c. In such words as वत्स and अप्सरस्, the prevailing sound is that of स् which, with the complete contact of the preceding त् and प्, ought to become थ्, as श् becomes छ् in the above case, on the theory that स् is a dental. But it is not properly a dental, since it is formed not at the root of the upper teeth as त्, थ्, द्, &c. are, but considerably above, and not by the tip of the tongue but by a part of it further inwards, which is made into a curve, having its convex side upwards, and brought near to that position. In this last respect it resembles the palatals, though the part of the tongue employed in their case is still further inwards, *i. e.* the middle. The sibilant स् therefore, has no mute corresponding to it in the sounds of the Sanskrit and Pâli languages. The Marâṭhî dento-palatals ·च्, ·छ्, ·ज्, ·झ् answer to it completely, being formed in the same position as itself; so that स्, when the organic contact is complete, should become the Marâṭhî ·छ्. But these sounds are unknown to the Pâli; the speakers of that language could not pronounce the Marâṭhi dento-palatals, as the Gujarâtîs and other northern nations cannot at the present day and just as these turn them into pure palatals, so did their ancestors. Hence, that sound which should properly be the dento-palatal ·छ् become the palatal छ्, and we have वच्छ for वत्स, अचछरा for अप्सरस् and मच्छर for मत्सर.

The dentals following a र् in a Sanskrit word are in Pâli often changed to cerebrals; as in वड्ढति for वर्धते, वट्टति for वर्तते, छड्डेति for छर्दयति अट्ठ for अर्थ &c. Here, as in the cases we have examined, the distinct sound is by the general rule the second, as we may observe even from the optional form वत्तति for वर्तते, and अत्थ for अर्थ. But, as before remarked, in all these Pâli transformations of Sanskrit conjuncts we see an attempt to pronounce both the members. When the speaker, being about to put the vocal organs into the position necessary for the utterance of the first letter, which he has first heard though indistinctly, sees that the second which he has distinctly heard cannot be produced there, he gives it up, and then passes immediately to the next position. But if, at the first, he thinks he can produce something like the second sound, which he has distinctly heard, he pronounces the letter there, and does not give up that position. Thus in pronouncing तर्प्, he feels that nothing like the sound प् can be produced at the position of र्, and hence gives it up and passing on to the lips forms तप्प्; but in वर्द् the द् that he pronounces at the cerebral point sounds a great deal more like ड् than प् and therefore he does not pass on to the dental position. But such of the Pâli speakers as could distinguish between ड् and द् did not stop at the cerebral position to pronounce their conjunct, but passed on to the dental; hence the optional forms we have noticed. Such words as मित्र, सत्र, भद्र, &c., differ from वर्धे, वर्द् &c., in having the र् after the distinct sound, so that the speaker resorts first to the dental position, and uttering the distinct sound there, is not carried away by the following र् to the cerebral position, the sound of र् being weaker. But if in the same word a dental follows such a conjunct, that dental is changed to the corresponding cerebral; as in पटि for प्रति and पठम for प्रथम. The cerebral element of these words has made a distinct impression on the speaker's ear, and he is conscious that his transformation of प्र into प, which was necessitated by his inherent inability to pronounce the two consonants together, has not brought it out. He therefore realizes it by changing the following ति and थ to टि and ठ. But if a consonant of another species follows, or if the conjunct ends the word, he cannot give effect to this impression.

The conjuncts in which the second sound is weak and consequently gives way to the first are क्य्, ख्य्, ग्य्, प्य्, भ्य्, श्य्, स्य्, क्र्, ग्र्, त्र्, द्र्, ध्र्, प्र्, भ्र्, श्र्, स्र्, क्ल्, क्व्, ज्व्, त्व्, द्व्, ध्व्, स्व्, &c., which have a semi-vowel for their latter member, and ग्न्, त्म्, प्न्, ष्ण्, &c., which have a nasal. Thus, we have सक्क for शक्य or शाक्य, अक्खान for आख्यान, योग्ग for योग्य, कुप्प for कुप्य, अब्भन्तर for अभ्यन्तर, पस्सति for पश्यति, तस्स for तस्य, सक्क for शक्र, अग्ग for अग्र, मित्त for मित्र, अद्दक for आर्द्रक, गिद्ध for गृध्र, विप्प for विप्र, अब्भ for अभ्र, अस्सम for आश्रम, अस्सव for आस्रव, सुक्क for शुक्ल, पक्क for पक्व, पज्जलति for प्रज्वलति, नीलत्त for नीलत्व, विद्देस for विद्वेष, अद्धा for अध्वा, अस्स for अश्व, &c., and अग्गि for अग्नि, अत्ता for आत्मा, छद्द for छद्म, सोप्प for स्वप्न, &c. The semi-vowel य् after न् in going out turns the न् into the palatal ञ्, this latter representing the combined effect of both; as in अञ्ञ for अन्य, राजञ्ञ for राजन्य, &c.

We have noticed above the change of क्ष् to च्छ्, but more frequently it is transformed into क्ख्. This change is due to the latter ष् being pronounced not incorrectly like ष् but correctly as a cerebral sound, which being hollow and undistinguishable is lost in the sound of क्. This last is distinctly heard, and the effect of ष् is only to add heavy *s'vâsa* to it and render it ख्; and thus the whole becomes क्ख् as in रुक्ख for वृक्ष, लक्खण for लक्षण, पक्ख for पक्ष, &c. Upon the principles we have laid down, it does not matter whether the Sanskrit conjunct is composed of two or three consonants, since what is done in the Pâli is to reproduce only the distinct consonantal sound with the other attendant characteristics; and thus we have ण्ह for क्ष्ण or ष्णं as in सण्ह for श्लक्ष्ण and पण्हि for पार्ष्णि, and म्ह for क्ष्म as in पम्ह for पक्ष्म in which words the last is the distinct sound, and क्ख for क्ष्म as in लक्खी for लक्ष्मी where the म् must have been pronounced so as to merge into the preceding क्ष्.

A Sanskrit conjunct at the beginning of a word is reduced to a single letter; and the reason is obvious. For as I have already observed the distinctive characteristic of a conjunct consists in the previous vowel being pronounced with rapidity and force, and in the subsequent strong pressure of the vocal organs which is rendered possible by the momentum acquired by that forcible utterance. It is the reproduction of this characteristic, that makes a single consonant that is pronounced at any one of the vocal positions look like a double. When a previous vowel does not exist, that is, when a conjunct begins a word, this characteristic cannot be reproduced; hence there is no double consonant. Thus, we have खलित for स्खलित, कमेण for क्रमेण, भमर for भ्रमर, फस्स for स्पर्श, &c.

You will have seen that in all the changes of conjunct consonants which we have examined, no element of the two sounds is omitted by the Pâli speakers. They had not the patience to hear and reproduce the two consonants immediately after each other, by putting their vocal organs into two different positions, or laboured under a physical inaptitude for doing so, their tongue not being sufficiently trained for the successive movements. But short of this, all the constituents of the sound, the *s'vâsa*, light and heavy, the completeness of contact, and the force of utterance, are represented in their pronunciation, and the amount of muscular exertion involved is the same as in the case of the original. This may be called the energetic mode of pronouncing conjuncts. There are, however, a few instances in which the components are separated by inserting a vowel between them. Thus Sanskrit सूक्ष्म is changed to सुखुम, औष्मिक to ओसमिक,

श्लेष्म to सिलेसुम, स्मरति to सुमरति, श्री and ह्री to सिरी and हिरी, बैल्व to बेलुव and औपश्लेषिक to ओपसिलेसिक. The separating vowel is generally such as can be easily pronounced along with the previous or the following consonant, that is, belongs to the same organic position as either. Thus in the first four instances we have the labial उ in the syllables सु and owing सु to the influence of the following म्. The conjuncts र्य् and र्ह् are almost invariably dissolved into रिय् and रह् as in कारिय, अरिय, सुरिय, विरिय &c. and अरह, गरहा, बरिह &c. for कार्य, अर्य or आर्य, सूर्य, वीर्य &c. and अर्ह, गर्हा, बर्ह &c.; and in one or two instances we have the first change when the य् is preceded by a consonant other than र्, as in चैतिय for चैत्य. This change is to some extent due to the य् being pronounced weak, *i. e.* almost like इ. In the same way, we have सिलोक, सिलेस, सिलाघा, किलेस, किलन्त, गिलान, मिलान, पिलवति, सुपिन, सिनिद्ध, नहान or सिनान &c. for श्लोक, श्लेष, श्लाघा, क्लेश, क्लान्त, ग्लान, म्लान, प्लवति, स्वप्न, स्निग्ध, स्नान &c. This mode of utterance wants the force of the one we have examined, but both the sounds of a conjunct are clearly reproduced in it. You will have observed that the second member of the conjunct dissolved in this way is what may be called an imperfect consonant, *i. e.* a semi-vowel, aspirate, or nasal, in pronouncing which the breath is not completely stopped. They therefore act like a vowel, and render the sound of the first consonant comparatively distinct and audible, but are not so weak themselves as to melt away into that sound. Hence both the sounds are audible but the Pâli speaker not being able to put his vocal organs into two consonantal positions successively, as we have seen, reproduced the two sounds by interposing a vowel between them. But when in some cases the second member was weakly pronounced it melted away into the first, and so we have the optional forms विस्सरति for विस्मरति, सेह्म for श्लेष्म, सोप्प for स्वप्न &c. When, however, its pronunciation became stronger than that of the first, it prevailed, and so we have कय्य for कार्य and अय्य for आर्य.

Some conjuncts appear also unchanged in this dialect; as ब्र in the words ब्रह्म, ब्रवीति, and ब्रूहेति, व्य in व्याधि, व्यग्घ, व्यग्ग &c., प्ल in प्लवङ्ग, प्लवति, and प्लव, स्न in स्नेह &c. Such as have a nasal for their first member and a mute for the second are also unchanged, since the nasal, even according to the rules of Sanskrit, belongs to the same organic position as the mute.

We will now proceed to notice the changes of single consonants. An unaspirate is changed to an aspirate when it is followed in the same word by a sibilant; as in फरसु for परशु, फरुस for परुष, फुस्स for

पुष्य, सुखुमार for सुकुमार, थुस, for तुष &c. The heavy *s'vâsa* that forms a constituent of the sibilant sound has made such a strong impression on the ear of the hearer, that he immediately prepares himself to let it out, and thus uses it even in pronouncing the letters which precede the sibilant and do not require it. The pronunciation of a word is rendered easier by transferring one of the elements of a sound to another or others, that is, by assimilating them to each other as much as possible. In a few instances the simple breath or *s'vâsa* of a previous surd is transferred to the following, originally a sonant, as in थकेति for स्थगयति. The cerebral unaspirated sonant ड् between two vowels is softened into the corresponding semi-vowel ळ्, as in ताळन for ताडन, पीळन for पीडन, तळाक for तडाक &c. This peculiarity distinguished the old Vedic Sanskrit also; and the sound exists in the modern Marâṭhî and Gujarâtî, though it is unknown to the other vernaculars.

I have already given instances in which the cerebral ऱ् of a previous syllable in going out changes the dental of the following to a cerebral, and to these I may now add निगण्ठ for निर्ग्रन्थ, वण्ट for वृन्त, कट for कृत &c. In some instances, this change takes place without such an influencing cause, as in डसति and डंस for दशति and दंश, and डाह for दाह. The same phenomenon is observable in some conjuncts, as in विदड्ढ for विदग्ध, हेट्ठा for अधस्तात्, and ठा or ट्ठा for स्था in the several derivatives from that root as ठाति, ठायी, उट्ठान &c. The dental nasal न् is also similarly changed to ण् in a few cases, as in याण, ओणत, ओणीत, सणिकं for ज्ञान, अवनत, अवनीत, शनकैः &c. The operation of this process is very limited but still it exists and cannot be accounted for in any other way than by supposing that the vocal organs or the vocal habits of the Pâli speakers were more adapted for the production of cerebral sounds, or, in other words, the people had a natural aptitude for them.

Sanskrit श् and ष् are changed to स्, which is the only sibilant in the language. This change involves an economy of effort. The tongue in its several movements becomes a lever with the fulcrum at the inner end where it is fixed in the mouth, and the weight in its centre of gravity. The advantage increases with the distance from the fulcrum of the point which is moved, that is, the point where power is applied. Hence gutturals are the most disadvantageous, palatals next, and dentals, the least. The cerebrals being pronounced by rounding the tongue and raising it very high, it is a question whether this additional effort does not neutralise the advantage they possess over the palatals by their position being more distant. Thus स् is the weakest of the sibilants. But in the Pâli the change is so universal that we must suppose a special inaptitude in the speakers of that language for pronouncing श् and ष्, as we had to suppose in the case of the conjuncts. When, however, in a few cases the peculiarity of the palatal श् was distinctly preceived, and it was felt that the substituted स् did not bring it out, that sibilant was changed to the corresponding mute of its psoition, *i. e.* to छ्, which resembles श् in the heaviness of the simple breath required for pronouncing it. We have thus छव for शव, छक for शकृत्, and छाप for शाव. The change of षष् 'six' to छ is also to be similarly accounted for. I have already remarked that sometimes ष् must at an early period have been pronounced very much like श्. Besides these changes there are solitary instances of others, such as the softening or toning of surds as in मूग for मूक, or the dropping of the mute element of the sonant aspirates as in होति and हेट्ठा for भवति and अधस्तात्. But these will be more fully discussed in connection with the Prâkṛits and the vernaculars, in which these processes have a much wider range.

The vowel ऋ is changed to अ as in कसि for कृषि, तण्हा for तृष्णा, गह for गृह, घत for घृत, मच्चु for मृत्यु &c.; to इ as in दिट्ठ for दृष्ट, तिण for तृण, मिग for मृग, तित्ति for तृप्ति, गिद्ध for गृध्र &c.; and to उ as in भुस for भृश, मुदु, for मृदु, मुसा for मृषा, वुस for वृष, वुट्ठि for वृष्टि &c. The last change generally takes place when the vowel is preceded by a labial; so that the vocal position of the consonant influences that of the vowel. When there is no such influence, it is changed to अ and इ. Now, the vowel ऋ is composed of a consonantal and a vowel element, the former of which is subordinated to the latter. On this account it does not give to the consonant to which it is added the character of a conjunct, and the preceding vowel is not rendered heavy[8]. In Pâli this consonantal element disappears in virtue of the inherent inability, which we have considered at such length, of passing from one vocal position to another without letting off the breath; but the previous consonant is not doubled because the usual character of a conjunct is absent. Or the disappearance may be accounted for by the fact that the consonantal element is so subordinated to the vowel element as to escape

8. This fact is accounted for by the authors and the commentators of the Prâtis'âkhyas by supposing that the vowel element envelopes the र on all sides *i.e.* precedes it and follows it. (See Vâj. Pr., Ind. St. V. 145 and Ath. Pr., Whitney, I. 37.)

notice, and that the letter, as a whole, is difficult to pronounce. The vowel element of ऋ is pronounced by bringing the root of the tongue in contact with the root of the palate, *i. e.* in the position of the gutturals; and is unrepresented independently in the Sanskrit or Pâli Alphabet. Hence it is pronounced either lower down, in the position of अ, or higher up in that of इ, while it is sometimes carried so far to the outside as the position of उ, especially when a labial precedes. That the cerebral or र् element did exist, and was occasionally preceived by the Pâli speakers is proved by such examples as रिते for ऋते and रुक्ख for वृक्ष, and also by the circumstance that in some cases, though it disappears, it changes the following dental to a cerebral, as in वड्ढि for वृद्धि, विसट for विसृत, कट for कृत &c. From these observations it would appear that the vowel we have been considering must have been in those days pronounced just in the manner in which Marâṭhí Pandits of the present day pronounce it, and not like अर्, इर्, र or रि as is supposed by several European scholars. If घृत were really घर्त, or मृग, मिर्ग, the Pâli corruptions would be घत्त or मिग्ग; and if सुकृत were सुक्रत, or तादृश, ताद्रिश we should have सुक्कत or तद्दिश instead of सुकत and तादिस, and there is no reason why ऋतु and ऋषि should have lost their र् and become उतु and इसि if they were really pronounced like रितु or रतु and रिषि or रषि.[9]

The sounds of the Sanskrit diphthongs ऐ and औ are like those of अइ and अउ uttered rapidly, *i. e.* without allowing any appreciable time to elapse between the two elements. In forming अ, the tongue and the lips are in a natural position, the lips, however, not being closed but a little opened; while इ requires that the middle of the tongue should be brought close to the palate, and उ, that the lips should be completely rounded. Hence, in pronouncing ऐ and औ it is necessary to pass from one vocal position *immediately* to another, a process of which, as we have seen, the Pâli speakers were incapable. These diphthongs are therefore changed to ए and ओ which partake of the character of both the components. In the formation of ए the tongue is not horizontal as in the case of अ; its middle is raised up but not brought so close to the palate as in the case of इ. Similarly, in pronouncing ओ the lips are not so completely rounded as in the formation of उ; neither are they in a natural position as in the case of अ. These sounds, therefore, being produced in a position between those of

9. The explanation of this vowel souud and the others that follow is based upon the mode in which we Marâṭhâs pronounce them at the present day, and which is sanctioned by the Prâtis'âkhyas,

अ and इ, and अ and उ, combine the characteristics of both, but are simple, *i. e.*, formed in one position only. Thus we have सेल for शैल, तेल for तैल, केवट्ट for कैवर्त, खोम for क्षौम, कोसेय्य for कौशेय, मोलि for मौलि &c. Similarly अय and अव frequently become ए and ओ; as in कथेति for कथयति, पूजेति for पूजयति, नेति for नयति, ओधि for अवधि, ओकास for अवकाश, नोनीत for नवनीत &c. The sounds of these dissyllables differ from those of ऐ and औ in this respect that the अ of the former is not rapidly pronounced as is that involved in these diphthongs; or, in the words of the grammarians, the value of the first अ is one *mâtrâ* and of the other one-half. In the same way the अ of the two dissyllables is followed by the semi-vowel य् and व्, while that of ऐ and औ has the corresponding vowels इ and उ after it. When अय and अव are hastily pronounced, this distinction disappears, and these dissyllables assume the form of the diphthongs ऐ and औ, which by the rule just discussed become ए and ओ.

A long vowel is shortened when it is followed by a double consonant; as in मग्ग for मार्ग, पत्त for प्राप्त, इक्खण for ईक्षण, कित्ति for कीर्ति, तिब्ब for तीव्र, रुक्ख for रूक्ष, सुत्त for सूत्र &c. The strong pressure that is necessary for the pronunciation of a conjunct cannot be properly exerted, as formerly observed, without momentum, for the acquisition of which the previous vowel has to be uttered with force and with a jerk. For this purpose a short vowel alone is fitted, but if a long one precedes, its utterance being by its nature slow and weak, the organs for want of momentum do not strike against each other with force, and hence the pressure they exert is weak. But the Pâli speaker, catching from his Sanskrit teacher only the generally strong nature of the pressure involved in the utterance of conjuncts, realized it to the fullest possible extent, without stopping to observe how much it was impaired by the length of the previous vowel, by pronouncing the previous vowel with force and rapidity, and thus rendering it short. And in this way the real quantity of the syllable is not diminished. Though the vowel is short the vocal organs take some time to emerge from the close contact and the strong pressure resulting from its forcible utterance, and hence the whole syllable इक्, for instance, in इक्खण, has the metrical value of a long vowel, *i. e.* is equal to two *mâtrâs* or syllabic instants. In the original ईक्षण, on the contrary, the pressure in the pronunciation of क्ष being weaker in consequence of the slowness of the previous vowel utterance occupies less time; so that in the one case the shortness of the vowel is accompanied by a longer duration of the contact, and in the other the length of the vowel is attended by a shorter duration of the contact. The change, then, we have been considering, is due to the pressure necessary for the formation of the conjunctal sounds in these words having made a strong impression on the ear of the Pâli speaker. When, however, the length of the vowel prevailed, and neutralized the pressure to such an extent as to render it incapable of attracting attention, the conjunct came to be in the condition of one standing at the beginning of a word; and like it preserved only the more distinct sound and dropped the other, leaving the long vowel unchanged. We have thus सीस for शीर्ष, दीघ for दीर्घ, सासप for सर्षप, &c. It is, however, clear that a long vowel followed by a double consonant is an impossibility in Pâli. A Sanskrit conjunct, whenever it made a distinct impression, was pronounced with the usual characteristics of that sound, *viz.*, the previous rapid and forcible vowel utterance and the subsequent strong contact and strong pressure, the perceptible effect of which was the shortening of the previous vowel and the doubling of the following consonant.

Without the momentum acquired from the force and rapidity of the previous vowel utterance, the Pâli speaker could not form a strong contact and exert strong pressure, that is, without a short preceding vowel they could not pronounce a double consonant. If then the Pâli has such words as तेत्तिस (त्रयस्त्रिंशत्), सेट्ठि (श्रेष्ठिन्), नेत्त (नेत्र), सोत्थिय (श्रोत्रिय), योग्गा (योग्या), मोक्ख &c., it follows that the vowels ए and ओ were in such cases pronounced short. Similarly, when before doubles इ and उ are changed to them, as they often are, they must be short. This change of इ and उ to ए and ओ arises from the fact that the force and rapidity of the jerk with which the current of breath is sent up to pronounce the former vowels is apt to prevent the tongue from rising as close to the palate or the lower lip to the upper, as is necessary for the formation of इ or उ, or they are apt to be forced down by the current. And ए and ओ differ from इ and उ simply in the distance between the pronouncing organs being greater. This change, therefore, really involves an economy, since the effort to raise up the tongue and the lower lip across the strong current of breath blowing above is saved. We have thus, ओट्ठ for उष्ट्र, पोक्खर for पुष्कर, पोत्थक for पुस्तक, सोण्ड for शुण्ड, नेक्ख for निष्क, नेत्तिंस for निस्त्रिंश, वेस्सभू for विश्वभू &c. In some cases both vowels are in use, as in the word नेक्ख which has another form निक्ख. Sometimes, especially before य्, ए was invariably pronounced short, though no conjunct followed, and to make up for the loss of quantity thus occasioned the consonant was doubled; as in थेय्य for स्थेय, गेय्य for गेय, कोसेय्य for कौशेय &c. The vowel ओ was also similarly treated in a few cases, as in ओस्सजति for अवसृजति. Thus then not only has the Pâli a short ए and ओ, but the speakers of the language seem to have possessed a predilection for those sounds. Besides the changes we have examined, there are stray examples of others, such as उसु and उच्छु for इषु and इक्षु, in which the उ of the following syllable influences the utterance of the first vowel, सोप्प for स्वप्न, in which the semi-vowel व् is dissolved into the corresponding vowel उ, and thence transformed to short ओ, मोर for मयूर, in which the य् being lightly pronounced loses its consonantal character and the vowel ऊ with the preceding अ forms ओ, and others.

You will thus have observed that the phonetic changes which Sanskrit words undergo in passing into the Pâli may be brought under a few general rules. There are not such various and extensive corruptions both of vowels and consonants as we find in the later dialects and in the modern vernaculars. It has been estimated that two-fifths of the Pâli vocabulary are composed of pure Sanskrit words, and the remaining three-fifths, of words altered in one or other of the modes explained above. The conclusion to be drawn from these facts is, that when the Pâli was in use, the tradition of the original Sanskrit was not distant; the words, so to say, did not stray away long from the mother-language, so as to undergo extensive alterations. If so, how is it that some of the changes such as the transformation of ऐ and औ into ए and ओ and the assimilation of consonants are so universal, the first being without any exception, and the second with but a few unimportant ones? The principle which guides phonetic change is the economy of effort, understanding the word in its widest sense. This economy is observable in the two kinds of changes, as well as in the transformation of surds into sonants, the elision of consonants or of some of their elements, the assimilation of the vowels or the single consonants that make up a word, and in several other processes. But in the Pâli there are very few instances of some of these, and none at all of others. The language had not a sufficiently long duration of independent existence to bring them into extensive operation. If, then, the two processes we have noticed are found in full play in that dialect, the reason must be sought for in the vocal peculiarities of the people who spoke it. Though they heard conjunct consonants and the diphthongs

ऐ and औ pronounced by the speakers of Sanskrit, as correctly as the other letters which they did not corrupt, their organs were not fitted to utter them. These peculiarities may have been natural or acquired. If natural, the people who first corrupted Sanskrit into the Pâli must have belonged to an alien race which came into close contact with the Âryas and learnt their language. If they were acquired, a branch of the same Âryan race must be supposed to have been isolated in some part of the country, and to have developed them, in consequence of being cut off from the main body. But this supposition must be rejected for the reasons that have been already given. Such complete isolation as could give rise to new vocal peculiarities must be expected to have occasioned greater phonetic decay in other respects than is observable in the Pâli. And our analysis of the Sanskrit conjunctal and the Pâli double sounds favours the first view. For, we have seen that these latter represent all the elements of the former, but they are combined in a sound produced in one vocal position only. The Pâli speakers endeavoured to reproduce the sound of a conjuct faithfully, their pronunciation was not weak, as is that prevailing in modern times, but energetic and correct in every other respect; but they could not combine energy of utterance with two successive movements of the vocal organs. This could only be because their organs were not sufficiently trained for the purpose; in other words, because the sounds were foreign to them. The condition of men who have to learn the language of others is similar to that of children, whose organs of speech are being exercised for the first time. Healthy children, whose utterance is energetic, pronounce the conjuncts almost in the same way as the Pâli speakers did. And there is another instance in History of an alien race having treated the sounds of the language of a civilized community in just the same way. The Barbarians who overran Italy and developed the Italian from the Latin, showed the same inability to pronounce the Latin conjuncts, and assimilated them as our Pâli ancestors did.

If this supposition is correct, we must find other traces of the peculiarities of this alien race. And such we do find. The existence of the short ए and ओ in the Pâli, and the predilection the people showed for them, as well as the change of dentals to cerebrals without any influencing cause, are similarly to be attributed to the natural vocal tendencies of the people. These sounds must have existed and played an important part in the original language of this people, so that they were unable to shake them off entirely, even when they left their own tongue and learned that of the more civilized Âryas with whom they came to be closely incorporated. If the original Pâli speakers belonged to the same race as the Dravidians of Southern India of the present day, we have a reason to believe that their native tongue contained them; for they exist in the Dravidian languages and are very characteristic of them.

We shall also find in the Pâli, and even in the passage placed before you, examples of another phenomenon presented by a growing language. Several new words, unknown to Sanskrit, but formed from Sanskrit roots, have come into use. Such is मनापो, derived very likely from मनस् 'mind' or 'heart', and आप् 'to obtain' 'to meet,' so that the word signifies 'something that comes up to the wishes of the heart', 'pleasing'. The word सचे is from चेत् with स prefixed, which स seems to be the same as the nominative singular of the masculine of तद्. For, it is so used in Sanskrit before चेत्, though it has there an independent sense; as in स चेन्मुनिदौहित्रस्तल्लक्षणोपपन्नः (Śâkuntala). Often used together in this way, the two words formed a compound expression, and, the independent character of स being forgotten, it came to be looked upon as one word. In the same way, सन्तिक must have come into existence from the frequent use of such expressions as तस्सन्तिकं, ब्राह्मणस्सन्तिकं &c. made up of the genitive singular of a nouu or pronoun ending in अ and अन्तिक. The portion सन्तिक then came to be regarded as an independent word, and was used as such. Another new word is फासु or फासुक 'agreeablc', 'pleasant', corresponding to such a Sanskrit word as स्पर्शु or स्पर्शुक formed from the analogy of such verbal derivatives as भिक्षु, इच्छु, or लाभुक, पातुक &c., and meaning 'that which is or deserves to be touched', or 'pleasant to the touch'. Other instances are पिलन्धन 'an ornament', पेय्याल 'plentiful' &c.

We will now proceed to the examination of Pâli grammar. When after years of successive creative efforts, the language of our Âryan ancestors came to be so rich in all kinds of grammatical forms, as the Vedic or middle Sanskrit is, it became cumbrous, and the tendency set in, as we have seen, of dropping away some of them and rendering the grammar simpler. The duals of both nouns and verbs are unnecessary; the occasions for using them do not often present themselves. Hence, even in Sanskrit, their use must have been rare, and the Pâli, which, in its original form at least, must be taken to represent the current usage, has dropped them away altogether. But the manner in which the process of simplification is principally carried on is by the use of false analogies. Thus in Sanskrit, nouns ending in इ and उ of the neuter gender prefix न् to the terminations of the vowel cases. But in Pâli it is added to those of the corresponding cases of masculine nouns also, as in मच्चुनो for मृत्योः in the passage before us. Similarly, from the analogy of neuter nouns in अ which form their nominative and accusative singular by adding म्, the pronouns यद् and तद् come to have यं and तं for the corresponding cases, instead of the Sanskrit यद् and तद्. In Sanskrit, the conjugation that is very often used is the first in which अ is tacked on to the root in the special tenses, and it embraces a large number of the most ordinary roots. Here, in our passage, we find the analogy extended to the root हिंस् the present tense of which is in the mother dialect ordinarily formed by inserting न between the two letters, and adding the termination to the final (हिनस्ति 3rd person singular), and we have हिंसति. The root ज्ञा takes the form of जा in the present and other special tenses, and to it is added the conjugational sign ना, so that it becomes जाना. Now, this special form is generalized, and used in other tenses also, such as the Aorist and the Future. Thus, we have here संजानिंसु, the Aorist 3rd person plural of ज्ञा, and in other places we find जानिस्सति as one of the forms of the Future. The special forms इच्छ, पश्य, शृण, बुध्य, and पद्य are similarly generalized, the last four being phonetically changed to पस्स, सुण, बुज्झ, and पज्ज. In the same way in forming the causative of a root प or आप is added in Sanskrit to roots ending in आ and to a few others. It is extended to all roots in the Pâli, and thus we have तिकिच्छापेहि for चिकित्सय in the above. The termination त्वा of the absolutive is, in Sanskrit, replaced by य when a root has a preposition prefixed to it. But here no such distinction is observed, and त्वा is used in all cases. The operation of this law of false analogies is very extensive in the grammar of the Pâli and the later Prâkṛits ; and by its means new forms have been made up instead of those current in the primitive language. But side by side with these, we often find the latter also in use corrupted by the usual phonetic laws, and having a sort of isolated existence, since they transgress the general rule that has newly come into operation. Thus we have जानिस्सति, पस्सिस्सति and लभिस्सति according to the law of analogy; but ञस्सति from ज्ञास्यति, दक्खति from द्रक्ष्यति, and लच्छति from लप्स्यते are also in use. These three processes then, *viz*, the dropping away of forms not required for the expression of the current ordinary thought, the formation of new ones on the principle of analogy, and the preservation of the old ones in what may be called an isolated or petrified condition, have contributed to the formation of the grammar of this and the succeeding languages. With these preliminary observations, I will now hastily pass under review the principal points in the grammar of this dialect.[10]

The Pâli has lost the dual, and also the dative and ablative cases, except of masculine and neuter nouns ending in अ.* The only occasion when the first is ordinarily used is when 'giving' is expressed, but the genitive case has such a comprehensive signification in Sanskrit that it denotes the dative relation also, and is often used in that sense. Most of the relations expressed by the ablative are denoted by the instrumental, and for the expression of the peculiar ablative sense, *viz.*, the separation of one thing from another, the particle तस् had come into very general use, even in the parent language. The genitive and instrumental thus took up the place of those two cases. But people do not forget what they have frequent occasion to use. The great majority of nouns in Sanskrit end in अ, and of these the singular is oftener used than the plural. Hence the singulars of the dative and ablative of these nouns are preserved in the Pâli, notwithstanding the operation of the causes that drove away these cases from other places. The भ् of the termination of the instrumental plural is optionally changed to ह्. The locative singular of masculine and neuter nouns ending in a vowel is formed by adding the pronominal termination स्मिन्, phonetically changed to स्मिं and म्हि; and the ablative स्मात् in the form of स्मा or म्हा is used optionally in the case of nouns in अ. The termination स्य of the genitive singular of this class of nouns is generalized, and in the form of स्स applied to all nouns of the masculine and neuter genders. It should be remembered that in accordance with the general rule, the Sanskrit grammatical forms drop the final consonant, including a visarga, in passing into the Pâli. The nasal म् is changed to an anusvâra, and since this, like a conjunct consonant, necessitates the rapid utterance of the preceding vowel and renders it heavy, the vowel is shortened. We have thus नं for नाम्, स्सं for स्याम्, यं for याम्, &c. The न् of स्मिन् and of the syllable अन् occurring in some of the cases is also changed to an anusvâra.

Masculine Nouns ending in अ. The nominative singular always ends in ओ. In Sanskrit we have this form before a short अ or a sonant only. Here it is generalized. The accusative plural ends in

10 My authority in this portion of my subject is Kachchâyana, as edited by M. Senart.

* The ablative अग्गिस्मा-म्हा, भिक्खुस्मा-म्हा do, however, occur in the literature.

ए as बुद्धे. When the final consonant is dropped according to the usual phonetic rules, the Sanskrit nominative and accusative plurals become exactly alike. To distinguish the one from the other, therefore, this form is appropriated in the Pâli for the latter. The ए appears to be the termination of the nominative plural of pronouns, and it is transferred to nouns in the same way as the others we have noticed above. But it is used here in an accusative sense. The forms of the singular and plural of the nominative of neuter nouns, and of the plural of many more, are the same as those of the accusative in Sanskrit, and this fact must have led to a tendency to liken the two cases in other places also. Hence the pronominal nominative came to be used like an accusative. We shall directly see this tendency to confuse the two cases manifested more clearly as regards the plural, and it may be remarked that as regards both the numbers it went on increasing at each successive stage, until in the latest Prâkṛit and in the vernaculars the distinction has entirely disappeared. The termination of the instrumental plural is एभि as in बुद्धेभि, or, with the mute element dropped, एहि which is traced to the Vedic एभिः in such forms as देवेभिः. But it may be explained otherwise. The Sanskrit बुद्धैः becomes बुद्धे by the dropping of the visarga and the change of the diphthong to ए, and this is the same as the locative singular, and is by no means distinctive of an instrumental sense. Hence to बुद्धे was added the instrumental termination भि or हि which all other nouns in Sanskrit and Pâli take. The other cases are the same as in Sanskrit, subject to the general remarks made above. The ablative and locative singulars have the new pronominal forms in स्मा or म्हा and स्मिं or म्हि in addition to the old ones. In the vocative singular, the final अ is optionally lengthened.

—*Nouns in* इ *and* उ. The nominative and accusative plurals have two forms and they are the same for both the cases, as अग्गी and अग्गयो, भिक्खू and भिक्खवो. Now अग्गी and भिक्खू are the Sanskrit accusative plurals अग्नीन् and भिक्षून्, and अग्गयो and भिक्खवो the nominative plurals अग्नयः and भिक्षवः The distinction between the two is lost, and both are used indifferently in the sense of the nominative and accusative. The termination of the instrumental plural is भि or हि. The singulars of the genitive and locative are, like those of the corresponding neuter nouns or nouns ending in इन् such as दण्डिन्, formed by the addition of न्, as अग्गिनो and भिक्खुनो, अग्गिनि and भिक्खुनि. They have also the forms indicated in the general remarks, *viz.*, अग्गिस्स and

भिक्खुस्स, and अग्गिस्मिं—म्हि and भिक्खुस्मि—म्हि; and the dative and ablative are, as usual, like the genitive and instrumental. The vocative is like the nominative, except in the plural of nouns in उ which ends in वो or वे as भिक्खवो or भिक्खवे. The rest are old or Sanskrit, the final vowel being, however, lengthened in the plural of the instrumental and locative, and the syllable ग्नि of अग्नि being optionally dissolved into गिनि in the nominative singular.

—*Nouns in* ऋ. The nominative has the old Sanskrit forms; as सत्था and सत्थारो for शास्ता and शास्तारः from शास्तृ. The accusative plural is the same as the nominative plural. The augmented form of the Sanskrit nominative plural, *viz.* सत्थार for शास्तार, is taken as the base for the plural of the instrumental, genitive, and locative, and declined like nouns in अ. The genitive plural is also formed by taking the nominative singular as the base, as सत्थानं. The instrumental singular has the new base and the old termination आ; and thus we have सत्थारा. The genitive singular has three forms, one of them being the old one with the final र् dropped, as सत्थु, and the other two made up by taking this form as the base, and appending the terminations which nouns in उ as भिक्खु take, as सत्थुस्स or सत्थुनो. The singulars of the accusative and locative have the Sanskrit forms, as सत्थारं and सत्थरि; and the vocative singular has besides the old one another with the vowel lengthened, as सत्थ or सत्था. You will thus see that there are four bases, the old one which gives the old forms, and three new ones, सत्था and सत्थार generalized from the nominative, and सत्थु, from the genitive.

—*Nouns ending in a consonant.* There can be no consonantal declension proper, since a final consonant is dropped, and the noun treated as one ending in the preceding vowel. But relics of the Sanskrit forms of the consonantal bases are preserved and used along with the others. In the declension of the noun आत्मन् there are two new bases अत्त and अत्तन, generalized from the forms of the singular of the Sanskrit nominative and of the instrumental and others आत्मा and आत्मना &c. and declined like nouns in अ. The first is used in the singular of the accusative and the plurals of the genitive and locative which are अत्तं, अत्तानं and अत्तेसु; and the second in the plural of the instrumental which is अत्तनेहि-भि. The remaining forms are old, the portion आत्म being corrupted to अत्त; they are अत्ता nominative singular, अत्तानो nominative and accusative plural, अत्तानं accusative singular, अत्तना instrumental singular, अत्तनो genitive singular, and

अत्तनि locative singular. The vocatives is अत्त or अत्ता, like that of nouns in अ.

In the declension of the noun राजन् the base राज in used in the singulars of the accusative, the instrumental, and perhaps the ablative also, and the forms are राजं, राजेन, and राजस्मा or राजम्हा. The old forms are found in the nominative (राजा, राजानो), and in the singular of the accusative which has thus two forms राजं and राजानं, and the plural of this last case is, as usual, the same as that of the first. The singulars of the instrumental, genitive, and locative are the same as those in Sanskrit, but ज्ञ being changed to ञ्ञ, we have रञ्ञा, रञ्ञो, and रञ्ञि. In the last two cases the conjunct is also dissolved into ञिन, wherefore we have राजिनो and राजिनि also. The genitive plural is रञ्ञं and, ज्ञ being dissolved into ञुन, the form राजूनं is used, in addition. This राजु is made the base of the plurals of the instrumental and locative; and thus we have राजूभि-हि and राजूसु. The vocative singular is like that of nouns in अ.

The suffixes वत् and मत् of such nouns as गुणवत् and सतिमत् are regarded as if they were वन्त and मन्त, and the nouns declined like those ending in अ in the sigulars of the nominative, accusative, and genitive, and in the plurals of the accusative, instrumental genitive and locative; and, according to the commentator of Kachchâyana, in the singulars of the instrumental and locative also; as गुणवन्तो, गुणवन्तं, गुणवन्तस्स, गुणवन्ते, गुणवन्तेभि-हि, गुणवन्तानं and गुणवन्तेसु; also गुणवन्तेन and गुणवन्तस्मि-म्हि. The old forms are preserved in both numbers of the nominative and genitive, and in the singulars of the instrumental, locative, and vocative; as गुणवा, गुणवन्तो, गुणवतो, गुणवतं, गुणवता, गुणवति, and गुणवं. The nominative singular is made the base of other forms of the singulars of the accusative, genitive and vocative, as गुणवं, गुणवस्स and गुणव or गुणवा. The present participles, Parasmaipada, are similarly declined, the only difference being in the nominative singular, as गच्छं.

Feminine nouns. The nominative, besides the old forms, has another transferred from nouns in ई; as कञ्ञायो. The singulars of the instrumental and the succeeding cases, excepting the vocative, have one same form made up from the Sanskrit genitive by dropping the visarga and shortening the final vowel; as कञ्ञाय, instrumental, dative, ablative, genitive, and locative singular. The others and also the locative singular have the old forms; as कञ्ञाभि-हि instrumental, and ablative plural, कञ्ञानं genitive and dative plural, and कञ्ञायं and कञ्ञासु locative singular and plural. The final member य of the conjunct which appears in the case-forms of nouns in ई such as नदी, is dissolved into इय, and thus we have नदियो from the Sanskrit नद्यः; and this and नदी from the Sanskrit नद्यः are both of them the plurals of the nominative and accusative; नद्या the singular of the instrumental is dissolved into नदिया, and also नद्याः of the ablative and genitive which after dropping the visarga becomes नद्या;* and this is extended to the locative singular, which has also another form नदियं, from नद्याम्. There is nothing particular about the rest. Nouns in short इ are declined in exactly the same way, except that Kachchâyana gives such forms as रत्या and रत्यं in addition to रत्तिया and रत्तियं for the singular of the ablative and locative. Nouns in उ or ऊ follow completely the analogy of those in ई; the forms of वधू, for instance, are not derived from the corresponding Sanskrit forms of the noun, but are made up by adding the final syllables of those of नदी; as वधुयो nominative and accusative plural, वधुया singular instrumental, ablative, genitive, &c.

Neuter Nouns.—The singular of the nominative and accusative of neuter nouns ending in a vowel is the same as in the parent tongue, but the forms of the plural are optionally like those of the corresponding masculine nouns; as रूपा or रूपानि nominative plural, and रूपे or रूपानि accusative plural; अट्ठी (like अग्गी) or अट्ठीनि nominative and accusative plural, आयू or आयूनि nominative and accusative plural. As in the case of masculine nouns, such as have a final consonant in Sanskrit drop it and are treated as if they ended in the preceding vowel. But in the singulars the old forms are preserved; as मनो or मनं nominative and accusative, मनसा or मनेन instrumental, मनसो genitive, मनसि, मने or मनस्मि-म्हि locative.

Pronouns.—As pronominal terminations have been transferred to nouns, a few nominal ones have been extended to pronouns, thus carrying on the process of unification a step further. The plural of the nominative of feminine pronouns has a form ending in यो, and the singulars of the instrumental and genitive end in आय or या and that of the locative in यं, as in the case of the corresponding nouns; as तायो nominative plural, ताय or तस्सा, इमाय or इमस्सा, अमुया or अमुस्सा genitive singular, and तायं or तस्सं, इमायं or इमिस्सं, अमुयं or अमुस्सं locative singular, of तद्, इदम्, and अदम्. All pronouns of the third person, of whatever gender, form the genitive plural by adding सं from

* The Sanskrit form नद्या corrupted to नज्जा is also found used.

the Sanskrit साम्, and also सानं which is made up of सं the pronominal and नं the nominal termination, so that the second form is the genitive of the first taken as a base, as तेसं or तेसानं, तासं or तासानं, &c. Similarly, the bases एती and इमी which are substituted for एता and इमा in the singulars of the genitive and locative, and ती which optionally replaces ता in these cases, have a genitive singular with a double termination; as तस्सा, तिस्सा or तिस्साय, एतिस्सा or एतिस्साय, इमिस्सा or इमिस्साय, where स्सा, Sanskrit स्याः, is the pronominal, and आय the nominal termination. The plurals of the nominative and accusative have the same form as ते, सब्बे, ता or तायो, &c., and the instrumental plural of the masculine has, like that of nouns, the termination एभि or एहि. The remaining terminations are the same as in Sanskrit. The correlative or remote demonstrative तद् has, besides the usual Sanskrit base, another न which has all the cases नं, नेन, &c., except the nominative singular. This base is generalized from the एनम्, एनेन &c. of the accusative, the singular of the instrumental, and the dual of the genitive and locative, which are used in making *anvâdes'a* as it is called by Pâṇini, *i. e.* in referring to one who has already been spoken of. The near demonstrative इदम् has two bases, अ and इम. In Sanskrit this latter is used in the nominative dual and plural and in the accusative. Here it is extended to all the cases except the nominative singular, and so we have इमे, इमिना, इमेहि, इमस्मा, इमस्स, इमेसं, इमस्मिं, and इमेसु; इमाय, इमिस्सा, &c. The first base is used, as in Sanskrit, in all cases except the plural of the nominative and accusative and the forms are अयं, अनेन, एहि, अस्मा &c. The pronoun अदस् has the base असु for the nominative singular, and अमु for all other cases which is lengthened in the plural; as अमुना, अमूहि, अमुस्मा, अमुस्स, अमूसं; अमुया, अमुस्सा, &c. The nominative and accusative of the neuter is अदुं.

The singulars of the pronouns of the first and second persons are the same as in Sanskrit; as अहं, मं, मया, मम or मे, and मयि; त्वं, त्वं, त्वया, तव or ते, and त्वयि. The syllable त्व is optionally dissolved into तु in the nominative and accusative which have thus तुवं, and changed to त in the latter as well as in the instrumental and locative; and so we have तं, तया and तयि also. The dative and genitive being confounded, the Sanskrit मह्यम् and तुभ्यम् of the former are in the form of मय्हं and तुय्हं used for both cases. The latter has also the forms ममं and अम्हं and तुम्हं, the anusvâra being inserted from the analogy of the plural. The plural of अहं is मयं in which the initial व of the Sanskrit form is changed to म; and in the accusative, instrumental, and locative, the Sanskrit base अस्म in the form of अम्ह is declined like the masculine तद्, and the forms are अम्हे, अम्हेहि, and अम्हेसु. The यु of युष्मद् was probably weakly pronounced, hence the singular base तु has been transferred to the plural and the peculiar syllable of this number स्म tacked on to it, and the whole in the form of तुम्ह is declined like तद् in all the cases except the genitive; as तुम्हे, तुम्हे, तुम्हेहि &c. The forms of the plurals of this last are like those in Sanskrit; as अम्हाकं and तुम्हाकं. The accusative singulars of these pronouns have the forms ममं and तवं, besides those mentioned above. These are made up by adding anusvâra, the sign of the accusative, to the form of the genitive used as a base. On the same principle we have अम्हाकं and तुम्हाकं for the plural, but as the genitive forms have an anusvâra already, the addition of the accusative sign makes no difference. This is an isolated instance in this dialect of a method of constructing new case-forms, which is, we shall find as we proceed in our investigations, largely used in the later dialects and especially in the modern vernaculars.

You will have seen how naturally the new formations we have noticed grew up. A language is well learnt by others or correctly transmitted to them only when they are in constant and close intercourse with those who know it, or when they are deliberately taught. When for some reason or other this is not the case, and the linguistic tradition is imperfect, men proceed from what is more in use and consequently better known to that which is less used and less known. Nouns in अ, for instance, constitute a very large portion of the ordinary Sanskrit names. Their case forms were most used, whence they were well known and those of other nouns not being so often used were less known. In these cases these less known forms had to conform to the model of the more known, and thus we see a tendency to bring nouns as close as possible to the अ declension, as you have seen in such nouns as आत्मन्, गुणवत्, गच्छत्, शास्तृ, and even अग्नि. And it is also clear that the new अ base is generally taken from the nominative, which case is oftener used than others; as अत्त, गुणवन्त, इच्छन्त, and सत्तार *i. e.* शास्तार. In the same way we have observed a strong tendency to obliterate the distinction between the nominal and pronominal declensions, and fuse them into one, and this tendency has succeeded everywhere except in the genitive plural. Still at the time when the Pâli arose the traditions of the original Sanskrit were not entirely lost, wherefore we have often old forms used side by side with the new ones. The same process is observable in the conjugations of verbs, as I have already remarked. It will thus be seen how groundless is the opinion of those who maintain that these Prâkṛits or derived languages were simply literary languages, or were constructed by Pandits. But this point will be discussed at length hereafter.

Inattention to this law of false analogies or generalization, and to the wide range of its operation in the formation of Pâli grammar has led some scholars to set down as Vedic certain forms which exist in this dialect but are not to be met with in classical Sanskrit. Such are इमस्स the genitive singular masculine of इदम्, फला the nominative plural of फल, अट्ठी and मधू nominative and accusative plural of अस्थि and मधु, अम्हे the general plural base of the pronoun of the first person, and गोनं genitive plural of गो. I see no reason why इमस्स should be regarded as Vedic and not the other forms that have इम for their base, such as इमस्मा, इमेसं, &c., or why फला should be so and not फले the accusative plural; अम्हे and not तुम्हे, अट्ठी and not अट्ठिस्स, or गोनं and not अभिभूनं. If these latter forms and a host of others must be explained with reference to a thoroughly different principle, why should the former which are kindred to them and are as completely capable of that same explanation, be traced to a Vedic origin? The fact that they happen to resemble certain Vedic forms does not prove their derivation from them. The same process of generalization and the same natural tendency to construct the less known forms from the analogy of those that are more known brought them all into use. The forms फला and फले, and अट्ठी and मधू are, as stated before, made up upon the analogy of the corresponding masculine, and herein we observe the beginning of a tendency to obliterate the distinction between the masculine and neuter, which went on progressing until now, in the Hindî, Sindhî, and other vernaculars of Northern India, the neuter gender has totally disappeared, while in the Marâṭhî the distinction remains in the case of pronouns and certain nouns, and in the Gujarâtî only in the latter.

We will now examine the Pâli verb. The distinction between the special and general tenses and moods is almost lost, the special form being used in the general, as in गच्छिस्सति the future of गम्, or the general form in the special as गमेति. We have also गमिस्सति and गच्छति. A large number of roots used in ordinary intercourse belong in Sanskrit to the first conjugation; this and the sixth are the easiest of the ten; in many cases there is no practical distinction between them, and in others they are so greatly like each other that they are capable of being confused together. Hence the rule of constructing verbal forms common to these two conjugations, *viz.* the addition of the personal terminations through the intervention of अ, has become general in Pâli. A good many roots belonging to the other classes are conjugated according to this rule; as दोहति, विदति, and रवति, for दोग्धि, वेत्ति, and रौति, of the second class; पोसति for पुष्यति, मुसति and बन्धति for मुष्णाति and बध्नाति, &c. The tenth conjugation is almost equally common in Sanskrit, whence a great many roots are conjugated necessarily or optionally in this way; as वदेमि or वदामि, गमेति or गच्छति, सिलेसेति, वेदेति or विदति, विगाहेति, &c. from वद्, गम्, श्लिष्, विद्, गाह् with वि, &c. The ए in these forms stands, you will remember, for the Sanskrit अय, which is the characteristic of the tenth class. The second conjugation has gone out, except in isolated forms such as अत्थि for अस्ति, and the third has left some reduplicated roots, as ददामि, जहाति, &c. The fourth has preserved a good many of its roots but its य is corrupted according to the usual phonetic rules; thus बुध्य becomes बुज्झ; पद्य, पज्ज; नृत्य, नच्च; मन्य, मञ्ञ, &c. The fifth and the ninth are confounded, and roots of the former take the termination of the latter also; as पापुणोति or पापुणाति for प्राप्नोति; सुणोति or सुणाति for शृणोति; सक्कोति or सकुणाति for शक्नोति &c. In the last instance the base is सक्क derived from सक्कोति the corruption of शक्नोति, thus showing that the forms in ना are a later growth. The seventh inserts, as before remarked, a nasal in the body of the roots and transfers them to the first; the eighth remains in a few cases such as तन् and कृ, though this last takes a peculiar form also, as तनोति, करोति or कयिरति; and the ninth adds ना as in Sanskrit, as किणाति, धुनाति, लुनाति, पुनाति, &c. But it is to be observed that the more common of the roots belonging to these conjugations only have preserved their peculiar forms; the rest are conjugated according to the rules of the first, sixth, or tenth. Since the distinction between the special and general tenses and moods is lost, the effect of these conjugational peculiarities is only to constitute a new or augmented root.

Of the ten tenses and moods in Sanskrit, the Pâli has lost two, the first future and the precative. The two Padas or voices remain, but the distinction is lost in most cases, such forms as वुच्चति, लब्भति, पच्चति, &c., though passive, taking Parasmaipada terminations.

The following are the terminations:—

Present Tense.

	Parasm.		Âtm.	
	Singular.	Plural.	Singular.	Plural.
1st pers.	मि	म	ए	म्हे
2nd „	सि	थ	से	व्हे
3rd „	ति	अन्ति	ते	अन्ते
Ex.	पचति	पचन्ति &c.	पचते	पचन्ते &c.
		Imperative.		
1st pers.	मि	म	ए	आमसे
2nd „	हि, or none	थ	स्सु	व्हो
3rd „	तु	अन्तु	तं	अन्तं
Ex.	पचतु	पचन्तु &c.	पचतं	पचन्तं &c.
		Imperfect.		
1st pers.	अ	म्हा	ईं	म्हसे
2nd „	ओ	त्थ	से	व्हं
3rd „	आ	ऊ	त्थ	त्थुं
Ex.	अपचा	अपचू &c.	अपचत्थ	अपचत्थुं &c.
		Potential.		
1st pers.	एय्यामि	एय्याम	एय्यं	एय्यम्हे
2nd „	एय्यासि	एय्याथ	एथो	एय्यव्हो
3rd „	एय्य or ए	एय्युं	एथ	एरं
Ex.	पचे or पचेय्य	पचेय्युं &c.	पचेथ	पचेरं &c.
		Aorist.		
1st pers.	ईं	म्हा	अ	म्हे
2nd „	ओ	त्थ	से	व्हं
3rd „	ईं	उं or ईंसु	आ	ऊ
Ex.	अपची	अपचुं or अपचिंसु &c.	अपचा	अपचू &c.
		Perfect.		
1st pers.	अ	म्ह	इ	म्हे
2nd „	ए	त्थ	त्थो	व्हो
3rd „	अ	उ	त्थ	रे
Ex.	पपच	पपचु &c.	पपाचित्थ	पपचिरे &c.
		Future.		
1st pers.	स्सामि	स्साम	स्सं	स्सम्हे
2nd „	स्ससि	स्सथ	स्ससे	स्सव्हे
3rd „	स्सति	स्सन्ति	स्सते	स्सन्ते
Ex.	भविस्सति	भविस्सन्ति &c.	भविस्सते	भविस्सन्ते &c.

Conditional.

1st pers.	स्सं	स्सम्हा	स्सं	स्साम्हसे
2nd „	स्से	स्सथ	स्ससे	स्सव्हे
3rd „	स्सा	स्संसु	स्सथ	स्सिंसु
Ex.	अभविस्सा	अभविस्ससु &c.	अभविस्सथ	अभविस्सिंसु &c.

The terminations of the Present of both Padas are the same as in Sanskrit, with the exception of the plural म and म्हे, the व्हे of the second person plural of the Âtmanepada being a corruption of ध्वे. This tense is most in use; hence the Pâli speakers learned it well, so to say, from their Sanskrit teachers. The other tenses, except the Future which, like the Present, is also entirely Sanskrit, and the moods have preserved such of their forms as are more frequently used in ordinary life. There is, for instance, greater occasion for the use of the second person singular of the Imperative Mood, and also for the third person. Hence these are the same as in Sanskrit, but the second person plural termination थ, and the first person singular मि and the plural म, Parasmaipada, have been transferred from the Present. As to these, even in Sanskrit we find the Present used very generally for this Mood in the first person; as in किं ते भूयः प्रियमुपहरामि S'âk., किं ते भूयः प्रियं करोमि Mṛich., &c. where the forms should be उपहराणि, करवाणि &c. The rest are the same as in Sanskrit. The second person singular is formed in two ways, *viz.* without adding any termination as in the conjugations which give an ending अ to the base, and by appending हि as is done in the others. The Âtmanepada स्व is changed to स्सु, the व being dissolved into उ, and since स्व renders the previous vowel heavy, the resulting सु is doubled to preserve that effect. The plural ध्वम् is altered to व्हो; the म् and the mute element being dropped, we have व्ह the final vowel of which is transformed into ओ through the influence of the preceding व्. The ऐ of the first person singular becomes ए, or this may be considered to have been transferred from the Present, and for the plural we have आमसे which is an old Vedic termination of the Âtmanepada first person plural corrupted in Sanskrit to आमहे. The तं and अन्तं of the third person are the same as the ताम् and अन्ताम् of the parent language.

The Potential has preserved the old forms of the third person only, *viz.*, पचे for पचेत्, and पचेय्युं for पचेयुः. The य is doubled as in थेय्यं for स्तेय according to a general rule which we have noticed before. The singular of this person is also formed by adding एय्य made up on the analogy of the plural एय्यु and also of such forms as स्नुयात्. The final vowel is, however, shortened, but in such cases as जानीया for जानीयात् it remains long. This form with the final long is used as a base, and the terminations of the first person and second person of the Present added to it to form the corresponding persons of the Potential. The Âtmanepada एथ, एरं, and एथो are the same as एत, एरन्, and एथाः of the Sanskrit अ-conjugations, the त of एत being rendered an aspirate and the आ of एथाः shortened. The Parasmaipada singular एयम् as in पचेयम् is adapted for the Âtmanepada in the form एय्यं and the plurals of the second and first persons are formed by taking एय्य as the base and appending ध्वम् corrupted to व्हो and म्हे of the Present.

In the Imperfect the आ and ऊ of the third person seem to be generalized from such forms as अयात् and अयुः. The termination उस् is, as you know, applied in Sanskrit optionally to roots ending in आ and necessarily to विद् and such as are reduplicated. The आ of the singular, however, may be considered as due to the lengthening of the previous अ of such Sanskrit forms of the अ-conjugations as अपचत्, when the final consonant was dropped. This lengthening was brought about by the forcible pronunciation of the अ rendered necessary in Sanskrit by the final consonant. The second person singular is ओ, which corresponds to the Sanskrit अः, and अ of the first person singular to the अम् with the nasal dropped. The Âtmanepada second person singular से is transferred from the Present, व्हं is ध्वम्, and इ is generalized from the forms of the non-अ-conjugations, such as अलुनि, अददि, &c. The Perfect has preserved the third person singular अ and plural उ and the first person singular अ, of the Parasmaipada; and रे of the Âtmanepada. Of the rest, ए second person singular Parasmaipada is perhaps the ए of the Sanskrit Âtmanepada singular of the first and third persons; and the इ of the Âtmanepada is transferred from the Imperfect.

In the Aorist the third person singular ई is the termination of the fifth form of the Sanskrit Aorist with the final त् dropped as usual; and the plural उं is generalized from such forms as अस्थुः. Some roots, such as भू and कृ have सि for the singular as अहोसि, and अकासि, the सि of which is to be traced to सीत्. Another plural termination is इसुं in which we can recognize the Sanskrit इषुः. The second person singular ओ is from the अस् of the second Aorist; and the first person singular is ईं resulting from the fusion of the augment इ with the अम् of the second Aorist. The third person singular and plural and the first person singular of the Âtmanepada are the same as the corresponding ones of the Parasmaipada Imperfect, both numbers of the second person are the same as the corresponding Âtmanepada of the Imperfect, and the म्हे of the first person plural is transferred from the Present.

The terminations of the Second Future are made up as in Sanskrit by prefixing स्स = स्य to those of the Present. The Âtmanepada first person singular has however स्सं instead of स्से. In one instance, *viz.*, होहिति, होहिन्ति from हो, the स्स is corrupted to ह. In the Conditional terminations the स्स occurs everywhere, but the other portions are transferred from other tenses. The ending आ of the third person singular स्सा is of course the आ of the Imperfect; the अंसु of the plural has been transferred from the Aorist, Imperfect, or Potential; the से and थ of स्से and स्सथ are brought over from the Âtmanepada and Parasmaipada of the Present; स्सं is स्यम्, and the म्हा of स्सम्हा the plural is from the Imperfect. In Sanskrit, the short terminations of the Imperfect and other tenses are added to the स्य in the Conditional; but here there is a mixture of both the short and the long, and also of the two Padas. We find the same mixture in the Âtmanepada.

It will thus appear that the Present and Future have preserved most of the Sanskrit terminations, and the other tenses only about two or three. Besides the terminations that have thus been preserved or transferred by analogy from one tense to another, there are others which cannot be thus explained. Such are म्हे Âtmanepada first person plural of the Present; त्थ and म्ह of the Parasmaipada second and first person plural, and त्थ third person singular, त्थो second person singular and म्हे first person plural of the Âtmanepada of the Perfect; त्थ second person plural and म्हा first person plural Parasmaipada, and त्थ and त्थुं third person singular and plural and म्हसे first person plural Âtmanepada, of the Imperfect; त्थ second person plural and म्हा first person plural Parasmaipada of the Aorist, and म्हे first person plural of the Âtmanepada of the same; म्हे first person plural Âtmanepada of the Future; and म्हा Parasmaipada and म्हसे Âtmanepada of the first person of the Conditional. These are unquestionably forms of the root अस् tacked on to the base in the particular tenses when the old terminations were forgotten, or some of them may be traced directly to the terminations of the Sanskrit Aorist स्त, स्थाः, and स्म which themselves, as you know, are forms of अस्. Of these, the Parasmaipada second person plural त्थ is to be traced to the corresponding Sanskrit स्थ of the Present of अस्, and म्ह and म्हा first person plural to the स्म of आस्म of the Imperfect and स्मः of the Present respectively. The penultimate अ of स्मः is lengthened for the same reason as that of अपचत् is in forming अपचा. The Âtmanepada त्थो of the second person singular comes from the स्थाः of आस्थाः of the Imperfect, त्थ third person singular, from the स्त of आस्त of the same; and म्हे and म्हसे first person plural are to be referred to such Âtmanepada forms as स्मे and स्मसे. Of the last two, स्मे appears to be a new formation from स्म, and स्मसे is the old Vedic archetype of स्महे.

You will thus see that when the original Sanskrit forms were forgotten, new ones corresponding to them were constructed in the Pâli, not only by the use of false analogies, but also by taking one form distinctively expressive of the sense of a particular mood or tense as a base, and appending first only the personal terminations of the Present, as in the case of the Potential; and secondly, the forms of the root अस्. You will hereafter find that the modern vernaculars have resorted to one at least of these two modes of reconstruction; and similarly the beginnings in the Pâli of a mode of constructing new case-forms widely prevalent in the modern dialects was brought to your notice before; so that the spirit or turn of mind which has been in operation in the formation of the vernacular speech of the country has been the same since very remote times.

The terminations with an initial consonant are in the general tenses appended through the intervention of the vowel इ; but in some cases there are forms directly corrupted from Sanskrit; as दक्खति, Sanskrit द्रक्ष्यति, मोक्खति=मोक्ष्यति. The temporal augment अ is often omitted, as गमा or अगमा, गमी or अगमी, गमिस्सा or अगमिस्सा. The several varieties of the Aorist and the many special forms of the Perfect have for the most part gone out of use. The Passive is formed by the addition of य as in Sanskrit, sometimes with the augment इ, sometimes without, in which last case the conjunct consonant is corrupted according to the prevailing rules; as बुज्झियते, पचते, लब्भते, करियते. The forms in a good many cases are the same as in Sanskrit, only phonetically altered; as थीयते, उच्चते, इज्जते, in which cases we see that the आ of स्था is changed to ई, and वच् and यज् undergo Samprasâraṇa. The causal is formed by adding आपे or आपय and ए or आय; as कारापेति or कारापयति and कारेति or कारयति. These forms I have already explained. The Past Passive Participle is formed as in Sanskrit, and in many cases the forms are the same. The Absolutive is fòrmed by using the terminations तून, त्वान, and त्वा. The first is the same as the second, the semi-vowel व् having only undergone Samprasârana; and they are to be traced to such Vedic forms as इष्ट्वीन, कृत्वान &c., which have disappeared in classical Sanskrit. The Infinitive is formed by adding तुं as in Sanskrit, or तवे which, I have already observed, is one of the many ways in which the Vedio Infinitive is formed. It has become obsolete in the later Sanskrit.

Now if the Pâli grew up naturally in the manner I have described, it could not come to possess the several grammatical forms it exhibits unless they were in use in Sanskrit at the time when it branched off. It has, as we have seen, preserved eight of the ten Tenses, and Moods whence it follows that verbal forms of these were then current in the language. Pâli therefore represents Middle Sanskrit or the usage that prevailed during the period between the composition of the Brâhmaṇas and Yâska or Pâṇini, and must have begun to be formed during that period. We shall hereafter find that the later Prâkṛits represent the third stage in the development of the Sanskrit, that in which a good many of the verbal forms ceased to be used; and thus bear to what I have called classical Sanskrit the same relation that the Pâli does to Middle Sanskrit.

We will now proceed to consider those valuable specimens of the ancient languages of the country which have been preserved in inscriptions. The most important of these are the edicts of As'oka, the pious king of Pâṭaliputra in Magadha, the modern Behar, who flourished in the middle of the third century before Christ. These edicts contain the king's religious and moral injunctions to his subjects, and set forth his own ideas, belief, and conduct in these matters. Five different versions of them have been discovered, inscribed on rocks in different parts of the country. There is one at Girnâr, near Junâgaḍ, in Kattiawar, another at Dhauli in Kattak, and a third at Kapurdigiri or Śahbazgarhi in Afghanistan. These have been published and examined. The Girnar version has been copied several times, but the other two only once, and hence there are a good many imperfections in our existing copies of them. Another version has recently been discovered at Jaugaḍ near Ganjam, in the Northern Circars, and copied by a Madras

Civilian. It is unfortunately greatly mutilated, not more than two of the fourteen edicts being found complete, and but a few words left of some. The fifth has recently been discovered by General Cunningham at Khalsi, near Masuri in the Himalayas, and has not yet been published.* Other edicts of the same king are found inscribed on columns which exist at Delhi, Allahabad, and other places. At Dhauli and Ganjam there exist, along with the edicts mentioned above, others which answer to these. Another inscription of As'oka has been found at Babhra in Rajputana, which consists of a letter to the Buddhist congregation. These inscriptions are in three different dialects, closely related to each other. The Girnâr dialect is very much like the Pâli. That of the Dhauli, Ganjam, and Khalsi versions presents peculiarities which are found in a later Prâkṛit called Mâgadhî by the grammarians. Such are the substitution of ल् for र्, ए for the ओ of the nominative singular of masculine nouns in अ, सि the termination of the locative instead of the Pâli म्हि, and हकम् for अहम्. The Babhra and the column inscriptions are also in this dialect. The S'ahbazgarhi recension admits of some conjuncts such as प्र, and the sibilants श् and ष् which in the others and in Pâli are changed to स्. But it is a question whether these are dialectic peculiarities, or are to be attributed to a confusion of the vernacular with Sanskrit. I will now place before you short specimens of these dialects.

Girnâr, edict VIII.

अतिकातं अंतरं राजानो विहारयातां ञयासु। एत मगव्या अञानि च एतारिसानि अभिरमकानि अहुंसु। सो देवानंपियो पियदसी राजा दसवसाभिसितो संतो अयाय संबोधिं। तेनेसा धंमयाता एतयं होति ब्राम्हणसमणानं दसणे च दाने च थैराणं दसणे च हिरंणपटिविधाने च जानपदस च जनस दसनं धंमानुसस्टी च धंमपरिपुछा च। तदोपया एसा भूयरति भवति देवानंपियस प्रियदसिनो राञो भागे अंञे.

Sanskrit:—

अतिक्रान्तमन्तरं राजानो विहारयात्रां निरयासिषुः। अत्र मृगयान्यानि चैतादृशान्यभिरामकाण्यभूवन्। स देवानांप्रियः प्रियदर्शी राजा दशवर्षाभिषिक्तः सन्नयासीत्संबोधिम्। तेनैषा धर्मयात्रा। अत्रेदं भवति ब्राह्मणश्रमणानां दर्शनं च दानं च स्थविराणां दर्शनं च हिरण्यप्रतिविधानं च जानपदस्य च जनस्य दर्शनं धर्मानुशास्तिश्च धर्मपरिपृच्छा च। तदौपयांदेषा भूयोरतिर्भवति देवानां प्रियस्य प्रियदर्शिनो राज्ञो भागेन्यस्मिन्।

Translation:—

"Some time ago kings went on pleasure excursions. Hunting and such others were the diversions here. But Priyadars'in, the favourite of the

* Published since in Corp. Insc. Ind. A sixth version existing at Manshera in the Panjab was discovered after the above was published. I have made use of the latest readings of the versions.

gods, began the search of enlightenment when he had been a crowned monarch for ten years. Hence this excursion (course) of righteousness. It consists of this, *viz.* seeing Brâhmaṇas and Śramaṇas, and bestowing gifts, seeing the religious elders and presenting gold, and seeing country-people and giving instruction in righteousness and in the investigation of the law. Since that time king Priyadarśin has been taking great delight in the glories of the next world."

It is not usual in these inscriptions to mark the double or assimilated consonants. Hence we do not find them here except in the case of double nasals which are indicated by an anusvâra followed by the nasal. There is, as in Pâli, no other phonetic change; प्रति we see becomes पटि and भू becomes optionally हू; and राजानो the nominative plural, राञो for रञ्ञो the genitive singular, सन्तो the nominative singular, and all other cases are just like those in that dialect. We have the Aorist forms ending in an anusvâra followed by सु, as in Pâli. But there are some differences; एतारिस is एतादिस in Pâli as it is in the other recensions of this same inscription, अहुंसु is अहेंसु, though अहुंसु agrees with the rules of Pâli grammar and must have existed in the language; the ऐ of थैराणं is opposed to Pâli usage, but the engraver may have committed a mistake; नेयासु is for निय्यासु, इ being changed to ए before the conjunct according to the rule we have noticed. बाम्हण is ब्राह्मण in Pâli; but the inscription perhaps represents the prevailing usage more correctly; and the अ is lengthened in राञो probably through mistake. There are thus very few cases of real difference, and though they might be considered to point to a dialectical variety of the nature of those we find in the different versions of the edicts, still the language is in the same stage of growth as the Pâli.

The following is the Dhauli version collated with that at Khalsi and completed:—

अतिकंतं अंतलं[1] लाजानो विहालयातं नाम निखमिसु। हिदा मिगविया अंनानि च [2] एदिसानि अभिलामानि [3]हुवंति नं। से देवानं पिये पियदसी लाजा दसवसाभिसिते [4] संते निखमि[5] संबोधिं। तेनता धंमयाता [6] हेता इयं होति समनबा[7]भनानं दसने च दाने च [8] वुढानं दसने च हिलंनपटिविधाने च।

We here observe the varieties mentioned before, the change of र to ल and the nominative in ए. We also see निखमिसु for नेयासु, एदिसानि

1. देवानं पिया Kh.
2. हेडिसानि Kh.
3. हुसु for हुवंति नं Kh.
4. Dh. om.
5. निखमिठा Kh.
6. ततेस for हेता इयं Dh.
7. बंभ Kh.
8. वुधानं Kh.

for एतारिसानि, वुधानं or वदानं(=वृद्धानां) for थैरानं, and बंभन or बाभन for ब्राम्हण. So then here we have another dialect.

Kapurdigiri or Śahbazgarhi version:—

अतिक्रंतं अंतरं देवनंप्रिय विहरयत्र नम निक्रमिषु अत्र मुगय अञ्ञनि च हेदिशानि अभिरमनि अभवसु सो देवनंप्रिय प्रियद्रसि रज दशवषभिसितो सतो निक्रमि संबोधिं तेनदं ध्रमयत्र अत्र इयं होति श्रमणब्रमणनं द्रशने दनं &c.

Here we have the conjuncts प्रि, त्रा, ब्रं &c., and the three Sanskrit sibilants; and also हेदिशानि for ईदृशानि. The reason why we have not one same version at all the three places must be that it was the intention of the king to publish the edicts in the dialect of each particular place. The Dhauli-Khalsi dialect is, as observed before, used in the column inscriptions, and also in that found at Babhra. The king's predilection for it can be plausibly accounted for only on the supposition that it was his own native tongue. If so, this dialect must have prevailed in Magadha, which country was under his immediate rule, and the capital of which was Pâṭaliputra, where he reigned. And this accounts for the fact that it is used in the inscriptions at Dhauli and Ganjam, since they are situated in the contiguous country. One peculiarity of this language, *viz.* the nominative singular of nouns in अ ending in ए is met with even in the Girnâr recension, which may be explained by the supposition that the edicts were drawn up first in the king's dialect but were translated into the dialect of each province, the translation however being not executed carefully enough to expunge all peculiarities of the original draft. It would thus appear that the grammarians of the later languages had more solid grounds than mere fancy for calling that Prâkṛit which bears close resemblance to this language by the name of Mâgadhî. Here then we find specimens of three dialects prevalent in three widely distant provinces; but we should bear in mind that the difference between them is small, while in the languages that are spoken in these countries at the present day it is so great as to make it difficult for the natives of one province to understand those of another.

In the many other ancient monuments existing in the country we often find inscriptions which are principally in two languages, the Sanskrit and the Pâli or Prâkṛit, understanding by this term simply a dialect derived from the Sanskrit. Those in the latter (Pâli) are mostly connected with Buddhism; though some Buddhistic inscriptions also, such as those discovered by General Cunningham at Mathurâ several years ago, are in Sanskrit. In the caves at Kânherî, Nâsik, Junar, Nânâghâṭ, Kârleṁ, and some other places in this Presidency, and in the Bhilsâ topes, we have Pâli or Prâkṛit inscriptions. Most of these are short, but at Nâsik we have long ones, in the caves of Ushavadâta and Gotamîputra. The language of these latter is Pâli; and but a few forms are peculiar, such as दत्त and कित for which the Pâli has दिण्ण and कत, Past Passive Participles of दा and कृ; and बे for the numeral two, the Pâli form being द्वे or दुवे. In Ushavadâta's caves we have one inscription entirely in Sanskrit, the rest are in Pâli or Prâkṛit, but we have an intermixture of Sanskrit words, and the conjuncts प्र, त्र and क्ष often appear. In these and smaller inscriptions we have such words as वार for द्वार, बारसक for वार्षिक, वरिस for वर्ष, उदिस for उद्दिश्य, while the Pâli forms of these words are द्वार, वस्सिक, वस्स, and उद्देसेत्वा. Some of these inscriptions were engraved so late as the third century, when the Pâli could hardly have been the vernacular; but it had become the sacred language of the Buddhists; the mendicant priests for whom the caves were intended and even educated lay members of that persuasion understood it; and hence it was used in these inscriptions as Sanskrit was in others. The style of Gotamîputra's charters, abounding as it does in long compounds and elaborate expressions, is very unlike the plain and simple language of As'oka's edicts. And at the end of these and that of his son, we are told that the officers of these kings who caused the charters to be engraved acted under the command, *i. e.* wrote to the dictation of "respected persons who were the compilers of all such documents." It thus appears that the Pâli was at that time a sacred and a literary language among the Buddhists. And as to the language of the other inscriptions, which like those of Gotamîputra and his son were not composed by learned men, one can easily understand how ignorant persons, not knowing Sanskrit or Pâli well, but still not ignorant enough to know nothing of those languages would confound together Sanskrit, Pâli, and vernacular words. Even in our days we find the phenomenon in the *patrikâs* or horoscopes written by our Jos'îs or astrologers, which are neither in pure Sanskrit nor in pure vernacular, but contain a mixture of them both, and the Sanskrit words and forms in which are incorrectly written. And an explanation of this nature I have also to give of another variety of language that is found in the writings of the Northern or Nepalese Buddhists. These unlike those of the Ceylonese and Burmese Buddhists are written in Sanskrit, but in such works as the Lalitavistâra or the life of Buddha we find, along with prose passages in pure Sanskrit, a number of verses which contain words or forms which are not Sanskrit. Thus, for instance, we have:—

सर्वशुभकर्महेतोः फलमिदं शृणुतास्य कर्मस्य
पूजारहो भवितुं सर्वजगे अनुवन्धत इममनन्तयशं ॥

You will here see that कर्मस्य, जगे, and यशं are as in the Pâli treated like nouns in अ, अर्ह is dissolved into अरह, and there are a few other instances of this process, such as किलेश for क्लेश, शिरि for श्री, हिरि for ह्री &c., but that generally the conjunct consonants are retained as they are in Sanskrit, and not assimilated. So also you have चोदेन्ति for चोदयन्ति, मायाय genitive singular of माया, उपजनित्वा, शुणिष्यति, निरीक्षथ Imperative second person plural, शमेथ for शमयत, &c., and even such words as तनाप which are Pâli in every respect. But along with these there are other peculiarities which must be attributed simply to carelessness. For instance, the case terminations are often omitted, a thing never done either in Sanskrit or Pâli, as काम सेवति for कामं सेवते, सुगत for सुगतं when governed by पूजयितुं, मोक्ष भोष्यति for मोक्षो भविष्यति, &c. Such constructions as क्षान्त्या सोरभ्यसम्पन्नाः for क्षान्तिसोरभ्यसंपन्नाः, शीलसमाधि तथा प्रज्ञमयं for शीलसमाधिप्रज्ञामयं, are often to be met with.

This language has therefore no fixed characteristics at all. We have seen that in such words as कर्म, जग and यश above, the final consonant is dropped, and these as in Pâli and Prakṛit made nouns in अ. But यशस् is used in the Sanskrit form also, as कीर्तिर्यशश्च; and there are instances in which other final consonants are preserved. Along with such a form as शुणिष्यति noted above, which is constructed on the same principle as the Pâli सुणिस्सति, such a Sanskrit one as शृण्वन्ति is found. It therefore appears to me that this is not an independent language; but that the writers of the Gâthâs knew the spoken language or Pâli, and that they were imperfectly acquainted with Sanskrit, knowing enough of it to see that the assimilation of consonants was a vulgarity, but not acquainted with its grammar. They intended to write in the more polished or literary language, but not knowing it well, often used unconsciously the grammatical forms and the peculiar words of the vernacular. At the time when the Gâthâs were written the claims of the Pâli to be considered a separate language were probably not recognised, and it constituted the speech of the uninstructed. Those who in this condition of things wished to write could not think of doing so in that form of speech, and therefore wrote in what they considered the language of educated men; but they knew it imperfectly, and produced such a heterogeneous compound as we have seen.

LECTURE III.

The Prâkrits and the Apabhrams'a.

On the last occasion we examined the language of the sacred books of the Southern Buddhists, and found that a large portion of the words it contains are pure Sanskrit and the rest are Sanskrit words corrupted or transformed according to certain laws of phonetic decay. Then by the law of false analogy the less used and less known declensional and conjugational forms have been in many cases brought over to the type of those more used in Sanskrit and consequently better known. So that in the vocabulary and the grammar the laws of growth I traced in the opening lecture are in operation, but their range is limited, and the dialect is in what may be called the first stage of departure from Sanskrit. We then examined the language of the Inscriptions of As'oka and found that it is either the same as Pâli or in the same stage of development, and that there existed in those times two or three varieties of speech slightly differing from each other. To-day I propose to examine certain other dialects which exhibit a much greater departure from the parent tongue. These are the so-called Prâkṛits. For a knowledge of these languages we have not to go beyond India, as in the case of the one we have examined. Prâkṛit dialects possessed a literature and a portion of it has come down to us.

There exist about six treatises on Prâkṛit grammar, the most ancient of which is Vararuchi's Prâkṛitaprakâs'a. Next comes Hemachandra, a Jaina scholar of Gujarat, who lived in the twelfth century. His work on grammar is known by the name of *Haimavyâkarana*, the eighth chapter of which he devotes to the grammar of the Prâkṛits. Hemachandra's treatment of these dialects is fuller than Vararuchi's; and his observation was wider. He shows a very intimate knowledge of the existing literature of these languages, both sacred and profane, Jaina or Brahmanical. His work and especially the last portion is full of quotations. He must have availed himself of the labours of former scholars, since he often mentions *Pûrvâchâryas.* Hemachandra also wrote a *Kosha* or thesaurus of the Des'î words existing in these languages. Vararuchi gives the grammar of four dialects, which he calls Mahârâshṭrî, Śaurasenî, Mâgadhî, and Pais'âchî. The names of the first three themselves would show that they were the languages spoken or used in the provinces from the names of which they are derived, but doubts have been raised as to their genuineness, which will be hereafter considered. The Mahârâshṭrî is called the principal Prâkṛit. For instance, Daṇḍin in his Kâvyâdars'a says—

"The language prevalent in Mahârâshṭra they regard as the Prâkṛit pre-eminent; it is the ocean of jewels in the shape of good literary works, and the Setubandha and others are written in it[1]."

Vararuchi devotes the first nine chapters of his work to the Mahârâshṭrî, and then a chapter each to the rest. The peculiarities only of the latter dialects and their differences from the Mahârâshṭrî are given, and in other respects they are to be considered similar to the first. Hemachandra follows the same method; but he does not mention the name Mahârâshṭrî and speaks of the dialect only as the Prâkṛit. These grammarians and all others who have written on the subject treat of the grammar of the language etymologically. They take Sanskrit as the original language or *Prakriti* and give rules about the various phonetical and grammatical changes which have reduced Sanskrit to the Prâkṛit form. The Pâli grammarian Kachchâyana treats the dialect not as one derived from Sanskrit as these writers do, but as an independent language, though it is very probable he knew Sanskrit, since he uses Sanskrit grammatical terms, and his Sûtras greatly resemble those in the Kâtantra and even Pâṇini. Vararuchi and Hemachandra derive Śaurasenî also from the Sanskrit as they do the Mahârâshṭrî or the principal Prâkṛit, but make the Śaurasenî the *Prakriti* or basis of the Mâgadhî and the Pais'âchî. This appears to be the tradition; whence it would seem that older and more developed language or the language of respectable people was the Śaurasenî, and the other two were the dialects of border countries used by persons in a lower scale of society. They have some of the peculiarities of the Śaurasenî, and come nearer to it than to the Mahârâshṭrî. Hemachandra gives the grammar of two more dialects, the Chûlikâ Pais'âchî and the Apabhrams'a, the latter of which was according to Daṇḍin, the language of Âbhîras (cowherds) and others. Another grammarian of the name of Trivikrama gives in his Prâkṛitasûtravṛitti the grammar of these six dialects. He lived after Hemachandra, since he mentions him in the introduction to his work,

---

1. महाराष्ट्राश्रयां भाषां प्रकृष्टं प्राकृतं विदुः ।
सागरः सूक्तिरत्नानां सेतुबन्धादि यन्मयम् ॥

and his book resembles Hemachandra's a good deal. There is another work by Chandra called Shaḍbhâshâchandrikâ which is a meagre production. Another still of the same nature, the author of which is Lakshmîdhara, mentions the same six dialects; so that the expression Shaḍbhâshâ seems to have become proverbial.

The Mahârâshṭrî derived its importance from its literature. From the manner in which Daṇḍin speaks of that literature it appears to have been very extensive and valuable. He himself mentions one work, the Setubandha, a poem attributed to Kâlidâsa but written by one Pravarasena, whose "fame," Bâṇa says in his Harshacharita, "reached the other side of the ocean by means of the Setu." I find in a Ms. in the colophon at the end of each âśvâsa or canto, sometimes इअ सिरिपवरसेणविरइए दहमुहवहे (thus in the Das'amukhavadha composed by the prosperous Pravarasena), and sometimes, इअ पवरसेनविरइए कालिदासकए दहमुहवहे (thus in the Das'amukhavadha, the work of Kâlidâsa, composed by Pravarasena). Some kings of Kas'mîr bore the name of Pravarasena, but there is nothing to show that any one of them was the poet who wrote this work. There is a collection of seven hundred songs, chiefly of an amorous nature, by a poet of the name of Hâla, which is called the Saptas'atî. We have an edition of this in Roman characters by Prof. Weber. Another long poem entitled the Gauḍavadhakâvya by a poet named Vâkpatirâja, who lived at the court of Yas'ovarman, king of Kanoj, in the early part of the eighth century, was discovered by Dr. Bühler about three years ago. And several other works may turn up, if diligent search is made for them. The Kâvyaprakâs'a contains about 75 Prâkṛit verses quoted to illustrate the rules laid down by the author, and S'ârngadhara also gives a good many in his Paddhati.

The religious books of the Jainas form another very extensive branch of Prâkṛit literature. Prof. Weber thinks the language of these to be later than the Pâli and earlier than the Prâkṛits, so as to occupy a middle position, and calls it Jaina-Mâgadhî. But Hemachandra himself, who must have known his religious books well, and was, as I have observed, a great Prâkṛit scholar, treats it as the principal Prâkṛit or Mahârâshṭrî, and in his grammar of this he in several places gives forms of words peculiar to his sacred language, which after the example of his Brahmanic brothers he calls Ârsha Prâkṛit[2]. In giv-

. आर्षम् । ३ । ऋषीणामिदमार्षम् । आर्षे प्राकृतं बहुलं भवति । तदपि यथास्थानं दर्शयिष्यामः । आर्षे हि सर्वे विधयो विकल्प्यन्ते । He has also said before, that the rules he

ing his first rule about the Mâgadhî dialect, *viz.*, that the nom. sing. of Masc. nouns takes the termination ए, he says:—"As to what the fathers have said about the Ârsha (works) being composed in the Ardha-Mâgadhî dialect in such words as these: 'the ancient Sùtra is composed in the Ardha-Mâgadhî dialect', they have said so in consequence of the observance of this rule and not of those that follow[3]. Thus if one chooses to call the sacred language of the Jainas Ardha-Mâgadhî on account of this Mâgadhî peculiarity and a few other archaisms, he may do so; and I shall presently have to observe that the great many dialects which writers on poetics give differed from each other in such insignificant particulars only. But it is clear that Hemachandra considers the distinction to be slight, and identifies the dialect with the principal Prâkṛit; and both he and the Jaina fathers refer it to the class of the Prâkṛits of the grammarians.[4]

---

is going to give even with regard to the ordinary Prâkṛit should not be considered universal.

3. यदपि पोराणमद्धमागहभासानिययं हवइ सुत्तमित्यादिनार्षस्यार्धमागधभाषानियतत्वमाम्नायि वृद्धैस्तदपि प्रायोस्यैव विधानान्न वक्ष्यमाणलक्षणस्य ।

4. The only specific grounds one can find in Prof. Weber's book in support of the assertion that the Jaina dialect occupies a middle position are these:—1. That uninitial क्, ग्, च्, ज्, त्, द् and other consonants are dropped in the Mahârâshṭrî leaving only the vowel, and preserved or softened in the Pâli, while in the Jaina books य् is substituted for them; *i. e.*, the different stages of phonetic corruption in this case are, the consonants in their original or softened forms, then य् for them, and lastly their elision. 2. That न् is preserved in the Pâli, and changed everywhere to ण् in the Mahârâshṭrî; while in the Jaina dialect initial न् remains unchanged except in enclytics. 3. That the loc. sing. of nouns in अ ends in सिं or सि which we find in the language of the column inscriptions; while it is स्मि and म्हि in the Pâli andम्मि in the Prâkṛit. Now as to the first, the य् is not prior to the elision, but contemporaneous or subsequent to it, being found even in the modern vernaculars. It was introduced simply to facilitate pronunciation; *i. e.*, it is a strengthened form of the vowel. Thus the Prâkṛit of पाद foot is पाअ, but in Marâṭhî we have पाय; so राजन् Skr., राअ Pr., राय H.; सोदर Skr., सोअर Pr., सोयरा M., &c. &c. The य् occurs not only in Jaina books, but everywhere in the Gauḍavadhakâvya; and Hemachandra does tell us in his sûtra अवर्णो यश्रुतिः that the अ that remains after the elision of a consonant is pronounced like a soft य. With regard to the second, initial न् is found unchanged in the Gauḍavadha in a great many places. Thus in stanza 242 we have the negative particle न, in 241 निवडइ for निपतति, in 245 नाह for नाथ, and in 251 नह नख. These instances I have found on simply opening the Ms. at random; and no great search

But it is in the dramatic plays that we find these dialects principally used. Writers on Poetics prescribe that a particular dramatic person should speak a particular dialect. Sanskrit is assigned to respectable men of education, and women in holy orders; Śaurasenî, to respectable ladies in their prose speeches, and the Mahârâshṭrî or the principal Prâkṛit, in the songs or verses put into their mouths. Śaurasenî is also assigned to inferior characters; and the Mâgadhî and Pais'âchî to very low persons. The general rule is that a dramatic person should speak the language of the country to which he or she is supposed to belong. Later writers give more minute rules. For

---

was necessary. Hemachandra also in his sûtra वादौ following another, नो णः, says that the initial न् is sometimes changed to ण्, sometimes not. As to the third, the termination सिं may constitute a peculiarity of the language, but it is by no means an index to its higher antiquity, since it occurs in the pronominal locative of the principal Prâkṛit. There are several peculiarities in the Jaina books, and a good many of them are noticed by our Grammarian, but they do not show an earlier stage of development.

This continues still to be my view, notwithstanding all that has since been published on the subject. Dr. Hoernle, in the introduction to his edition of Chaṇḍa's Prâkritalakshaṇa makes an elaborate attempt to prove that the dialect, the grammar of which is given in that book, is more ancient than the Prâkṛit of Vararuchi and Hemachandra. But it is not at all difficult to see that he is altogether on a wrong tack. He says there is nothing in Hemachandra corresponding to the rule given by Chaṇḍa about dropping the final vowel of the first member of a compound when the initial vowel of the second is followed by a conjunt consonant, in such words as *dhana+âdhya*, *deva+indra*, &c., which in that Prâkṛit have the forms *dhanaddha*, *devinda*, &c. This change, however, does come under Hemachandra's rule I. 84, which provides for the shortening of a long vowel when followed by a conjunct consonant. The short vowels corresponding to ए and ओ are इ and उ; and among the instances given by Hemachandra, we have *narindo* for *narendra*, *aharuṭṭha* for *adharoshṭha*, *Nîluppala for Nîlotpala* &c. Dr. Hoernle thinks the changes of *i* to short *e* and of *u* to short *o* are later Prâkṛit changes. But he will find many instances of them in the Pâli, which certainly is an older dialect than any Jaina Prâkṛit. They are, he says, unknown to Chaṇḍa. Chaṇḍa's work is a very meagre production, in which very little endeavour is made to classify facts; and thus he must be supposed to include these changes under his very general rule that *one vowel takes the place of another vowel* (II. 4). The instance *ginhati* incidentaly given by him in connection with another rule does not show that in his Prâkrit the form *genha* did not exist, much less that the change of *i* to *e* was unknown. Then with regard to consonants, Dr. Hoernle says there are five points in which the "older Prâkrit" of Chaṇḍa, as he calls it, differs from the Prâkṛit of Vararuchi and Hemachandra. One of these is "the preservation of the

instance, the author of the Sâhityadarpaṇa assigns Mâgadhî to the attendants in the royal seraglio, Ardhamâgadhî to footmen, royal children, and merchants, Prâchyâ to the Vidûshaka and others, Âvantikî to sharpers, warriors, and clever men of the world, Dâkshiṇâtyâ to gamblers, Śâkârî to Śakârs, Śakas, and others, Bâhḷikâ to celestial persons, Drâviḍî to Draviḍas and others, Âbhîrî to cowherds, Châṇḍâlikî to outcastes, Âbhîrî and Śâbarî, also to those who live by selling wood and leaves, and Pais'âchî to dealers in charcoal. Handmaids, if they do not belong to a very low class, should speak Śaurasenî. Some of the modern grammarians also mention as large a number of dialects. But whether these were actually used by writers

---

dental *n* in every case." For this statement the Doctor quotes the authority of a sûtra in which we are told by Çhaṇḍa that ङ् and ञ् do not exist in the Prâkṛit, as compared with another version of that stûra which says that ङ्, न्, and ञ् do not exist (II. 14). This last version no doubt provides for the change of न् in all cases; but the other which denies the non-existence or affirms the existence of न् cannot mean that it exists or is unchanged in *all* cases. The denial of non-existence or affirmation of existence only proves its existence or remaining unchanged in *some* cases. Besides we have a specific rule where we are told that a letter of the द् class takes the place of the corresponding letter of the त् class (III. 16), thus providing for the change of न् to ण्; and the instance given is धण्णं for धान्यम्. But this rule the Doctor thinks holds good in exceptional cases, for which however there is no authority whatever, and he gives none. Again, he says that his statement is proved by the uniform spelling of the Prâkṛit examples with *n* in Mss. A and B, which, according to him, contain the older version of the work. I, however, find that the spelling in his edition, which is the spelling of A and B, follows uniformly, with one or two exceptions, in which we must suppose a mistake, the rule laid down by Hemachandra, *viz.*, that initial *n* is optionally changed to *ṇ*, while medial *n* is necessarily so changed. The instances are:—all the case-terminations which are to be traced to the Sanskrit terminations having *n* in them, such as णो, णि, and णं; मुणिणो for मुनीन् (I. 1), गयणओ for गगनतः (I. 16), मणिस्सा A. (I. 21), नाणी (I. 24) for ज्ञानी, सक्कीसाणा for शक्रेशानौ (II. 1.), काणं (II. 15), गयणं for गगनम् (II. 21), पीलणं for पीडनम् (II. 24), नाणं for ज्ञानम् (III. 6), जुव्वणं for यौवनम् (III. 15), and रअणं for रत्नं (III. 30). The second point is "the preservation of the medial single surd unaspirate consonants with the only exception of *k*." This simply means the preservation of *ch*, *t*, and *p* which according to the other grammarians are *generally* dropped. Chaṇḍa agrees with these in dropping not only *k*, but *g*, *j*, and *d*. Whether therefore the preservation of *ch*, *t*, and *p*, supposing that Chaṇḍa really allows it, marks off his Prâkṛit as older than that of Hemachandra or Vararuchi is more than questionable. But, as a matter of fact in III. 12, he does provide for their change to *j*, *d*, and *b*; and the change of *t* to *d* is a S'auraseni, *i. e.*, a local change, and does not indicate priority of time. Besides, even the dropping of these consonants must have been contemplated by him.

of dramatic plays in accordance with the rules of Rhetoricians, or if they were, what constituted the exact difference between these various languages, it is impossible to determine so long as we have not got satisfactory editions of the plays. Still in those cases in which we have the assistance of the older Prâkṛit grammarians, the characteristics of each can be made out with fulness and certainty. To illustrate his rules about the Mâgadhî, Hemachandra quotes from the speeches of the fisherman and the two poilcemen in Śakuntalâ, of the Kshapaṇaka from the Mudrârâkshasa, and Rudhirapriyâ from the Veṇîsaṁhâra. The points in which the Mâgadhî chiefly differs from the principal Prâkṛit and Śaurasenî are these:—र् and स् of these are changed to ल् and श्; स्थ and र्थ of Sanskrit to स्त, and ष्ट to स्ट; and स् is not assimilated as in पस्खलदि from प्रस्खलति, the nom. sing. of masc. nouns ends in ए instead of ओ, which is the Prâkṛit ending; the gen.

For in the instances given in the book, they are dropped in all the manuscripts used by Dr. Hoernle, even in A and B, which according to him contain the older version. Thus we have एइ for एति (I. 12), गयणओ-उ or गयणाओ-उ for गगनतः (I, 16),' कयं for कृतम् (I. 23 and everywhere else), इहागओ-उ for इहागतः (II. 1.), इच्छिअं for इच्छितम् (II. 3), कायव्वं-व्वं for कर्तव्यम्, सुइणं for सूचीनाम् (II. 4), नेउरं for नूपुरम् (II. 4), घयं for घृतम्, काउण for कृत्वा, दीसइ for दृश्यते (II. 5), गच्छइ for गच्छति, वइ for पतिः (II. 10), सरिआणं or सरियाणं for सरिताम् (II. 11), गइ-ई for गतिः, मइ-ई for मतिः (II. 17), &c. &c. It is very much to be regretted that the Doctor should in all these cases have set aside the readings of his manuscripts and invented his own with the त्, च्, and प् standing in the words, instead of being dropped. This invention or restoration, as he calls it, is based on a singular inference that he deduces from a single word, कृतं given as a Prâkrit word in the book. He says it must originally have been कतं, but the copyist, not knowing of such a word being in the later Prâkṛit which he knew, took it as the Sanskrit कृतं, and wrote accordingly. If, therefore, कतं was the Prâkṛit word in this case, it must have been so in all those cases in which कयं occurs in the book, and so Dr. Hoernle makes it कतं throughout. But it did not strike him that if the copyist knew Prâkṛit enough to see that कतं was not a Prâkṛit word, he must have seen that कृतं also was not a Prâkṛit word; and could not have given it as such. Now the reason why these consonants were not admitted by Chaṇḍa, according to the manuscripts A and B, among those that are dropped, but only among those that are softened must be that all these rules are only general and not universal, and there were as many instances of softening as of dropping. Besides, I have already said that Chaṇḍa's work is perfunctory, and does not show accuracy of observation and statement. The third point is the preservation of the medial single surd aspirate consonants with the only exception of *kh*; *i. e.*, ठ्, थ्, फ्, are preserved. But III. 11 provides for t e change of these to ढ्, ध्, and भ्, if we look to the sense of the

sing. of masc. and neut. nouns optionally in आह as कम्माह; and the form of the nom. sing. of the first personal pronoun is हगे. If we apply the test furnished by these rules to the several dialects used by the characters in the Mṛichchhakaṭika as it is in the existing editions, which play contains a large variety of characters, and consequently of speech, we shall find that the language of the Châṇḍâlas, the Śakâra, his servant Sthâvaraka, and even Kumbhîraka and Vaṛdhamânaka, is Mâgadhî, though the rules about स्य, र्थं, and ष्ट are scarcely observed. There is hardly any dialectic difference in their speeches. But the Sâhityadarpaṇa would lead us to expect his Châṇḍâlikâ and Śâkârî respectively in the first two cases, and Ardhamâgadhí in the last three. As before observed, some admixture of Mâgadhî characteristics constitutes this last dialect. Under this view there are instances of the use of the Ardhamâgadhî, as Lassen remarks, in the Prabodhachandrodaya. The dialect used by Mâthura, the keeper of the gambling-house in the Mṛichchhakaṭika, is somewhat different. In his speeches, we sometimes find ल् and श् used for र् and स्, and sometimes not. The nom. sing. ends in ओ, as in the Mahârâshṭrî or Śauraseni, in some cases, in others it ends in ए as in the Mâgadhî, and sometimes in उ as in the Apabhraṁśa; and the gen. sing. sometimes ends in आह as in the Mâgadhî. If the text is to be depended on, the Dâkshiṇâtya which Vis'vanâtha[5] attributes to gamblers may be such a mixed language.

It would thus appear that if all these inferior dialects did exist and were used by dramatic writers, they differed from each other in unimportant particulars, and that most of them belonged to the Mâgadhî species, since the Mss. have confounded them with the Mâgadhî of the grammarians. Hence we are justified in taking the real number of Prâkṛit dialects used for literary purposes to be six, *viz.*, those mentioned by Hemachandra, Trivikrama, and Lakshmîdhara.

---

sûtra and also to some of the instances that are given. The change of थ् to ध्, is a S'auraseni peculiarity. Of the two remaining points one is the insertion of य् to avoid the hiatus caused by the dropping of a consonant, about which I have already spoken, and the other is unimportant.

There is, therefore, no question that the Prâkrit, a meagre grammar of whic his given in the work edited by Dr. Hoernle, is not older than Hemachandra's.—(1887).

5 Another gambler without a name is introduced in the same scene, whose language Prof. Lassen thinks is Dâkshiṇâtyâ and Mâthura's, Âvantikî. Very few speeches, however, are given to the former, and it is not possible to come to any

Daṇḍin mentions a work of the name of Bṛihatkathâ written in the language of the ghosts, *i. e.*, in the Pais'âchî. Dr. Bühler has recently obtained a trace of the work, and arrangements have been made for getting it copied[6]. It is traditionally ascribed to a poet of the name of Guṇâḍhya.

Let us now examine cursorily the principal Prâkṛit and the Śaurasenî which ranks next to it in literary importance, but as the model of the inferior dialects and as the language used by the higher class of Prâkṛit-speaking dramatic persons in their prose speeches is more important than the other. Here, as before, I will place a specimen of each before you:—

61. नियआए चियअ वायाइ अत्तणो गारवं निवेसेन्ता।
जे यन्ति पसंसं चियअ जयन्ति इह ते महाकइणो ॥

63. दोग्गच्चंमि वि सोक्खाइं ताण विहवे वि होन्ति दुक्खाइं।
कव्वपरमत्थरसियाआइं जाण जायन्ति हिययाअआइं ॥

67. सोहेइ सुहावेइ यअ उवहुज्जन्तो लवो वि लच्छीए।
देवी सरस्सई उण असमग्गा किंपि विणडेइ ॥

99. अत्थिं नियअत्तियअनीसेसभुवणदुरियाआहिनन्दियअमहिन्दो।
सिरि जसवम्मो त्ति दिसापडिलग्गगुणो महीनाहो ॥

Sanskrit:—

61. निजयैव वाचयात्मनो गौरवं निवेशयन्तः।
ये यान्ति प्रशंसामेव जयन्तीह ते महाकवयः ॥

63. दौर्गत्येपि सौख्यानि तेषां विभवेपि भवन्ति दुःखानि।
काव्यपरमार्थरसिकानि येषां जायन्ते हृदयानि ॥

67. शोभयति सुखयति चोपभुज्यमानो लवोपि लक्ष्म्याः।
देवी सरस्वती पुनरसमग्रा किमपि विडम्बयति ॥

---

definite conclusion from them; but so far as they go there is hardly any difference between his dialect and that of Mâthura. The Professor is led to attribute two languages to gamblers by the annotator on the Sâhityadarpaṇa whom he quotes, and who explains धूर्त by अक्षदेविन्. But if the word is to be so understood, दीव्यताम् in the next line is not wanted, and neither योध nor नागरिक. For, supposing the warriors and clever worldly men were gamblers, gambling was not confined to them; whence there is no reason to mention them in particular.

6. So Dr. Bühler told me at the time; and on a subsequent occasion I myself thought I had found a trace of the work. But up to this time all our search has proved fruitless. (1887).

99. अस्ति निवर्तितनिःशेषभुवनदुरिताभिनन्दितमहेन्द्रः ।
श्रीयशोवर्मेति दिशाप्रतिलग्नगुणो महीनाथः ॥

61. "Victorious are the great poets who, establishing their greatness by their own words, do obtain praise only."

63. "Those whose hearts appreciate the true beauty of poetry experience joys even in poverty and sorrows even in prosperity."

67. "Even a small degree of Lakshmî when enjoyed adorns and delights, but the divine Sarasvatî if imperfect is an unspeakable mockery."

99. "There lives a king named Yas'ovarman who delights Indra by removing all the distresses of the world and whose virtues have reached the ends of the quarters."

Śaurasenî:

कधं अणुगहीदम्हि । इअमालिङ्गामि । दंसणं उण पिअसहीए बाहुप्पीडेण णिरुद्धं ण लम्भीअदि । सहि कठोरकमलपम्हलो अण्णारिसो जेव्व दे अज्ज णिव्वावेदि सरीरफंसो । किं अ मउलिविणिविसिदञ्जली मह वअणेण विण्णवेहि तं जणं ण मए मन्दभाइणीए विअसन्त-पुण्डरीअलच्छीविलासहारिणो मुहचन्दमण्डलस्स दे सच्छन्ददंसणेण संभाविदो चिरं महूसवो लोअणाणं ।

Sanskrit:

कथमनुगृहीतास्मि । इयमालिङ्गामि । दर्शनं पुनःप्रियसख्या बाष्पोत्पीडेन निरुद्धं न लभ्यते । सखि कठोरकमलपक्ष्मलोन्यादृश एव तेऽद्य निर्वापयति शरीरस्पर्शः । किं च मौलि-विनिवेशिताञ्जलिर्मम वचनेन विज्ञापय तं जनं न मया मन्दभाग्यया विकसत्पुण्डरीकलक्ष्मी-विलासहारिणो मुखचन्द्रमण्डलस्य ते स्वच्छन्ददर्शनेन संभावितश्चिरं महोत्सवो लोचनानाम् ।

"What ! thou hast obliged me. Here I embrace. But I do not catch a glimpse of my dear friend, my sight being obstructed by the flow of tears. Friend, the contact of thy body, hairy like a ripened lotus, cools my body in a peculiar manner to-day. Moreover, with thy hands clasped and placed over thy head, do at my request, humbly say to that person, 'Unfortunate as I am, I have not feasted my eyes long, by looking freely at the moon of thy face which rivals the blown lotus in beauty".

In the Ms. of the Gauḍavadha, from which the first extract is given, अ and आ preceded by अ and इ are marked as य and या. In Mss. of other works the य does not appear; but there can be no question that it represent the later pronunciation correctly, since as already remarked in a note this य is observed in some of the modern vernnaculars. But it is to be pronounced like a strengthened अ or आ and not like the heavy semi-vowel that I mentioned in my observations on the Pâli.

From these extracts you will observe that phonetic decay has made greater progress in these dialects than in the one we have examined. The changes in the Pâli are, with a few exceptions, such as may be attributed to the circumstances and vocal peculiarities of a foreign race. But in the Prâkṛits the usual processes of corruption have a wider range of operation; though even here we shall, as we proceed, find it necessary to ascribe a good deal to an ethnological cause. And first as regards the phonetic transformations which we have noticed in the Pâli, I have to observe that Prâkṛits also exhibit the same with but slight differences. The vowel ऋ is changed to अ as in घअ, तण, मअ, &c. for घृत, तृण, मृग, &c.; to इ as in किवा, हिअअ, किस, &c. for कृपा, हृदय, कृश, &c.; to उ as in पुहई, पाउस, वुड्ढ, &c., for पृथिवी, प्रावृष्, वृद्ध, &c. When standing alone it is more often changed to रि than in Pâli; as in रिद्धी and रिच्छ for ऋद्धि and ऋक्ष; रिण or अण, रिजू or उजू, &c., for ऋण, ऋजु, &c., while the Pâli forms of these words are इद्धि, अच्छ, अण and उजु. The diphthongs ऐ and औ are as in Pâli changed to ए and ओ, as in केलास, वेज्ज, केढव, &c. for कैलास, वैद्य, कैटभ, &c.; and in जोव्वण, कोमुई, कोत्थुह &c., for यौवन, कौमुदी, कौस्तुभ, &c.; but in a good many instances they are dissolved into their elements अइ and अउ, as in दइच, भइरव, दइवअ, सइर, &c., for दैत्य, भैरव, दैवत, स्वैर, &c., and पउर, कउसल, सउह, मउली, &c., for पौर, कौशल, सौध, मौलि, &c. This change resembles the dissolution of conjunct consonants into the different members, and like it is due to a weak or languid way of pronunciation. In ऐ and औ the first element or अ is rapidly pronounced, and the temporal value assigned to it by the authors of the Prâtiśâkhyas is, you will remember, half a mâtrâ, while in the Prâkṛit transformations it is one mâtrâ. The long vowels are, as in Pâli, shortened when followed by double consonants; and there is the same or even stronger evidence of the existence of short ए and ओ. In Pâli short इ and उ followed by a conjunct are in certain cases changed to ए and ओ, and from that fact we inferred that they were short. Here in a great many more cases when so followed, short इ is optionally interchangeable with ए, and short उ is necessarily replaced by ओ, as in पिण्ड or पेण्ड, पिट्ठ or पेट्ठ, निद्दा or नेद्दा, &c., and तोण्ड, मोण्ड, पोक्खर, &c., for पिण्ड, पिष्ट, निद्रा, तुण्ड, मुण्ड, पुष्कर, &c. In several cases ए not followed by a conjunct is optionally changed to इ, as in विअणा or वेअणा for वेदना, दिअर or देअर for देवर, &c.

The ए in these words must for some reason that we will hereafter consider have been pronounced short and hence interchangeable with इ. Sometimes the consonant following an ए or ओ is doubled, as in तेल्ल, पेम्म, सोत्त, जोव्वन, &c., for तैल, प्रेमन्, स्रोतस्, यौवन, &c., which could only be because those vowels were pronounced short, and the loss of quantity thus occasioned made up for by rendering the pronunciation heavy and forcible. In other cases the ए was so pronounced by some and not by others; and so we have एक्क or एअ for एक, सेव्वा or सेवा for सेवा, &c. The syllables अय and अव are changed to ए and ओ oftener than in Pâli, the अय of the causative and the tenth class becoming ए necessarily throughout, as in कारेइ, हासेइ, कहेइ for कारयति, हासयति, कथयति &c.

All the sibilants are reduced to स् as in the Pâli, but in the Mâgadhî dialect to श्; as शालश, पुलिश for सारस, पुरुष, &c. These dialects do not possess the cerebral ळ्, and therefore we have ल् in the place of the Pâli ळ् and in some cases the original Sanskrit ड्; as in तलाअ, गरुल, कीलइ for the Pâli तळाग, गरुळ, कीळति and Sanskrit तडाग, गरुड, क्रीडति, &c., गुल or गुड, णाली or णाडी for the Pâli गुळ, नाळी, &c. and पीडेइ, नीड for the Pâli पीळेति, नीळ, &c. There are a good many more examples of the change of dentals to cerebrals than in the Pâli, both through the influence of a neighbouring र or without it. The ट् and ठ् which correspond to त् and थ् are in most cases softened to ड् and ढ्. Thus we have पडि for the Pâli पटि, as in पडिमा, पडिहार, for प्रतिमा, प्रतिहार, &c., and पहुडि, पडण, बहेडअ, for प्रभृति, पतन, बिभीतक; डोला or दोला, डम्भ or दम्भ, डब्भ or दब्भ for दोला, दम्भ, दर्भ, &c.; पढम (Pâli पठम), सिढिल, मेढी, ओसढ for प्रथम, शिथिल, मेथि, औषध, &c. In Pâli the dental nasal न् is changed ण् in but a few instances; but here it is so changed throughout, necessarily when uninitial, and optionally when at the beginning of a word; as कणअ, मअण, वअण, for कनक, मदन, वदन, &c., and णर or नर, णई or नई, णेइ or नेइ, for नर, नदी, नयति, &c. The opposite process is however observable in the Paiśâchî dialect, where not only have we no instances of this change but even the original Sanskrit ण् is changed to न् as in गुन, गन, for गुण, गण, &c. The conjunct consonants are transformed in the Prâkṛit in the same way as in the Pâli. In the former however, ज्ञ् and न्य् are changed to ण्ण् and not to ञ्ञ् as in the latter, as in णाण, सण्णा, अण्ण, सुण्ण, for ज्ञान, संज्ञा, अन्य, शून्य, &c. To be thus corrupted, ज्ञ् must in the original Sanskrit have been pronounced as if it were composed of ज् and न्; and sometimes the latter must have been so weakly pronounced that the sound of ज् prevailed over it and the whole became ज्ज्, as in जाण or णाण, सव्वज्ज or सव्वण्ण, मणोज्ज or मणोण्ण, for ज्ञान, सर्वज्ञ, मनोज्ञ, &c. In the Paiśâchî and the Mâgadhî, however, the Pâli transformation is retained; as in सञ्ञा, सवञ्ञ, कञ्ञका, अभिमञ्ञू, for संज्ञा, सर्वज्ञ, कन्यका, अभिमन्यु, &c. The conjunct र्य् is sometimes changed to ज्ज् corresponding to the य्य् of the older dialect, and ह्य् to ज्झ् in which case the heavy *nâda* of ह् is transferred to the ज् which takes the place of य् as in the change of ध्य् to ज्झ्. In Pâli the consonants of ह्य् only interchange places; *i. e.* it becomes य्ह्. From this and from the change of the initial uncombined य् to ज्, it appears that very often the Sanskrit य्, was pronounced heavily when the Prâkṛits arose. The Śaurasenî and the dialects allied with it have, however, both the Pâli and the Prâkṛit corruptions of र्य्.

A dental forming a conjunct with a following व् is in a few cases changed to the corresponding palatal; as in भोच्चा for भुक्त्वा, चच्चर for चत्वर, पिच्छी for पृथ्वी, विज्जं for विद्वान्, बुज्झा for बुद्ध्वा, झअ for ध्वज, झुणी for ध्वनि, सज्झस for साध्वस, &c. This seems to arise from the fact that व् was pronounced so lightly that it lost its distinctive character, and the conjuncts came to be confused with those containing a dental and य् which, you will remember, are changed to a double palatal. In Pâli the त्व् is retained in these instances, and the द्व् and and ध्व् are changed to द् and द्ध् according to the general rules, and the थ्व् of पृथ्वी becomes थव्. Besides the conjuncts disjoined in Pâli by the interposition of a vowel, we have र्श् and र्ष् also so treated in the Prâkṛit, sometimes optionally and sometimes necessarily. Thus आदर्श becomes आअरिस or आअंस, (P. आदास); सुदर्शन, सुदरिसण or सुदंसण, (P. सुदस्सन); वर्ष, वरिस or वास, (P. वस्स); परामर्श, परामरिस, (P. परामास); अमर्श, अमरिस, (P. अमस्स).

Having noticed the changes common to the Prâkṛits with the Pâli, we will proceed to consider others distinctive of the former. Most of these were due to the continuous operation of processes which come into play in a living language. The Pâli exhibits but few instances of these processes. The changes observable in it are mostly to be traced to one or two vocal peculiarities of the men who spoke it. At the time when the language received the form in which we now find it, the tradition of the original Sanskrit was still distinct; the Pâli had not lived an independent life detached from its mother for a long time. But with the Prâkṛits the case is different. They show a great many more instances of the usual processes, and consequently a much greater departure from the parent tongue. We will begin by noticing what may be called the softening process.

The vowels इ and उ are softened, as we have seen, to short ए and ओ before conjuncts. These latter sounds are, as indicated in the last lecture, more open than the former; that is, do not require the tongue to be raised so high as in the case of इ and उ. They are therefore softer. But since the change principally takes place before doubles, it may, I believe, be traced to their influence, as I have already observed. In that case this would be an instance of assimilation. But the change of long ई and ऊ to long ए and ओ is due to softening alone; as in पेऊस for पीयूष, आमेल for आपीड, बहेडअ for बिभीतक, केरिस for कीदृश, and एरिस for ईदृश, नेड for नीड, पेढ for पीठ, तम्बोल for ताम्बूल, तोणीर for तूणीर, थोर for स्थूल, and गलोई for गुडूची. In the same way, इ and उ are in rare cases softened to अ, as in हलद्दा for हरिद्रा, पडंसुअ for प्रतिश्रुत, and जहिट्ठिल for युधिष्ठिर. अ requires no movement of the tongue or lips, while इ and उ do. It is therefore softer than those two vowels. Both these changes contradict another principle to be hereafter noticed, the operation of which is wide, and they must therefore be considered special or peculiar changes. The manner in which ऋ is softened has been already detailed.

The semivowel य् is often softened to इ, as in विअण for व्यजन, विलिअ for व्यलीक, थीण for स्त्यान, उव्वीढ for उद्व्यूढ, जीआ for ज्या, &c. Here the effort necessary to bring the middle of the tongue closer to the palate is economized, while the position of the organs in other respects is the same. The य of the conjunct र्य is sometimes softened in this way to इ and sometimes to इअ. In the former case the resulting इ is transferred to the previous syllable and forms ए with the अ contained in it; as in पेरन्त for पर्यन्त, अच्छेर for आश्चर्य, बम्भचेर for ब्रह्मचर्य, सुन्देर for सौन्दर्य, &c. Similarly व is changed to उ as in झुणी for ध्वनि, वीसुं for विष्वक्, गउओ for गवय, सुवइ for स्वपिति, दु for द्वि, &c.

The surds are softened into sonants. The pronunciation of these requires, as you will remember, less exertion than that of the former. For sonants such as ग्, घ्, ड्, ध्, &c., are pronounced by means of *nâda*, or vocal sound which is produced when the glottis is in its natural condition and the chords vibrate, and the surds क्, ख्, ट्, थ्, &c. are uttered by sending forth simple breath or *s'vâsa*, to produce which it is necessary to stretch the glottis. This effort is saved by changing the surds to sonants. Thus क् is changed to ग् as in मरगअ for मरकत and गेन्दुअ for कन्दुक; ट् to ड् as in नड, भड, and घड; for नट, भट, and घट;

and in पडि for प्रति and the other instances given above; ड् to ड् as in मढ, सढ, कमढ, कुढार, and पढ, for मठ, शठ, कमठ, कुठार, and पठ; and त and थ to द and ध as in एद for एत, नाध for नाथ &c. (in Śaur.). The cerebral, and ड् resulting from the original dentals त् and थ् are also similarly softened to ड् and ढ् as in पडि for प्रति (पटि in Pâli), पहुडि for प्रभृति, बहेडअ for बिभीतक, हरडई for हरीतकी, मडअ for मृतक, &c., and सिढिल for शिथिल, पुढवी for पृथिवी. पढम for प्रथम, &c. The sonant answering to प् is ब् but this is further softened to व्, as in कूव, कवाल, कुणव, तवइ, &c., for कूप कपाल, कुणप, तपति, &c.

An original ड् is softened to ल्, in which case there is a saving of two efforts. The complete contact necessary for the pronunciation of ड् being avoided we have ळ. This sound is similar to ल् in the fact that the breath before the break of the contact or close approach is allowed to pass out by the sides of the tongue, but is more difficult or harder because its position being higher up, the tongue has to be raised higher than in pronouncing ल्, the position of which is near the root of the upper teeth. This additional exertion is saved by proceeding from ड्, at once to ल्. We have thus गरुल, तलाअ, कीलइ, दालिम, गुल, नाली, for गरुड, तडाग, क्रीडति, दाडिम, गुड, नाडी, &c. In the Pâli, however, you will remember and probably in some unwritten Prâkṛits also, the cerebral character of the letter was preserved and we have ळ् instead of ल्. Sometimes ड् is softened to र् only. The position of this is lower than that of ड् and the contact is incomplete. It is therefore softer than ड् but harder than ल्. This last sound is produced lower still, but a light close approach is formed, and the breath is allowed to escape by the sides of the tongue; while in uttering र् the tongue is kept in its position with greater force, and the breath is allowed to vibrate. This change is principally to be met with in the case of the ड् resulting from an original द् in such words as एआरह, बारह, तेरह, &c., for एकादश, द्वादश, त्रयोदश, &c., the द् of which must first have become ड्. In कलम्ब, दोहल, and पलित्त, for कदम्ब, दोहद, and प्रदीप्त, we have instances of an original द् passing into ल्. An original र् is changed to ल् which, as just observed, is softer than र्, as in हलद्दी, दलिद्द, मुहल, इङ्गाल, &c., for हरिद्रा, दरिद्र, मुखर, अङ्गार, &c. When the र् forming the first member of a conjunct is softened in this way, and the following member is weak, or is itself capable of becoming ल् the whole conjunct becomes ल्ल; as पर्यस्त becomes पल्लट्ट-त्थ; पर्याण, पल्लाण; आर्द्र, अल्ल or ओल्ल; मर्द, मल्ल, &c. The sibilant स्, which is the only one we have in the Mahârâshṭrî and Śaurasenî, is sometimes softened to ह्, that is, the simple heavy breath somewhat compressed at the dental position is made uncompressed heavy vocal sound; as in दिवह, पाहाण, दह, एआरह, बारह &c., for दिवस, पाषाण, दश, एकादश द्वादश, &c.

Another phenomenon characteristic of the Prâkṛits is the dropping away of single uninitial consonants. Thus क् is dropped, as in सअद, कुम्भआर, for शकट, कुम्भकार, &c.; ग् as in नअ, नअर, साअर for नग, नगर, सागर, &c.; च् as in वअण, सूई, for वचन, सूचि, &c.; ज् as in रअअ, राआ, गअ, for रजत, राजा, गज &c.; त् as in विआण, पआवई, गअ, for वितान, प्रजापति, गत, &c.; द् as in मअण, पाअ, कअल, for मदन, पाद, कदल, &c.; प् followed by any vowel except अ, as in रिऊ, कई, विउल, for रिपु, कपि, विपुल, &c.; य् as in वाउणा, णअण, for वायुना, नयन, &c.; व् as in जीअ, दिअह, for जीव, दिवस, &c. The vowel अ or आ that remains after the elision is when preceded by अ or आ pronounced like a light य. We find it written in Mss. also, as in सयढ, तित्थयरो, नयर, &c. In the same way, the mute element of the aspirates is dropped, except in the case of the palatals and of फ्, the ह् or the heavy *nâda* or vocal sound being alone preserved. Thus we have मुह, लिह, सही, for मुख, लिख, सखी, &c., मेह, माह पाहुण, for मेघ, माघ, प्राघुण, &c.; नाह, मिहुण, कहा, for नाथ, मिथुन, कथा, &c.; बहिर, वहू, साहु, for बधिर, वधू, साधु, &c.; लाह, सोहग्ग, सोहा, for लाभ, सौभाग्य, शोभा, &c. The range of the operation of these processes is very wide; and the number of words transformed in accordance with them is very large. Now, the principle which is at the bottom of this elision of consonants is the same as that which brings about softening, viz., economy of exertion. But in a growing language which knows of no accidents in the course of its history, there is another principle which counteracts this, viz., the necessity of pronouncing words in a manner to be understood by others. Hence a wholesale elision is impossible; and the natural course is to soften sounds away, until finally they are elided. This of course must be a very slow process. But in the Prâkṛit, and especially the Mahârâshṭrî, we do not find it to be slow. Elision seems to be a distinguishing characteristic which strikes one very forcibly on reading a Prâkṛit passage. It is too regular, systematic, and far-reaching, to have been the product of a long course of softening. In fact, because it is so systematic and general, some writers have doubted whether the Prâkṛits were genuine dialects, and have expressed their belief that they are the creation of Pandits. But we shall find that the modern vernaculars retain the words shorn of their elements by the Prâkṛits in this way; and that these latter dialects were the immediate parents of those we now speak in Northern India. If this general mutilation of words was brought about by a natural decay, we must suppose the process to have gone on for a great many centuries. The Prâkṛit vocables that have descended to the modern vernaculars have not, since the period when the Prâkṛits arose about fourteen centuries ago, suffered at all so much as Sanskrit words in passing into the Prâkṛits. We have not dropped away any of the elements of Prâkṛit vocables, though we may have re-arranged them in some cases. If, then, fourteen centuries have not been sufficient to make words lose any of their elements by the action of natural causes, the process by which Sanskrit words were mutilated and became Prâkṛit must, if it was natural and ordinary, have been in operation for a considerably longer period, a supposition which appears extremely improbable. And it is questionable whether a language which has not been exposed to accidents in the course of its history suffers so much, even after the lapse of any conceivable time. The Teutonic languages, though they have been going through an independent course of development since the period when the ancestors of the modern English and Germans separated from the ancestors of the Hindus in pre-historic ages, have preserved the elements of old Aryan vocables which the Prâkṛits lost. They may have transformed the words, but have not mutilated them to any great extent. The English words *father*, *mother*, *brother*, *foot*, and others, have all the elements of the old पितृ, मातृ, भ्रातृ, पद् (पाद), and others; while the Prâkṛit पीआ or पीउ, माआ, माइ or माउ, भाआ or भाउ, and पाअ, and the modern vernacular पिउ, माउ, मा, माँ, भाई, भाउ, and पा or पाय, have lost all except the first consonantal sound. The elision of consonants on a large scale in the Prâkṛits is therefore to be accounted for in another way than by attributing it to a natural process of decay. The Prâkṛit words must be taken to represent the pronunciation of the corresponding Sanskrit words by an alien race. The vocal organs of the people of that race were unused to the utterance of Sanskrit sounds, and in this respect they were in the condition of children making their first attempts at articulate speech, and elided uninitial consonantal sounds and assimilated conjunct consonants as these do. When a child or a barbarous foreigner listens to an elderly or more civilized person, he has not the patience to attend to all the sounds composing a word and to reproduce them carefully, or has not acquired the habit of doing so. The first letter only makes a strong impression on his ear, and this he faithfully reproduces; and as to the rest, he realizes their quantity by pronouncing the vowels, but his tongue being untrained, the peculiar movements necessary for uttering the consonantal sounds he cannot go through, and avoids. In going over the Pâli we had to attribute the assimilation of conjuncts and other peculiarities observable in that dialect to such a cause; and now the elision in the Prâkṛits that we have been considering must, I believe, be accounted for in the same way.

But what could be the historical events which led to the wholesale assimilation of consonants in the first place and to the similar elision of uninitial consonants in addition to the assimilation, in the next? I would put forward the following hypothesis. It would appear that when the Âryas moved from the land of the five rivers and settled in the country known afterwards as Brahmâvarta and Kurukshetra that is the country about Thânes'var, they formed a consolidated community in which an aboriginal or alien race was incorporated and the language represented by the Pâli was the language of this race. When, however, the consolidated community spread eastwards and southwards, they met other alien races and the dialect spoken by the lowest class of the consolidated community was learnt by these new alien races and the words which were in the Pâli stage were further corrupted into the forms which we find in the Prâkṛits. The dialects of the Aśoka edicts do not show instances of the Prâkṛit rule of elision, though some peculiarities of one or two later dialects are discernable in them. Does this necessarily show that the Prâkṛits had not developed in the time of As'oka? I think not. The dialects of the edicts represent the spoken language of the more cultured portion of the consolidated community and not that used by the races which were newly incorporated with the community and formed a class lower in the scale, though the Prâkṛits must have begun to be developed about the time of Aśoka. In the Nâsik cave inscriptions of about the second century of the Christian era we observe some instances of the Prâkṛit peculiarity of elision, whence it would appear that the Prâkṛits had then come into existence though they were still regarded as vulgar and were neglected, the principal inscriptions being in the Páli which had then become a learned language. The conclusion we came to in the last lecture, that the Pâli represents middle Sanskrit in a vernacular form while the Prâkṛits correspond to the last or classical stage, is in harmony with this view.

Another process which transforms the words of a language is assimilation. We have already discussed the assimilation of the members of a conjunct and of the diphthongal sounds ऐ and औ, and will now consider the application of the process to the different syllable, composing a word. The अ of the second syllable of ईषत्, वेतस्, and कृपण, is changed to इ, because the vowel in the first is ई or ए, the ऋ of कृपण being changed to इ; and we have ईसि, वेडिस, and किविण. Similarly, the अ of मरिच and वल्ली, and the इ of इक्षु are changed to इ, ए, and उ through the influence of the following इ, ई, and उ; and the forms are मिरिअ, वेल्ली, and उच्छु. Sometimes, when य् as a member of a conjunct is changed to a palatal, it influences the preceding vowel and brings it over to its own position, as in सेज्जा for शय्या, मज्झिम for मध्यम, गेज्झ for ग्राह्य, &c. An original palatal also produces similar effect, as in जिमइ or जेमइ for जमति. In the words पुढम for प्रथम, पोम्म for पद्म, and ओप्पेइ for अर्पयति, the adjoining vowel is changed to उ to make it go easily with the labial प. You will observe that it is अ that yields so readily to the influence of an adjoining letter, because in pronouncing it no movement of the tongue is necessary. It is sounded by letting off *nâda* or intonated breath, without offering any obstruction to it; and this current gives rise to the different vowels when it is obstructed in various degrees by various movements of the tongue and the lips; so that if the organic position of the previous consonant remains a little longer, or if the following is begun a little earlier, the अ current assumes the form that that position gives it. An aspirate or an aspirated mute existing in a word influences an adjoining vowel or a consonant; that is, the heavy breath that is necessary for the utterance of the aspirate mingles itself with the other sounds also. Thus कासित becomes खासिअ; परुष, फरुस; परिघ, फलिह; परिखा, फलिहा; पनस, फणस; and बिसिनी, भिसिणी, in which instances क्, प् and ब् are changed to ख्, फ्, and भ्. In other cases the heavy breath is transferred to an adjoining vowel which becomes ह्; as in फलिह for स्फटिक, निहस for निकष, विहत्थी for वितस्ति, वसही for वसति, भरह for भरत, in which cases by the dropping of the mute we should have, but for this heavy breath, फलिअ, निअस, विअत्थी, वसई, and भरअ. The words सटा and शकट become सढा and सअढ, the ढ् resulting from the transference of the heavy breath being softened to ढ्.

Another kind of assimilation must be noticed here. The vowels are open sounds and the consonants close. These being used together, the openness of the former has a tendency to diminish to assimilate them to the latter, and the closeness of the latter has a similar tendency to yield to the openness of the former. This latter change involves economy and is the same as softening; त् and प् for instance become more and more like vowels when they are changed to द् and ब्, and thence to ल् and व्; while the latter ultimately does become the vowel उ. But the former does not involve softening in itself but rather hardening, since ए or इ, and ओ or उ, to which अ is sometimes changed, occasion motions of the tongue and the lips which the latter does not. But in this change there is an ease of pronunciation such as is involved in assimilation. Immediately after one closing of the passage of the breath, it is easier to make a shorter opening for it such as इ and उ require before another closing, than a longer one such as the pronunciation of ए and ओ requires, or a complete one such as is necessary for अ. This last vowel therefore has a tendency to pass off into ए and इ, or ओ and उ. But whether the shorter opening is to be made at the middle of the palate or at the lips, that is, whether अ is to be changed to ए and इ, or ओ and उ depends on the vocal habits of a people. Some are accustomed to open their lips and round them, others not. Similarly, whether the opening shall be the least possible or a little more, that is, whether अ is to be changed to ए or ओ first, and then to इ or उ, or at once to इ or उ depends upon habit. And the ease of pronunciation involved in this kind of assimilation is also relative. Some people may feel the muscular effort required for इ and उ to be more intolerable than the wider or complete opening, and prefer ए and ओ or even अ, as in the instances given under vowel softening, and in others occurring in some of the modern vernaculars. The Prâkṛits change अ to इ in virtue of this law of assimilation, as in पिक्क for पक्क, इङ्गाल for अङ्गार, मुइङ्ग for मृदङ्ग, सिविण for स्वप्न, and णिडाल for ललाट; and to एं in गेन्दुअ for कन्दुक, एत्थ for अत्र, देक्ख for द्रक्ष, &c.

Opposed to this process of assimilation is dissimilation. When the same vowel occurs in two successive syllables, it is felt to be burdensome, and hence a dissimilar vowel is substituted for it in one of the two. We have thus बहेडअ for विभीतक, सढिल for शिथिल, पुहवी for पृथिवी, मउल, मउड and मउर for मुकुल, मुकुट and मुकुर, भिउडी for भ्रुकुटी, पुरिस for पुरुष, निउर or नेउर for नूपुर, दुअल्ल for दुकूल, सोअमल्ल for सौकुमार्य, अगरु for अगुरु, गलोइ for गुडूची, and गरुअ for गुरुक. The words अङ्गुदी and हरडई for इङ्गुदी and हरीतकी must also be considered as instances of the same law, though another syllable intervenes between the two containing the same vowel. Instances of this process must necessarily be few, since there are not many words containing the same vowel in successive syllables. But we have got so many here, that the substitution of a dissimilar vowel in such cases may be considered a general characteristic of the Prâkṛits. It will also be seen that in these instances, अ is subsituted for इ throughout, and for उ mostly; so that these may also be considered as instances in which the most open sound अ was preferred by the Prâkṛit speakers to इ or उ, as involving less exertion.

The first अ of समृद्धि, प्रसिद्धि, प्रकट, प्रतिपद्, सदृक्ष, &c., is lengthened optionally; and we have सामिद्धि or समिद्धि, पासिद्धि or पसिद्धि, प-पाअड, प-पाडिव, स-सारिच्छ, &c. On the other hand, the आ of यथा, तथा, उत्खात संस्थापित, प्राकृत, हालिक, कुमार &c. is optionally shortened; and these words become जह-हा, तह-हा, उक्खअ-खाअ, संठविअ-ठाविअ, पअड-पाअड, हलिअ-हालिअ, कुमर-मार &c. The ई of पानिय, अलीक, जीवति, गभीर, द्वितीय, तृतीय, &c., is necessarily shortened, and we have पाणिअ, अलिअ, जिवइ, गहिर, दुइअ, तइअ &c. Changes of this nature seem to be due to some kind of accent with which the words must have been pronounced. When one of the syllables of a word is accented, the whole vocal weight of that word gravitates towards that syllable. It is sounded with greater force and pitch and with a jerk which are apt to cause a wider opening between the organs of speech than is necessary. Hence the less open vowels अ, इ, and उ have a tendency to become more open, *i.e.*, आ, ए, and ओ. Similarly the force and the jerk tend to prolong the time occupied by the utterance of the vowel, that is, to lengthen it. And long vowels occurring in the unaccented syllables often become short, since they are uttered hurriedly or carelessly. Supposing प्रतिपद् was pronounced with the accent on प्र, that would be a reason why the प्र should become प्रा in the course of time; and if द्वितीय was pronounced with the accent on द्वि, we can understand why the ती should become short. But the real nature of the old Sanskṛit accents, notwithstanding the labours of the grammarians, is little understood. How words were actually pronounced in this respect it is difficult to say. If the *udâtta* was really the acute accent, it falls in some of the above words on syllables by being on which it could not have operated in the manner indicated above. The supposition that the *svarita* was the acute accent fails equally. But perhaps the old accents went out of use very early, and others took up their place. Whatever may have been the case, the changes we have been considering seem to have risen from an accent of some sort. The ए of वेदना, चपेटा, देवर, and केसर is optionally changed to इ; for supposing that the accent fell on the second or third syllable, the force necessary to pronounce it could not be successfully exerted if the mouth had to be previously opened wide for sounding ए. It is thus reduced to the close vowel इ; and so we have विअणा, चविडा, दिअर and किसर. The dropping of initial vowels as in रण्ण for अरण्य and लाबू for अलाबू must also be traced to those vowels being unaccented. The accent on the penultimate vowel which is very general in the vernaculars as will be noticed in the next lecture had probably its beginning in these Prâkṛits and of this fact these six words are instances. This penultimate accent seems to have had a wider range in the later stage of these dialects represented by the Apabhraṁśa.

There are several instances in these dialects of the interchange of consonants. The word स्नुषा becomes सुण्हा, while regularly it ought to be ण्हुसा; ण्हु and स् thus interchange places. Similarly, करेणु is transformed to कणेरू, वाराणसी to वाणारसी, अचलपुर to अलचपुर, आलान to आणाल, लघु to हलु (लहु also being used), महाराष्ट्र to मरहट्ठ, &c. In the case of विच्छुअ for वृश्चिक we have an interchange of vowels, for the उ resulting from ऋ is transferred to श्च and its to व. In ordinary life we often find that a man speaking hastily makes the sounds of a word thus interchange places. When several people happen to do so in the case of particular words, the new transformations come in the course of time to be regarded as the true words and acquire a recognized position.

The Prâkṛits sometimes change a labial to the nasal of its class as in नीम for नीप, आमेल for आपीड, कमन्ध for कबन्ध, नीमी for नीवि, समर for शबर, and सिमिण for स्वप्न. These are optional changes; the forms of the words with व or ब instead of म also existing. Though the change involves softening, since a portion of the breath is sent through the nose and the force of the contact weakened, it must be attributed to a tendency to speak through the nose. Similarly, they introduced an *anusvâra* into words which did not originally contain it; where also the breath was discharged through the mouth as well as the nose. In this manner, वक्र became वंक; अश्रु, अंसु; श्मश्रु, मंसु; स्पर्श, फंस; पुच्छ, पुंछ; मूर्धा, मुंढा; बुध्न, बुंध; दर्शन, दंसण; वृश्चिक, विंछुअ; मार्जार, मंजार; प्रतिश्रुत, पडंसुआ, &c. The last syllable of the absolutive termination ऊण and of the case endings एण and एसु is also sometimes nasalised, as in काऊणं or काऊण for कृत्वा, and वच्छेणं or ण and वच्छेसुं or सु for वृक्षेण and वृक्षेषु. On the other hand, the existing *anusvâra* of a few words is dropped, probably from a feeling that its existence in those words was due to a mistake and from a desire to correct it. Thus we have मास or मंस for मांस, कास or कंस for कांस्य, पासु or पंसु for पांसु, दाणि or दाणिं for इदानीं, and णं or ण as the termination of the gen. pl. The letter ल् is, in a few cases optionally, sometimes necessarily, transformed into ण्, as in णाहल or लाहल, णङ्गल or लङ्गुल, णङ्गूल or लङ्गूल, and णडाल or णिडाल, for लाहल, लाङ्गल, लाङ्गूल, and ललाट. In the last instance ट् is softened and made to exchange its place with the second ल्, and the अ of ण becomes इ optionally. This also points to the Prâkṛit characteristic of speaking through the nose.

The remarks I have hitherto made apply to the Mahârâshṭrî or the principal Prâkṛit. The Śaurasenî differs from it in but a few particulars. It does not drop त् and थ् but softens them into द् and ध्, as in पूरिद, मारुदि, तधा, नाध, &c., for पूरित, मारुति, तथा, नाथ, &c. The conjunct न्त् is often changed to न्द्, as in निचिन्दो, अन्देउर for निश्चिन्त, अन्तःपुर, &c. In addition to these peculiarities, in the Mâgadhî the र् and स् of the principal Prâkṛit are represented by ल् and श्, as in नल, कल, शालश, पुलिश, for नर, कर, सारस, पुरुष, &c. The स् of a conjunct is not assimilated but preserved, and the ष् changed to स्, as in पस्खलदि हस्ती for प्रस्खलति हस्ती, शुष्क दालु for शुष्क दारु, कस्ट for कष्ट, &c. The double ट् and the conjunct ष्ठ are changed to स्ट्, and स्थ् and र्थ to स्त; द् and ध् being thus softened to द् and त्. Thus we have भस्टालिका for भट्टारिका, सुस्टु for सुष्ठु, उवस्तिद for उपस्थित, शस्तवाह for सार्थवाह, &c. The consonant ज् whether original or derived, as in the Prâkṛit corruptions of द्य or र्य, was pronounced lightly, that is softened to य्, as in याणादि for जानाति, अय्य for अद्य &c. The conjuncts ज्ञ्, न्य्, and ण्य् are, as before mentioned, changed to ञ्ञ्, as in Pâli; and च्छ् to श्च्, as in गश्च, पुश्च for गच्छ, पुच्छ, &c. The क्ष् of प्रेक्ष् and चक्ष् is changed to स्क्, as in पेस्कदि for प्रेक्षते and आचस्कदि for आचक्षते. In the Pais'âchî, the changes of single consonants that we have noticed in the case of the Mahârâshṭrî and Śaurasenî do not take place; that is, the consonants are not dropped or softened, nor are they transformed by the process of assimilation. The dentals are not changed to cerebrals, but the original Sanskrit cerebrals are optionally changed to dentals, as in कुतुम्बक or कुटुम्बक for कुटुम्बक; and an original ण् to न् throughout, as in गुनगन for गुणगण. The sonant द् is hardened to त्, as in तामोतर for दामोदर, पतेस for प्रदेश, &c. The sibilants are changed to स् as in Pâli and the principal Prâkṛit, and ज्ञ् and न्य् to ञ्ञ् as in the former. In the Chûlikâ Paiśâchî,* the sonants are throughout changed to surds, as in नकर, मक्कन, मेख, वक्ख, राचा, चीमूत, &c., for नगर, मार्गण, मेघ, व्याघ्र, राजा, जीमूत, &c. Phonetically the Paiśâchî appears to be in nearly the same condition as the Pâli, but the hardening of sonants is peculiar, and may be compared to the change of Sanskrit sonants to surds in the Teutonic languages, as in *foot* for पद्, *tooth* for दत्, *know* for ज्ञा, &c. Such changes involve no economy whatever; and like the change of dentals to cerebrals they must be attributed to certain peculiarities of the vocal organs. Even in the operation of the usual processes we have, as you will have seen, found very wide scope for the play of similar special aptitudes. The characteristic of the dialect we have been considering of not changing dentals to cerebrals as the Pâli and the Prâkṛits do, and even the dentalizing of cerebrals, would appear to be truly Âryan. Perhaps then this was the language of an Âryan tribe that had remained longer in the original seat of the race, and was connected with the ancestors of the Teutons, so as to develop a phonetic peculiarity resembling theirs, and emigrated to India at a very late period and settled on the borders. Or it might be that the tribe came to India along with the others, but living in the mountainous countries on the border in a sort of rude independence, it developed this peculiarity of pronunciation, which to my mind betokens a rude and uncontrollable force of breath. Since under this supposition they could not have come in very close contact with their more civilized brethren of the plains, their language did not undergo some of those phonetic modifications which Sanskrit underwent in the mouths of the aboriginal races. And in a Sanskrit verse quoted by Mr. Ellis in his preface to Campbell's Grammar of the Telugu language, the countries where the Pais'âchî is said to have prevailed are such border countries as Gândhâra or Afghanistan, Nepal, Bâhlika or Balk, &c.[7]

We will now proceed to examine the Grammar of the Prâkṛits.

As in the Pâli the dual and the dat. case are wanting. The termination of the instr. pl. is हि, the other Pâli भि having disappeared. The ablative pl. which was lost in the older dialect is made up by adding तो, Skr. तस्, to the हि of the instr. pl., which was used in Pâli for the abl., and to सु, the termination of the locative, and using हिन्तो and सुन्तो as the terminations for all nouns. This तो in the form of दो and दु is also used to form the abl. sing. of all nouns. This is according to Vararuchi. But Hemachandra gives दो and दु as the Śaurasenî terminations, and ओ and उ as those in the principal Prâkṛit, which is according to the usual phonetic rules. This grammarian gives त्तो as an additional termination for both numbers, and extends ओ and उ to the plural also, and हिन्तो to the singular.[8] In Prâkṛit, sometimes consonants are doubled even when there is no conjunct in the original Sanskrit. Hence we have त्तो; and the reason why this and दो and दु or ओ and उ are extended to the plural is that in Skr. the expression made up of a noun and this termination has both senses; as ग्रामतः may mean *from a village* or *villages*. The gen. sing. स्स from the स्य of Sanskrit nouns in

7. Names of other countries in Central or Southern India also occur; but the reading of the verse is evidently corrupt.

8. I shall in all my observations on the Prâkṛits follow Hemachandra, since he is full and explicit. Vararuchi is indistinct in several cases, and his rules on that account have been misunderstood by all writers who have followed him; and he is incomplete.

अ is generalized as in Pâli and applied to all masc. and neut. nouns; and the pl. is formed by the old Skr. term. नाम् Prâkṛitized to णं, as in the older dialect. The Pâli pronominal abl. स्मा or म्हा has disappeared and the loc. स्मि or म्हि has assumed the form of म्मि and is used for all nouns of the masc. and neut. genders as in the other language. The voc. pl. is as in Skr. and Pâli the same as the Nom. pl.

Masculine Nouns in अ. The nom., acc., and instr. cases of nouns in अ are the same as in Pâli; but here the nom. pl. form वच्छा is optionally transferred to the acc. pl. also, thus giving another instance of the strong tendency to confuse the nom. and acc. that I have spoken of. The dat. sing. in आय like that in Pâli, is preserved in solitary instances in which it has the sense of "for the sake of". The abl. sing. besides the general forms mentioned above has the old one ending in आ, as in Pâli, and a new one in आहि which is used in the plural also. This आहि is used in Sanskrit in the words दक्षिणाहि and उत्तराहि,[9] which have an ablative signification. It must in its origin be considered the same as the instr. termination भिस्. The loc. sing. besides the general form has, as in Pâli, the old one in ए. The voc. sing. has also the two Pâli forms देव, देवा, and another देवो the same as the nom. sing.

—*Nouns in* इ *and* उ. The nom. pl. has a form made up according to the analogy of neuter nouns or nouns ending in इन्; as अग्गिणो and साहुणो. This does not exist in the Pâli, the analogy being there extended to the gen. and loc. sing. only. The Prâkṛit has also the two Pâli forms अग्गी and अग्गयो, which latter is transformed into अग्गओ and अग्गउ; and साहू and साहवो, the latter appearing also in the form of साहओ and साहउ. The acc. pl. has also the neuter form अग्गिणो or साहुणो in addition to the Pâli अग्गी or साहू. Besides the general forms mentioned above, the abl. has in the sing. the neuter form अग्गिणो or साहुणो also. The Pâli loc. sing. अग्गिणि does not appear. The other forms of these nouns are like those in the older dialect. The voc. sing. is अग्गि or साहु as in Pâli, and अग्गी or साहू. We here see the analogy of neuter nouns or nouns ending in इन् extended to all vowel cases except the loc. sing.

—*Nouns in* ऋ. Two bases, one ending in आर as in भत्तार from भर्तृ and the other in उ as भत्तु, are used, the former throughout all the cases and the latter in all except the sing. of the nom. and acc. The first is declined like nouns in अ, and the second like those in उ as साहु. The nom. sing. has also the old form भत्ता. In the Pâli, you will re-

9. Prof. Lassen derives them differently.

member, the first base is used in the plural of four cases, and the second in the gen. sing. only; while the singulars of three cases have the old Sanskrit forms. Here the two bases have been extended much further and one old form only that of the nom. sing. remains. Nouns expressive of relationship such as पितृ, भ्रातृ and जामातृ are declined similarly, the final syllable आर being shortened to अर as it is in Sanskrit and Pâli in those cases where the base is used. The voc. sing. is भत्त, and of the latter class of nouns it ends in अ or अरं, as पिअ or पिअरं.

—*Nouns in* अन्, अत् (*present participle*), वत्, मत् &c. राजन् has four bases. The old one राजन् with the old Sanskrit forms only phonetically corrupted (ञ् becoming ण्ण्) is used in all the singulars except that of the loc. and in the nom. pl.; as राआ, राआणो, राआणं, रण्णा, रण्णो and रण्णो. In Pâli it is used in the loc. sing. and gen. pl. also. The second राज, Prâkritised into राअ, is used in both numbers of all cases except the nom. sing., and in Pâli in all except the nom. sing. and pl. and the acc. pl. It is declined like a noun in अ; as राआ nom. pl., राअं acc. sing., राआ-राए acc. pl., राएण instr. sing., &c. The third राजिन् is employed in the gen. sing., in the older dialect; but here, as राइन, in all cases and numbers except the nom. sing. It is declined like an ordinary Sanskrit noun in इन्; as राइणो nom. and acc. pl., राइणं acc. sing., राइणा instr. sing., &c. The fourth is राजान, Pr. राआण, used in all cases and both numbers. Vararuchi, however, does not give this, and omits the others in some of the cases. This base is unknown to Pâli, but occurs in the word आत्मन् in the form of अत्ताण, and is used in the plurals of the instr. and loc., while here it is extended to all cases. This noun and such others ending in अन् are in the Prâkṛit declined like राजन्; the base in आण is general to all and used throughout, but the others occur in certain cases only. The voc. sing. of राजन् is राअं or राअ in the Śaurasenî, the former of which does not occur in the Mahârâshṭrî. The base of the present participles ends in अन्त and they are declined like nouns in अ. The Pâli, you will remember, uses the old base in some of the cases and has the old forms; but here they have disappeared. Similarly वत् and मत् become वन्त and मन्त throughout, *i.e.*, end in अ. Other final consonants are dropped and in feminine nouns sometimes आ is added.

Feminine and Neuter Nouns.—The Prâkṛit feminine declension differs from the Pâli in little more than a phonetic corruption of the terminations. The य of the instr., abl., gen. and loc. of nouns in आ, and the या of those in इ or ई, are weakened into ए or इ or dropped, leaving only अ and आ. In the latter class of nouns this आ is further optionally shortened to अ. Thus we have मालाए-इ-अ and नईए-इ-आ-अ, &c. The optional loc. forms in यं are lost; and the यो of the nom. plurals मालायो and नदियो leaves only the vowel ओ which is again shortened to उ. The abl. forms in दो-दु or ओ-उ are of course new. Fem. nouns in ऋ substitute आ for the final and are declined like nouns in आ; as, णणन्दा, णणन्दाओ, &c. मातृ, however, has another base मातरा when it signifies a "goddess." In the Pâli four bases are used, the old one, मातर declined like masc. nouns in अ, मातु, and माता. This last is used in the gen. pl. only along with मातराण, and मातूनं. The nom. and acc. of neuter nouns in अ are in the Prâkṛit the same as in Skr. only phonetically corrupted, as वणं sing., वणा-इँ-इं-णि pl.; while the sing. of those in इ and उ have an anusvâra optionally attached to them, as दहि or दहिं sing., दहीइँ-इं-णिं, pl. The optional Pâli plurals in आ and ए are lost. Sanskrit neuter nouns in अन् and अस् become nouns in अ, and are masculine.

Pronouns—The nom. pl. in ए is preserved, as in सव्वे, जे &c. The gen. pl. has सिं for its termination formed by adding a light इ to the साम् of Sanskrit, which according to the usual rules should be corrupted to सं, and is also formed upon the model of the corresponding nouns; as सव्वेसिं or सव्वाण-णं, जेसिं or जाण-णं, &c. The Pâli has सं, and its double gen. सानं is wanting. The loc. sing. has the termination स्सिं, a form not existing in the older dialect, in addition to the म्मि used for nouns, both of which are to be traced to the Skr. स्मिन्, as in सव्वस्सिं or सव्वम्मि, जस्सिं or जम्मि, &c. This स्सिं is further changed to हिं as in सव्वहिं, जहिं, &c., or better, this latter may be traced to the Pâli म्हि. Another loc. sing. term. is त्थ which reperesents त्र, as सव्वत्थ, जत्थ &c. The abl. sing. स्मात् is optionally used after किम्, यद्, and तद् only, in the form of म्हा, as कम्हा, जम्हा, and तम्हा; in Pâli it is necessarily used after all pronouns. In other respects pronouns are declined like the corresponding nouns; as सव्वं, सव्वे acc., सव्वेण, सव्वेहिं instr., सव्वत्तो-दो-दु, सव्वाहिन्तो-सुन्तो abl. The instr. sing. is optionally formed like that of nouns in इ in the case of some; as इमिणा, जिणा &c. You will thus observe, that except in the nom. pl. there is no distinction between the two declensions; the peculiar pronominal forms I have mentioned being only optional. Of the fem. of तद्, यद्, and किम्, the gen. sing. is optionally तिस्सा or तीसे &c., where the base is ती &c. The other forms are like those of nouns in ई, as तीआ-ई-ए &c. This base is used throughout along with the other in आ. In Pâli it is used in the gen. and loc. sing. only along with the other, and the gen. forms are तिस्सा and तिस्साय, the latter of which is, as I have said, a double genitive. This the Prâkṛit has preserved in the form of तिसे, originally तिस्से, where the ए represents the य of the older dialect, as it does in the feminine nouns. The other base of किम् and तद् has also its genitive singular in स, as तास, formed by transferring the masc. termination; or it is to be traced to तस्सा. The genitive plural forms of the masc., such as तेसिं and ताण, are also sometimes used in a feminine sense. The loc. sing. of किम्, यद्, and तद् is optionally formed by extending the masc. termination हिं to the base in आ, as ताहिं &c. These peculiarities are only optional; so that the feminine pronouns are declined like nouns in आ or ई. Thus we have जा, जाओ-उ, जीओ-उ nom., जं, जाओ-उ, जीओ-उ acc., जिणा, जाहिं, जीहिं instr., जादो-दु, जीदो-दु, जाहिन्तो-सुन्तो, जीहिन्तो-सुन्तो &c. abl. जस्सा, जिस्सा, जीसे, जासं, जासिं, जेसिं, जाण, जीसिं, जीणं gen., जाहिं, जासु, जीसु loc. The optional instr., abl., gen., and loc. singulars are जाए-इ-अ and जीए-इ-आ-अ.

The pronoun न in the form of ण exists as in the Pâli; इदम् has two bases, इम which is used throughout, as इमो, इमे nom., इमं, इमे acc., इमेण-मिणा, इमेहि, instr. &c; and अ from which we have optionally अअं nom. sing., अस्स and अस्सि, gen. and loc. sing., and एहिं and एसु instr. and loc. plural, and आहिं instr. pl of the feminine. इमो, इमस्स, इमस्सिं &c. are also in use. The base अ is used in the Pâli in the instr. sing., gen. pl., and abl. sing. also. The demonstrative अदस् has one base only, अमु, which is declined like nouns in उ; as अमू, अमुणो nom., अमुं अमुणो acc. अमुणा, अमूहिं instr., &c. The pronoun of the second person has, according to Vararuchi, five bases त, तुम् or तुम, तुज्झ, तुम्ह, तुम्म, वो and भे. The first is derived from the त्व of त्वम्; तुम् or तुम from the same with the व softened to उ; तुज्झ from तुभ्यम् through the intermediate Pâli form तुय्हं, the last conjunct of which is changed to ज्झ, by a rule formerly given; तुम्ह is made up by putting together the तु of the singular and the स्म of the plural, as explained in going over the Pâli; तुम्म is another form of तुम्ह; वो is the old Sanskrit वस्; and भे seems to be derived from the म्हे of तुम्हे as बम्भण is from ब्राह्मण. Hemachandra adds तुब्भ, to be derived from the Sanskrit तुभ्यम् or from तुम्ह, म्ह being changed to ब्भ; उज्झ from तुज्झ by the dropping of त्; तुय्ह and उय्ह other forms of तुभ्यम्; तुव from त्व by the insertion of उ; तुह from तुय्हं; उम्ह by the dropping of the त् of तुम्ह; and उब्भ by treating तुब्भ in the same way. The Pâli has only त, तु, and तुम्ह; and the several old forms it had are lost in the Prâkṛit. Nominal terminations are used in a good many cases. Thus we have तं, तुं, तुवं, तुह, and तुमं for the nom. sing., these and तुए and तुमे for the acc. sing., तइ, तए, तुमइ, तुमए, तुमे, तुमाइ, and also तुमं, भे, ते, दे, and दि for the instr. sing. The form तुमं properly belongs to the nom. and acc. cases and ते to the gen., दे and दि

being only ते softened; but several cases are here confounded. The abl. sing. has तइत्तो-ओ-उ-दो-दु-हि-हिन्तो, तुवत्तो-ओ &c., तुमत्तो-ओ &c., तुहत्तो-ओ &c., तुब्भत्तो-ओ &c., तुम्हत्तो-ओ &c., तुज्झत्तो-ओ &c., also तुय्ह, तुब्भ, तुम्ह, and तुज्झ. The gen. sing. has twenty-one forms, *viz.* तइतुं, ते, तुह, तुहं, तुव, तुम, तुमे, तुमो, तुमा, इ, दि, दे, इ, ए, तुब्भ, उब्भ, उय्ह, तुम्ह, तुज्झ, उम्ह, and उज्झ. The loc. sing. has तुमे, तुमए, तुमाइ, तइ, तए, तुम्मि, तुवम्मि, तुमम्मि, तुहम्मि, तुब्भम्मि, तुम्हम्मि, and तुज्झम्मि. The plurals are as follows:—भे, तुब्भे, उज्झे, तुम्हे, तुय्हे, उय्हे, तुम्हे, तुज्झे nom.; वो, तुब्भे, उज्झे, तुम्हे, तुज्झे, तुय्हे, उय्हे, भे acc.; भे तुब्भेहिं, तुज्झेहिं, तुम्हेहिं, उज्झेहिं, उम्हेहिं, तुय्हेहिं and उय्हेहिं instr.; तुब्भतो-दो-दु-हिन्तो -सुन्तो, तुय्हत्तो-दो &c., उय्हत्तो-दो &c., उम्हत्तो-दो &c., तुम्हत्तो-दो &c., and तुज्झत्तो-दो- &c. abl., भे, तुय्ह, तुब्भ, उब्भ, तुब्भाण-णं; तुवाण-णं, तुमाण-णं, तुहाण-णं, तुम्हाण-णं, तुम्ह, तुज्झ, उम्ह, उज्झ, तुज्झाण-णं, gen., तुसु, तुव-वेसु, तुम-मेसु, तुह-हेसु, तुब्भ-ब्भा-ब्भेसु, तुम्ह-म्हा-म्हेसु, तुज्झ-ज्झा-ज्झेसु loc. The points to be observed in these forms are these. The nom. sing. has mostly the same forms as the acc. sing. This is due to the fact that the Sanskrit त्वाम् of the acc. becomes, when the आ is shortened by a Prâkṛit phonetic rule, त्वं *i. e.*, the same as the nom. sing. Hence its Prâkṛit representatvies तं, तुं, तुवं and तुमं are the same for both the cases. But a more probable reason, which explains a similar fact in the case of the first personal pronoun also, is that the plurals of the nom. and acc. having by natural processes already explained become exactly alike, the two cases came to be confounded; and the sing. forms also of the one were used for the other. The forms तइ, तए, तुमइ, तुमए, तुमे, and तुमाइ are common to the instr. and loc. sing. This probably arises from the fact that the Sanskrit त्वया, when the य is softened to ए or इ, becomes तए or तइ, and so does the त्वयि of the loc.; and when the base त is seen to be interchangeable with तुम in the nom., the terminations ए and इ which are common to the two cases are applied to तुम also. ते and its softened forms दे and दि, and तइ are common to the instr. and gen. sing.; तुय्ह, तुब्भ, तुम्ह, तुज्झ are common to the abl. sing and the gen. sing. and pl.; and भे to the instr. sing. and pl. and the gen. sing. Such a confusion of the case-relations must be expected in course of time. Even in Sanskrit the gen. and instr. &c., are used alike in connection with some participles; and the identification of the abl. and the instr. we have already noticed in the Prâkṛits. The gen. forms तुय्ह, तुब्भ, तुम्ह, तुज्झ, उब्भ, उम्ह, and उज्झ, all derived from the Sanskrit dat. तुभ्यम् and referred to the gen. when that case was lost, are taken as bases, and the terminations ए of the nom. and acc. pl., हि of the instr. pl., त्तो, दो, दु, ओ, and उ of the abl., ण or णं of the gen. pl., and म्मि and सु of the loc. sing. and pl. are tacked on to them to form these cases. Here the tendency to use the genitive form as a base for the formation of the other cases, a trace of which only we observed in the Pâli, is seen more developed.

The pronoun of the first person has, according to Vararuchi, the following bases :—हं or अहं and म from the Sanskrit singulars, मम the gen. sing., अम्ह from अस्म and णो from नस्, of which अम्ह is used in the plural. Hemachandra adds मह and मज्झ from मह्यम्, and मे from म्हे or स्मे. He also gives अम्हि, अम्मि, and म्मि for the nom. sing. and अम्मि for the acc. sing. The first is clearly from अस्मि 1st pers. sing. present of अस्, often used in Sanskrit as an indeclinable particle; and the others are also corruptions of the same just as the termination म्मि of the loc. is a corruption of स्मिन्. The singular forms, therefore, are:—अम्मि, म्मि, अम्हि, हं, अहं, अहयं nom.; णे, णं, मि, अम्मि; अम्ह, मम्ह, मं, ममं, मिमं, अहं acc.; मि, मे, ममं, ममए, ममाइ, मइ, मए, मयाइ, णे, instr.; मइत्तो-दो-दु-ओ-उ-हि-हिन्तो, ममत्तो &c., महत्तो &c., मज्झत्तो &c., abl., मे, मइ, मम, मह, महं, मज्झ, मज्झं, अम्ह, अम्हं gen.; मि, मइ, ममाइ, मए, मे, अम्हम्मि, ममम्मि, महम्मि, loc. The plurals are:—अम्ह, अम्हे, अम्हो, मो, वयं, मे, nom., अम्हे, अम्हो, अम्ह, णे, acc.; अम्हेहिं, अम्हाहि, अम्ह, अम्हे, णे instr.; ममत्तो, अम्हत्तो, ममाहिन्तो-सुन्तो, अम्हाहिन्तो-सुन्तो, ममेसुन्तो, अम्हेसुन्तो abl., णे, णो, मज्झ, अम्ह, अम्हं, अम्हे, अम्हो, अम्हाण, ममाण, महाण, मज्झाण gen., अम्ह-म्हा-म्हेसु-मम-मेसु, मह-हेसु, मज्झ-ज्झेसु loc. Here also the same observations as those made in the case of the last pronoun are applicable.

In the Mâgadhî the ओ of the nom. sing. of nouns ending in अ is replaced by ए; as एशे पुलिशे for एष पुरुषः. The स्स of the gen. sing. is sometimes changed to ह and the preceding अ is lengthened; as शोणिदाह कुम्भे for शोणितस्य कुम्भः. The plural of this case is formed by adding आहं, as कम्माहं for कर्मणाम्. The anusvâra represents the ण of the original termination आण, and ह is introduced from the analogy of the sing. The regular forms शोणिदस्स and कम्माणं are also admissible. Such forms as these we shall meet with hereafter; and they belong to a later stage in the decay of our grammar.

Conjugations.—All the Skr. conjugations, with the exception of the second in the case of a few roots ending in a vowel, have been brought over to the अ type, *i. e.*, to the first, sixth, and the tenth. Some of the others have left a few traces; as, the fifth and the ninth their ण in such instances as सुण, किण, जाण, लुण पुण, धुण, both conjugations being, as you may remember, confounded in the Pâli, the third the root बीह—pres. tense बीहदि—the ह standing for भ, the fourth its य assimilated in a good many roots such as णच्च, बुज्झ, जुज्झ, तुट्ट, नस्स. &c., and the seventh its न् in रुन्ध and others. But you will see that to these forms अ is added and they are made roots ending in अ; while a great many have lost even such traces. In the Pâli, you will remember, the conjugational signs added to some of the roots are entire, as the ना of the sixth and the नो of the fifth, and अ is appended to roots of the seventh conjugation only, न् being inserted before the last consonant. But here the अ takes the place of the ending vowel of the signs of the fifth and other conjugations also, and so we have सुण, कीण, and चीह. Thus in the Prâkṛits most roots end in अ. There are some ending in other vowels, such as हो and ठा; but the rule of conjugation is the same for all, *viz.*, to add the terminations to the root directly. There can be no consonantal root. Some forms, such as those of अस्, have come down from the parent language only phonetically changed; but these are not formed in the Prâkṛit. They are really Sanskrit forms in what I have ventured to call a petrified condition. The roots ending in अ change it to ए optionally, *i. e.*, they are conjugated according to the model of the first and of the tenth, as is the case to a great extent in the Pâli also. The distinction between the special and the general tenses is of course forgotten.

The Prâkṛits have retained the Present and Future tenses and the Imperative mood entire; while the Potential and the Aorist have left the third person singular only. An isolated form of the Imperfect such as आसि from the root अस् remains.

The terminations of the Present Tense are—3rd pers. sing. दि and दे in Śaur. and इ and ए in the principal Prâkṛit, pl. न्ति and न्ते; 2nd pers. sing. सि and से, pl. इत्था and ह for which last the S'aur. has ध; 1st pers. sing. मि, pl. मो, मु, and म. Of these दे or ए, से and न्ते, of which the last is not given by Vararuchi, are remnants of the old Âtmanepada, and the first two are used after roots ending in अ only. With the exception of the first pers. pl. म and the 2nd pers. pl. इत्था, the terminations can readily be traced to the corresponding Skr. Parasm. The Sanskrit 2nd pers. pl. थ becomes ध in the Śaurasenî and ह in the Mahârâshṭrî by the phonetic rules already noticed, and मो or its shortened form मु is the Skr. मस्. In these points the primitive and derived languages perfectly agree; but म and इत्था are new terminations and were first used in Pâli, the latter however in the form of त्थ. The first is, as I have observed, transferred from the Imperative, Imperfect and other tenses, and त्थ is the Skr. स्थ 2nd pers. pl. of the root अस् To this is prefixed in the Prâkṛit the usual augment इ, which मो and मु also take optionally. The terminations मो and मु are unknown to the Pâli. Other forms of the first pers. sing. and pl. made up by adding म्हि and म्ह or म्हो, as in करेम्हि, करेम्ह, गच्छम्ह, &c., occur in the plays, though the grammarians have not noticed them. These terminations are evidently the Skr. स्मि 1st pers. sing. and स्मः or स्म pl. of अस्.[10] You will remember that a good many verbs are made up in the Pâli by adding forms of this root. Hemachandra notices also another termination of the 3rd pers. pl., *viz.* इरे, which is transferred from the Perfect. The Imperative forms are made up by adding दु S'aur. उ Pr. 3rd pers. sing. and न्तु pl.; सु and हि 2nd pers. sing. and ध S'aur. ह Pr. pl.; and मु 1st pers. sing. and मो pl. The original form of the root ending in अ is also used as the second pers. sing. Of these दु, न्तु, हि or अ, and सु from स्व Atm. are both Skr. and Pâli; ह (Skr. थ) transferred from the Present is used in Pâli; but मु and मो are peculiar to the Prâkṛit, the Pâli using only the terminations of its present. Of these मो is transferred from the Prâkṛit Present, and मु is made up by adding the उ which is peculiar to the Imperative and distinguishes it from the present. The first pers. pl. takes म also sometimes as in the Pâli, but it is not noticed by the grammarians. The consciousness that the future is made up by prefixing स्य=स्स Pr. & Pâli to the terminations of the present has never been lost, and whatever changes these terminations undergo are transferred to the future; so that the S'aurasenî and Mâgadhî future differs from the Pâli in those respects only in which the Present tenses of the two differ. The मि of the first person sing., however, is optionally changed to an anusvâra; or the anusvâra may be a remnant of the conditional terminations; as हसिस्सं. In the principal Prâkṛit the स्य is still further corrupted to हि, य being dissolved into इ and स changed to ह, as in होहिइ for भविष्यति, होहिन्ति for भविष्यन्ति, &c. In the first pers. we have, in addition to this हि, स्स which is lengthened as in Skr. and also its other form हा as well as स्सं for the whole as in the S'aurasenî, *e. g.*, होहि-स्सा-हामि or होहिस्सं, &c. A beginning in the direction of the हि was, you will remember, made in Pâli. We have also a few petrified Skr. forms such as दच्छं for द्रक्ष्यामि, मोच्छं for मोक्ष्यामि which are more conditional than future in their origin; and to these as bases are added the terminations of the present and also of the future to form new futures; as दच्छिइ, दच्छिहिइ, &c. We have also काहं and दाहं from कृ and दा. The only Potential form left is that of the 3rd pers. sing.; as हसेज्ज or हसेज्जा, होज्ज or होज्जा. The termination is the same as in Pâli, the य्य of the 3rd pers. sing. being altered to ज्ज, and the general form of the termination य्या to ज्जा. After bases ending in अ, ज्ज or ज्जा

10. Prof. Lassen traces these to the root अस्, but इत्था to the Skr. थ to which इ is, he says, prefixed because the previous vowel must have been pronounced with some accent. But considering that many forms of अस् are used as terminations it is more natural to take this also as such a form.

becomes एज्ज or एज्जा, as in Skr. and Pâli.[11] This being an isolated form and derived from the Potential, which does not signify any particular time, it is used in the sense of the Present, Future, or Imperative in all numbers and persons; and after roots in अ the terminations सु and हि of the second pers. sing. of the Imperative are added to ज्ज to make up new forms of that mood, as हसेज्जसु, हसेज्जहि; and another form हसेज्जे is also mentioned.[12] This Potential form of roots ending in vowels other than अ is used as a base, and the terminations of the two tenses and one mood are attached to it to make up new forms for them; as होज्जइ, होज्जाइ; होज्जउ, होज्जाउ, &c. The Aorist also has left its 3rd pers. sing. only; the termination to be added to roots ending in a vowel, is सी, ही, or हीअ and ईअ to those ending in a consonant or अ, *i. e.*, such as take the augment इ or change the अ to इ. Of these सी and ही are derived from the Parasm. सीत् of the fourth form; the first is found in Pâli, and ही is only another form of it. The Pâli has ई also for the 3rd pers. sing. corresponding to the ईत् affixed to Sanskṛit roots that take the augment इ. This is very likely the origin of ईअ also since we have it after the roots which necessarily admit the augment; but the अ of this and of हीअ is difficult to explain. हीअ must correspond to some such form as सीय or सीत which, the स् being dropped after the augment इ, is reduced to ईअ. These सीय and सीत are forms of the Potential Âtm. of अस्, and they may have been added as terminations to form the Aorist as other forms of अस् are in this and other tenses in the Pâli. Or the सी of the Aorist may have been confounded with सीत the pot. of अस् from its resemblance to it.

These are rare and isolated forms, and past time is mostly expressed by the past participle passive which in the case of intransitive and some transitive verbs has also an active sense. The Sanskrit termination त is only phonetically changed to द in the Śauraseni and to अ in the Prâkṛit. Roots ending in अ change it to इ before the past participial termination. The past participles of some roots are not newly formed, but the old Skr. forms have come down only phonetically altered. This fact should always be remembered, that there are in all these derived

11 This fact strongly supports my derivation of the forms. Prof. Lassen derives them from the Precative. But the Precative was lost at an early stage, since it does not exist even in the Pâli. The ए is not the अय of the 10th conj. as the Prof. thinks, but the ए which bases ending in अ take in the Pot. in Skr.

12 Prof. Lassen derives these also from the Precative, and against the argument that that mood is rarely used in Skr. itself and was lost in the Pâli states that the Precative is found in the Vernaculars. But I have not found it. The forms करजे, करजो G. करिये, करियो H. I trace to the Prâkṛit Potential forms spoken of above.

dialects new formations called by Hemchandra साध्यावस्थ, as well as old formations, सिद्धावस्थ. This arises from the fact of the analogies not being made applicable throughout, as they would have been if the languages had been artificial. Contingency or condition is expressed by the present participle, as we do in our modern vernaculars. The infinitive is formed as in Skr. by the addition of तुम् changed to उं, the Pâli तवे being lost, and the absolutive by affixing the termination ऊण (दूण Śaurasenî) from the Pâli तून and the Vedic त्वान or त्वीन. But the termination that is most used in the Śaurasenî is इअ from the Sanskrit य of roots with prepositions prefixed. Hemachandra also gives for the principal Prâkṛit तूण and तुआण the origin of which is the same as that of ऊण, त्ता from त्वा, तु by the dissolution of the semi-vowel of त्वा, तुम् by a confusion with the infinitive, and इअ which is used in the Śaurasenî. Of these, however, ऊण is the one that prevails; the others are rare. The passive is formed by adding ईअ and इज्ज, both of which come from the Sanskrit य with the augment इ prefixed as in Pâli, the य being transformed to ज्ज in one case and leaving its अ only in the other or being dissolved into इअ. Hemachandra gives a good many roots which preserve the Skr. forms, only phonetically changed, as दीसइ from दृश्यते, वुच्चइ from उच्यते, गम्मइ from गम्यते, लब्भइ from लभ्यते, बज्झइ from बध्यते, &c. The causal terminations are ए from अय, and आवे from आपय. These two are the same as in the Pâli, the Sanskrit forms also existing in the latter being lost. Hemachandra adds अ and आव, *i. e.*, the ए answering to अय is lost. But the Sanskrit vowel changes are preserved even when the अय gives place to अ; as दरिसइ. The terminations of the absolutive, the infinitive, the potential participle (अव्व from Skr. तव्य), and of the Future take the augment इ which also is transformed into a short ए of the same nature as that which is found before conjunct consonants, as in पेण्ड or पिण्ड. We have thus हसिऊण or हसेऊण, हसिउं or हसेउं, &c.

You will thus have observed a much greater progress in the operation of those principles which we found at work in the construction of the Pâli. Here as before we find that the less known forms are made up on the model of the more known. The number of old forms which still remained in some of the Pâli declensions and conjugations has been greatly reduced in the Prâkṛits, and a further advance been made in the introduction of uniformity and simplicity in the grammar of the language. It is also worthy of remark, that in a great measure the same false analogies which are used in the Pâli have come down to the Prâkṛit, and their range extended. Thus the analogy of nouns in इन् or neuter nouns in इ or उ has been carried much further in the declension of masculine nouns ending in इ or उ. Nouns in ऋ, अन् and वत् have adapted themselves more closely to the model of those ending in अ, their Sanskrit nom. case supplying the new अ base; and the अ conjugations have more generally prevailed over the rest. The device of using such case-forms as मम and मह्यम् as bases, and making up the cases by appending the proper terminations has also been more largely availed of. Some of these phenomena may be attributed to the operation of the same invariable laws in the development of either without being an index to a more intimate connection between the two dialects. But there are individual forms in the two languages which, though they might be different, are yet the same in both. Such, for instance, are वच्छे acc. pl., the loc. sing. ending in the pronominal म्हि or म्मि, the double gen. तिस्साय, the 2nd pers. pl. ending in इत्था of the present tense, and a good many others. The consonantal and vowel changes also, so far as they go in the older language, are the same. We may therefore safely conclude that the Pâli represents generally an earlier stage of the same language which afterwards became the Prâkṛit or Prâkṛits. But there are again in the Prâkṛits such forms as those of the ablative in दो and आहि instead of the old pronominal म्हा, the first pers. pl. of the Pres. in मो or मु instead of the Pâli म, the 1st pers. sing. of the Imperative in मु instead of the Pâli मि, the S'aurasenî absolutive in इअ corresponding to the Sanskrit य, which does not exist in the older dialect, and others. These Prâkṛit forms cannot have been developed out of the Pâli forms, but must have grown independently from the Sanskrit originals. In the same way, though the Prâkṛit sounds are generally the same as or further developments of the Pâli sounds, there are a good many which could not have grown out of the latter. Thus the रि in the Prâkṛit words रिद्धि, रिच्छ, रिण, रिज्जू, &c. cannot have been developed out of the इ or अ of the Pâli इद्धि, अच्छ, अण, उज्जू, &c., or the अइ and अउ of such words as दइच्च, भइरव, पउर, कउसल, &c., from the ए and ओ of the corresponding Pâli words, or the ण्ण् for Sanskrit ज्ञ् from the Pâli ञ्ञ्, though this latter exists in some of the Prâkṛit dialects, or the रिस for र्श or र्ष in such words as आअरिस, सुदरिसण, वरिस, and परामरिस from the स्स or स of the Pâli आदास, सुदस्सन, वस्स, and परामास. The Prâkṛit sounds must in these cases be traced directly to the corresponding Sanskrit sounds. It therefore appears that the Prâkṛits had also an independent development, which may be accounted for on the supposition that they sprang not from the Pâli but a sister dialect or dialects; or that, though originally they were the same as the Pâli, their subsequent development was influenced by the parent language, and thus other sounds and forms not

14

existing in the earlier dialect came in fresh from Sanskrit. But the first supposition is discountenanced by the fact that the resemblance between the Pâli and the Prâkṛits extends even to isolated cases; and the second is supported by the circumstance that in one important particular the Prâkṛits resemble the Sanskrit in the last stage of its development, while the Pâli differs in that particular from both and agrees with an earlier form of the parent language. We have seen that in later Sanskrit verbal forms especially of the past tenses were rarely used, and participles were employed instead; and we find that the Prâkṛits have mostly lost all the Sanskrit tenses and moods except three, and past time is generally expressed by the past participle and contingency by the present; while the Pâli has, as we have seen, preserved eight, including all the past tenses and the conditional. Middle Sanskrit bears to later or classical Sanskrit the same relation, in this respect, that the Pâli bears to the Prâkṛits. The change that came over Sanskrit between the two periods left its impress on what may be called the Vernacular speech. This could not have been the case unless Sanskrit had continued to influence that form of speech represented first by the Pâli and afterwards by the Prâkṛits. And it was because it continued so to influence it, that the Prâkṛits came to have sounds and grammatical forms also derived direct from Sanskrit and not through the Pâli. This leads to the conclusion, which will be developed in detail in the last lecture, that when the Pâli and the Prâkṛits came into existence Sanskrit had not been dead but was as much a living language as either of the other two and both were spoken or used for ordinary purposes, one by men of culture and the other by ordinary people.

Sanskrit writers distinguish three elements in the Prâkṛit vocabulary which they call Tadbhava, Tatsama, and Des'ya. Such words as are derived from Sanskrit are called Tadbhava, such as दंसण, फस, मग्ग, कण्ण, &c. Tatsamas are those that are the same in Sanskrit and Prâkṛit as कमल, मण्डल, &c., the phonetic laws of the Prâkṛits not necessitating a change in them, and Deśyas are such as cannot be derived from Sanskrit and must be referred to another source. A good many words of this nature we find used in Prâkṛit literature; and there exists a *kosha* or thesaurus of Deśya words by Hemachandra. A large number of these Deśya words exist in the modern vernaculars, such as:—

अक्का a sister, M.[13] आक्का, a term of honour used for an elder sister.

13 M.—Marâṭhi; G.—Gujarâti; H.—Hindi.

अग्घाडो an herb ; आघाडा M.
अवडो a well ; आड M.
उडिद a kind of pulse; the same, M. H.
उङ्घइ sleeps ; उंघना H. उंघवुं G.
कुडं, कुड्डं, कोड्डुं, wonder ; कोड old M.
कोट्टं a town ; कोट a fort M.
कोडिम्बो a basin of wood for water ; कोठंबा M.
कोलित्त a firebrand ; कोलीत M.
कालविअं to mix a liquid with a solid substance and stir it up; कालवणें M.
गोहो a man, a warrior ; घोव husband, M.
चोप्पडइ rubs, anoints ; चोपडणें M.

छिण्णो, छिण्णी, छिण्णालो, छिण्णाली } an adulterer or adulteress ; शिंदळ M.

पोआलो an ox ; पोळ M.
पडच्छी a cow that has no milk ; पाडशी M.
पासलं slanting ; पासलें lying down with the face upwards, M.
पोट्टं belly ; पोट M. पेट H. G.
फंसइ deceives ; फसविणें M.
फुक्का false, vain ; फुका M.
बाउल्ली a doll ; बाउली M.
बप्पो father, a brave man; बाप M. G. H; बाप्या an able-bodied man, M.

There are a great many words set down as Deśyas, which on close examination will be found to be Tadbhavas. They differ from ordinary Tadbhavas in having undergone great corruption. The following are instances. Some of the words in the above list may also be considered to be of the same nature. Thus फंसइ 'deceives' is a denominative or nominal verb from the word पाश 'a snare,' which in our modern dialects has the form of फांस; whence फंसई is 'to ensnare' or 'entrap.' So also कुडं, कुड्ड, कोड्डुं and the old M. कोड are in all likelihood to be traced to the Skr. कौतुक.

उव्वड्डिओ thrown upwards ; उद्वर्तित: Skr.
कन्दोट्ट a lotus ; from कन्दोत्थ Skr.
कुहुडो humpbacked. This may be traced to Skr. कुब्ज-कुब्भ-कुह ; and ड is a termination which is used in a great many nouns.
कुरुच disliked, evidently from कु and रोच्य.
कोणो black ; Skr. कृष्ण-कण्ह-कोण्ह-कोण.

उज्जड desolate; from Skr. उज्ज्वल bright, pure, cleared of every thing, desolate.

बइल्ल a bullock; from Skr. बलीवर्द.

छल्ली rind, bark; may be from Skr. शल्य, शल्यक.

छासी whey; may be from Skr. तक्र.

छिवइ touches; from Skr. छुप् by a change of vowel.

छिप्प a tail; from पुच्छ, by the consonants interchanging places, and the palatal छ having its vowel इ.

पडोहर the hind part of a house; from Skr. पृष्ठगृह.

पेयाले, पेजल, a measure, a certain quantity, occurs in the Pàli and is traced to Skr. प्राय. It may also be connected with प्राज्य.

बोल्लइ speaks; from ब्रू by the change of र to ल and the transference of the vowel to the first consonant—a thing often observable; ब्लु—बुल्ल—बोल्ल.

The Sanskrit etymology of some of the words given by the lexicographers is evident; and one does not know how they came to be regarded as Deśyas. Other words changed their sense in the course of time and so were referred to this class.

पम्हुसइ forgets; from प्रमुष् to steal,—a thing forgotten is as it were stolen.

बहुमुहो a wicked person; from बहुमुख, because a wicked person puts on many faces or appearances.

कामकिसोरो an ass;—a son of Kâma or love, devoted to pleasure, is often a donkey.

कुच्छिमई pregnant, कुक्षि originally 'side,' came to signify 'womb;' and that womb is worthy of the name which bears a child, hence कुक्षिमती *lit.* 'having a womb' came to have the signification given. A good many of the words given by Hemachandra do not occur in the modern Vernaculars, and we have regular Tadbhavas instead; as, इल्ली a tiger, ईस a nail, &c.

The number of Des'ya words, if properly examined, would be greatly reduced. Still a Des'i element in the Prâkṛits and the Vernaculars must be admitted. These words must have come into the dialects from the language of the aborigines whom the Aryas conquered; and some are found in Sanskrit also.

THE APABHRAṀŚA.

The dialect called the Apabhraṁs'a by the grammarians presents Indian speech in a further stage of decay and occupies a middle position between these Prâkṛits and the modern vernaculars to some of which, especially to the old Hindî, the Brajabhâshâ, and the Gujarâtî it bears striking resemblances, as I shall hereafter show.

As mentioned before, we have the grammar of this dialect from Hemachandra, Trivikrama, and Kramadîśvara; but Vararuchi does not mention it. The Apabhraṁśa had a literature of its own. Hemachandra illustrates each of his rules about this dialect by quoting a verse. In the fourth Act of the Vikramorvaśî the Prâkṛit speeches of the king in his madness are in this dialect. But it is a question whether they existed there originally, since in several manuscripts on this side of India they do not appear. The metres employed in these and in Hemachandra's quotations are the same as those popularly used in old and modern Hindî or Braj, *viz.*, *dohâ* or *chopai*. Pandit Vrajalal mentions a work of the name of Muñjarâsa, written in the Apabhraṁśa, from which he gives a short extract, and another the hero of which is a king of the name of Prasenajita. He also quotes from another work; but the language of all these appears to be more modern than Hemachandra's Apabhraṁśa, and that of some of the verses makes a very near approach to the Gujarâtî. As before, I will introduce my remarks on this dialect by a specimen: –

एत्तहे तेत्तहे बारि घरि लच्छि विसंठुल धाइ।
पिअ पब्भट्टव गोरडी निच्चल कहिंवि न ठाइ॥
जे महु दिण्णा दिअहडा दइएं पवसन्तेण।
ताण गणन्तिए अङ्गुलिउ जज्जरिआउ नहेण॥
जीविउ कासु न वल्लहउं धणु पुणु कासु न इट्ठु।
दोण्णि वि अवसरि निवडिअइं तिणसम गणइ विसिट्ठु॥
जो गुण गोवइ अप्पणा पयडा करइ परस्सु।
तसु हउं कलिजुगि दुल्लहहो बलि किज्जउं सुअणस्सु॥
गङ्ग गमेप्पिण जो मुअओ जो सिवतित्थ गमेप्पि।
कीलदि तिदसावासगउ सो जमलोउ जिणेप्पि॥

Sanskrit:

अत्र तत्र द्वारे गृहे लक्ष्मीर्विसंष्ठुला धावति।
प्रियप्रभ्रष्टेव गौरी निश्चला क्वापि न तिष्ठति॥
ये मह्यं दत्ता दिवसा दयितेन प्रवसता।
तेषां (तान्) गणयन्त्या अङ्गुलयो जर्जरिता नखेन॥
जीवितं कस्य न वल्लभं धनं पुनः कस्य न इष्टम्।
द्वे अप्यवसरे निपतिते तृणसमे गणयति विशिष्टः॥

यो गुणान्गोपायत्यात्मीयान्प्रकटान्करोति परस्य।
तस्याहं कलियुगे दुर्लभस्य बलिं करोमि सुजनस्य ॥
गङ्गां गत्वा यो मृतो यः शिवतीर्थं गत्वा।
क्रीडति त्रिदशावासगतः स यमलोकं जित्वा ॥

"The unsteady goddess of wealth runs to this door and that, this house and that; like a fair one separated from her lover she does not remain firm anywhere."

"My fingers have worn away rubbed against by my nails, while counting, again and again, the days named by my lover [as the period of his absence], when he set out on his journey."

"To whom is life not dear and to whom is wealth not an object of desire? But when the occasion comes, a worthy man regards them as straw."

"I worship that good man so rarely to be met with in this Kali age, who conceals his own merits and gives publicity to those of others."

"He who dies after having gone to the Gangâ and to Śivatîrtha, triumphs over the power(world) of death and sports in the habitation of the gods."

The vowel अ of the derivatives of the pronouns यद्, तद्, किम्, and इदम् is changed to इ or ए. In the principal Prâkṛit we have noticed a tendency to such a change, and one of our instances was एत्थ for अत्र. From the same tendency we have in the Apabhraṁśa जेत्थु for यत्र, तेत्थु for तत्र, and केत्थु for कुत्र, the उ of the latter being replaced by ए in virtue of the analogy of the other pronouns. In the same way तद्वत् "in that manner," which after dropping the final consonant becomes तद्व, is changed to तेम, यद्वत् to जेम, and किम्वत् to केम. This ए is also rendered a more close vowel and changed to इ, and thus we have तिम, जिम, and किम. Thus the bases of these pronouns came to be considered as ते or ति, जे or जि, and के or कि, and so we have तिध for तथा, जिध for यथा, and किध for कथम्. The mute element being dropped these forms become तिह, जिह, and किह, and further तेहु, जेहु and केहु. For similar reasons we have तेत्तिअ or तित्तिअ for तावत्क, जेत्तिअं or जित्तिअ for यावत्क, केत्तिअ or कित्तिअ for कियत्क, &c., even in the Prâkṛits. The nom. sing. termination of nouns in अ is shortened to उ, and since a great many nouns were pronounced with this final उ and its original sense was forgotten, it was transferred by way of analogy to other words or grammatical forms that did not possess it before; and thus we have पुणु and विणु for पुनः and विना, and

जेत्थु, तेत्थु, जेहु, &c., in the above. The long vowels are sometimes shortened as in the word गङ्ग in the last of the above verses. The consonants क् and ख् are sometimes softened to ग् and घ्, instead of being dropped, त् and थ् to द् and ध्, as in the S'aurasenî, and प् and फ् to ब् and भ्. In the principal Prâkṛit also this is sometimes the case. The labial, व् is changed to म् in a few more instances than in the Prâkṛits as in जाम and ताम for यावत् and तावत्, and जेम or जिम, तेम or तिम, &c., in the above for यद्वत्, तद्वत्, &c. The complete contact of the lips necessary for the pronunciation of म् is avoided in a great many cases, and thus we have वँ for म as in भवँरु for भ्रमर, कवँलु for कमल, &c. This is the prevailing rule in most of the vernaculars, as we shall hereafter find. The conjunct म्ह् is changed to म्भ्; that is, the aspirate ह् has been labialized and assimilated to the preceding म्, as in गिम्भ for Prâkṛit गिम्हं and Sanskrit ग्रीष्म. A few instances of this change we did find in the Prâkṛits and we shall find more in the vernaculars. The Sanskrit conjunct त्व् is changed to प्प्; for as व् was often pronounced as ब्, this ब् instead of merging into the preceding mute, as semi-vowels often do, acquired prominence as य् does when preceded by a dental; and the त् being assimilated to it, the whole become प्प् as त्य् becomes च्च्, as in पइं for त्वया, प्पण or पण for the abstract termination त्वन, and प्पिण for त्विन, the suffix of the absolutive. In the Prâkṛits the त्म of आत्मन् similarly becomes प्प and so we have अप्पा for आत्मा. The letter र् when the latter member of a conjunct is sometimes not assimilated, as in ब्रोप्पि, प्राउ for प्रायः, &c., and sometimes it is introduced even when it does not exist in the original, as in ध्रुं for तद्, भ्रस्स for पस्स, &c. With these few exceptions, the rules about the assimilation of conjuncts, the elision of consonants, and others hold good generally as in the Prâkṛits, as you will see from the above extract.

DECLENSIONS—*Nouns in* अ—The decay of the case terminations is, however, a distinguishing feature of this dialect. The distinction between the nom. and acc. case forms which we observed lessening at each stage in the growth of our languages is here altogether lost. The ओ of the nom. sing. of masculine nouns in अ is shortened to उ, and used in both the cases, as मुअउ nom. for मृतकः, गउ for गतः, जमलोउ for यमलोकम्; and applied to neuter nouns as well, as कमलु. The nasal of the neuter is preserved only in nouns which are augmented by the addition of क changed to अ; as कमलउं for कमलकम्. The nom. and acc. pl of the masculine ends in आ; as दिअहडा, पयडा &c. in the above. The neuter nouns preserve the Prâkṛit इं of the plural, as in कमलइं. Sometimes words are used in these two cases without any terminations; as विसंठुल nom. sing., निचल nom. sing., गुण acc. pl., गड्ड acc. sing., तित्थ acc. sing., in the above extract. The principle observable in the other cases is the same as we have noticed in the older dialects, viz., a gradual reduction of all the declensions to a uniformity. The instrumental singular of nouns in अ has two forms, one in एं as देवें, and the other the old one देवेण. The former is derived from this old form, the final अ being dropped, and the nasal assuming the form of an anusvâra. This new termination is transferred to nouns in इ or उ also, as अग्गिएं. The instrumental pl. is the old one in हिं, but the change of the ending vowel to ए is only optionally made; as गुणेहिं or गुणहिं. One ablative termination is हे which is appended to all nouns, and the other हु as in वच्छहे गृण्हइ फलइं or वच्छहु गृण्हइ, "gathers fruits from trees." Of course we may trace the first to हिन्तो by supposing it first to be changed to हेन्तो by the usual Prâkṛit rule, and afterwards to have dropped its second syllable; and हु to something else. But it appears to me that a good many of the terminations having been reduced to ह् by natural phonetic changes, the others also had this inserted in them by analogy, just as the nominative termination उ is introduced in words and forms in which it did not exist. This process we shall necessarily have to suppose when we examine the forms of the present tense. Or the ह् may have been introduced simply to prevent a hiatus and connect the vowel-termination with the base. And this is rendered probable by Hemachandra's rule that the ending syllables उं, हुं, हिं, and हं, are to be lightly pronounced, as the य् that is introduced in the place of a dropped consonant is. The real syllables in these cases are therefore अं, उं, इं, and अं; and this is confirmed by the fact that the remnants of these Apabhraṁśa terminations existing in some of the modern vernaculars are destitute of this ह् and are mere vowel-terminations, as will be seen in a subsequent lecture. Thus, then, हे may be considered the aspirated form of the ए of the Prâkṛit feminine ablative, and हु of the उ of the masculine ablative.[14] The operation of the law of false analogies is very wide. The abl. pl. हुं, as in गिरिसिङ्गहुं, may with Lassen be traced to सुन्तो, the स् being changed to ह् and the syllable तो dropped, as ति is in the case of the 3rd pers. pl. of the present, as we shall see. The genitive singular सु, and स्सु as in सुअणस्सु and परस्सु in verse 4 above, I trace to the स्स of the Prâkṛits, the उ being added by analogy as observed before. Lassen

14. Kramadis'vara in Lassen's extract gives द् instead of हु; but this is an evident misreading.

traces is to स्व, which, he says, must have been added to these nouns to form the genitive; and the व being softened to उ, it is reduced to सु. But this does not account for the double स्स of the other form; and the addition of such a word as स्व to make up a case-form is altogether unexampled. The suffix हो, as in दुल्लहहो in the same verse, is but another form of सु. The genitive plural हं, as in माणुसहं for मनुष्याणाम्, may with Lassen be derived from the साम् of the Sanskrit pronominal declension. But the transference of this termination to nouns is nowhere seen in the Prâkṛits; हं is optionally appended to nouns in इ or उ also; and the characteristic णं of the gen. is wanting in this dialect. The more probable explanation, therefore, is that the ण lost its cerebral element and was reduced merely to a nasal अ, or अ with an anusvâra, as is the case in the instrumental singular, and the ह् is added, as observed before, simply to facilitate the pronunciation. The loc. sing. ends in ए, as in तले, which we see is the old termination, or in इ, as in तलि, which is a shortened form of ए. Kramadîśvara gives also ह्निं which might be traced to the Pâli म्हि, the Sanskrit स्मिन्, or the स्सिं of the Prâkrit pronominal declension. The language of Jaina works has this स्सिं in the case of nouns also. But even here the Prâkṛit म्मि, may, with reason, be supposed to have changed to इं, and the ह् to be as before, a mere *spiritus lenis*. We have this locative इं in the Marâṭhî. The हिं is extended to the plural also of these nouns; The vocative is formed by using हो which is evidently an interjection; as तरुण हो "O young men."

Nouns in इ *or* उ.—There is no distinction between the nom. and acc. sing. and pl., the original base being used without any modification or addition. The instrumental singular is formed by adding एं or ण, as in the last class of nouns, or simple anusvâra; as अग्गिएं, अग्गिण, अग्गिं. As एण becomes एं by dropping the final vowel, so does the इणा of the Prâkṛit instrumental here become इं. The abl. sing. ends in हे as in गिरिहे and तरुहे; and the gen. sing. also according to Kramadîśvara, Hemachandra being silent. These have been transferred from the feminine. Kramadîśvara also gives हो and हं as the terminations of the sing. of these two cases; but there must be some misreading here in Lassen's extract from the author, since हं is a distinctive plural termination, The gen. pl. termination is हुं or हं as in तरुहुं, सउणिहं (शकुनीनाम्). The latter has been traced to the old gen. ण, and the former appears to be only another form of it with the addition of the usual उ. The loc. sing. has हि, as in कलिहि; and the pl. has हिं and हुं, as in तरुहिं, and उदुहुं. The first must be considered to be the same as

हिं derived from स्सि or स्मि with the anusvâra dropped; or as the इ of Prâkrit feminine nouns with the *spiritus lenis* ह. This explanation seems to be probable, since we have seen other feminine terminations also used for the cases of these nouns. The third is to be traced to the Prâkrit सुं. Kramadîśvara in Lassen's extract gives हूं for the हुं of the abl. pl., and हूं for that of the gen. pl.; but I have to make the same remark here as before. The instr. and abl. plurals are the same as those of nouns in अ; as तरुहिं and तरुहुं. Thus the plural of three cases ends in हुं, derived separately of course, and the plurals of two in हिं.

Feminine nouns.—The. plurals of the nom. and acc. of feminine nouns preserve the old ओ, or its shortened form उ, as in अङ्गुलिउ जज्जरिआउ in the second verse, and सुन्दरसव्वङ्गाओ विलासिणीओ. The sing. is the original base, as जज्जरिआ, विलासिणी &c. The instr. sing. termination is ए, the old one, as in ससिमण्डलचन्दिमए, कन्तिए, &c.; the. abl. is हे, as in बालहे for बालायाः, which is an aspirated ए; and the gen. हे as in मुद्धडहे for मुग्धायाः (ड being a nominal suffix) may be similarly explained or traced to the से of the gen. sing. fem. of the pronoun, किम्, यद्, and तद्, in the Prâkrit. I prefer the former explanation. This हे has been transferred to masculine nouns in इ or उ as we have seen. The abl. and gen. pl. ends in हु, as in वयसिअहु for वयस्याभ्यः or वयस्यानाम्. The anusvâra of the हु of the other classes of nouns is here omitted; and if correctly so, the हु of the abl. may be considered an aspirated form of the उ which is the ablative termination in the Prâkrit; and that of the genitive may be traced to the सु of the singular of masculine nouns. The instr. pl. and the loc. sing. and pl. take the same terminations as masculine nouns in इ or उ; as मइहिं, मइहि, and मइहिं-हुं. Lassen gives other terminations; but he appears to me not to have interpreted Kramadîśvara correctly. Those I have given are all that I have been able to find.

You will thus see how by the various influences at work, the natural transformation of स् to ह्, the elision of some of the elements, and the aspirated pronunciation of the vowels, most of the old terminations have been reduced to syllables composed of ह् and a vowel with or without an anusvâra. Terminations with such weak sounds are not adapted to serve the purposes of ordinary intercourse, since they require on the part of the speakers such care in pronunciation to render themselves intelligible to each other as we have not seen displayed in the course of our lingual history. The nominative and accusative throughout, and in certain classes of nouns the other cases also, have come to have the same forms. So that the purpose of expressing the different relations can be no longer performed by these poor remnants of the old declensional system; and a process of reconstruction must take place. It has already begun in the Apabhraṁśa; but we shall find it carried on much further in the vernaculars, which may now be said to have completed their new declensional system.

Pronouns.—The abl. sing. of pronouns ends in हां, as जहां, &c., which is to be traced to the Sanskrit स्मात् and the Prâkṛit म्हा, and the loc. sing. in हिं which has been explained. The gen. sing. of यद्, तद्, and किम् are optionally जासु, तासु, and कासु, made up by adding the usual उ to जास, तास, and कास, which again are other forms of जस्स, तस्स, and कस्स, with one of the consonants dropped and the preceding vowel lengthened as a compensation, a phenomenon to be noticed in going over the vernaculars. In the feminine these pronouns have जहे, तहे, and कहे optionally for the gen. sing., which are derived from the Prâkṛit जिसे, तिसे and किसे and the Pâli जिस्साय, तिस्साय, and किस्साय. The base, however, in the Apabhraṁśa ends in अ and not ई, or the more probable explanation is that this हे is the aspirated form of the ए of feminine nouns. इदम् has आय for its base; the instr. and gen. singulars, for instance, are आयेण and आयहो. This seems to be taken from the nom. sing. अअ, or अय by the rule of the substitution of य for अं. The neuter nom. and acc. sing. is इड. एहो is nom. and acc. sing. masc. of एतद्, corresponding to एसो, एह fem. to एसा, and by the application of उ to these we have the neuter एहु. एइ is the nom. and acc. pl. answering to एए Prâkṛit, with the latter ए shortened; and ओइ of अदस which corresponds to the form अमुके, the अमु being changed to अउं by a rule before mentioned, and afterwards to ओ; and के to ए shortened to इ. In other respects all these pronouns are declined like the corresponding nouns. The pronouns of the 1st and 2nd persons are thus declined:—

	1st pers.		2nd pers.	
	sing.	*pl.*	*sing.*	*pl.*
Nom.	हउं	अम्हे, अम्हइं	तुहं	तुम्हे-तुम्हइं
Acc.	मइं	— —	तइं	— —
Instr.	—	अम्हेहिं	पइं, तइं	तुम्हेहिं
Abl.	महु-मज्झु	अम्हहं	तउ, तुज्झ, तुध्र	तुम्हहं
Gen.	— —	—	— — —	—
Loc.	मइं	अम्हासु	पइं, तइं	तुम्हासु

Here we have not the wilderness of forms which we observed in the principal Prâkṛit. The nom. sing. of the 1st per. is हउं corresponding to अहकम्, the initial अ and the क् being elided and the usual Apabhraṁśa उ added. In the Prâkṛit अहकम् is represented by अहअं or अहयं. मइं is to be traced to the Sanskrit instr. मया and the loc. मयि both of which are reduced to the form of मइ in the Prâkṛit. Here it is extended to the acc. also. The pl. base is अम्ह which has been explained. The nom. pl. अम्हइं corresponds to such a form as अस्मके nom. pl., not loc. as Lassen says, through अम्हए; and the gen. pl. has the Apabhraṁśa termination हं. The rest are old. तुह is a base derived, as I said in going over the Prâkṛits, from तुय्हं and is used in the Prâkṛit also. पइं and तइं of the acc. instr. and loc. are from त्वया and त्वयि. The second is found in the older dialects, the first is peculiar to this. Of the corruption of त्व to प्प I have already spoken. The abl. and gen. तउ corresponds to a form त्वक which with the Apabhraṁśic उ is तउ, the क being dropped. Or it may be traced to तव with the व dissolved into उ. तुज्झ is a form found in the Prâkṛits also and explained by me as a corruption of the dat. तुय्हं in the Pâli and Prâkṛits, derived from the Skr. तुभ्यम्. The dative forms, you will remember, are put under the gen. in the older dialects. The ध्र of तुध्र is a peculiar Apabhraṁśic conjunct formed from ज्झ. The neuter of तद् is similarly त्रं and ध्रं. The base of the plural is तुम्ह, the same as in the Prâkṛit; and the nom. pl. तुम्हइं is to be traced to तुष्मके for युष्मके nom. pl. All the forms are similar to those of the first personal pronoun.

The Present tense of the Apabhraṁśa verb admits besides those of the corresponding Prâkṛit or Śaurasenî tense, the following forms:—1st pers. sing. लहउं, pl. लहहुं ; 2nd pers. sing. लहहि, pl. लहहु; 3rd pers. sing. लहइ, pl. लहहिं. It appears that some of these forms have arisen from a confusion of the Present Indicative with the Imperative. The prevailing and distinguishing final of the latter is the vowel उ; and here we see it is appended to the forms of the 1st pers. sing. and 2nd pers. pl., though it does not occur in those forms in any of the older dialects. The ह is another characteristic of these paradigms. That of the second pers. sing. we get from the old सि, and that of the pl. exists in the Prâkṛit, being derived from the Skr. थ. But the 3rd pers. pl. and the 1st pers. pl. get it simply by an extension of the analogy; or it my have been introduced to pervent a hiatus and thus may, like those of the cases, have been simply a *spiritus lenis*. The हुं of the latter, however, may be traced to म्हो, ओ being shortened to उ, just as म्हा and म्हि of the declensions become हां and हिं. Instead of the 3rd pers. pl. न्ति we have हिं, in which, though the ह is due to analogy, the characteristic इ and the nasal are preserved. You will thus see that in the declensions as well as conjugations the

हु prevails in this dialect. The Imperative second pers. sing. ends in इ, ए or उ. The first two may be traced to the Prâkṛit and Sanskrit हि, ह being dropped as in the Vernaculars; and the last seems to be substituted for the अ of one of the forms in the original dialects by analogy; or it may be the remnant of सु changed first to हु, and then to उ. But a better and, I may say, the true explanation of these forms will be given in going over the Vernaculars. Hemachandra does not give any more forms for the Imperative; but Kramadîśvara gives ज for the second person plural which must very likely be हु, the same as in the present, and हुं for the first pers. pl. which we have in the Present also. In one of the verses quoted by Hemachandra occurs पिअहुं which seems to correspond to पिबन्तु, if the reading is correct. The truth seems to be that the forms of the Imperative were lost, and the sense confounded with that of the Present, but the distinctive forms were those of the second pers. sing.; and in this respect there is an analogy with the Hindî and the Gujarâtî which resemble the Apabhraṁśa the most. The Future has the Prâkṛit and Śaurasenî forms in हि and इस्स; but one स् of this latter is dropped, and then the terminations of the Apabhraṁśa Present are added. The terminations of the absolutive are इ, इउ, अवि, इवि, एवि, एविणु, एप्पि, एप्पिणु. इ is the same as the Śaurasenî इअ from the Skr. य, इउ is the same, with the usual उ added to it, or is to be traced to the तुम् or इतुम् which is, as we have seen, confounded in tha Prâkṛit with the absolutive, and the rest are various forms of the Vedic त्वीन with the Prâkṛit augment इ or ए. This त्विन is, by a rule before mentioned, changed to प्पिण which with उ becomes प्पिणु; and by dropping the final न we have प्पि. This, however, may be derived also from such a form as त्वी found in the Vedas. This प्पि or प्पिणु is then softened to वि or विणु, as प् is so softened in many cases. When the augment इ or ए is not prefixed, we have वि in the form of अवि the अ being the final vowel of the root. Some of the terminations of the absolutive are also used to form the infinitive, on account of the prevailing confusion between the two. In consequence of this very confusion, recourse is had to other ways of forming the latter which are similar to those existing in the Prâkṛits; but these will be noticed hereafter.

The termination तव्य of the potential participle assumes the forms of इएव्वउं, एव्वउं, and एवा. The first two represent the form with the addition of क; and the इ of इएव्वउं is the usual augment. The अ of the त of तव्य which remains after the consonantal portion is dropped, is by the influence of the preceding इ changed to ए. In those points which are not noticed here, the Apabhraṁśa follows chiefly the Śaurasenî, and the principal Prâkṛit also to some extent. Thus in a great measure it represents those dialects in a further stage of decay; but it must be considered to have derived some words or forms independently also. Thus the पइ of the second personal pronoun cannot be derived from the Prâkṛit तइ, nor प्पिण of the absolutive from तूण or ऊण, or प्पण of abstract nouns from त्तण, but directly from the Sanskrit त्वया, त्वीन, and त्वन. This corruption of त्व must have existed in some of the older dialects too, since, as observed before, we have it in Aśoka's inscriptions; and the Apabhraṁśa derived it as well as a few such peculiarities from them.

LECTURE IV.

Phonology of the Vernaculars of Northern India.

We have now traced the gradual decay of Sanskrit from the form in which it is presented to us in the oldest literary records to that which it assumed in the Apabhraṁśa dialect. We have seen how words lost some of their vocal elements on account of the natural tendency of men to economize effort, as well as in consequence of the fact that the vocal organs of the people, who through historical accidents had to speak that language though it was not theirs, were untrained to utter the sounds of that language, and that they imported into it some sounds to which they themselves were previously accustomed. We have also observed the effects of the operation of the law of analogy in simplifying the grammar of the language—an operation, the range of which, in consequence of the ignorance of those same foreigners, was very extensive. The declensions and conjugations gradually lost their variety and became reduced to one or two types by the generalization of the rules originally applicable only to the nouns and verbs frequently used in ordinary intercourse. At the same time the terminations themselves of some of the cases, tenses, and moods came through numberless analogies to have the same or similar forms, and their vocal body gradually became attenuated and in some instances they were altogether dropped. Thus these processes of simplification were carried on much further than was consistent with intelligibility in ordinary intercourse. Hence the necessity arose of inventing new modes of expression for those relations which came to be imperfectly expressed or ceased to be expressed in the old way. As observed in the last lecture such new expressions are to be met with in the Apabhraṁśa dialect. If the Prâkṛits and the Apabhraṁśa which we have examined really represent the speech of the Indian people at certain periods of their past history, we should expect to find a relation of continuity between them and the prevailing speech of modern times. The words and grammatical forms in the modern vernaculars should either be the same as those existing in those dialects, or should be easily deducible from them by laws which we have observed to be in operation; and if in the Apabhraṁśa the grammatical forms came to be in a condition in which reconstruction was necessary, and if accordingly it was begun, we should find it carried on much further in the vernaculars and on principles used in the Apabhraṁśa and the older dialects and out of materials existing in them. We will therefore proceed now to the examination of the vernaculars with a view to trace this continuity.

The varieties of speech prevailing in Northern India at the present day are almost innumerable. If even a few peculiarities were to be regarded as giving individuality to a language, the number of dialects spoken in this part of the country would exceed even the proverbial fifty-six. But they may be divided into classes on the principle of resemblance; and generally the dialects spoken in the adjoining provinces are so alike each other that they may be regarded as constituting one class or even one language. Thus we have nine principal languages; and starting from ourselves, and going northwards, first on the western side of the country and then turning to the east and south-east, I may state them as the Marâṭhi, the Gujarâtî, the Sindhî, including the Kachchhî, the Panjabî, the Kaśmîrî, the Hindî, the Nepâlî, the Bangâlî, and the Oriyâ. Of these the Kaśmîrî and the Nepâlî have not yet been studied, and no grammars or books are available. Hence my observations will not extend to them. Each of these has its dialects; but those of some, such as the Gujarâtî and the Sindhî, differ from the main language in unimportant particulars. The same is the case with the Marâṭhî, except in some corners of the Maratha country. But in these there are five dialects differing in a great many important particulars from the main Marâṭhî. Thus, the Goanese prevails in Goa; the Mâlvaṇî, my own native tongue, and the Sâvantvâḍî, both of which, notwithstanding some minor differences, may be considered as one, are spoken in the Mâlvan, Vingorla, and Sâvantvâḍî districts. The Chitpâvnî is used only by the caste of Chitpâvan Brahmans in the district about Ratnâgiri; the Salsettî is spoken by the original inhabitants of that island and of Bombay; and the Khândeśî, which is a mixture of Marâṭhî and Gujarâtî, and contains to an appreciable degree a barbarous element, probably from a Bheel source, prevails in Khândeśa.

The Hindî has a great many dialects. Two at least may be distinguished among the variety of speech prevalent in Rajputana, the Mewârî spoken in Mewar and the adjoining districts, and the Mârwârî which prevails in Marwar, Jesselmere, and the other provinces. These, as may be inferred from their geographical position, are midway between the Gujarâtî and the Hindî dialects of the North, displaying some of the peculiar characteristics of both. Further north, we have the Braj prevailing in the country about Mathurâ; and to the east the Kanojî. There is not much difference between these. The language of the history of 84 Vaishṇavas and other books of the Vallabhâchâryan sects, which is ordinarily supposed to be the Braj, has grammatical forms identical with those mentioned by a recent grammarian as peculiar to the Kanojî. There is a good deal of confusion as regards this matter, the characteristics of one being found in the printed books together with those belonging to another. Then further north, we have the Garhawâlî and the Kumaonî spoken in the provinces of Garhawal and Kumaon. To the east, we have the Avadhî or the dialect of the province of Avadha or Ayodhyâ, and to the south of this again is the Rewâî spoken in the State of Rewâ. Further to the east is the Bhojpurî, and kindred dialects prevailing in Bihâr and the adjacent districts on the confines of Bengal. The old literature of the Hindî is principally written in two dialects, the Braj, and what is called the Pûrbî. Sûradâsa's works, Behârilâl's Satasâî, and others are written in the former; and to these I may add the Vallabha works I have already mentioned. The Râmâyaṇa and Tulasîdâsa's other works are written in the latter. The chief distinction between the idioms of Sûradâsa and Tulasîdâsa appears to me to be, that the latter uses a great many grammatical forms which are old, and from which those used by the former are derived. In this respect Pûrbî might be considered to be a very old form of the Braj. But there are a few other distinctions, though it is questionable whether they are enough to justify the Pûrbî being considered an independent dialect. The language of Kabîra's Ramainî and Sâkhîs presents a few peculiarities found in neither of the above. But the characteristics of Sûradâsa and Tulasîdâsa are also to be found in it; so that if we leave out of consideration the other works of Kabîra, in which there is probably another variety of speech, the dialect used by these Hindî poets may be considered to be the same. This has come to be regarded as the poetic dialect, and most of the other Hindî poets have written in it. Its modern representative is the Braj, in which the commentaries on Tulasîdâsa's, Kabîra's and Behârilâl's works, and on the tenth book of the Bhâgavata that I have seen, are written. This then is the Hindî literary dialect. The language, however, which is used as the medium of instruction in the Government schools in the North-Western Provinces, and in which the books published by the Educational Department are written, is now regarded as the Standard Hindî and its grammatical structure is identical with that of the Urdu spoken by the Mussalmans. This is rather the dialect in which the Hindus of the different provinces in Northern India communicate with each other, than that which they speak in their own provinces. The Panjâbî has also several dialects; but little is known about them. Oriyî resembles the Bangâlî in so many respects that one of them may be considered a dialect of the other. The similarity between the Hindî and the

Panjâbî is also very great. I will now give short specimens of these dialects.

I. Marâṭhî :—

कित्येक लोक मुत्सद्दी याणीं पदर पसरोन प्रार्थना आईसाहेबांची केली जे तुम्ही अग्निप्रवेश केलिया नंतर संपादिलेलें राज्य लयास आजच जातें प्राण महाराज कांहीं ठेवीत नाहींत हा प्रकार घडतो शाहाजी महाराजांचें व शिवाजी महाराजांचें नांव जगीं नाहींसें होतें सर्वांवर साहेबीं दृष्टि देवून राजयांस वोसंगास घेऊन साहेबीं अग्नि न घेतां मानस कठिण करून राहावें । हें काम करून गेलिया वंशक्षय महाराजांचा वडिलींच केला ऐसें जगीं प्रसिद्धता दिसतें तेव्हां आई साहेबांस राहविलें।

(*From an old Bakhara or Chronicle of S'ivâjî.*)

Some counsellors supplicated the lady-mother in an humble attitude saying: 'If you will burn yourself by fire, the kingdom which has been acquired goes to ruin this very day; and it will happen that the king will not bear life; the name of S'âhâjî Mahârâj and S'ivâjî Mahârâj will not remain in the world. Therefore, your ladyship, looking to all these things, should make the king sit in your lap (protect him), and, not resorting to fire, render your mind firm, and live. If you do this (burn yourself), it will plainly appear to all the world that you destroyed the race of the Mahârâj.' Thus they prevailed on her to live.

2. Gujarâtî :—

दमयंतीने तो महा आश्चर्य लाग्युं अने भ्रान्ति पडी के आ ते स्वप्न के साचुं । एवा अनेक विचार करती चालेछे एवामां एक अशोक वृक्ष दीठो त्यां दीन दमयंती आवीने कहेछे के ओ प्रियदर्शन अशोक तारा नामनो महिमा राखी मारा शोकनो नाश करी सत्यनामी था । पण कोण उत्तर आपे ।

(*From Mr. Mansukharâma's Nala-Damayanti.*)

Damayantî felt greatly astonished and was in doubt whether it was a reality or a dream. While moving on, engaged in various such thoughts, she saw an Aśoka tree. Going there she said; "O lovely Aśoka, having regard to the greatness of thy name, destroy my *S'oka* (sorrow) and deserve that name." But who would answer?

3. Sindhî:—

गिरनार कोटमे राइ ड़िआचु नाले हिकिडो पातिशाहु हो। तहिंजे भेणु फकीरखां सुयों साईं मूखे पुटु डे। फकीर हुनखे चिओ पुटु तोखे थींदो पर राइ डिआचजो सिरु वढींदो । हुन चिओ उहो पुटु ईं बनि पिओ जो मूजे भाउजो सिरु वढे। पर फकीरजो चवणु थिओ सो टरे की न। थोरे घणे ड़िहाडे माइअ पुटु जण्यो।।

(*From the story of Râi Diâcha in Major Stack's Grammar.*)

There was a Pâtiśâha (king) of the name of Râi Ḍiâcha. His sister begged of a Fakir: "Sire, give me a son." The Fakir said to her: "A son will be (born) to thee, but he will cut off the head of Râi Ḍiâcha." She said, "Accursed be (*lit.* fall into a wilderness) the son who should cut off my brother's head." But the Fakir's word cannot prove vain. In a few days the woman gave birth to a son.

4. Panjâbî:—

तां फेर बाबे नानकजी कहिआ हे पंडतजी तूं सुण ब्राहमणखतरीदा धरम जनेऊते रहिंदा है या भले करमांते रहिंदा है। सुण पंडत जे जनेऊ पावे अर बुरे करम करे तां उह ब्राहमणखतरी रहिंदा है या चंडाल हुंदा है। जां इह गल्ल स्रीगुरु बाबेजी कही तां जितने लोक बैठे से सभ हैरान हो गए। तां कहिण लग्गे ऐ स्रीपरमेसुरजी अजां इह बालक है अते केसीआं बातां करदी है।

(From the Janamasâkhî.)

Then again Bâbe Nânakajî said: "O Pandit, hear. Is the religious holiness of Brahmans and Kshatriyas preserved by the sacred thread or by good deeds? Hear, O Pandit, if one who is invested with the sacred thread does wicked deeds, does he remain a Brahman or Kshatriya or become a Chaṇḍâla?" When Śrî Guru Bâbejî spoke thus, all the people that were sitting there were astonished. Then they began to exclaim: "O God, he is still but a child, and how wonderfully he speaks!"

5. Hindî:—

इतना कह उसने बहुतेरे उपाय हाथ निकालनेको किये पर एक भी काम न आया। निदान सांस रुककर पेट फट गया। तो पछाड खाय के गिरा तब उसके शरीरसे लोहु नदीकी भांति वह निकला। तिस समैं ग्वालबाल आय आय देखने लगे और श्रीकृष्णचंद आगे जाय बनमें एक कदम की छांहतले खड हुए।

(Premasâgara, chap. 38.)

Having said so much, he made many attempts to throw out his (Kṛishṇa's) hand, but none was of any use. At last, he was suffocated and his belly burst out. Then he fell down, and blood flowed from his body in torrents. At that time the cowherd boys came one after another and began to see; and Śrî Kṛishṇa went forward and stood in the shade of a Kadamba tree in the forest.

6. Braj:—

जब सब ब्रजवासीनने सुनी जो श्रीदेवदमनको गाय बहोत प्रिय है तब सबनने मिलिके यह विचार कियौ जो जाके गाय होय सो सब एक एक तथा दोय दोय भेट करो। और श्रीगिरिराजके आसपास जो चौबीस गाम हैं तिनके पाससौं सब ब्रजबासी

मिलिके एक एक दोइ दोइ गाइ भेट करवाई । और यह ठहरी जो बीस गाममें जाके प्रथम गाय ब्यावै सो बछिया तो देवदमनको भेट करै। ऐसें सहस्रावधि गाय श्रीजीके भेट भई। तब दूध दही माखन और मठा सब घरकी गायनका आरोगें।

(From the Story of the Manifestation of Govardhananâthji.)

When all the inhabitants of Vraja heard that Devadamana was greatly fond of cows, they all joined and resolved that all who had cows should each present one or two. And the inhabitants of Vraja joined and caused each of the twenty-four villages about the mountain (Govardhana) to present one or two cows each. And it was resolved that in the twenty villages he whose cow should first calve should present the calf to Devadamana. In this way thousands of cows were presented to the Prosperous One. Then he used the milk, curds, butter and whey of the cows in his home.

7. Bangâlí:—

तबे शुन्बे ? आर वत्सर जखन आमि पाला ज्वर भुगते छिलु–दिबारात्रि बिछानाय पड़े थाकितुम–उठिया दांडाइबार शक्ति छिल ना, से समय स्वामी आसिया उपस्थित हलेन। स्वामी केमन ज्ञान हओया अवधि देखि नाइ, मेये मानुषेर स्वामी न्याय धन नाइ । मने करिलाम दुइ दण्ड काछे बसे कथा कहिले रोगेर यन्त्रणा कम हबे। दिदि बल्ले प्रत्यय जाबे ना–तिनि आमार काछे दांडाइयाइ अमनि बल्लेन षोल वत्सर हइल तोमाके बिबाह करे गियाछि–तुमि आमार एक स्त्री—टाकार दरकारे तोमार निकटे आसितेछि–शीघ्र जाब–तोमार बापके बल्लाम तिनि तो फांकि दिलेन—तोमार हातेर गहना खुलिया दाओ।

(From Peary Chand's Âlâler gharer dulâla—a Kulina Marriage.)

Will you hear then? That year at the time when I was suffering from intermittent fever, remained lying in bed day and night, and had no strength to rise and stand, my lord (husband) came. I had not seen what sort of a man my husband was since I ceased to be an infant. Nothing is more valuable to a woman than her husband. I had thought that my suffering would become alleviated, if he sat by my side for a few minutes (*lit.* two daṇḍas) and spoke with me. Dear sister, you will not believe me when I say that, as soon as he stood by my side, he said, "It is sixteen years since I married you and went away. You are one of my wives. I come to you, being in need of money, and will go back soon. I spoke to your father; but he put me off. Do pull out the ornament in your arm (round the wrist), and give it to me."

8. Oriyî ;—

गोटि ए मशा एक षण्डशृङ्ग उपरे बसि अहङ्कारे आपणाकु भारी बुझि षण्डकु कहिला भाइ षण्ड आम्भ बासवारु जेबे तुम्भकु भारी लागे तेबे कह आम्भे अन्य

स्थानकु उडि जाउं । ए कथा शुणि वृष कहिला आरे मशा तु जे आम्भ उपरे बासि अच्छु ए कथार टेर सुद्धा पाइ नाहुं

(*Fables published by the Calcutta School Book Society.*)

A certain gnat sitting on a horn of an ox, and with pride thinking itself heavy, said, "O ox, if in consequence of my sitting, you feel heavily weighted, tell me, and I will fly away to anther spot." Hearing these words the ox said, "O gnat I had not even the slightest idea that you were sitting on me."

In these extracts there are a great many words which on examination will be found to be derived from Sanskrit through the Prâkṛits; in other words, the vernacular forms will be found to be the same as, or further developments of, the Prâkṛit forms.

Thus we have in No. 1:—

किति, Pr. केत्तिअ or कित्तिअ, Skr. कियत् with the termination इक changed to इअ.

या of याणीं, Pr. अअ or अय in अअं nom. sing., Skr. अयम्.

पसर, Pr. पसर, Skr. प्रसर in प्रसरति.

के of केली, from Pr. कअ or कय, Skr. कृत, ल being a termination often used in the Prâkṛits.

जे, Pr. जअ or जय, Skr. यकत्, क being a suffix used in the Prâkṛits generally, and sometimes in Sanskrit also.

तुह्मी, Apabhr. तुम्हइं, Pr. तुम्हे or तुम्हए, Skr. such a form as तुष्मके, by analogy, for यूयम्,

आज, Pr. अज्ज, Skr. अद्य.

जा of जातें, Pr. जा, Skr. या.

कांहीं, Pr. केहिं, Skr. केभिः.

ठेव of ठेवीत, Pr. ठव, Skr. स्थाप in स्थापयति.

हा, Apabhr. एहो, Pr. एसओ, Skr. एषकः.

घड of घडतो, Pr. घड, Skr. घट in घटते.

नांव, Pr. नाम, Skr. नाम.

जग, Pr. जग, Skr. जगत्.

हो of होते, Pr. हो, Skr. भव in भवति.

वर, Pr. उवरि, Skr. उपरि .

दे of देवून, Pr. दि as in दिण्ण, Skr. दत्त.

वोसंग or ओसंग, Pr. उच्छङ्ग, Skr. उत्सङ्ग. The छ् of Sanskrit, Prâkṛit, Hindî &c., is in Marâṭhî changed to स्.

घे of घेऊन and घेतां, Pr. घे as in घेत्तूण, Skrî. गृह as in गृहीत्वा.

न, Pr. and Skr. same.

कर of करून, Pr. कर as in करइ, Skr. करोति.

काम, Pr. कम्म, Skr. कर्म.

गे of गेलिया, Pr. गअ or गय, Skr. गत.

वडिल, Pr. वड्ढ, Skr. वृध्द, इल being a Prâkṛit suffix.

ऐसें, Apabhr. अइस, Pr. ईदिस, Skr. ईदृश.

दिस of दिसतें, Pr. दिस in दीसइ, Skr. दृश्यते.

In No. 2:—

तो, Apabhr. तउ, Pr. ताव, Skr. तावत्.

लाग, Pr. लग्ग, Skr. लग्न.

अने, Pr. अने?, Skr. अन्य.

पड, Pr. पड, Skr. पत् in पतति.

ते from such Pr. and Skr. forms as ते, तं, तेण or तेन &c.

के, Pr. कय or कअ, Skr. कक for the crude किमकद्.

साचुं, Apabhr. सचउं, Pr. सचअं, Skr. सत्यकम्.

एवो sing. of एवा, Apabhr. एहु or एहउ and अइसो, Pr. इदिसो, Skr. ईदृश.

कर as in No. 1.

चाल, Pr. चल, Skr. चल.

दीठो, Apabhr. दिठ्ठउ, Pr. दिठ्ठओ, Skr. दृष्टकः.

त्यां, Pr. तहिं, Skr. तस्मिन्.

आव, from Pr. आअओ, or Skr. आगतः.

कह, Pr. कह, Skr. कथ as in कथयति.

छे, Pr. आच्छइ, Skr. आस्ते.

तार of तारा, Apabhr. तुहार for तुहआर, तुह being the Skr. तुभ्यम् and आर, कार.

नाम, Pr. नाम, Skr. नाम.

राख, Pr. रक्ख, Skr. रक्ष.

मार of मारा, Apabhr. महार for महआर, मह being the Pr. of Skr. मह्यम् and आर for कार.

था, Pr. था, Skr. स्था.

पण, Pr. पुणो, Skr. पुनः.

कोण, Pr. कउण, Skr. कः पुनः.

आप, Pr. अप्प, Skr. अर्प.

In No. 3:—

ना of नाले, Pr. and Skr. नाम, ल being suffix.

हो, Apabhr. हुअउ, Pr. हुअओ, Skr. भूतः (भूतकः)

तहिं of तहिंजे, Pr. तेसिं, Skr. तेषाम्.

भेणु, Pr. भइणी, Skr. भगिनी.

साईं, Pr. सामी, Skr. स्वामी.

मू of मूखे, Apabhr. महु, Pr. मह, Skr. मह्यम्.

पुट्ठ, Pr. पुत्तो, Skr. पुत्रः

तो of तोखे, Apabhr. तउ, Pr. तुह, Skr. तुभ्यम्.

डे, Pr. दा, Skr. दा.

राइ, Pr. राअ-राय-राआ, Skr. राजा.

सिर of सिरु, Pr. सिरं, Skr. शिरस्.

वढ, Pr. वड्ढ, Skr. वर्ध.

भाउ, Pr. भाउओ, Skr. भ्रातृकः

चवण, from Pr. चव for Skr. वच.

थिअ, Pr. थिअ, Skr. स्थित.

सो, Pr. सो, Skr. सः.

की, Pr. कहिं, Skr. कस्मिन्.

माइ, Pr. माइआ, Skr. मातृका.

थोरे, थो from Pr. थोअ, Skr. स्तोक, and र or ड, a suffix.

डिहाड, Apabhr. दिअहड, ड being a termination often used, Pr. दिअह, Skr. दिवस.

जण, Pr. जण, Skr. जन of जनयति.

In No. 4:—

तां, Pr. तहिं, Skr. तस्मिन्.

कइ, as in No. 2.

तूं, Pr. तुं, Skr. त्वम्.

सुण, Pr. सुण as in सुणइ, Skr. शृण as in शृणोति.

जनेउ, Pr. जण्णोवीअ, Skr. यज्ञोपवीत.

है, from अस, Pr. and Skr.

भला, Apabhr. भल्लउ, Pr. भल्लओ, Skr. भद्रकः, *i. e.* भद्र with suffix क.

जे, Pr. जे or जए, Skr. ये or यके.

पाव in पावे, Pr. पाव, Skr. प्राप as in प्राप्नोति.

अर, Pr. अवर, Skr. अपर.

कर, as in Nos. 1 and 2.

हु of हुंदा, as in No. 1.

जां, Pr. जहिं, Skr. यस्मिन्.

इह, Apabhr. एह, Pr एस, Skr. एष.

जित of जितने, Pr जित्तिअ, Skr. यावत् with suffix इक.

बैठा, Pr. उवइट्ठओ, Skr. उपविष्टकः, *i. e.* उपविष्ट with suffix क.

से, *plural* from Pr. सो, Skr. सः.

सभ, Pr. सब्ब, Skr सर्व.

गआ, Pr गअओ, Skr. गतकः, *i. e.* गत with क.

लग, Pr. लग्ग, Skr. लग्न.

अज of अजां, Pr. अज्ज, Skr. अद्य.

कैस of कैसा, Apabhr. कइस, Pr. कीदिस, Skr. कीदृश.
बात, Pr. वत्त, Skr. वृत्त.

In No. 5 :—

इत of इतना, Pr. इत्तिअ, Skr. इयत् with इक.
कह, as in Nos. 2 and 4.
हाथ, Pr. हत्थ, Skr. हस्त.
किय of किये, Pr. किअ, Skr. कृत.
भी, Pr. वि, Skr. अपि.
काम, as in No. 1.
न, Pr. Skr. same.
आय of आया, Pr. आअअ, Skr. आगत.
गय of गया, Pr. गअ, Skr. गत.
तो as in No. 2.
खा of खाय, Pr. खाअ, Skr. खाद.
लोहु, Pr. लोहिअ, Skr. लोहित.
वह, Pr. Skr. same.
तिस, Pr. तस्स, Skr. तस्य.
ग्वाल, Pr. गोआल or गोवाल, Skr. गोपाल.
बाल, Pr. Skr. same.
देख, Pr. देक्ख, Skr. द्रक्ष or दृक्ष.
लग of लगे, as लाग in No. 2 and लग्ग in No. 4.
औ, Pr. उअ, Skr. उत.
आग of आगे, Pr. अग्ग, Skr. अग्र.
जा as in No. 1.
छांह, Pr. छाआ, Skr. छाया.
हुअ of हुए, as हो in No. 3.

In No. 6:—

सब, Pr. सब्ब, Skr. सर्व.
सुन of सुनी, Pr. सुण, Skr. शृण.
गाय or गाइ, Pr. गावी, Skr. गाव as in गावम् &c.
मिल of मिलिकै, Pr. Skr. same.
किय as in No. 5.
जो, Pr. जओ, Skr. यकः *i. e.* य with the suffix क or अक.
हो of होय or होइ, as in No. 1.
सो, Pr. सो or सओ, Skr. सः or सकः *i. e.* स with क or अक.
दोय or दोइ, Pr. दुवे or दो, Skr. द्वे or द्वौ.
कर as in Nos. 1, 2 and 4.
और, Pr. अवर, Skr. अपर.

चौबीस, Pr. चउबीसा, Skr. चतुर्विंशति.
गाम, Pr. गाम, Skr. ग्राम.
है as in No. 4.
तिन of तिनके, Pr. ताण, Skr. तानाम्, by analogy, for तेषाम्.
पास, Pr. पस्स, Skr. पार्श्व.
यह, Apabhr. एह, Pr. एस, Skr. एष.
ठहर of ठहरी, Pr. ठिर, Skr. स्थिर.
बीस, Pr. बीसा, Skr. विंशति.
ब्या of ब्यावै, Pr. and Skr. वी.
बछ of बछिया, Pr. वच्छ, Skr. वत्स.
तो as in Nos. 2 and 5.
ऐसें as in No. 1.
भूअ of भई, Pr. भूअ, Skr. भूत.
दूध, Pr. दुद्ध, Skr. दुग्ध.
दही, Pr. दहि, Skr. दधि.
माखन, Pr. मक्खण, Skr. म्रक्षण.
मठ of मठा, Pr. मत्थ, Skr. मथ्य.
घर, Pr. घर, Skr. गृह.

In No. 7.

शुन of शुन्बे or शुनिबे, as सुण and सुन in Nos. 4 and 6
आर, Pr. अवर, Skr. अपर.
आमि, Apabhr. अम्हइ, Pr. अम्हे, Skr. such a form as अस्मके or अस्मे for वयम्.
पाला, Pr. पल्लाअ, Skr. पर्याय.
पड़ of पड़े or पड़िया, as in No. 2.
उठ of उठिया, Pr. उट्ठा, Skr. उत्था.
आछे in छिल, छिनु &c., Pr. आच्छइ, Skr. आस्ते.
से, Pr. सो, Skr. सः
आस of आसिया, Pr. आगच्छ or आअच्छ, Skr. आगच्छ.
हो of हलेन or होलेन, as in No. 1, 4 and 6.
देख of देखि as in No. 5.
नाइ, Pr. नाइ, Skr. नहि.
मन, Pr. मन, Skr. मनः.
दुइ, Pr. दुवे, Skr. द्वे.
काच्छ of काच्छे, Pr. कच्छा, Skr. कक्षा.
बस of बसे, Pr. उवइस, Skr. उपविश.
कह, as in Nos. 2, 4, and 5.
बल or बोल, Pr. बोल्ल, Skr. ब्रू.
तिनि, Pr. ताण, Skr. तानाम्, by analogy for तेषाम्.
षोल, Pr. सोलह, Skr. षोडश.

तोमा of तोमाके, Apabhr. तुम्हहं, Pr. तुम्हाणं, Skr. तुष्माणं, by analogy, for युष्माकम्.

कर as in Nos. 1, 2, 4 and 6.

गे or गय of गियाछि as in Nos. 1 and 5.

जा of जाब, as in Nos. 1 and 5.

हात, Pr. हत्थ, Skr. हस्त.

तो as in Nos. 2, 5, and 6.

दि as दे in No. 1.

In No. 8.

माशा, Pr. मसअ, Skr. मशक.

बस of बसि, as in No. 7.

आपणा, Pr. अप्पण, Skr. आत्मन as in आत्मना &c.

बुझ of बुझि, Pr. बुज्झ, Skr. बुध्य as in बुध्यति.

कह as in Nos. 2, 4, 5 and 6.

आम्भे, Apabhr. अम्हइ, Pr. अम्हे, Skr. such a form as अस्मके or अस्मे, for वयम्, as in No.7.

तुम्भ as तुम्ही in No. 1.

लाग as in No. 2, and as लग्ग and लग in Nos. 4 and 5.

उड of उडि, Pr. उड्ड, Skr. उड्ड as in उड्डयते.

जा as in Nos. 1, 5, and 7.

शुण as in Nos. 4, 6, and 7.

तु, as तूं in No. 4.

पाअ of पाइ, as पाव in No. 4.

जे as in No. 1.

ए, Apabhr. एह, Pr. एह, Skr. एष, as इह in No. 4, and यह in No 6.

You will find that in the Marâṭhî passage there are about 58 different words of which 26 or a few less than a half are derived from the Sanskrit through the Prâkṛits; in the Gujarâtî there are 42 out of which 23 or a few more than a half are of the latter description; in the Sindhî the proportion is 38 to 21 or somewhat greater than a half; in the Panjâbî 44 to 23 or a half; in the High Hindî 48 to 23 or a little less than a half; in the Braj 45 to 29, *i. e.*, about two-thirds; in the Bangâlî 71 to 27, *i. e.*, about two-fifths; and in the Oriyâ 32 to 15 or a little less than a half. I have not taken into consideration other words which do come to us undoubtedly through the Prâkṛits, but the etymology of which is not so obvious. These would increase the proportion and bring it to more than one-half in most of the cases. In this list there are three or four words such as नाम and वह which may be called old Tatsama, since they exist unchanged in the Prâkṛits, and the rest may be called old Tadbhavas. Now in these passages you will also have seen a large number of words such as प्रार्थना, अग्निप्रवेश, आश्चर्य, स्वप्न, बालक, शरीर, नदी, प्रिय, प्रथम, ज्वर, दिवारात्रि, शृङ्ग, स्थान &c., which are exactly the same as in Sanskrit. They could not have existed in those forms in the Prâkṛits, and hence it is clear that they were introduced long after the Prâkṛit period; and the tendency now-a-days in our languages is to introduce more of such words. These may be called modern Tatsamas. But some of these have uudergone a corruption since they were adopted. Thus कर्म is pronounced as करम; धर्म, धरम; क्षत्रिय, खतरी; कार्य, कारज; and कृपा, कर्पा or कुर्पा; while the Prâkṛit corruptions of these are कम्म, धम्म खत्तिअ, कज्ज, and किवा. Such words therefore are modern Tadbhavas. At the end of my observations on the Prâkṛits in the last lecture I gave a list of vocables existing in those dialects which are called Deśyas by native grammarians, and showed that several of them existed in our vernaculars also. We observe from the above passages, which contain such words as मुत्सद्दी, साहेब, and पातिशाह, that there are in the modern dialects words of an Arabic or Persian origin also. Thus we may distinguish these elements in the vocabulary of the vernaculars of Northern India:—1. Old Tadbhava, 2. Old Tatsama, 3. Modern Tadbhava, 4. Modern Tatsama, 5. Deśya, 6. Arabic, and 7. Persian. In its nature the old Tatsama element is but a small quantity and the main skeleton of our languages is made up of the old Tadbhava. It forms the principal constituent of the speech of the middle classes. The higher classes, however, use the Modern Tatsama and Tadbhava element to a much larger extent; and the language spoken by learned men is heavily loaded with pure Sanskrit words. This element has succeeded in driving out a very appreciable portion of the first in some of the languages. The Bangâlî contains the largest number of pure Sanskrit words, and hence one who knows Sanskrit can master the language in but a few weeks. The old Tadbhava element is reduced to the smallest minimum in what is called the *sâdhu bhâshâ* or the speech of the educated. According to the extent of the modern Tatsama or Tadbhava element, the other languages may be arranged in the following order:–Oriyâ, Marâṭhî, Hindî, Gujarâtî, Panjâbî, Sindhî. It must, however, be remarked that the modern Tatsamas appear in a pure or correct Sanskrit form only in the written language. The Bengalis in actually pronouncing these words corrupt them in a manner which renders them unrecognizable as Sanskrit words; and often in the same way as the old Prâkṛit speakers did. Thus आत्मा is pronounced अत्ता, ईश्वर इस्सर, मोक्ष मोक्ख, &c. The same is the case more or less with the speakers of the other languages, so that the pure Sanskrit words that we meet with in the written modern vernaculars may be considered modern Tadbhavas and in rare cases Prâkṛit Tadbhavas. The educated classes, however, in Mahârâshṭra and Gujarât and to a certain extent in the Hindî provinces pronounce the Sanskrit words correctly. The Sindhî however contains but a few pure Sanskrit words; hence it is rich in the old Tadbhava element, while it draws largely upon the Persian and Arabic. This foreign element is used in our dialects, principally in political matters. Persian and Arabic words are also used in the concerns of ordinary life, but their number is limited. The higher classes and learned men very rarely use them; while that element enters largely into the speech of the Mahomedans in the different provinces and of the Parsis. And the Mahomedans in the Hindî area use such a large number of these words that their language is by some considered an independent dialect and called Urdu, but it differs from the High Hindî in nothing further than in the use of these foreign words.

But though the vocabulary of our languages is thus composite the grammar is in every way the same that they have inherited from the Prâkṛits. Here there is no mixture of different elements. A good many of the forms now in use have been constructed since the Prâkṛit period; but, as I hope to show you, they are simply combinations or adaptations of existing Prâkṛit forms. Thus we will divide our examination of the vernaculars into three branches. In the first we will trace out the Sanskrit words which were transformed in the Pâli and the Prâkṛits in the various ways we have noticed, and discover the operation of the same or other laws in their further transformation, if they have undergone any, as also in the transformation of other words which remained unchanged in the Prâkṛits or were imported from Sanskrit at a later period. In the second we will trace out the Prâkṛit or Apabhraṁśa grammatical forms, and in the third, examine the new or reconstructed forms and find out the principles upon which they have been made up.

The phonetic changes which the words of a living language undergo involve, as a general rule, economy of exertion in its widest sense; but there are some which do not, or which require increased effort. Economy may sometimes be effected in more ways than one. For instance, the assimilation of vowels to consonants may be effected by changing अ to ओ and thence to उ, or to ए and इ. Some people have a predilection for the former, others for the latter. Again, one mode of change may be economical to some, and another opposed to it to others.

Thus the assimilation involved in the less open vowels इ and उ is of importance to some, but of little consequence to others; and they prefer the economy arising from the change of these vowels to अ, since this does not require any movement of the tongue or the lips. Here then we have two kinds of peculiarities. Again, if an ordinary change has a very comprehensive range or is almost universal in a language, and if other ordinary changes do not keep pace with it, and are to be found only in a limited number of instances, that ordinary change must be considered to be due to a peculiar vocal habit or incapacity. The assimilation of conjuncts and of the diphthongs in the Pâli and the Prâkṛits, and the elision of uninitial consonants in the latter, are changes of this nature. And finally, there is all the greater reason for attributing changes that involve no economy or necessitate greater exertion, such as the change of dentals to cerebrals or of sonants to surds, to vocal peculiarities. These several kinds of peculiarities give distinct individualities, so far as the external forms of words are concerned, to languages derived from one and the same primitive language. Thus then, some phonetic changes are special or peculiar, and others ordinary. We will now take up in order the instances observable in the Pâli and the Prâkṛits of these two kinds of changes and trace them in the vernaculars, and also endeavour to find out whether these dialects have preserved any of the Pâli and Prâkṛit peculiarities or developed new ones.

And first as regards vowels. The following are some of the instances in which Sanskrit ऋ is changed to अ, इ, or उ in the Prâkṛits with the vernacular forms of the words:—

अ.

1. Skr. कृत्तिः skin, Pr. कत्ति, M. कात in कातडें.
   Skr. घृष्टः rubbed away, slender, Pr. घट्ठो, G. and H. घट as a verbal base in घटवुं and घटना.
   Skr. मृदु soft, Pr. मउ, M. and G. मऊ.
   Skr. वृषभः bull, Pr. वसहो, H. बसह.
   Skr. कृष्णः proper name, Pr. कण्हो, M. G. H. कान्ह or कान्हा.
   Skr. तृणम् straw, Pr. तणं, M. तण.

इ.

2. Skr. कृपा pity, Pr. किवा, M. कींव.
   Skr. हृदयम् heart, Pr. हिअअं, H. B. O. हिय or हिया, old M. हियें, Mod. M. हिय्या, S. हिओ, हिआउं, G. हइया, P. हियाउं.
   Skr. मृष्टम् sweet, Pr. मिट्ठं, P. मिट्ठा, H. मीठा, B. O. मिठा, G. मीठुं, S. मिठो.

Skr. { दृष्टः seen, Pr. दिट्ठो, G. दीठो, S. डीठो.
दृष्टिः sight, Pr. दिट्ठी, M. H. दीठ or दीठी.
दृश्य of दृश्यते is seen, Pr. दिस्सइ, M. दिस in दिसणें, P. दिस in दिसणा, S. ड़िस in ड़िसणु, O. दिश in दिशिवार.

Skr. शृगाल: jackal, Pr. सिआलो, G. B. शियाल, H. सियार.

Skr. घृणा pity, disgust, Pr. घिणा, H. घिन, P. घिण.

Skr. शृङ्गम् horn, Pr. सिङ्ग, M. B. O. शिंग, G. H. सींग, P. सिंग, S. सिङु.

Skr. कृषिः husbandry, Pr. किसी, H. P. किस in किसान and किसाण.

Skr. तृषा thirst, Pr. तिसा, P. तिहा, S. टिह.

Skr. गृध्रः a vulture, Pr. गिद्धो, P. गिद्ध, M. G. H. गीध, M. गिधाड or गिधाड; also, B. गिधर, ड and र being the same termination, S. गिझ.

Skr. मृत्युः death, Pr. मिच्चू, H. मीच.

Skr. घृतम् ghee, Pr. घिअं, O. घिअ, G. H. P. B. घी, S. गिहु.

Skr. बृहस्पतिः name of a deity, Pr. बिहप्फई, H. बिफै.

Skr. मातृगृहम् mother's house, Pr. माइघर, or माइहरं, M. माहेर, G. महीरुं or महियर.

Skr. पितृगृहम् father's house, Pr. पिइघर, or पिइहर, H. पीहर, G. पीयर.

उ.

3. Skr. पृच्छ to ask, Pr. पुच्छ, P. पुच्छ in पुच्छणा, S. पुछ in पुछणु, H. G. पूछ in पूछना-वुं, M. पुस in पुसणें.

Skr. वृष्टः rained, Pr. वुट्ठो, P. वुट्टा, S. वुठो, G. वुठ in वुठवुं.

Skr. प्रावृष् rain, Pr. पाउसो, M. पाऊस, H. पावस.

Skr. ऋजु straight, Pr. उज्जू, M. उजू.

Skr. पितृकः father, Pr. पिउओ, S. P. पिउ.*

Skr. मातृष्वसृका mother's sister, Pr. माउसिआ, H. मौसी, M. मावशी. The others have मासी, probably by dropping उ.

Skr. भृङ्गः a bee, Pr. भुङ्गो, M. भुंगा.

The word घृतम् has घअं in the Prâkṛits according to the grammarians, but घिअं also must have existed; so also भृङ्ग has भिङ्गो. Some of the above words have two forms in the Prâkṛits, but since one of them does not occur in any of the vernaculars, it has been omitted. There are other words having two or even three Prâ-

* Mr. Beames considers the उ of the S. पिउ, भाउ, &c., to be the nom. sing. termination and not a transformation of the Sanskrit ऋ. But he is evidently wrong, since this उ appears in the oblique cases also, as पिउजो, भाउजो, &c.; while the nom. sing. उ does not, as in देहजो, gen. sing. of देहु "a country." The words have उ even in those languages, such as the P. and M., which have discarded the nom. sing. उ and it appears even in the feminine word माउ which cannot take the masculine termination उ.

kṛit forms, one of which occurs in one of the vernaculars, and the other or others in another. Thus :—

4. Skr. तृणम् straw.	Pâli तिणं, H. तिन in तिनका. Pr. तणं, M. तण, P. तुण in तुणका.
Skr. कृतम् done, Pr.	किदो or किओ, G. कीदो, H. किया, P. कीता S. कियो or कितो. कओ, S. कयो, M. के for कय or कअ in केला, B. कै or कै in कैलें*, O. कला.
Skr. मृतः dead, Pr.	मुओ, G. S. मुओ, H. मुआ. मओ, M. मे for मय in मेला.
Skr. वृद्धः old, Pr.	वुड्ढो, G. बुड्ढो, S. बुढो, H. P. बुड्ढा, O. बुढा B. बुडा. वड्ढो, S. वडो, H. P. बडा, B. O. बड, M. *dial.* व्हड in the sense of "large," G. वडो, M. G. S. वड in वडिल and वडेरो, meaning "elder."
Skr. पृष्ठम् back, Pr.	पट्ठ, M. पाठ, G. पाठ, as in पाठुं a carbuncle. पिट्ठ, P. पिट्ठ, G. H. पीठ, O. पिठ, B. पिठ or पिट. पुट्ठ, G. पूठ, S. पुठि.
Skr. मृत्तिका earth, Pr.	मत्तिआ or मट्टिआ, M. माती, H. मट्टी or माटी, G. B. O. माटी. मिट्टिआ, G. H. P. मिट्टी, S. मिटी.
Skr. मातृका mother, Pr.	माइआ, G. S. P. H. माइ or माई, G. H. माए, O. B. माई and माइया contracted to मेये, meaning 'a woman' generally. माउआ, S. P. H. माउ or माऊ. M. माय and G. P. H. B. O. मा are from Pr. माआ, Skr. माता.
Skr. भ्रातृकः brother, Pr.	भाइओ, G. S. P. H. B. O. भाइ or भाई. भाउओ, M. S. P. भाउ or भाऊ.

As the Pâli and the Prâkṛit alphabet, on account of these changes, has no ऋ, so do the vernacular alphabets not possess it. Sanskrit words containing the vowel have, however, been recently imported into the languages; but since even in those words, it is not correctly pronounced except by a few learned men, it cannot be said really to exist in vernacular speech, notwithstanding the use of those words. The usual modern pronunciation of the vowel is र, रि, रु, or अर्.

---

* चारि भाग कैल वेदव्यासते कारण B. Mahâbhârata.

Another characteristic change we noticed in the Prákṛits is the softening of इ and उ to ए and ओ before double consonants. A good many words so changed have descended to the vernaculars. Thus:—

5. Skr. सिन्दूरः red lead, Pr. सिन्दूरो or सेन्दूरो, M. शेंदूर, H. सेंदूर, G. B. सिंदूर, S. सिंधुरु.

Skr. शिग्रुः a kind of tree, Pr. शेग्गू or शिग्गू, M. शेगूल or शेगट.

Skr. पिण्डः a ball, a bundle, Pr. पिण्डो or पेण्डो, M. पेंडा-पेंडी, H. P. पिंडा, G. पिंडो, S. पिंडो or पिंडी.

Skr. पुस्तकम् a volume, Pr. पोत्थओ, H. P. पोथा and पोथी, M. G. पोथी, S. पोथु and पोथी, O. पोथी, B. पुथी or पुती .

Skr. मुद्गरः a mallet, Pr. मोग्गरो, M. H. मोगरा, G. मोगर, S. मुङ्गिरो, B. O. मुगुर.

Skr. मूल्यम् value, Pr. मोल्लं, H. M. मोल, O. मूल, G. मूल.

Skr. मुस्ता a kind of grass, Pr. मोत्था, M. मोथा in नागरमोथा, H. P. मोथा, S. G. मोथ, O. मुथा.

Skr. मुक्तः free, Pr. मोक्को, M. P. मोक in मोकळा, G. मोक in मोकळुं, S. मोकल, O. मुकुळा.

Skr. कुक्षिः a side of the belly or abdomen, Pr. कोक्खी, H. कोख, P. कुक्ख or कोख, G. कुख, S. कुखि, M. कूस, from Pr. कुच्छा.

Skr. गुच्छः a bunch, Pr. गोच्छो, B. गुचि, गुछि, or गोछा, O. गेाछ, M. घोंस, H. P. गुच्छा, G. गुच्छो, S. छुगो (by transposition) or गोष.

Skr. कुष्ठम् white leprosy, Pr. कोट्ठं, M. कोड, H. G. कोढ, S. कोढ़, B. कोठ, कुठ or कुढ, O. कोढ or कुढें.

Skr. कूर्परः elbow, Pr. कोप्परो, M. कोंपर, G. कोपरियुं.

Skr. शुण्डा the trunk of an elephant, Pr. सोण्डा, M. सोंड, P. सुंड, H. सुंड or सूंढ, G. सूंढ, S. सूंढि. B. O. शुंड, O. शोंड ?

Skr. तुण्ड mouth, Pr. तोण्डं, M. तोंड.

Skr. कुण्डम् a puddle, Pr. कोण्डं, M. कोंड, G. कुंडी, कुंडुं.

Skr. मुग्ध foolish, Pr. मोद्ध or मोग्ग, H. P. मोधू, S. भोंदू, मोंगो, M. भोंदू ?

Skr. तुन्द a pot-belly, Pr. तोन्द, H. P. तोंद, M. दोंद, G. दुंद.

The G. ओचरवुं 'to pronounce' from Skr. and Pr. उच्चार, ओळंगवुं 'to transgress' from Skr. Pr. उल्लङ्घ, G. ओकवुं, M. ओकणें, H. ओकना 'to vomit' from Pr. उग्गिर, Skr. उद्गिर, are also later instances of the operation of the same law.

The change of इ to ए is according to the grammarians optional in the Prâkṛits and that of उ to ओ necessary. But in both cases we find two forms in the vernaculars. Still the prevailing forms in the latter are those in ओ, while those in उ are rare and mostly to be found in the Bangâlî and Oriyâ, which languages, and more especially the first, have a predilection for उ, in which case it is possible they may have changed the Prâkṛit ओ to उ. In the Pâli and Prâkṛits the ए and ओ in these cases are short; but the vernaculars having dropped one of the following double consonants have, according to a general rule to be noticed hereafter, lengthened the vowels. When instead of a double consonant, there is a conjunct of a nasal and a mute as in सेन्दूर and तोण्ड, the nasal consonant is reduced to a simple anusvâra or nasal sound so as to give to the conjunct the character of a simple consonant, and the ए or ओ is pronounced long as in सेंदूर and तोंड. In this manner, though the Prâkṛit short ए and ओ are, in the instances in which we possess an evidence of their existence, lengthened, I think in some of the vernaculars at least we have these vowels. For in a good many instances in Marâṭhî and Gujarâtî ए and ओ are pronounced short. There is a rule which in Marâṭhî is almost universal, and in Gujarâtî often observable, in virtue of which the accent or the whole weight of the sound of a word falls on the final आ or एं of nouns in the former and the final ओ or ऊं in the latter; and the preceding vowels are rendered short while in the original Sanskrit and in Hindî they are long. Thus:

6. Skr. कीटकः a worm, Pr. कीडओ, H. कीड़ा, M. किडा.
 Skr. कीलकः a nail, Pr. कीलओ, H. कीला, M. खिळा.
 Skr. कूपकः a well, Pr. कूवओ, H. कूआ, G. कुवो.
 Skr. चित्रकः leopard, Pr. चित्तओ, H. चीता, M. चिता, G. चित्तो.
 Skr. चूडकः a bangle, Pr. चूडओ; H. चूड़ा, M. चुडा, G. चुडो.
 Skr. चूर्णकः lime, Pr. चुण्णओ, H. चूना, M. चुना, G. चुनो.

And many more instance might be given. Similarly in Marâṭhî the preceding long vowels are shortened when the terminations of the oblique cases are applied, as in भिकेस, पिकास, किडीस, पिठास, उनास, भुकेस, गुळास, &c., dative singulars of भीक 'beggary,' पीक 'crop,' कीड 'a worm,' पीठ 'flour,' ऊन 'sun,' भूक 'hunger,' गूळ 'molasses,' &c. If so, then by a necessary law of Marâṭhî speech, the ए and ओ of गेला 'gone,' केला 'done,' मेळा 'a gathering,' जेवढा 'as much,' पेढा 'sweetmeat,' घोडा 'a horse,' कोळसा 'charcoal,' गोफा 'the ankle,' जोडा 'a pair,' &c., and of शेणास 'to cowdung,' शेतास 'to a field,' पेठेस 'to a market,' लेंकरास 'to a child,' गोतास 'to a race,' चोरास 'to a thief,' पोरास 'to a boy,' &c., must be short. And if the Marâṭhî speaker will compare his pronunciation of मेळ, शेत, शेण, गोत, पोर, &c., with that of मेळा, शेतास, शेणास, गोतास, पोरास, &c., he will find that the quantity of ए and ओ in these latter words is shorter than in the former. Similarly, in Gujarâtî the first ए and ओ of केवी 'how large,' घेलो 'a mad man,' छेडो 'end,' मेडो 'an upper storey,' मेळो 'a gathering,' खोळो 'lap,' घोडो 'a horse,' चोखा *pl.* 'rice,' पोळो 'broad,' पोणा *pl.* 'three-quarters,' मोगरो 'jessamine,' कोळसो 'charcoal,' &c., must be short. In Gujarâtî the penultimate vowel of a monosyllabic root is, as in Hindî, shrotened in the causal, as in लागवुं 'to adhere,' लगाडवुं 'to cause to adhere,' 'join,' धाववुं 'to run,' धवाडवुं 'to cause to run', सीखवुं 'to learn,' सिखाववुं 'to teach,' शीववुं 'to sew,' शिवाडवुं 'to cause to sew,' बीहवुं 'to fear,' बिहवाडवुं 'to terrify,' &c. But in Hindî the short vowels that take the place of ए and ओ are इ and उ, as in दिखाना 'to show' from देखना 'to see,' धुलाना 'to cause to wash' from धोना 'to wash,' &c. But in Gujarâtî the ए and ओ are not changed to इ and उ but remain, as in देखाडवुं 'to show,' लेवाडवुं 'to cause to take' from लेववुं 'to take,' धोवाडवुं 'to cause to wash' from धोववुं 'to wash,' जोवाडवुं 'to show' from जोववुं 'to see,' &c., which they cannot do by the general rule if they are long. They must therefore be pronounced short. And as a matter of fact it will be found that the Gujarâtî people in these and several other cases give a short sound to these vowels. In the Mâlvaṇî dialect of the Marâṭhî ओ is very often pronounced like the English *o* in *pot*, and ए like *e* in *pet*. In Bangâlî the ओ to which अ is converted in ordinary speech is also broad and short, and we have reason to believe that both ए and ओ when they really occur in words are often pronounced short in that and the Bhojpurî and other dialects of Bihâr and Mithilâ.

It may be urged against one of the arguments I have used that if the ए and ओ in शेतास and गोतास are short, the first आ in हातास 'to the hand,' कानास 'to the ear,' &c., must also be short, and consequently these vowels must be changed to अ. But अ is not necessarily the short form of आ, or आ the long form of अ. For in pronouncing आ the lips and the upper and lower parts of the mouth are much more widely apart from each other than in pronouncing अ; so that the difference between the two is not simply of quantity but of quality also. The first आ of such words as हातास and मातला 'maddened,' is therefore short आ; that is, in pronouncing it the vocal organs are in the same condition as in pronouncing long आ, but the time occupied is shorter than in the case of the latter. The अ that we have got in Sanskrit is short, but in most of the vernaculars we have a long अ which takes longer time to pronounce than the Sanskrit अ, while the condition of the vocal organs is the same. The final अ of words is silent in the vernaculars, but at the same time the vowel of the preceding syllable is lengthened. Thus गुण 'virtue' is, as a Sanskrit word, pronounced *gu-ṇa*, but in Marâṭhî and Gujarâtî it is *gûṇ*; and in Hindi *gûn*; Sanskrit गुड *gu-ḍa* 'molasses' is in Marâṭhî *gûḷ*; Sanskrit तिल *ti-la* 'sesamum' is in Marâṭhi and Gujarâtî *til* and Hindî *til*. In the same way, the word रथ is in Sanskrit pronounced *ra-tha*, but when in vernacular pronunciation it becomes *rath*, the *a* is not the short अ, but अ pronounced long, as if the word were *ra-ath* without a pause between the two *as*. The long अ and the short are found side by side in such a word as मदन, which as pronounced in Sanskrit is *madana* with three consonants each followed by the Sanskrit or short अ. In the modern languages, however, the first syllable has its अ as in Sanskrit, but that of the second is lengthened, and in the last it is dropped, and the word thus becomes *madaan*.

This peculiarity of softening इ and उ to ए and ओ has been preserved by the vernaculars. It is not necessary that a conjunct consonant should follow. Thus:

7. H. बिराना or बेराना to mock, from Skr. विडम्बन; बिहान or बेहान morning, from Skr. विभानम्, Pr. विहाणं; नेवता invitation, from Pr. निमन्त, Skr. निमन्त्र; सोहर pleasing, from Skr. सुखकर, Pr. सुहअर; सुहावन or सोहावन agreeable, from Pr. सुहावन for such a Sanskrit form as सुखापन; मोहरा or मुहरा front or van-guard the first part of which is from Pr. मुह, Skr. मुख; उखल or ओखल a wooden mortar, from Skr. उलूखल.

G. मोह in मोहडुं face, from Pr. मुह, Skr. मुख; भोय ground, the M. and H. form being भुंई; ओर in ओरडा, Pr. उवरओ, Skr. उपरकः or अपवरकः; गोर a family priest, from Skr. Pr. गुरु.

M. मेहुण a couple, from Pr. मिहुण, Skr. मिथुन; वेडावणें to mock, Skr. विडम्बन; शेंडी the lock of hair on the head from Pr. शिहण्डिआ, Skr. शिखण्डिका; मोहरे or म्होरे in front, of which मोह is from मुह as above; ओवरी (dial.) from Pr. उवरओ as above; तिरडा or तेरडा a kind of flower.

P. विह or वेह poison, from Pr. विस, Skr. विष; पिउ or पेउ father for Pr. पिउओ, Skr. पितृकः; नेउंदा invitation, from Pr. निमन्त, Skr. निमन्त्र; मोहर van-guard, as above; ओडक end, from Pr. उदक, Skr. उदर्क.

B. दोयार door, for Pr. दुआर; छोरा a razor, for Pr. छुरओ, Skr. क्षुरकः; B. O. मोंच mustache, for मुछ, Pr. मस्सू, Skr. श्मश्रु; शोन or शुन to hear, for Pr. सुण; शियाल or शेयाल a jackal, for Pr. सिआलो, Skr. शृगालः.

The ए and ओ to which इ and उ are thus reduced must be short, since there is no reason here why the quantity should be increased.

Of the instances in which long ई and ऊ are softened to long ए and ओ in the Prâkṛits, the vernaculars have retained the following :—

8. Skr. बिभीतक myrobalan, Pr. बहेडओ, M. बेहडा, G. बेहडुं, H. P. बहेडा, S. बहेडो.

Skr. ताम्बूल betel leaf, Pr. तम्बोल, H. P. तम्बोल, M. तांबोळ in तांबोळी a seller of betel leaves, G. तंबोळ in तंबोळी.

Skr. स्थूल, Pr. थोर, M. थोर.

More modern instances of this change are:—

9. H. लीमु or लेमु, B. लेबु, a lemon; H. मूछ or मोछ mustache, Pr. मस्सु or मसु; G. पेठे in that manner, from Skr. पीठिकया; वेरवुं to scatter, from Pr. विइर, Skr. विकिर; खेचवुं to pull, for H. खींचना; O. भोक hunger, for the भूक or भूख of the others.

Of the few instances in which इ is softened to अ in the Prâkṛits, the vernaculars have retained हलद्दा in the M. G. हळद, H. हलदी, O. हळदी and P. हल्हदी or हळदी. Though पडंसुआ does not occur, still पड which stands for प्रति in this word is preserved in several words, as M. पडसाद 'echo,' for Skr. प्रतिशब्द, पडजीभ 'the uvula' for Skr. प्रतिजिह्वा, पडछाया or पडसावली, H. परछाईं for Skr. प्रतिच्छाया &c. No more instances of this change are given by the grammarians, but, as observed in the last lecture, the substitution of अ for इ or उ in one of the two or more places in which it occurs in some words indicates a tendency in the Prâkṛits towards this change. The vernaculars have got more instances. Thus:—

10. M. G. S पारख examination, test, H. P. B. O. परख, Skr. परीक्षा, Pr. परिक्खा; also the verb पारखणें.

M. H. P. G. निरखणें-ना-णा-वुं to see closely, Skr. निरीक्षण, Pr. निरिक्खण.

M. H. G. विखरणें-ना-वुं, P. विक्खरना to scatter, Skr. विष्किर, Pr. विक्खिर, (S. विखेरणुं).

H. बहलना to divert, amuse, Skr. विहर.

H. भभूत holy ashes, Skr. विभूति.

H. बहन, also बहिन, sister, Skr. भगिनी, Pr. भइणी; also बहरा or बहिरा, Skr. बधिर, Pr. बहिर.

H. पहरना or पहिरना, S. पराहणुं, B. परण, to wear, Pr. परिहाण, Skr. परिधान.

M. G. पण but, also, Pr. पुणो, Skr. पुनः

M. H. जथा an herd, Skr. यूथकः.

P. पंडत a learned man, Skr. पण्डित.

P. सगन an omen, Skr. शकुन.

But in Gujarâtî the tendency has operated very widely, as will be seen from the following:—

G.	Skr. or Pr.	M. or H.
11. लखवुं to write........	लिख	H. लिखना.
बगडवुं to be spoilt........	विघट	M. बिघडणें, H. बिगडना.
मळवुं to be got	मिल.....................	M. मिळणें, H. मिलना.
वक्रो sale	विक्रय	M. विक्रा, H. बिका.
कठण difficult	कठिन	M. कठिण, H. कठिन.
वकासवुं to yawn	विकास..................	H. विकसना.
तळसी a kind of plant ...	तुलसी	M. तुळशी, H. तुलसी.
माणस a man	मनुष्य	M. माणूस, H. मानस.
नरो mere	Pr. णवरि, Apabhr. निरु	H. निरा.
अजवाळो light.............	उज्ज्वाल	M. उजेड or उजवड (dial.). H. उजियाला.
मडदुं a corpse..............	मृत with ड..........	M. मुडदा.
वसमुं difficult	विषम	M. H. विषम.
गळवुं to swallow...........	गिल	M. गिळणें.
समणुं a dream..............	Pr. सिमिण, Skr. स्वप्न	H. सपना, M. सपन or स्वप्न.
पंडे one's self, bodily	पिण्ड body	M. पिण्ड.
मस pretext..................	मिष	H. मिस, M. मिष.
चंता thought, anxiety......	चिन्ता	M. चिन्ता.
गण virtue, quality.........	गुण	M. गुण, H. गुन.
मकण name of Krishna, of a man................	मुकुन्द	M. मुकुंद.
परशोत्तम	पुरुषोत्तम............	M. पुरुषोत्तम.

And there are many other instances, such as फरवुं 'to walk,' टकवुं 'to last,' and मरडवुं 'to twist,' the Marâṭhî forms of which are फिरणें, टिकणें, and मुरडणें. Thus Sanskṛit, Prâkṛit, and even foreign words such as मालूम 'known,' which becomes मालम, change their इ or उ to अ. The Gujarâtî people have thus got a habit of careless pronunciation. After forming the contact necessary for pronouncing a consonant, they emit the breath without compressing it at the palatal or labial position, and thus save the trouble of raising the middle of the tongue to the palate, or of rounding the lips.

Under the head of assimilation the first characteristic vowel change observable in the Pâli and the Prâkṛits which we have to notice is that of the Sanskrit ऐ and औ to ए and ओ. Most of the nouns having ऐ and औ are in Sanskrit attributives formed from other nouns, and as these are formed in other ways in our languages we cannot expect to find many instances of them. Still there are a good many, and enough to show that our vernaculars have inherited these Pâli and Prâkṛit transformations of the Sanskrit ऐ and औ. Thus:—

12. Skr. गैरिक red chalk, Pr. गेरिअ, M. H. गेरू; Skr. कैवर्त pilot, Pr. केवट्ट, H. केवट; Skr. तैल oil, Pr. तेल्ल, M. G. H. तेल; Skr. वैवाहिक parties to a marriage, Pr. वेवाहिअ, G. वेवइ, B. वेहाइ, M. (dial.) वेइ; Sk. शैवल moss, Pr. सेवल, M. शेवळ, G. शेवाळ, H. शेवाल, B. शेयाला; Skr. सैन्धव rock-salt, Pr. सेन्धव, H. P. सेंधा, M. सेंधे in सेंधेलोण, S. सेंधोलूण; Skr. वैदिक: learned in the Vedas, Pr. वेदिओ, G. वेदिओ; Skr. सौभाग्य good fortune, husband's love, Pr. सोहग्ग, H. B. O. सोहाग,—S. P. shorten the ओ to उ and H. also optionally;—Skr. पौत्र son's son, Pr. पोत्त, P. पोत or पोत्ता, H. पोता, S. पोटो; Skr. मौक्तिकम् a pearl, Pr. मोत्तिअं, M. मोतीं, G. S. P. H. मोती; Skr. वैद्य:, Pr. वेज्जो, S. वेजु; Skr. गौर:, Pr. गोरो M. H. गोरा, S. गोरो.

The Sanskrit syllables अय and अव are, you will remember, often changed to ए and ओ in the Pâli and the Prâkṛits. The following instances of this change have come down to the vernaculars:—

13. M. ने to carry, H. ले, Pr. ने, Skr. नय; M. G. तेतीस thirty-three, H. तैंतीस, P. तेती, B. तेत्रिश, O. तेतिश, Pr. तेत्तीसा, Skr. त्रयस्त्रिंशत्; M. केळें a plantain, G. केळुं, H. केला &c., Pr. केलं for कयलं, Skr. कदलम्; M. लोण salt, Pr. लोण, Skr. लवण; H. ओस dew, Pr. ओस्साय, Skr. अवश्याय; M. ओणवा bent, Pr. ओणअ, Skr. अवनत; M. G. ओळंबा a plumb, Pr. ओलम्बअ, Skr. अवलम्बक:; M. बोर jujube fruit, Pr. बोर for बवर or बअर, Skr. बदर.

The Pâli and the Prâkṛits on account of these changes lost the Sanskrit diphthongs ऐ and औ. But several of the vernaculars have got them back by combining the vowels अ and इ, and अ and उ, short or long, brought together by the elision of consonants in the Prâkṛits. A hiatus, which requires the intonated breath to be let off twice successively without being stopped or compressed, is mostly felt to be burdensome, and is in consequence avoided in several ways. Where the two vowels can combine into one sound, a diphthong is formed out of them. Thus ऐ and औ are combinations of अइ and अउ. In pronouncing these last the breath has to be emitted twice, while in sounding the former the same current is first let off through the position of अ, and afterwards through that of इ and उ. The first part of the diphthong is thus a very short अ, to which half a mâtrâ, as previously observed, has been allowed by the grammarians. The following are instances of this formation:—

14. Skr. प्रविष्ट entered, Pr. पइट्ठ, H. old M. पैठा.

Skr. उपविश sit, Pr. उवइस, M. H. बैसणें-ना by the dropping of the initial उ.

Skr. उपविष्ट sat, Pr. उवइट्ठ, H. P. बैठा.

Skr. खदिर name of a tree, Pr. खइर, M. H. P. खैर.

Skr. कपित्थ name of a tree, Pr. कवित्थ, H. कैथ by dropping व्.

Skr. बलीवर्द a bull, Pr. बइल्ल, M. H. P. बैल.

Skr. तादृश like that, Pr. तादिस, Apabhr. तइस, M. H. P. तैसा.

Skr. महिषी a female buffalo, Pr. महीसी, M. म्हैस, H. भैंस, P. मैंह or भैंस.

Skr. भगिनी sister, Pr. भइणी, P. M. (dial.) भैण, H. बैन (more commonly बहिन.)

Skr. बृहस्पति a certain god, Pr. बिहप्फई, H. बिफै.

Skr. मलिन dirty, Pr. मइल, H. P. मैल, old M. मैळ.

Skr. पवित्रक holy thread, Pr. पवित्तअ, B. पैता.

In this manner the Hindî, Marâṭhî, and Panjâbî combine अ and इ or ई into ऐ. Sometimes the ऐ so formed is dropped by the Marâṭhî, and we have optionally बसणें for बैसणें, म्हस for म्हैस, and तसा for तैसा. Bangâlî and Oriyâ have बस for बैस. The former has बैस in addition, so that these languages also seem to have once formed ऐ out of the two vowels.

अ and उ.

15. Skr. मुकुट a chaplet, Pr. मउड, H. P. मौडा, B. O. मउड.

Skr. चतुर्थ fourth, Pr. चउत्थ, M. H. P. चौथा, O. चौथ.

Skr. चतुष्क a square, Pr. चउक्क, M. H. P. चौक. Similarly other compounds of चतुर्; as चौरस, चौकोन, चौमास &c., B. O. S. also have चौ.

Skr. ज्येष्ठपुत्र the son of an elder brother, Pr. जेट्ठउत्त, H. जेठौत.

Skr. मधुमक्षिका a bee, Pr. महुमक्खिआ, H. मौमाखी by dropping ह्.

Skr. वधू a girl, a daughter-in-law, Pr. वहू, O. बौ.

When sometimes the Prâkṛits combined अ and इ or अ and उ, they formed ए and ओ out of them. For, as we have seen, the passage from one position to another in the same breath was impossible to the speakers of the Prâkṛits and the Pâli. Thus we have मोर for मऊर, Skr. मयूर; थेर for थइर, Skr. स्थविर; चोत्थ for चउत्थ, Skr. चतुर्थ; चोग्गुण for चउग्गुण, Skr. चतुर्गुण &c.

Similarly अय and अव from ऐ and औ in the vernaculars. When the final अ of य and व is not pronounced, these semivowels easily pass into इ and उ which with the previous अ form those diphthongs.

16. Skr. मदन god of love, Pr. मअण or मयण, H. मैन.

Skr. रजनी night, Pr. रअणी or रयणी, H. P. रैन.

Skr. नयन the eye, H. नैन, P. नैण.

Skr. भय fear, H. P. भै.

Skr. जय victory, H. P. जै.

Skr. शत a hundred, Pr. सअ or सय, H. P. सै.

Skr. वचन speech, Pr. वअण or वयण, H. बैन.

The Marâṭhî does not follow the Hindî and Panjâbî here. For, according to the modern way of pronunciation as observed before, the final अ of words not being pronounced, the vowel of the preceding syllable is lengthened. The अ of the first syllable of भय and जय being thus long prevents the formation of ऐ; while that of य being so in such words as नयन that semivowel is not reduced to इ, and hence we have no ऐ. But these obstacles are set aside in the Hindî and the Panjâbî, the tendency to form the diphthongs being strong. When however the Marâṭhî was in a state of formation it retained the Prâkṛit peculiarity and changed the syllable अय to ए, as in शें for शतम्, भे (old) for भय, एं of neuter nouns such as केळें and ताम्बें for the अयं of the Prâkṛit केलयं and तम्बयं, के and गे of केला and गेला for the Prâkṛit कय and गय, &c. This change is due to a weakened pronunciation of य. In modern times even य is often sounded like ए. For, in producing these two sounds the middle of the tongue being raised, the forepart falls lower, than in sounding इ. When, therefore, in prononncing य the middle is not raised sufficiently high, the sound becomes ए and not इ, because this requires the forepart also to be raised higher.

In the following instances अव forms औ :—

17. Skr. धवल white, Pr. धवल, H. P. धौला, M. धवळा.

Skr. नवशिक्षित newly learned, Pr. नवसिक्खिअ, H. नौसिख, M. नौशिका or नवशिका.

Skr. भवन a dwelling, Pr. भवण, H. भौन, P. भौण.

Skr. कवल a mouthful, Pr. कवल, H. कौर or कौल.

Skr. नवनीत butter, Pr. नवणीअ, H. नौनी, P. नौणी, M. लोणी from the Pr. णोणीअ.

Skr. नमन bowing, Apabhr. नवँन, H. नौना, P. नौणा, M. लवणें.

Skr. लवन cutting, Pr. लवन, H. लौना.

Skr. कपर्दिका a shell, Pr. कवड्डिआ, H. P. M. कौडी, M. कवडी also.

Skr. सपत्नी a fellow-wife, Pr. सवत्ती, H. सौत, M. सवत.

Skr. भ्रमर a bee, Apabhr. भवँर, H. P. भौंरा, M. भौंवरा from another derivative of भ्रम.

Skr. समर्प to deliver, Apabhr. सवँप्प, H. सौंपना, P. सौंपणा, M. सोंपणें Here the Panjâbî and the Hindî agree perfectly; but the Marâṭhî is not decided, sometimes changing the syllable to औ but more often, for the reasons given in the case of अय, retaining it as it is in the original the अव, however, being pronounced like अव् in some cases, and अव with long final अ in others. Hindî and Panjâbî similarly treat अाइ or आई and आय, and आउ or आऊ and आव, while the Marâṭhî here completely parts from them. For the आ in these syllables is too strong a sound for the Marâṭhî ear to pass off into the very short अ of half a mâtrâ. Even the Hindî preserves आय unchanged in a good many cases, as बाय for Pr. वाय, Skr. वात 'wind.'

18. आइ or आय.

Skr. पाद foot, Pr. पाअ or पाय, H. P. पै in पैर foot, पैदल foot-soldiers, पैकड़ shackles, &c., M. पाय in पायदळ foot-soldiers, पायरी a step.

Skr. कायस्थ name of a caste, Pr. कायत्थ, H. कैथ in कैथी name of the characters prevalent in some parts of Northern India.

Skr. नाविक a boatman, Pr. नाविअ, H. नैया by dropping व् as H. usually does and reducing नाविअ to नाइअ.

Skr. ज्ञातिगृह a woman's family of birth, Pr. नाइहर, H. नैहर.

19. आउ or आव.

Skr. भ्रातृजाया brother's wife, Pr. भाउजाआ, H. भौजाई, M. भावजई, S. भाजाई.

Skr. मातृष्वसृका mother's sister, Pr. माउसिआ, H. मौसी, M. मावशी, S. P. मासी.

Skr. वातूल under the influence of wind, mad, Pr. वाऊल, H. P. बौरा, M. बावळा, O. बाउळा, B. बाउडा, S. वांविरो.

Skr. श्वापद a prey, a beast of chase, Pr. सावज, H. सौजा, M. सावज.

Skr. वामन a dwarf, Apabhr. बावन, H. बौना, P. बौणा, B. बाउनिया.

Skr. पादोन three-quarters, Pr. पाओन or पाऊन, H. पौने, P. पौणिआ.

There are a few instances in Hindî such as पेरना, from Pr. पइर 'to sow', Skr. प्रकिर; पोत 'nature,' Pr. पउत्ति, Skr. प्रकृति; पतोहू 'son's wife', Pr. पुत्तवहू, Skr. पुत्रवधू; भादो 'name of a month', Pr. भद्दवअ, Skr. भाद्रपद &c., in which अइ forms ए, and अउ and अव, ओ; but it will appear that the prevailing rule in that language and in the Panjâbî is to change these vowels and semivowels into ऐ or औ. The Braj dialect of Hindî is thoroughly consistent in this respect, having ऐ and औ even in its grammatical terminations, as कौ for High H. को, करै for करे, करौं for करूं, करौ for करो, &c. The Marâṭhî agrees with these dialects perfectly only as respects अ+इ, and अ+उ; and the Bangâlî and Oriyâ, if we look to the few traces that they have retained of these Prâkṛit syllables, seem to agree with the Marâṭhî. But the Gujarâtî has throughout ए and ओ for the Hindî and Panjâbî ऐ and औ; and the Sindhî follows the Gujarâtî a great way. The Gujarâtî and Sindhî forms of the words occurring in tables 14-19, are as follows :—

	H.	G.	S.	H.	G.	S.
20.	पैठा	पेठो	पेठो	जै	जे	
	बैसना	बेसवुं		सै	से in सेंकडा	
	बैठा	बेठो		बैन	वेन	वेणु
	खैर	खेर		मौडा	मोड	मोडु
	बैल	बेल		चौथा	चोथो	चोथो [&c.,
	भैस	भेस	मेंहि	चौक	चोक	चौक, चौपैरो
	बैन (P. भैण)	बेन	भेणु भेण	चौरस	चोरस &c.	
	मैल	मेल	मेरो-मैल	धौला	धोळो	धैरो
	मैन	मेन		कौडी	कोडी	कोडी
	रैन	रेन		सौत	सोक्य	
	नैन	नेन	नेणु	सौंपना	सोंपवुं	सौंपणु
	भै	भे		पैदल	पेदल	

H.	G.
भौजाई	भोजाई
पौने	पोणा

The Gujarâtî has ए or ओ even in words of a foreign origin where the other languages have ऐ or औ ; as,

	H.	G.	H.	G.
21.	पैदा करना	पेदा करवुं	मैदान	मेदान
	दौलत	दोलत	फौज	फोज

Similarly, though a few Sanskrit words containing ऐ and औ do occur in Gujarâtî dictionaries, these diphthongs are generally pronounced like ए and ओ; as in जेन for जैन 'a follower of the Jaina sect', वेर for वैर 'enmity', &c. The Gujarâtî, therefore, like the old Prâkṛits combines अय and अव and अइ and अउ into ए and ओ, and since it did not receive the diphthongs ऐ and औ from the old Prâkṛits, its alphabet really does not contain them. As observed before, the syllables अइ and अउ differ from ऐ and औ only in two currents of breath being emitted instead of one; in other respects they are alike, both the vowel sounds being contained in the diphthongs. Those syllables as well as अय् and अव् should, therefore, naturally pass into those diphthongs as involving the least possible change. If, notwithstanding, the Gujarâtî people make ए or ओ out of them, and also give those forms to the ऐ and औ of Sanskrit and foreign words, it must be so, because their vocal organs are in this respect in the same condition as those of their Pâli and Prâkṛit ancestors. On the other hand, the Hindî, and especially the Braj form of it, presents the old Âryan tendency of pronouncing the diphthongs in a somewhat exaggerated form; while the other dialects take up a position between these two in this respect.

Of the words in which an open vowel is changed to one more close and an approach towards an assimilation to a consonant is thus effected, the vernaculars have preserved the following:—

22. Skr. पक्वम् ripe, Pr. पिक्कं or पक्कं, M. पिकें, G. पाकु, H. P. पका, S. पको, B. पाका, O. पका or पाक in पाकला.

Skr. अङ्गारः ember, Pr. इङ्गालो or अङ्गारो, M. (dial.) इंगळ, इंगळे, M. आंगारा, the rest अंगार.

Skr. ललाटम् forehead, Pr. णिडालं or णडालं, M. निढळ, S. निराड़ु.

Skr. दत्तम्, Pr. दिण्णं, H. दिन, P. दित्ता.

Skr. कन्दुकः a ball, Pr. गेन्दुओ, H. गेंदा, P. गेंद, M. गेंद.

Skr. अत्र, Pr. एत्थ, M. एथ.

In a great many more instances अ is thus changed in the vernaculars, and not only before conjuncts as is mostly the case in the Prâkṛits, but before simple consonants also.

	S.	Skr. or Pr.	M.
23.	किहाणी a tale	कथानिका—कहानिआ	कहाणी.
	मुङ्गिरो a mallet	मुद्गरः—मोग्गरो	मोगर.
	सांविरो dark	श्यामलः—सामलो	सांवळा.
	पजिरणु to be lit up	प्रज्वलन—पज्जलण	पाजळणें.
	पुखिराजु a topaz	पुष्कराज	
	विरिरणु to forget	निस्मरण—विस्सरण	विसरणें.
	विञ्णु a fan	व्यजन	विंजणा.
	खिण a moment	क्षण—खण	
	खिमा forgiveness	क्षमा—खमा	
	पघिरणु to melt	प्रगलन	पगळणें.
	पिंगुलो lame	पङ्गु with ल	पांगळा
	पिञ्जिरो a cage	पञ्जर	पिंजरा.
	पिपिरु the pîpal tree	पिप्पल	पिंपळ.

S. Skr. M.

किलाटु the forehead... ललाट.......................ललाट

विरिलो rare ....विरलः.......................विरळ

H. P. Skr. or Pr

छिन a moment..........छिन...............क्षणः—खणो...................

किवाड door ....कवाड.........कपाटम्–कवाड......M. कवाड

डिम्भ vanity ....दम्भः.................M. डंभ

गिनना to count ....गिणना.........गणनम् ....M. गणणें

.... डिम्भ or दम्भ...दर्भः दब्भो ....H. डाभ

पिघलना to melt ......पिघलना ......प्रगलनम्.............M. पगळणें

हिलना to move ....हिलना.........हलनम् ?............M. हालणें

रींधना to cook ....रिण्हना, ...रन्धनम् ....M. रांधणें

खिमा or छिमा forgive- खिमा ....क्षमा ....

ness.

पिंजरा a cage ....पिंजरा, ...पञ्जर .... G. पांजरुं

जीमना to eat ....जमनम्............. G. जमवुं

बिंगा or बांका crooked...बिंगा ....वक्र-वंक .... M. वांक

M. Skr. or Pr.

खिण (dial.) .... क्षण—खण

पिंजरा as above,

मिशी .... श्मश्रू—मसू............ M. मूछ.

B. Skr.

पिंजरा as above, O. also

काछिम tortoise .... कच्छप .... M. कासव

काहिनी a tale .... कथानिका .... M. कहाणी

The Sindhî has the largest number of instances, and this change of अ to इ constitutes a peculiarity of that language. The Hindî has got a good many, and the Panjâbî follows it in almost all cases. Marâṭhî has but a few stray instances, but sometimes, as in शिवणें 'to touch', H. छूना, Skr. छुप, but Pr. छित्र, and मिशी, इ takes the place of उ also. The Gujarâtî has पिगलवुं for प्रगलनम् and इंडुं 'an egg', for अण्डकम्, but not many more cases. Bangâlî and Oriyâ have also but few instances, and even in most of these, and in those of the Marâṭhî, as well as in the Hindî पिंजरा and जीमना, the इ may be regarded as arising from the influence of the neighbouring palatal consonant. The following are instances in which अ and in one case आ are changed to ए :—

24. H. मेंडुक or मेडुक, P. मेंडुक, G. मेंडक, M. बेडूक, Skr, मण्डूक.

H. सेंबल or सेमल, M. शेवरी or सांवरी, Skr. शाल्मली, Pr. सामरी or सिम्बली.

H. नेवना to bow, P. नेउणा, M. लवणें, Skr. नमन.

H. नेवल a mungoose, P. नेउल, Skr. नकुल, Pr. नउल.

H. जेवना to eat, P. जेउणा, M. जेवणें, G. जमवुं, Skr. जमन.
M. उजेड light, Pr. उजाल, Skr. उज्ज्वाल.
M. शेण cowdung, G. छाण, Skr. शक्ना instr. sing.
M. ठेवणें to keep, Skr. स्थापन, Pr. ठावण.

G. केहवुं to tell, सेहवुं to endure, रेहवुं to dwell, &c., before ह् followed by अ, for कथ, सह, &c.

But even here the ए of the Marâṭhî शेवरी, शेण, जेवणें, and उजेड, as of the Hindî जेवना, may be attributed to the influence of the preceding palatal.

In the Prâkṛits there are two instances of the change of अ to उ, viz., चुडं and खुडिओ for Skr. चण्ड 'fierce' and खण्डित 'plucked out'. The latter we have in the vernaculars in the from of खूट M. G., खुटि S. 'deficiency', खोट H., खोड M. 'blemish', and खुडणें or खुटणें M., खुटना H., खुंटवुं G. 'to pluck out', or खुटवुं G. 'to be deficient'. The Bangâlî, changes अ to उ in a good many cases as :—

	B.	Skr. or Pr.	M. or H.
25.	हलुद turmeric	हरिद्रा-हलद्दा	हळद M.
	आगुन fire	अग्नि-अगणी	आग M.
	बामुन Brahman	ब्राह्मण-बम्हण	बामण.
	थुअन to place	स्थापन-ठावण..................	ठेवणें M.
	शिमुल the silk-cotton tree.	शाल्मली-सामरी	सेमळ H., शेवरी or सांवरी M.
	पुकुर a pond	पुष्कर-पोक्खर	पोखर H.
	मुगुर a mallet	मुद्गर-मोग्गर	मोगरा M.

And where the Sanskrit or the sister dialects have ओ, the Bangâlî has उ as in the following words :—

26. B. चुरि theft, Skr. चोरिका, M. H. चोरी.
B. मुचि a shoemaker, M. H. मोची.
B. पुलि a cake, Skr. पोलिका or पुलिका, M. पोळी.
B. छुडी a girl, G. छोडी.
B. पुडन burning, M. पोळणें.
B. खुदन digging, H. खोदना, M. खोदणें.
B. खुजन searching, H. खोजना.

Thus उ whether for अ or ओ is a characteristic of the Bangâlî. But this characteristic is very likely connected with another which distinguishes the Bangâlî language, *viz.*, to pronounce the non-final अ in all cases as a short and broad ओ like that in the English word *pot*. I have observed before that the assimilation of vowels to consonants might be effected by narrowing the passage of the breath by an upward movement of the tongue near the palatal position, or by rounding the lips. Which of these modes is resorted to, depends on the peculiar vocal tendencies of a people. Thus then, to change अ to ए or इ is a peculiarity of the Sindhî, the Panjâbî, and the Hindî, and to short ओ and उ of the Bangâlî.

The following Prâkṛit instances of the assimilation of the different vowels of a word have come down to the vernaculars :—

27. M. G. P. वेल a creeper, H. P. बेल, Pr. वेल्ली, Skr. वल्लि, S. व लि, Pr. वल्ली.

M. ऊंस a sugarcane, H. ऊख, Pr. उच्छू, Skr. इक्षु. H. has ईख also, and P. इक्ख.

H. P. S. सेज a bed, M. G. शेज, Pr. सेज्जा, Skr. शय्या.

M. मिरीं, S. मिरी pepper, Pr. मिरिअं, Skr. मरिचम्.

M. ओपणें to give over, assign, Pr. ओप्प, Skr. अर्प.

There are a few modern instances as in:—

28. S. मेहि a buffalo, Pr. महिस.

H. इम्ली a tamarind tree, Skr. अम्लिका.

H. P. कोहू blood, Pr. लोहिअ, Skr. लोहित.

H. जुगून a glow-worm, Pr. जोइङ्गण ?, Skr. ज्योतिरिङ्गण.

H. तिरिच्छ askance, Pr. तिरच्छ, Skr. तिरश्च in तिरश्चः, तिरश्चा &c.

P. इंगुळ or इंगुळी a finger, Skr. अङ्गुलि.

Examples of the change of अ to इ or ए under the influence of a palatal consonant have been given in Table 24.

Of the words in which one of two similar vowels is made dissimilar or changed to अ in the Prâkṛits the vernaculars have preserved the following:—

29. Skr. बिभीतक, Pr., &c., as in Table 8.

Skr. शिथिलम् loose, Pr. सढिलं or सिढिलं, M. सढळ in the sense of 'loose of hand' or 'liberal', H. B. O. ढीला, S. ढिरो or ढरो, G. ढीलुं. In these the first syllable स is elided.

Skr. हरीतकी myrobalan, Pr. हरडई, M. हरडी, S. हरीड.

Skr. मुकुटः a crown, Pr. मउडो, H. मौड, G. मोड.

Skr. मुकुलः a bud, Pr. मउलो, P. मौल in मौलना to bud.

Sindhî has हिलिड़ो also for सिढिल in which the last two consonants have interchanged places, and स् is changed to ह्.

Modern instances of this change are:—

30. M. इंदीर a rat, G. इंद्र, H. B. O. इंदूर, Skr. उन्दुरु.

H. B. चूंची nipple, Skr. चूचुकम्.

H. गेहूं, घेऊं or गोहूं wheat, P. घेऊं, G. घऊं, M. गहूं or गंव, B. गम, O. गहम, Skr. गोधूम.

P. रेहू a kind of fish, for रोहू, Skr. रोहित.

G. मुगट a crown, S. मुकिटु or मूटिकु, P. मुकट, M. मुगुट, Skr. मुकुट.

H. महुरत an auspicious time, Skr. मुहूर्त.

P. G. कुटंब family, Skr. कुटुम्ब.

P. परोहत priest, Skr. पुरोहित.

H. पतोहू for पुतोहू a son's wife, Pr. पुत्तवहू, Skr. पुत्रवधू.

H. सपूत, Pr. सुपुत्त, Skr. सुपुत्र.

H. P. पुरखा an ancestor, Skr. पुरुष.

M. तुंबळ, Skr. तुमुल.

H. P. जनेऊ, from जण्णोऊअ, Pr. जण्णोवईअ ?, Skr. यज्ञोपवीत.

Here, as well as in the Prâkṛits, one of the two similar vowels is oftener changed to अ than to इ or उ.

In the Prâkṛits, you will remember, there are a few instances in which the vowels of the different syllables composing a word exchange places, or the close vowel of one is transferred to another. Of these the M. has विंचू 'scorpion', H. and P. बिच्छू, S. विछुं and B. and O. बिछा. There are a good many more modern instances :—

31. H. अकेला alone, Pr. एकल्लअ.

H. उंगली a finger, Skr. अङ्गुलि.

H. P. मौत death, from such a Pr. form as मतु, Skr. मृत्यु; the उ being transferred to the preceding syllable forms औ with अ; G. मोत.

H. हौले slowly, from Pr. हलु, Skr. लघु; and P. कौड़ा bitter, from Pr. कडुअ, Skr. कटुक.

H. M. S. बूंद, G. P. बुंद, Skr. बिन्दु, the इ transferred to the second syllable being dropped in virtue of a general law to be presently noticed in the vernaculars.

H. G. मूछ mustache, S. मुछ, P. मुच्छ, B. O. मोच, Pr. मस्सु, Skr. श्मश्रु.

H. हिरन a deer, Skr. हरिण.

H. सेंध, B. O. सिंध a hole made in a wall by a thief, Skr. संधि.

G. केड the waist, Skr. कटि.

G. पीरसवुं to distribute food, from Skr. परिवेष.

G. बनेवी sister's husband, बने for बेन sister, Pr. भइणी, and वी for वई, Skr. पति.

B. शेल a dart, from Skr. शल्य, the इ arising from the softening of य being transferred to श.

P. पुर above, Skr. उपरि.

M. ओंजळ a cavity made by joining the hands, from the word अंजुळी existing in old Marâṭhî, and अंजुली existing in H. made up on the analogy of the Skr. अङ्गुलि.

M. हिरवा green, from Skr. हरित or हरितक.

M. चोंच a beak, M. (dial.) and B. टोंच, Skr. चंचु.

Of the Prâkṛit words with a syllable lengthened or shortened through the influence of an accent of some sort, the vernaculars have preserved a few words. Thus:—

32. M. पाडवा the 1st day of the moon's increase, Pr. पाडिवो, Skr. प्रतिपद्. H. has the form with short प, पडिवा.

M. सारिखा like, Pr. सारिच्छो or सारिक्खो ?, Skr. सदृक्षः.

M. हल्या a buffalo used for ploughing, Pr. हलिओ; H. P. हाली one who ploughs, Pr. हालिओ, Skr. हालिकः.

H. गहिरा deep, Pr. गहिरो, Skr. गभीरः.

G. कुंवर, H. कुंवर or कुंअर, Pr. कुमरो, Skr. कुमार.

In modern vernacular pronunciation there is a law of accentuation which has produced important results. The penultimate syllable of a word is in all our dialects pronounced with a stress, the tendency of which is to lengthen that syllable and drop the final vowel. In most of them this tendency has worked itself out thoroughly. The preceding vowel, however, is not always written long, but still the long or at least the emphasized pronunciation does exist I have already given instances* in which while the final अ is silent or dropped, the इ or उ of the preceding syllable is lengthened, and have shown that when that syllable has अ, it also is pronounced long though not changed to आ. The final इ or उ of Sanskrit words recently imported into the languages have been dropped in virtue of this law of accentuation. Thus:—

33. M. H. G. पद्धत method, mode, Skr. पद्धति.

M. H. G. P. गत condition, Skr. गति.

M. G. विपत, H. P. बिपत misery, Skr. विपत्ति.

M. H. P. G. B. रीत manner, Skr. रीति.

M. H. G. P. B. जात species, caste, Skr. जाति.

M. H. कीर्त, H. G. P. कीरत fame, Skr. कीर्ति.

M. H. P. G. रास a heap, Skr. राशि.

M. H. P. उपाध injury, annoyance, Skr. उपाधि.

* See p. p. 138-9.

M. H. P. G. नीत morality, Skr. नीति.
H. P. कव a poet, Skr. कवि.
M. G. वस्त, H. P. बस्त a thing, Skr. वस्तु.
H. P. साध a good man, Skr. साधु.
M. G. H. P. मध honey, Skr. मधु.

Bangâli and Oriyâ authors hardly represent the proper vernacular pronunciation. Such words as the above, therefore, do not occur, but probably they do exist. In Sindhî, however, here as well as in other instances to be given, the tendency of this law of accentuation is but partially realised, and such of the above words as exist in that language preserve their Sankrit endings; as राहि or रासि, जाति, रीति &c. Not only does this law characterise the vernacular speech of the day, but it must have been in operation for centuries, since the old Prâkṛit words, which like the above have not recently been imported but have descended to the modern languages from the spoken dialects of ancient times, have also been similarly changed. Thus:—

34. M. B. भूक, H. G. B. भूख, P. भुक्ख, O. भोक hunger, Pr. बहुक्खा Skr. बभुक्षा.

M. H. P. G. जीभ, B. O. S. जिभ tongue, Pr. जिब्भा, Skr. जिह्वा.
H. P. सेज, M. G. शेज, S. सेज–सेजा a bed, Pr. सेज्जा, Skr. शय्या.

M. भीक, H. G. भीख, P. भिक्ख or भीख, B. O. भिक alms, Pr. भिक्खा. Skr. भिक्षा.

M. नीज, H. P. नींद, S. निंड sleep, Pr. निद्दा, Skr. निद्रा.

M. सोंड, H. सूंड, G. सूंढ, P. सुंड, B. O. शुंड, S. सुंढि trunk of an elephant, Pr. सोण्डा, Skr. शुण्डा.

M. G. दाढ, H. डाढ, S. डाढ a jaw, a grinder, Pr. दाढा, Skr. दंष्ट्रा.
H. P. सैन, S. सैण, G. सान a sign, Pr. सण्णा. Skr. संज्ञा.
H. S. साध, B. साद or साध, O. साध wish, longing, Pr. सद्धा, Skr. श्रद्धा,
M. G. धूळ, H. धूल, S. धूडि, B. O. धूला dust, Pr. धूलि, Skr. धूलि.

M. H. G. आग, P. आग or आगन, B. आगुन, S. आगि fire, Pr. अग्गी or अग्गिणी, Skr. अग्नि.

M. H. दीठ sight, Pr. दिट्ठि, Skr. दृष्टि.

M. बहिण or भैण, P. भैण, H. बहिन, बहन, or बैन, G. बेन, S. भेण or भेणु, B. बोन sister, Pr. भइणी, Skr. भगिनी.

M. म्हैस, H. भैंस, G. भेंस, P. मैंह or भैंस, S. मेंहि a buffalo, Pr. महिसी, Skr. महिषी.

H. P. कोख, G. कुख, M. कूस, S. कुखि a side of the abdomen, Pr. कुक्खि, Skr. कुक्षि.

H. B. रैन, G. रेन night, Pr. रयणी, Skr. रजनी.

M. सवत, H. सौत, G. सोक a fellow wife, Pr. सवत्ती, Skr. सपत्नी.

M. खाण, H. खान a mine, Pr. खाणी, Skr. खनि or खानि.

M. H. P. G. B. O. रात, S. राति night, Pr. रत्ती, Skr. रात्रि.

M. G. P. वेल, H. P. बेल, S. वलि a creeping plant, Pr. वेल्ली, Skr. वल्लि.

H. सास, P. सस्स, M. G. सासू, S. ससु mother-in-law, Pr. सस्सू, Skr. श्वश्रू.

M. G. वीज, P. बिज्ज, S. विजु lightning, Pr. विज्जु, Skr. विद्युत्.

M. ऊंस, H. ऊख or ईख, P. इक्ख, Pr. उच्छू, Skr. इक्षु.

H. G. आंख, P. अक्ख, S. अखि, B. O. आखि the eye, Pr. अक्खि, Skr. अक्षि.

M. G. B. O. हाड, H. हाड, हड्डु, or हड्डी, P. हड्ड or हड्डी, S. हडु or हडी, Pr. अट्ठी, Skr. अस्थि.

M. हत्तीण, H. G. हाथीन, Pr. हत्थिनी, Skr. हस्तिनी.

Here also the Sindhî preserves the old endings in some cases, and has dropped them in others. In this manner, the final आ, इ, ई, उ and ऊ of Sanskrit and Prâkṛit nouns have been dropped in the vernaculars or changed to a silent अ. Final ओ is similarly treated. Even in the Apabhraṁśa period this rule of accentuation must have prevailed, since the ending vowels are similarly shortened in a good many cases. You will remember that the Prâkṛit ओ of the nominative singular of masculine nouns is mostly shortened to उ in that dialect, and sometimes altogether dropped. The modern vernaculars have thus got a great many masculine nouns ending in the silent अ, such as हात or हाथ 'hand,' कान 'ear,' दांत 'tooth,' धीट 'bold,' वड 'the Bunyan tree', &c. But as before the Sindhî has in all these cases preserved the उ; as हथु, कनु, डंदु, डीठु, बडु, &c. When the final vowel is preceded by another and not by a consonant as in these words and the others given in the above lists, that other vowel being accented by our rule shows a tendency to become long, and the original unaccented final being dropped, the accented vowel becomes final. Thus:—

35. Skr. मौक्तिकम् a pearl, Pr. मोत्तिअं, M. मोतीं, G. S. P. H. मोती.

Skr. पानीयम् water, Pr. पाणिअं, M. G. पाणीं, H. पानी.

Skr. यूथिका a flowering bush, Pr. जूहिआ, M. H. G. जुही or जुई' H. जूही.

Skr. घोटिका a mare, Pr. घोडिआ, M. G. H. P. घोडी.

Skr. शाटिका a garment, Pr. साडिआ, M. G. H. साडी.

Skr. मृत्तिका earth, Pr. मत्तिआ, मट्टिआ or मिट्टिआ, M. माती, H. मट्टी as in Table 4, all ending in ई.

Skr. ताम्बूलिकः a seller of betelnut, Pr. and Ap. तम्बोलिओ-उ, M. तांबोळी, G. तंबोळी, H. तंबोली.

Skr. तैलिकः a seller of oil, Pr. and Ap. तेल्लिओ-उ, M. तेली.

Skr. हालिकः a peasant, Pr. हालिओ, Ap. हालिउ, H. हाली, S. हारी.

Skr. नापितः a barber, Pr. and Ap. न्हाविओ-उ or नाविओ-उ, M. न्हावी, H. नाई.

Skr. वृश्चिकः a scorpion, Pr. विच्छुओ, Ap. विच्छुउ, M. विंचू, H. P. बिछू, S. बिछु, B. O. बिछा.

Skr. गुदः ordure, Pr. गुओ, गुउ, M. H. G. गू.

Skr. युगम्, Pr. जुअं, M. जूं.

Skr. यूका a louse, Pr. जूआ, H. P. G. जू, M. ऊ.

Skr. वाटिका an enclosure, Pr. वाटिआ or वाडिआ, M. G. H. वाडी, B. वाटी.

Skr. वीटिका a roll of betel leaf, &c., Pr. वीडिआ, M. विडी, G. बिडी, H. बीडी.

Skr. सूचिकः a tailor, Pr. सूचिओ, Ap. सूचिउ, H. सूजी.

Skr. मक्षिका a fly, Pr. मच्छिआ or मक्खिआ, M. माशी, G. H. माखी, माछी.

Skr. जीवः life, Pr. जीओ, Ap. जीउ, H. जी.

Skr. लोहितम् blood, Pr. लोहिअं, G. लोही, H. P. लोहू.

Skr. जलौका a leech, Pr. जलोआ, M. जळू, H. जलू, G. जळो.

Skr. वालुका sand, Pr. वालुआ, M. G. वाळू, H. बालू.

Skr. पितृकः, मातृका, and भ्रातृकः as in Tables 3 and 4.

Thus then the Sanskrit and Prâkrit penultimate vowels become final in the vernaculars, and being originally accented in consequence of the law we have been considering, retain that accent in most cases, and are thus lengthened. When the penultimate happens to be अ it is lengthened to आ as in the following:—

36. Skr. घोटकः a horse, Pr. घोडओ, Ap. घोडउ, M. H. P. B. O. घोडा.

Skr. पारदः mercury, Pr. पारओ, Ap. पारउ, M. H. P. B. O. पारा.

Skr. आमलकः a kind of myrobalan, Pr. आमलओ, Ap. आवेलउ, M. आंवळा, H. P. आवला or आमला.

Skr. आम्रातकः hog-plum, Pr. अम्माडओ ?, Ap. अम्बाडउ, M. आंबाडा, H. अंबाडा.

Skr. बिभीतकः beleric myrobalan, Pr. बहेडओ, Ap. बहेडउ, M. बेहडा, H. P. बहेडा.

Skr. पुस्तकम् a volume, Pr. पोत्थओ, Ap. पोत्थउ, H. P. पोथा.

Skr. कण्टकः a thorn, Pr. कण्टओ, Ap. कण्टउ, M. H. B. कांटा.

Skr. गोलकः a ball, Pr. गोलआ, Ap. गोलउ, M. P. गोळा, H. B. गोला.

Skr. श्यालकः brother-in-law, Pr. सालओ, Ap. सालउ, M. P. साळा, H. साला.

Skr. दीपकः a lamp, Pr. दीवओ, Ap. दीवउ, M. दिवा, P. दीवा, H. दिया, B. दीया.

Skr. मञ्चकः a bedstead, Pr. मञ्चओ, Ap. मञ्चउ, M. मांचा.

Skr. मस्तकम् head, Pr. मत्थअं, M. (Goan., Mâl., and Chit.) माथां; Pr. मत्थओ, Ap. मत्थउ, by a change of gender, M. H. B. माथा, P. मत्था.

Skr. कटकम् a wristlet, Pr. कडअं, M. (Goan., Mâl. and Chit.) कडां.

Skr. कीटकः a worm, Pr. कीडओ, Ap. कीडउ, M. किडा, H. P. कीडा, B. कीडा, and the other words given in Table 6.

It may be urged that in modern pronunciation when the penultimate अ is accented, it does not become आ even though pronounced long, as observed before.* How is it then that it becomes आ here? In modern times several new modes of pronunciation have arisen, but as regards the matter in hand, to lengthen अ into आ was the old process. And often when the old processes have disappeared from what is considered the standard form of a language, they are found preserved in some dialect of that language. Thus, while in the standard Marâṭhî the penultimate अ is simply pronounced long, it becomes आ in the Goanese and Mâlvaṇî dialects.

Thus—

	St. M.		Mâl. Goan.
37.	पातळ	a garment, or thin.	पाताळ.
	कापड	cloth.	कापाड.
	वतन	hereditary property,	वतान.
	जतन	careful preservation.	जतान.
	धोतर	garment.	धोतार.
	खडप	a rock.	खडाप.

In this manner then the penultimate अ in consequence of the accent became आ, and the final उ and the अ of the final अं being dropped, itself became final, and has preserved its accent.

An unaccented अ, आ, or उ is, you will have observed from the above instances, dropped after a close or dissimilar vowel. For, if preserved, its effect would be to change the preceding close vowel to the corresponding semivowel. But being accented that vowel resists the

* Supra, p. 139.

influence and in its turn overpowers the unaccented, and consequently weak, vowel. But when it is possible to combine both into one sound the final is sometimes not dropped. Thus the अ and उ in the above examples are combined into ओ in the Gujarâtî, the Sindhî, and the Goanese, Mâlvaṇî, and Chitpávni dialects of the Marâṭhî, and the Mârvârî, Mevârî, Kumaonî, and Garhavâlî dialects of the Hindî; and we have घोडो, पारो, आंवळो or आंवलो, आंबाडो, वेहडो, कांटो, गोळो, साळो, दिवो, मांचो, and किडो. When अ follows another अ, the former, you will remember, is generally changed to a light य in the Prâkṛits. Those dialects tolerated a hiatus when one or both of the vowels were close. But अ or आ followed by अ or आ require two complete openings of the mouth which could not be borne, and hence a close sound य् was interposed. Thus मत्थअं and कडअं, in the above, became मत्थयं and कडयं, and the य being almost as light as the vowel इ and being unaccented, is dropped in the Mâlvaṇî and the other dialects; but in the standard Maràṭhî, as formerly observed, the अ and यं are combined into एं, and so we have माथें and कडें. In the Apabhraṁśa, you will remember, the masculine termination उ is transferred by analogy to neuter nouns, and Hemachandra tells us that neuter nouns having a क at the end do not drop their nasal termination. Thus, we have मत्थउं and कडउं from which by combination we have the Gujarâtî माथूं and कडूं. Here the nasal sound gives a sort of fixity to the vowel, and hence it does not pass into ओ as in the case of masculine nouns, but absorbs the preceding अ. The ओ, एं, and ऊं thus formed are accented like the आ of the masculine nouns in the Marâṭhî and others, since they contain the accented penultimate.

Similarly, final unaccented इ is not dropped after अ or आ, but is slurred over and the least possible time is allowed to it, in consequence of which it sounds like the consonant य्, and thus forms a sort of diphthong with the preceding अ or आ.

38. M. वइ or वय् a hedge, Pr. वइ, Skr. वृति.

M. सइ or सय् remembrance, Pr. सई, Skr. स्मृति.

M. (Mâl. and Chit.) नइ or , H. नइ, S. नइ, Pr. नइ, Skr. नदी.

M. शेणवइ or य name of a caste, Pr. सेणावइ, Skr. सेनापति.

H. बहनोइ sister's husband, Pr. भइणिवइ, Skr. भगिनीपति.

Sometimes the final vowel इ absorbs the preceding अ, as in G. बेनवी for बहनोइ, M. शेणवी, and M. दळवी for Pr. दलवइ, Skr. दलपति.

You will have seen that the Sanskrit nouns, composed of three or more syllables given in Table 36 with अ for their penultimate vowel and क or any other similar syllable ending in अ for the final, have dropped one syllable and become nouns ending in आ in Marâṭhî, Hindî, Panjâbî, and Bangâlî, and in Oriyâ also in some cases, and in ओ in Gujarâtî, Sindhî, and the dialects of the Marâṭhî and Hindî spoken of above. Such of them as are neuter have acquired the ending एं or आं in Marâṭhî and ऊं in Gujarâtî. But these are not the only nouns with a final आ and ओ and एं, आं and ऊं in these languages. There are a good many more, both substantives and adjectives, which have these endings. In the Brajbhâshâ also a great many adjectives, nominal and verbal, end in ओ or औ. The Sanskrit words from which they are derived are not composed of three syllables, with क or another syllable like it preceded by an अ, as the final. Thus the substantives H. M. चेला 'a disciple,' पुडा 'a parcel,' काढा 'a decoction,' adjectives, H. नीला, M. निळा 'blue,' H. पीला, M. पिवळा 'yellow,' and past participles, H. गया 'gone,' मुवा 'dead,' M. गेला, मेला, &c., and the corresponding Gujarâtî, चेलो, पुडो, काढो, नीळो, पीळो, गयो and मुवो are derived from the Sanskrit चेटः, पुटः, क्राथः, नीलः, पीतलः, &c. Similarly such neuter nouns as M. केळें (dial. केळां), G. केळुं, M. सोनें (dial. सोनां), G. सोनुं, are derived from the Skr. कदलम् and सुवर्णम्. How then did they get their आ and ओ and आं, एं and ऊं? A great many nouns in our languages end in अ, which has now become silent; and these, as I have explained, are derived from the Sanskrit nouns ending in अ, the nominative termination ओ being, because it was unaccented, at first reduced to उ, and afterwards dropped in most of them, but preserved in Sindhî. By that same law of accentuation which brought about the elision of this ओ, we have seen, that nouns ending in क or such other syllable preceded by अ come to have आ-ओ and एं-आं-ऊं for their final. By an obvious inference, therefore, those other substantives and adjectives also must have got कः or कम् in the Prâkṛits and the Apabhraṁśa in the forms of ओ or अं and उ or उं, though in Sanskrit they do not possess them. The suffix क, though actually found in certain words only in Sanskrit, must have been largely used in the spoken language of ancient times, since Pâṇini and his expositors allow of its being appended to all nouns and even verbs and participles, to indicate littleness,* contempt,† tenderness, ‡ the state of being unknown, § resemblance or copy, || and a species $ founded on

* Pâṇ. v. 3, 85-86; v. 4, 4.

† Pâṇ. v. 3, 74-75.

‡ Pâṇ. v. 3, 76-77. § Pâṇ. v. 3, 73.

|| Pâṇ. v. 3, 96-97. $ Pâṇ. v. 3, 75, 87, 97.

some of these particularities. Words formed by the addition of such a suffix in such senses cannot, of course, be much used in literary works. They are adapted for colloquial purposes, such as our Marâṭhî राम्या for Râma and गोंद्या for Govinda are. Accordingly in the Prâkṛits and Apabhraṁśa, which were derived from the spoken languages, we find the practice of adding the suffix to be very common. Thus in the fourth act of the Vikramorvaśî we have लिद्दअं for लिद्दकं formed from the analogy of स्निग्धकम् but properly लीढकम्, सिणिद्धअं for स्निग्धकम्, जुअलअं for युगलकम्, जुआणओ for युवकः, आणत्तओ for आज्ञप्तकः, परिमंथरओ for परिमन्थरकः, काननए for काननके, कुसुमुज्जलए for कुसुमोज्ज्वलके, लालसओ for लालसकः, परवारणओ for परवारणकः, लीणओ for लीनकः, गइन्दओ for गजेन्द्रकः and many others. So also in Hemachandra's quotations from Apabhraṁśa works, we have घडिअउ for घटितकः, विप्पिअयारउ for विप्रियकारकः, उड्डावन्तिअए for उड्डावयन्तिकया, दिट्ठउ for दृष्टकः, वल्लहउं for वल्लभकम्, मुअउ for मृतकः, &c.

Now the question is, why is it that certain nouns only which have आ and ओ or अां, एं and उं in our vernaculars had क appended to them in the Prâkṛits and not others? The suffix was used only where some additional sense was intended to be expressed. Hence there were some words to which it was not appended at all, and of those to which it was two forms existed, of which the one augmented had an augmented sense. And in our modern dialects a good many words have these two forms, and of these that with आ conveys an additional sense, such as is attributed to क by the Sanskrit grammarians. Thus दांत in Marâṭhî expresses a 'tooth,' but दांता *a copy of the animal tooth* that is, 'the tooth' of such an instrument as a saw; मेळ signifies 'union,' 'agreement,' but मेळा expresses *a certain union*, viz. a concourse of people in a fair or on some festive occasion; कोंपर signifies 'the elbow,' but कोंपरा *any corner*, resembling that made by the elbow; दोर means 'a string,' generally, but दोरा a *particular string*, that is, 'thread,' used for sewing; पाट denotes generally 'a strip,' and thence *the piece of wood* used for sitting on, but पाटा *a slab of stone* used for pounding spices; फांस signifies 'a noose,' generally, but फांसा *a snare* for birds or beasts, and also '*a catch*,' for fastening anything. In the Hindî, Panjâbî and Gujarâtî बांस or वांस means a *bambu*, as does बांसु in Sindhi; but in Marâṭhi वांसा means 'a bambu used as a *rafter*' and thence a rafter generally, &c. In Marâṭhî and Hindî गाभ signifies 'fœtus' or 'womb,' but गाभा the *internal spadix or fruit-receptacle* of the plantain-tree *or the core* or *heart* of anything. The Panjâbî गब्भ and गब्भा also mean 'the womb' and the *heart* or *core* of anything respectively. Thus then क was appended to a word in the Prâkṛits to denote some additional sense; and both the augmented and unaugmented forms of it were in use; and these in some cases have descended to the vernaculars. But in the course of time, in consequence of the frequent use of the augmented forms, the things expressed by the unaugmented words came to be thought of with the additional property to denote which the क was in the first instance affixed. Hence the forms without क went out of use, and gradually those with it lost the additional sense. It was not possible to preserve this sense except by a comparison with the signification of the unaugmented forms. But as these disappeared, the comparison was impossible. And in some cases the additional sense was so slight, that in the course of time it gradually dropped away, though the two forms of the word did exist. Thus we have in Marâṭhî चूर or चुरा 'fragments,' घेर or घेरा 'circumference,' खांद or खांदा 'the shoulder,' जोड or जोडा 'a pair,' भूस or भुसा 'chaff,' and others; but there is no perceptible difference in the sense of the two forms, though in the last three cases usage has restricted one of them to one state of things and the other to another. So also one of our dialects has the augmented form, and another the original, the sense being the same. Thus:—

39. B. बड, H. P. बडा large or great.

M. खेळ, H. P. खेल, B. खेला a play.

H. दहिना, B. डाइन, O. डाहाण right hand.

M. खांब, M. (dial.) खांबो, G. खंभ, H. P. खंभ or खंभा, B. खंबा, O. खंब a pillar.

B. आम, H. आम or आम्ब, P. अंब, M. आंबा, G. आंबो the mango tree.

P. मच्छ, H. B. माछ, M. मासा a fish.

B. भाल, H. P. M. भला good.

It thus appears that originally the suffix क was not necessarily applied to any nouns, but optionally to such as admitted of the additional signification. This additional signification has been preserved in some cases, but lost in others.

You will now have seen that the Sanskrit and Prâkṛit final vowels having, for the most part, been dropped by the influence of the accent, the final आ, आं, ई, ईं, ऊ, ऊं, एं, and ओ that we have now got were originally penultimates or have arisen from a combination of the penultimate and final. The accent which originally fell on the penultimate falls now in consequence of this change on these new finals. Thus, these two accents, that on the penultimate when a word ends in the silent अ, and that on the new final, are now to be met with in the vernaculars. The first may be called the original accent, and the second derivative. The Marâṭhî is of all our dialects the most sensitive to them, and shortens all the other vowels of the word in order to throw the whole force of utterance on the accented syllable. The Sanskrit सूतक 'mourning', नूतन 'new', पीतल 'brass,' and the Sanskrit and Prâkṛit जीवन्त (from जीवन्तः or जीवन्तो) are pronounced as सुतक्, नुतन्, पितळ्, जिवन्त्, &c., with the penultimate अ long and the first vowel short. In this way, in a word composed of three syllables with the final अ silent, the first syllable must be short in Marâṭhî. When a word is composed of more than three syllables, the अ of the antepenultimate is elided, as in अडचण, शहाणपण, pronounced as अड्चण् शहाण्पण्, &c.

Similarly, when a word ends in the accented आ and the other vowels, the preceding vowels are shortened as in the following :—

40. किडा, Skr. कीटकः, Pr. कीडओ, and the others in Table 6. Also चुरा and भुसा which without the आ are चूर and भूस (see p. 160), विडी, जुई and such others occurring in Table 35.

पिढी a step in the scale of descent, a generation, Skr. पीठिका.
जुवा gambling by means of dice, Skr. द्यूतकः (by change of gender).
निळा-ळें-ळी blue, Skr. नीलकः-कं-लिका.
पिवळा-ळें-ळी yellow, Skr. पीतलकः-कं-लिका.

When together with the accented final a word is composed of three or more syllables, or, more generally, when the accented syllable is preceded by two others or more, the अ of that which immediately precedes is silent or elided, as in the case of अड्चण above, and any other vowel in its place is shortened and sometimes dropped. The other vowels are also pronounced short. Thus :—

41. शीक *imper.* 2*nd per. sing.* the original form of the root.	शिकणें *inf.* to learn,	pronounced as शिक्णें.
पूस........................	पुसणें *inf.* 'to ask' ...	पुस्णें.
रूस	रुसतो *pres. part.* 'he is angry'	रुस्तो.
शीव........................	शिवला *past part.* 'touched'	शिव्ला.

शीव has similarly शिव्णें 'to sew' *inf.*, शिव्तो 'he sews,' शिव्ला 'sewn.'

कर 'do,' *pres. part.* unaugmented करीत, augmented करितो or करतो pronounced as कर्तो.

So also अङ्गुष्ठकः is आंगूठा, and मधुरकः, सामुरा the penultimate उ being dropped.

When the final is unaccented, it is the penultimate that is emphasized, but when it is accented, the penultimate is slurred over. Thus the accentuation of the penultimate leads to the elision of the final vowel, and the accentuation of the final brings about an elision or shortening of the penultimate.

In Hindî also the accent leads to the elision of the अ of the previous syllable when more than one precede the accented syllable. Thus उबटन 'a cosmetic' is pronounced as उब्टॅन्, मूरखपन as मूरख्पॅन, उबटना *inf.* 'to rub the body with a cosmetic,' as उबट्ना, करना as कर्ना. The Braj present participle करत is pronounced as करॅत् since one syllable only precedes the accented penultimate; but the Hindî करता is कर्ता as two syllables precede the accented ता. The accent leads to the shortening of the preceding vowels in some cases. Thus गोपाल 'a cowherd,' and पाताल 'the lower regions,' are sometimes pronounced and written as गुपाल and पताल; so does आशिष् become असीस. In such words as उपज 'produce,' उसास 'respiration,' and उबटन 'a cosmetic,' from the Pr. उप्पज्ज, उस्सास, and उब्बट्टण, Skr. उत्पद्य, उच्छ्वास, and उद्वर्तन, it prevents the lengthening of the initial उ, as by the general rule it should be long, since one member of the following double consonant is dropped. The derived accent also shortens the preceding vowels in such instances as the following :—

42. H. दहिना southern, Pr. दाहिणओ, Skr. दक्षिणकः.

H. दिया a lamp, Pr. दीवओ, Skr. दीपकः.

H. जुआ gambling, Pr. जूअओ, Skr. द्यूतकः (by a change of gender).

H. अगला foremost, the first part of which is आग, from Pr. अग्ग, Skr. अग्र.

H. अपना one's own............................आप from Pr. अप्प, Skr. आत्म.

H. इकट्ठा together....................................एक.

H. फिरा walked, पिया drunk, सिया sewn, छुआ touched, past participles of फीरना, पीना, सीना, छूना, &c.

In the same way it prevents the lengthening of a preceding vowel in such cases as उपजना 'to be produced,' उठना 'to rise,' उड़ना 'to fly,' the last two being derived from the Prâkṛit उत्थाण and उड्डयन.

But in a great many cases the accent does not affect the preceding close vowels. The Sanskrit words सूतक, पीतल, &c., the first syllable of which is shortened in Marâṭhi, retain it long in the Hindî. The words उपज, उपजना, उसास, and others have their initial vowel optionally lengthened, and in a few cases, such as ऊपर and ऊखल, it is lengthened without any apparent reason. Similarly, the Hindî forms of कीटक and the other words in Table 6 retain the long vowel. It has also बीड़ी, जूही, and सूजी as in Table 35, and नीला 'blue,' पीला 'yellow,' सीखा, 'learnt,' भीगा 'wet,' मीठा 'sweet,' पूछा 'asked,' मूआ 'dead,' सीखना 'to learn,' पूछना 'to ask,' दूसरा, &c., while in all these cases the Marâṭhi has short इ and उ. Perhaps this weakening of the accent as regards previous ई and ऊ is due to the development of another accent in Hindi on the initial syllable. To such an accent as this might be attributed the almost universal change of अय and अव to ऐ and औ that we have already noticed. The अ of the initial syllable, being accented, draws to itself the य or व of the following and deprives it of its अ, in which cases the य or व becomes इ or उ, and then the two form ऐ and औ.

The Gujarâtî follows the Hindî completely, sometimes shortening the preceding vowels as in कुवो, सुवो, and कुमळो 'delicate,' 'tender,' and dropping it as in सस्रो 'father-in-law' (Skr. श्वशुरकः), and आंगळी 'finger' (Skr. अङ्गुलिका), sometimes preventing their being lengthened, as in उपज, उठवुं, &c., and very often preserving them long, as in पूरो 'full,' शीकवुं, शीक्यो, &c. The Panjâbî also keeps the short vowel in such cases as उचार 'utterance,' उजाला 'light,' though a member of a double is dropped, and preserves the long in such cases as दीया or दीवा, जूआ, कीड़ा, पूरा, पूरी 'a cake,' &c. It has even fewer instances of shortening than the Hindî. The Sindhî has जुआ 'gambling,' डिओ 'a lamp,' पितल &c., but has such words as सतकु 'mourning,' कीडो 'a worm,' बीडो 'a roll of betel leaves,' Skr. वीटकः, पीतो 'drunk,' &c. In a great many words such as सुको 'dried,' सुधो 'heard,' छुतो 'touched,' दुधो 'milked,' the vowel of the preceding syllable is short; but that is due not to the accent on the last syllable but to the peculiarity of the Sindhî not to lengthen the preceding vowel even when a member of a double is dropped.

The Bangâlî is more like the Marâṭhî in this respect than like the Hindî. Thus we have भितर, H. भीतर 'in the interior;' शुका dry, H. सूखा; भिजा or भिगा 'wet,' H. भीजा or भीगा; किडा 'a worm,' H. कीड़ा; जुता 'shoes,' H. जूता; खिला 'a nail,' H. कीला; उपजन 'to be produced,' &c. It thus shortens इ and उ in the unaccented syllables like the Marâṭhî. The Oriyâ follows the Bangâlî, having जुडा, Skr. जूटक 'a knot of hair,' जुता 'shoes,' भिजा 'wet,' भितर 'in the interior,' &c.

All these languages, however, treat the unaccented अ in words of three or more syllables as the Marâṭhî and Hindî do.

In Marâṭhî the termination of the oblique form of cases and that of the plural of neuter nouns in ए are also accented. The reason why they bear the accent will be considered hereafter. The accent on the causal termination, in consequence of which the preceding vowels are shortened in the Hindî and the Gujarâtî, has already been mentioned. This also seems to be the same accent that we have been considering. Thus in G. शिवडाव 'make him sew,' or धोवडाव 'make him wash,' the आ being penultimate bears the accent and the final अ is dropped. Similarly in धोवडावडुं by the general rule, the final vowel being accented the penultimate अ is silent. It is because it is so, and the वडुं forms the conjunct व्डुं that the आ looks as if emphasized just as the first अ of अड्चन and कड्ता is. In the Marâṭhî and other dialects also there is this accent in the case of the causal, and the preceding ई and ऊ are shortened; as in निजव् 'make him sleep,' निजव्णें 'to make one sleep,' from the original नीज 'sleep,' in करीव् 'cause him to do,' करिव्णें or करव्णें 'to cause one to do,' &c. In the standard Hindî the व is dropped but still the way of pronunciation remains the same as it was when it existed. In दिखाना 'to show,' for instance, the खा is pronounced as it would have been if the word had been दिखावना. And the forms with व exist in the Braj.

Compounds in the vernaculars, most of which belong to the Tatpurusha, Karmadhâraya, or Dvandva class have an accent on the penultimate or final of the last word, as in the H. पन्साल 'a place where water is provided for passengers,' in which the first word पानी becomes पन्, अम्राई 'a forest of Mango-trees' in which the आ of आम is shortened, घुड्साल 'a stable,' in which we have घुड् for घोडा, रन्वास 'harem' the रन् of which is a shortened form of रानी, and in the G. अधमुई 'half dead,' and the M. अधमण 'half a maund.' In the Marâṭhî आम्राई, रान्माणूस, काळमांजेर, the आ of the first syllable is short though not changed to अ; and in तिर्कांबटें 'an arrow and a bow,' the first word is तीर with the ई shortened.

An unaccented initial vowel is dropped in the following instances:—

43. Skr. उपविश sit, Pr. उवइस, M. H. B. O. बैस, G. बेस, S. विह.

Skr. उपविष्टकः sat, Pr. उवइट्ठओ, H. P. बैठा, G. बेठो, S. वीठो.

Skr. अभ्यन्तर inside, H. भीतर, B. M. (dial.) भितर.

Skr. अरघट्ट a water-wheel, Pr. अरहट्ट ?, H. रहट, M. रहाट.

Skr. अभ्यञ्जनकम् to soak, M. भिजणें, H. भीजना, G. भिजवुं, B. भिजिवा.

Skr. एकस्थकम् in one place, Pr. एकट्ठअं, H. P. कट्ठा, or इकट्ठा.

Skr. उपरि above, Pr. उवरि, M. वर.

Skr. उत्सृष्टकः left, Pr. उच्छुट्ठओ, H. जूठा 'what is left after eating.'

Skr. उपाध्याय a preceptor, M. पाध्या, P. पाधे.

Skr. उदूढकः, Pr. उदूढओ a bridegroom, H. P. दूल्हा.

Of the two instances of this change in the Prâkṛits लाबू 'a pumpkin' exists in Hindî, and रण्ण in the form of रान in M. and P. and of रन in H. Medial ऐ is dropped in Marâṭhî, Bangâlî, and Oriyâ in the word बैस, and the others enumerated before. It is dropped in the G. माशी for H. मौसी (see p. 134). This elision does not appear to be due to accent since according to our theory it must fall on the ऐ in some at least of the cases. The change is due to the process of softening, since what takes place here is the simple dropping away of the close element of the diphthong.

We will now briefly notice the manner in which the hiatus caused by two vowels coming together in consequence of the elision of uninitial consonats in the Prâkṛits is avoided. We have seen that अ and इ and अ and उ are combined into ऐ and औ in some of the dialects, and into ए and ओ in others.* Final unaccented अ and आ are dropped when preceded by इ or उ as in the words given in list No. 35, and unaccented उ preceded by अ is dropped in some of the vernaculars, as in list No. 36, and combined into ओ or ऊ in others.† Final इ is preserved or changed to य् after अ in some cases, and combined with it to form ई in others.‡ Final accented आ and उ or ऊ are preserved and a hiatus is tolerated; as in H. P. जुआ or जूआ for द्यूतक and S. P. पिउ, माउ, and the M. भाऊ for पितृक, मातृका, भ्रातृक, &c. Sometimes य् or व् is inserted in such cases after इ and उ, as in H. दिया for दिआ 'a lamp,' and M. जुवा, H. जूवा for द्यूतक. The syllable अय formed in the Prâkṛits by interposing a य् betwen अ and अ is changed to ऐ in modern Hindî as in the words in list No. 16 and to ए in the Gujarâtî and tho Sindhî. This latter was the older process; and hence even in the Prâkṛits we have केल for कयल, Skr. कदल, and तेरह, तेवीसा, तेत्तीसा for त्रयोदश, त्रयोविंशति, त्रयस्त्रिंशत्, &c. And in Hindî also we have ए in बेर 'a plum' from बयर for Skr. बदर, which must have existed in the Prâkṛits, though the form given by the Grammarians is बोर for बवर. Though the Marâṭhî does not, like the Hindî or Gujarâtî, now change अय to ऐ or ए, still as formerly observed, when in a state of

* Pp. 142-7. † See 157. ‡ P. 157.

formation, it did form ए out of it, as in the instances there given, and in the neuter singular temination एं.* The termination नेर occurring at the end of the names of Gujarâtî and Marâṭhî towns such as चांपानेर, बडनेर, संगमनेर, पिंपळनेर, &c., is derived from Pr. नयर for Skr. नगर 'town.' The syllables अया arising from अ and आ are also sometimes changed to ए, as in H. अंधेर or अंधेरा, M. अंधेर, Pr. अन्धयार, Skr. अन्धकार. After आ the य is sometimes changed to ऐ and ए in the Hindî and Gujarâtî as in the instances in Nos. 18 and 20, and also in the Marâṭhî in the instance शेळी from Pr. छाअलिआ, Skr. छागलिका; but often आय and अया remain unchanged as in:

44. H. G. कायर timid, Pr. कायर, Skr. कातर.
H. G. M. घाय a wound or blow, Pr. घाअ or घाय, Skr. घात.
H. वाय wind, Pr. वाअ or वाय, Skr. वात.
M. पाय the foot, Pr. पाअ or पाय, Skr. पाद.
M. H. G. राय a king, Pr. राआ or राया, Skr. राजा.
H. गया gone, G. गयो, Pr. गअओ or गयओ, Skr. गतकः.
G. शियाळो the cold season, S. शियारो, Pr. शीअआ(या)लओ, Skr. शीतकालकः.
H. बरात, M. वरात a bridal procession, Skr. वरयात्रा.

Sometimes the interposed य् is so light that it is dropped and the vowels अ and आ or आ and अ and in rare cases अ and अ combine and form आ as in:

45. B. पा, and B. G. घा for पाय and घाय in the above.
M. आ of आला, Pr. आअअ, Skr. आगत.
M. कुंभार a potter, Pr. कुम्भआर, Skr. कुम्भकार, and generally the termination कार as in सुवर्णकार 'a goldsmith' and others; also M. अंधार for अंधकार.
M. आर a Boa constrictor, Pr. अअअर, Skr. अजगर.
G. वानुं a promise, Pr. वअणअं, Skr. वचनकम्.

In some cases व् is inserted instead of य् to prevent the hiatus, as in M. राव for राअ 'a king'; H. पाव for पाअ 'the foot;' M. साव in सावली for छाअ in छाया; कावरा for Pr. काअरअ, Skr. कातरक; काव in कावळा for Pr. काअ from Skr. काक; and a few others. In the principal Prâkṛit also we find पीवलअं for Skr. पीतलकम् 'yellow,' from which we have the Marâṭhî पिवळें, and बोर mentioned above.

A medial अ is dropped after इ, ए, or उ short or long, as in M. दीर for Pr. दिअर 'husband's brother'; G. पीळुं, H. पीला 'yellow' for Pr. पीअलअं,

* P, 144.

Skr. पीतलकम्; M. शिळें 'stale', H. सीला 'damp,' 'cool,' Pr. सीअलअं, Skr. शीतलकम्; M. वेण 'a throe,' Pr. वेअणा, Skr. वेदना; M. जूळ or जुळें 'twins,' Pr. जुअलं or जुअलअं, Skr. युगलम् or युगलकम्. Sometimes with the previous इ, it forms ए; that is a vowel partaking of the character of both is substituted for them; as in the S. नेड़ु 'a fetter,' Pr. निअडो, Skr. निगड:; H. P. नेड़े or नेरे 'near,' Pr. निअडे, Skr. निकटे; M. शेंडी 'the tuft of hair on the head,' Pr. सिहण्डिआ, Skr. शिखण्डिका, the इ being softened to अ; H. बेना 'a fan,' Pr. विअणअ, Skr. व्यजनक. नेड़े has the form नीड़े also in which case अ is simply dropped and the vowel rendered long as in the M. दीर. The long आ is preserved and changes the preceding इ to इय or य as in the H. सियार or स्यार 'jackal,' for Pr. सिआल, Skr. सृगाल; याह 'marriage,' for Pr. विआह, Skr. विवाह, &c.

We will now proceed to the consideration of consonantal changes; and first of those due to the process of softening. The semivowel य् is often softened to इ. In the Prâkṛits व्यजन 'a fan' becomes विअण which is preserved in the H. बेना, and स्त्यान is changed to थीण. This word does not occur in the vernaculars, but the Hindî and Marâṭhî have got थिजना, and थिजणें 'to congeal' from the verb स्त्यायते, in which या is softened to इ. From व्यजन or rather such a word as व्यंजन we have by a similar softening M. विंजणा, H. बिंजना, G. विजणो, S. विञ्णु. More modern instnces are :

46. H. P. सलाई, P. सळाई, Pr. सलाया, M. सळई a pencil, probe, Skr. शलाका.

B. शेल a dart, Skr. शल्य; the य being changed to इ is transferred to the preceding syllable.

H. P. जनेत a bridal procession, Skr. जन्ययात्रा.

H. छाईं shadow, P. छाइया, Skr. छाया.

H. P. बितीत passed, Skr. व्यतीत.

H. P. बिथा pain, Skr. व्यथा; बिवहार business, performance, Skr. व्यवहार.

H. P. कलिआण welfare, Skr. कल्याण, बिदिआ learning, Skr. विद्या.

P. पतीज faith, belief, Skr. प्रत्यय.

H. पतिछ visible, Skr. प्रत्यक्ष.

The Panjâbî always dissolves a Sanskrit य contained in a conjunct into इ+अ, or sometimes into इ simply, while the Hindî often resorts to the latter change. The other languages do not seem to possess many instances of this process. The change of अय or अया to ए fromerly noticed is also due to this softening process.

In the Prâkṛits व् is dissolved into उ in झुणी for Skr. ध्वनि, सुवइ for स्वपिति, दु for द्वि, तुवर for त्वर, &c. In Hindi we have झुन in the sense of 'a slight resemblance,' a remote *sound* of the property possessed by another. But another derivative from the word exists in the form of धुन or धून in that language, and of धून or धुनक in Marâṭhi. From सुव H. has सो 'to sleep,' P. सौ, G. सुव, and B. and O. शु or शुइ. दु occurs in the forms of दो or दु when the word stands alone or is compounded, as in H. दूना, B. दुना, M. दुणा, &c., for Pr. दुउण, Skr. द्विगुण 'two-fold;' and तुवर by a further dissolution becomes the P. तुरना 'to go,' H. P. तुरंत, G. तरत 'instantly, *pr. part.*, M. तूर्ते 'at present'.

More modern instances are:—

47. H. P. परोस to serve food, Skr. परिवेष.

H. P. M. पडोसी a neighbour, Skr. प्रतिवेशी.

H. अंगोछा a towel, Skr. अङ्गवस्त्र.

H. पतोहू son's wife, Pr. पुत्तवहू, Skr. पुत्रवधू.

H. P. जनेऊ, Pr. जण्णोवीअ, Skr. यज्ञोपवीत.

The व and वं to which प and म are softened are similarly changed to उ or ओ.

H. P. बहनोई sister's husband, Pr. बहिनीवई, Skr. भगिनीपति.

H. P. भादो name of a month, Pr. भद्दवअ, Skr. भाद्रपद.

H. P. G. खो·[ना-णा-वुं] to lose, Pr. खव, Skr. क्षप.

H. P. B. छू to touch, Pr. छिव, or छुव, Skr. छुप.

H. अनोखा unexpected, Pr. अणवेक्ख-[अ], Skr. अनपेक्ष-[क].

H. नोता, P. नेउंदा, G. नोतरुं, invitation, Ap. निवंत-[उ] or निवंत्र-[उ], Skr. निमन्त्र-[कः]. H. has नेवता also.

H. पुन्यों the full-moon day, Ap. पुण्णिवां, Skr. पूर्णिमा.

H. सोंह (of सोंहीं) face to face, Ap. संवुंह, Skr. संमुख.

M. सोंप to entrust, Ap. सवंप्प, Skr. समर्प.

It will be seen that the ओ or उ to which व् is softened often prevails over the preceding and following vowels, as in the words परोस and पडोशी. The change of अव to औ fromerly noticed I consider as due to the elision of the final अ of व consequent upon an accent on the first syllable, though afterwards there is a softening of the व् to उ. But in the above instances the change of व् to ओ or उ is due to a weak pronunciation or softening alone. The diphthong औ requires, as I have several times observed, a passage from one vocal position immediately to another which involves energetic utterance. The Pâli, Prâkṛit, Gujarâtî, and Sindhî substitute for it, viz., ओ is due to assimilation. The Hindî औ and the corresponding Gujarâtî ओ, therefore, are not due to a weakening of the व्; but the ओ in the above instances is, since it is not a substitute for औ and consequently does not arise from an assimilation of the two sounds, involved in that diphthong.

The following are still more modern instances:—

48. H. P. परमेसुर God, Skr. परमेश्वर.

M. H. P. सुर or सूर a musical note, Skr. स्वर.

H. P. सुभाउ nature, Skr. स्वभाव.

P. सुआमी master, Skr. स्वामी.

In this manner the Panjâbîs always pronounce the व् of Sanskrit words and to a smaller extent the Hindî people. The Marâṭhî has not many instances of this softening of व्.

In the Prâkṛits there are according to the grammarians but three instances of the change of क् to the sonant ग्. Of these गेन्दुअ for Skr. कन्दुक occurs in the vernaculars.* With these exceptions the initial क् remains unchanged and the medial is dropped. But the vernaculars, adopting pure Sanskrit words again and again in the course of their history, have changed them as we have seen or changed the Prâkṛit words that came down to them in virtue of the general or special laws which regulate the development of human speech. Thus, though they did not receive more words with a softened क् from the Prâkṛits they have now come to possess a good many. Thus:—

49. M. सगळा, P. सगरा, सगला, or सगळ, H. सगल or सगला, G. सगळो all or whole, Skr. सकल or सकलकः.

M. बगळा, H. P. बगला, G. बगलो, S. बगो, B. O. बग, Skr. बक or बककः a crane.

M. H. P. G. परगट or प्रगट, S. प्रघटु visible, manifest, Skr. प्रकट.

H. P. G. B. काग, S. कांगु a crow, Skr. काकः. H. has कौवा or कौआ from Pr. काअ with the suffix कः *i. e.*, ओ, M. काव, of कावळा, also.

H. लोग, S. लोगु or लोकु people, the world, Skr. लोकः. The others have लोक.

H. P. साग, S. सागु greens, culinary herbs, Skr. शाकः. The others have शाक.

H. सगुन, P. सगन, G. सगन or शगन, S. सगुणु, B. शगुन an auspicious omen, Skr. शकुनः, M. शकुन. S. has सोणु, also from the Pr. सउणो.

H. P. सोग, S. सोगु grief, Skr. शोकः. The others have शोक.

*See Table 22.

H. P. विंगा crooked, Pr. वङ्कअ, Skr. वक्रक. The others have बांक or बांक.

P. सगरांद passage of the sun into a sign, Skr. संक्रान्ति. The others have. संक्रांत.

P. संगोच contraction, bashfulness, Skr. संकोच; H. सकोच or सकुच M. संकोक.

च् is softened to the sonant ज् as in the following :—

50. H. सूजी a needle, Skr. सुचि; also 'a tailor' from Skr. सुचिक.

H. G. सूज-or सूझ-[ना and वुं] to be suggested, Skr. सूच्य.

H. कुंजी a key, Skr. कुञ्चिका.

P. S. पंज five, Skr. पञ्च; P. मंजी a small bedstead, Skr. मञ्चिका. There are not many instances of this process.

The Prâkṛits change an uninitial ट् to ड् when preceded by a vowel; and the vernaculars have preserved the words so changed. For instance:—

51. Skr. घटकः a jar, M. H. घडा, G. S. घडो, H. P. घडा.

Skr. घट to happen, to occur, to forge, to fashion, M. S. G. घड-[णें-णु-वुं], H. P. घड़-[ना].

Skr. घटिका a measure of time, M. G. S. O. B. घडी, H. P. घड़ी.

Skr. घोटकः a horse, M. O. B. घोडा, G. S. घोडो, H. P. घोड़ा.

Skr. तट a bank, M. तड, O. तडा, S. तडो in an altered sense.

Skr. कपाट a door, M. कवाड, H. किवाड, G. कमाड.

Skr. कटु bitter, M. कडु, G. कडवुं, H. कडुवा, S. कडो.

Skr. कटि waist, M. कड, G. केड.

Skr. कटकम् a bracelet, M. कडें, H. O. कडा, G. कडुं.

Skr. रट् or आरट् to cry, M. रड in रडणें or आरडणें, G. S. रड-[वुं-णु]

Skr. शाटिका a garment, M. G. साडी, H. P. साड़ी, S. शाड्ही, B. O. शाडी.

Skr. वटः the Banyan tree, M. G. वड, H. P. बड़, S. बडु.

Skr. त्रोट in त्रोटयति to snap, तोड in M. तोडणें, G. तोडवुं, H. P. तोड़ना, S. तोडणु.

Skr. स्फोट in स्फोटयति to break, फोड in M. फोडणें.

Skr. मुकुट or मुकुटक a crown, H. P. मौडा, B. O. मउड.

Skr. कुटज a kind of tree, M. कुडा.

Skr. पटोल a kind of cucumber, M. पडवळ, H. परवल, G. परवळ.

Skr. कीटकः a worm, M. किडा, G. किडो, H. कीडा.

The instances in which the cerebral ट् resulting from an original त् has been softened in the Prâkṛits to ड् have been preserved by the vernaculars. The following are some of these :—

52. पड for Pr. पडि, Skr. प्रति, in such words as H. G. पडोसी a neighbour, M. पडोशी, Skr. प्रतिवेशी; M. पडसाद, Skr. प्रतिशब्द echo; M. पडसें, Skr. प्रतिश्याय cold, catarrh, and also in M. पडछाया reflection, and पडताळा proof; G. पडसाळ, Skr. प्रतिशाला a penthouse; G. पडघा, Skr. प्रतिघात echo or resonance; हरडा or हरडी and बेहडा as in Table 29; M. पुढें forward, so forth, Pr. पहुडि, Skr. प्रभृति; पड of M. पडणें, G. पडवुं. H. पडना to fall, Pr. पड, Skr. पत्; मडें M. a corpse from Pr. मडअं, Skr. मृतकम्; उखाडना to dig out, to root out, from the Skr. उत्खात.

Of the change of त् to द् there are some instances in the Śaurasenî, and corresponding to these we have a few in the Panjâbî, Sindhî, and Gujarâtî, thus:—

53. P. जीउंदा 'living,' Śaur. *pres. part.* जीवन्दो, Skr. जीवन्त; दा of the present participle of roots, as करदा *masc.* 'doing,' आखदा *masc.* 'saying' &c. A modern instance is सगरांद for the Sanskrit संक्रान्ति. The Sindhî preserves the Śaurasenî present participial affix न्दो or अन्दो sometimes changed to इन्दो throughout, as in हलन्दो 'moving,' करीन्दो 'doing,' हुन्दो 'being,' &c. The same change is observable in other words also as in खांदि for Sanskrit क्षान्ति. The Gujarâtî has a few instances of the Śaurasenî past passive participle in द as in खादुं 'eaten,' पीदुं 'drunk,' कीदुं 'done,' &c. Marâṭhî has दोंद for Skr. तुन्द 'belly,' and Gujarâtî दुंद.

The labial surd प् is, when uninitial, softened in the Prâkṛits to व्. The व् is preserved by the Marâṭhî unchanged, but the Hindî softens it in some cases still further to उ as already shown (p. 168), and drops it in a great many more cases, according to a very general rule to be hereafter noticed, while the Gujarâtî changes it sometimes to म्. The Śindhî and Bangâlî follow the Hindî to a large extent in this latter respect.

54. Skr. वापी a well, Pr. बावी, M. बाव, G. H. बाव in बावडी, S. वाइ, P. बाउ in बाउडी.

Skr. कूपकः a well, Pr. कूवो. G. कुवो, H. कुआ, S. कुहो for कुओ.

Skr. कपाट a door, Pr. कवाड, M. कवाड, H. किवाड, G. कमाड.

Skr. प्राप to reach, attain, Pr. पाव, M. पाव (in पावणें), G. पाम-[वुं], H. पा-[ना], S. पाइ-[णु], B. पाओ-[वा].

Skr. प्रस्थाप to send, Pr. पट्ठाव, M. पाठव-[णें], old H. पठव-[ना], H. पठा-[ना], S. पठ-[णु].

Skr. छुप् to touch, Pr. छिव or छुव, M. शिव-[णें], H. P. B. छू-[ना &c.], O. छुं or छुंइ, S. छुअ-[णु] or छुह-[णु].

Skr. ताप to heat, Pr. ताव, M. G. H. ताव-[णें-वुं-ना], S. ताइ-[णु].

Skr. नापित a barber, Pr. नाविअ or न्हाविअ, M. न्हावी, G. नावी, H. S. नाई.

Skr. गोपाल-लिक a cowherd, Pr. गोवाल-लिअ, M. गोवळा, M. G. गवळी. G. गोवाळियो, H. गोवाली, ग्वाल (=गोआल), ग्वाली, S. गवारु.

Skr. कच्छपः a tortoise, Pr. कच्छवो, H. कछूआ, S. कछउं, कछूं, M. कासव.

Skr. सपत्नी a fellow-wife, Pr. सवत्ती, M. सवत, H. सौत.

Skr. भाद्रपद name of the sixth month, Pr. भद्दवअ, M. भादवा, H. भादो, S. बड़ो.

The lingual surd aspirate ठ् is, it will be remembered, changed in the Prâkṛits to ढ्, and the vernaculars, especially the Hindî, have preserved the instances and even added to them, as will be seen from the following :—

55. Skr. पठ to read, Pr. पढ, M. H. P. S. पढ in पढणें-ना-णु. In H, and P., however, the pronunciation of ढ is somewhat different from what it is in M., and in S. it sounds like the conjunct ड्ढ.

Skr. पीठक a stool, Pr. पीढअ, H. पीढा.

Skr. पीठिका a series (of generations), Pr. पीढिआ, H. पीढी, M. पिढी, G. पेढी.

Skr. मठ or मठिका a small temple, Pr. मढ, H. P. मढी, old M. मढ.

Skr. दंष्ट्रा, Pr. दाढा, H. डाढ, M. G. दाढ.

Similarly we have H. लुढना 'to roll' from Skr. लुठ्. In the word दाढा the ढा does not represent ष्ट्र but ट्ठ to which that Skr. conjunct must by the general rules, be reduced in the Prâkṛits. One of the two ठ् is dropped and the preceding vowel lengthened according to a general rule in the vernaculars to be hereafter noticed. The remaining ठ् is then softened to ढ्. There are other instances of the same change in our dialects.

56. वेढ of M. वेढणें, S. वेड्हणु, बेढ of H. बेढना, बेड़ of B. वेडन 'to surround' from Skr. वेष्ट through Pr. वेढ. The Gujarâtî, however, has वीटवुं.

काढ of M. काढणें, G. काढवुं, H. काढना; कढ of S. कढणु, B. काढ 'to draw out,' from Pr. कड्ढ, Skr. कृष्ट.

कूढ of H. कूढना to mourn, from Pr. कुड्ढ, Skr. क्रुष्ट. Even here the Gujarâtî has कूटवुं.

H. कोढ, M. G. कोड, S. कोड्हु white leprosy, from Skr. कुष्ठ through Pr. कोट्ठ.

The ठ् arising from the Sanskrit थ् is also similarly changed to ढ्. M. सढळ, H. ढीला, &c., from the Skr. शिथिल as in Table 29.

M. कढणें to boil, काढा decoction, कढी curry, कढई a cauldron, G. कढवुं, काढो, &c., H. कढना, काढा, कढी, &c., all from the Skr. root क्वथ्.

We have noticed the change of ड् to ट् and ल् and of ट् to ल् in the Prâkṛits. Not only have the vernaculars preserved the words so changed, but have carried on the process to such an extent that ल् and ट् have become mutually interchangeable in some of them, especially the Hindi.

57. Skr. तडाग a tank, Pr. तलाअ, M. G. तळाव, M. तळें, H. तलाव, S. B. तलाउ.

Skr. दाडिम pomegranate, Pr. दालिम, M. डाळिंब, G. दाळम, H. B. डालिम, H. दालिम.

Skr. गुड molasses, Pr. गुल, M. गूळ.

Skr. पीड of पीडयति to torment, to twist, Pr. पील, M. पिळणें, G. पीळवुं, H. पिलना, &c.

The numerals with their द् changed in the Prâkṛits to ट् through an intermediate ड् have come down to the vernaculars:—

	Skr.	Pr.	H.	P.	S.	M.	G.	O.	B.
58.	एकादश	एआरह	ग्यारह	यारां or गिआरां	यारहं कारहं	अकरा	अग्यार	एगार	एगार
	द्वादश	बारह	बारह	बारां	बारहं	बारा	बार	बार	बार
	त्रयोदश	तेरह	तेरह	तेरां	तेरहं	तेरा	तेर	तेर	तेर
	चतुर्दश	चउद्दह	चौदह	चौदां	चौडहं	चौदा	चौद	चौद	चौद
	पञ्चदश	पण्णरह	पंद्रह	पंदरां	पंद्रहं-पंध्रां	पंधरा	पंधर	पंधर	पनेर
	षोडश	सोलह	सोलह	सोलां	सोरहं	सोळा	सोळ	षोहल	षोल
	सप्तदश	सत्तरह	सत्रह	सतारां	सत्रहं	सतरा	सत्तर	सतर	सतेर
	अष्टादश	अट्ठारह	अठारह	अठारां	अडहं	अठरा	अढार	अठर	आठार

The other Prâkṛit words दोहल and कलम्ब in which the द् of the Sanskrit दोहद and कदम्ब is changed to ल् are preserved in Marâṭhî in the forms of डोहाळा and कळंब. Similarly हरिद्रा and अंगार with the ट् so changed appear in the vernaculars as shown before.*

The following are later instances:—

59. B. कोल, G. खोळो, Skr. क्रोड, lap; B. चुल, Skr. चूडा lock of hair; H. मरा for Pr. मडअ, Skr. मृतक a corpse; H. परछाईं, Pr. पडिछाआ, Skr. प्रतिच्छाया; H. बेराना or बिराना, Skr. विडम्बन mocking; G. वाळवुं, from Skr. वार to resist; G. पालवुं from Skr. पार to tide over; H. बहकना from Skr. विहरण to amuse one's self; S. निअर, नेर, or नेडु fetters, from Skr. निगड; H. P. नेरे, Pr. निअडे, Skr. निकटे near.

*See 140 and Table 22.

Though the change of ल् to ड् does not involve softening but must be considered to be due to a predilection for the sound, it would be convenient to notice it here. There is only one instance of this change given by Hemachandra as existing in the Mahârâshṭrî, but there are a great many in the vernaculars, so that this appears to be a peculiarly modern process. The Hindî and the Sindhî have, however, of all the vernaculars, the largest number of examples, the rest presenting but a few stray ones. Sometimes both the forms with ल् and ड् are in use, especially in the Hindî.

60. Skr. स्थूल, Pr. थोर, M. थोर large, great.

H. G. लंगर, M. G. नांगर, S. लंगरु, Skr. लाङ्गल a plough, or anchor.

H. कौर or कौल, Skr. कवल a morsel; धूर or धूल, Skr. धूलि dust; सियार, Skr. शृगाल, a jackal; सराहना, Pr. सलाह, Skr. श्लाघ् to praise; दुलार, Skr. दुर्लल a spoilt child; सिकरी, Skr. शृङ्खला a chain; बारना, Skr. ज्वाल (*caus.* of ज्वल) to burn; सांवरो Braj for सांवला, Skr. श्यामलक dark.

S. सांविरो, Skr. श्यामलकः dark; पिपिरु, Skr. पिप्पलः a certain tree; पजिरणु, Skr. प्रज्वल to light or burn; पघिरणु, Skr. प्रगल to melt; हरु, Skr. हलः a plough, &c.

G. अटारी, Skr. अट्टालिका a high mansion; M. शेवरी or सांवरी, Skr. शाल्मली the silk cotton tree.

Notable instances of the interchangeableness of ड्, ड़् and ल् are afforded by the causal forms of verbal roots in some of the vernaculars. In Hindî the causal of roots ending in a vowel is formed by inserting ल् between it and the termination आ which is the remnant of the old Prâkṛit आव preserved in the Braj and other dialects; as पिलाना caus. of पी 'to drink,' खिलाना of खा 'to eat,' दिलाना of दे 'to give,' धुलाना of धो 'to wash,' &c. In Gujarâtî we have ड् for ल् as खवाडवुं 'to cause to eat,' देवाडवुं 'to cause to give,' 'न्हवाडवुं', to cause to bathe,' 'wash,' &c. Sometimes instead of ड्, ड़् is optionally used as in खवराववुं 'to cause to eat,' बीहीवराववुं 'to threaten,' &c. But in Sindhî ड़् always represents the Hindî ल् and the Gujarâtî ड्, as in दिआरणु 'to cause to give,' धुआरणु 'to cause to wash,' वेहारणु 'to cause to sit.' What the origin is of the ड् of these forms, which is more primitive than the ल् and ड़् to which it was afterwards changed, will be considered in the next lecture.

Another peculiarly vernacular process, of which Hemachandra gives only one instance, is the transformation of न् into ल् in which न् is deprived of its nasal element, and the complete contact of the vocal organs avoided. Thus :—

61. Skr. निम्ब a certain tree, Pr. लिम्ब or निम्ब, M. लिंब.

M. लवणें to bow, Skr. नमन; लोणी butter, Skr. नवनीत; H. लौटना to return, Skr. निवर्त, Pr. निवट्ट; G. लील blue, Skr. नील; P. लेर, a cocoanut, Skr. नारीकेल, H. नारियेल.

But there are more instances of the opposite process in the Prâkṛits; and these have come down to the vernaculars.

62. M. G. नांगर a plough or anchor, P. नङ्गल or लङ्गल; M. निढळ, S. निराडु, Pr. णिडाल or णडाल, Skr. ललाट forhead. The H. नून salt, Skr. लवण, is a later instance.

The sibilant स् whether original or derived from the Sanskrit श् or ष् is in a few cases changed to ह् in the Prâkṛits. For दिवस 'a day,' we have दिवह or दिअह, for पाषाण 'a stone,' पहाण, and for दशन् 'ten' दह. These words, so changed, have come down to the vernaculars, and are found in one or other of them. The various forms of the numerals having the word दश at the end have been given above. Of the other words G. has दिह 'a day,' and दिहाडो with the suffix डो, P. दिंह and दिहाड़ा, and S. ड्डिंहु and ड्डिहाडो; and S. पहणु 'a stone.' The Sindhî and the Panjâbî have given a wider range to this process, as will be seen from the following :—

63. S. बुहु or बुहो chaff, Skr. बुस, M. भुसा.

S. बिहु lotus-stalk, Skr. बिस, M. भिसें.

S. मेंहि a buffalo, Skr. महीषी, M. भैस.

S. वेहणु to sit, Skr. उपविश, M. बैसणें, G. बेसवुं.

S. वेसाहु trust, Skr. विश्वास.

P. बीह, S. वीह twenty, Skr. विंश-[ति], M. वीस.

P. विह or विस, S. विहु or विसु poison, Skr. विष, M विख.

P. सहुरा, S. सहुरो, Skr. श्वशुर, M. सासरा father-in-law.

P. तिहा thirst, Skr. तृषा.

P. फाहा or फाही, S. फाहो or फाही a snare, noose, Skr. पाश, M फांस.

Gujarâtîs, especially of the uneducated classes, pretty freely pronounce स् as ह्, as in हमजवुं for समजवुं 'to understand,' वरह for वरस 'a year,' हाचुं for साचुं 'true,' &c., but the forms with स् are also in use. The other dialects do not seem to have many instances of this change. The termination स् of verbs of the future tense is in several dialects of the Hindî changed to ह as in करिहै, G. करसे 'he will do.'

The change of म to वँ seems to be an almost entirely later process of which there are scarcely any instances in the Prâkṛits. It is seen in full operation in the Apabhraṁśa.

64. Skr. नाम name, M. नांव, H. नाओं, old H. नाउं, also नाम, P. नांडं, S. नांडं also नामु and नालो.

Skr. दाम a tying rope, M. दावें, P. दांड, H. दांव in दांवरी.

Skr. ग्राम a village, M. H. गांव, H. गाम, also; S. गांड, गामु.

Skr. भ्रमण to turn round, M. भोंवणें, P. भौंणा, S. भौंणणु; from the same root, M. भोंवळ, H. भंवर, S. भौंरी.

Skr. नमन, M. लवणें, H. नवना-नौला-नेवना.

Skr. अवनमन to bow down, M. ओणवणें.

Skr. आचमन to rinse the mouth, M. आंचवणें, H. अंचवना, also अचाना.

Skr. विश्राम rest, M. विसांवा, S. वेसांहि,

Skr. श्यामल dark-complexioned, M. सांवळा, H. सांवला-रा, P. सांवला, and सामला, S. सांविलो.

Skr. जामातृक son-in-law, M. जांवई, but H. जमाई, P. जवाइ or जमाइ,

Skr. उद्गमन rising, M. उगवणें, but P. उग्गमणा.

Skr. आमलक a kind of myrobalans, M. P. आंवळा, H. P. आंवला. P. आमला also, S. आंउरी.

Skr. सामन्त a chief, M. H. सावंत.

Skr. चामर *n.* a sort of fly-brush, M. चौरी, H. P. चवंर, S. चंवरु.

Skr. कमल a lotus, H. P. कंवल, M. कमळ, S. कंवलु.

Skr. गमन *caus.* spending, wasting, H. गंवाना, P. गवाउणा, S. गंवाइणु but M. गमवणें.

Skr. भ्रमर a bee, H. भंवरा or भौंरा, P. भौंर or भौंरा, S. भौंरु.

Skr. पञ्चम fifth, M. पांचवा, H. पांचवां, P. पंजवां, &c., and other ordinals.

Skr. कोमल delicate, tender, M. कोंवळा.

Skr. जमन eating, M. जेवण, H. जेवन, P. जेंउणा.

Skr. कर्दम mud, H. कांदो, G. कादव.

From the fact that the Marâṭhî, Hindî, Sindhî, and Panjâbî contain many instances of this change it is to be gathered that though it does not appear in the Prâkṛits proper it must have begun very early before the vernaculars received their distinctive forms and were isolated from each other. Of all the dialects the Marâṭhî alone has preserved the व् of this वं in most cases; the Hindî, and the others having dropped it or softened it to उ in a good many instances; while the Gujarâtî changes it back again to म्. Thus, such of the above words as exist in Gujarâtî have the following forms :—

65. नाम name. corresponding to M. भोंवळ.
गाम a village. चमरी a fly-brush.
भमवुं to turn round, भमरी giddiness, कमळ a lotus.

गमावडुं wasting.
विसामो rest.
सामळो dark-complexioned.
जमाइ son-in-law.
आमळा myrobalans.
भमरो a bee.
पांचमो, सातमो, &c., fifth, seventh, &c.
कुमळो delicate, tender.
जमवुं eating.

The reason why I consider this as a change of वँ back to म, and not a preservation of the original Sanskrit and Prâkṛit म, is that the Gujarâti changes व् to म् in other cases where there is no question as to the व् (or प्) being the original sound. Thus :—

66. G. कमाड a door, H. किवाड, M. कवाड, Pr. कवाड, Skr. कपाट;
G. शिसम blackwood, M. शिसवा, Pr. सिंसव, Skr. शिंशप.
G. पामवुं to attain, M. पावणें, Pr. पाव, Skr. प्राप.
G. धाम in दोडधाम running, Skr. धाव्.

Where in Marâṭhi we have व् or ब् the Gujarâti has in some cases म् as in G. मुक्की 'a blow,' M. बुकी, G. ठाम 'a place of residence,' M. ठाव, derived in some way from Skr. स्थाप. There are traces of this change in some of the other dialects too, as in S. P. मिंनत, B. मिनति, corresponding to M. विनंति, H. बिनति, Pr. विण्णत्ति, Skr. विज्ञप्ति 'solicitation;' B. काछिम, Pr. कच्छव, Skr. कच्छप 'a tortoise;' H. धीमर, Skr. धीवर 'a fisherman;' old M. मात, G. वात, Skr. वार्ता 'news;' B. मुछ, H. पुंछ-[ना], Skr. प्रोञ्छ् 'to wipe away.' This phenomenon of the change of व् to म् the vernaculars, and especially the Gujarâti, have inherited from the Prâkṛits. Of the words so changed the Gujarâti has preserved समणुं 'a dream,' the Prâkṛit form being सिमिण or सुमिण, and some of the others, नीम 'kind of tree.' This last is नीप in Sanskrit; but probably there was an intermediate form नीव.

The vernaculars have thrown away the aspiration of hard and soft aspirate mutes in a good many cases. Thus :—

67. M. शीक	learn,	Pr.	सिक्ख,	H. सीख.
M. भीक	beggary,	Pr.	भिक्खा,	H. भीख.
M. सुकणें	to dry,	Pr.	सुक or सुक्ख,	H. सूखना.
M. भूक	hunger,	Pr.	बुहुक्खा,	H. भूख.
M. हात	hand,	Pr.	हत्थ,	H. हाथ.
M. हत्ती	elephant,	Pr.	हत्थी,	H. हाथी.
G. बीनो	afraid,	Pr.	भीदो or भीओ,	M. भ्याला.
G. बडाई	greatness from	Pr.	वड्ढ,	H. बढाई.
G. बगाडवुं	to spoil,	Pr.	विघड,	M. बिघडणें.
		S. सुकणु	to dry.	
		S. बीख	beggary.	

S. बुख hunger.

B. पुति a book, Pr. पोत्थिआ, H. M. पोथी.
B. पड to learn, Pr. पढ, H. M., &c. पढ.
B. वाड to grow, Pr. वड्ढ, M. वाढ-[णें], H. बाढ-ढब-[ना].
B. वेड to surround, Pr. वेढ, M. वेढ-[णें], H. बेढ-[ना], &c.
B. पातर stone, Pr. पत्थर, M. पाथर, H. पत्थर or पाथर.
B. पिट back, Pr. पिट्ठ or पट्ठ, H. पीठ, M. पाठ.
B. साद wish, Pr. सद्धा, S. P. साध.
B. शुक (in शुकान) to dry, Pr. सुक्ख or सुक्क, H. सूखना.
B. काड (in काडिया) to take out, Pr. कड्ढ, H. M. &c. काढ.
B. पुकुर a pond, Pr. पुक्खरिणी.

And in such forms as पराइले 'worn' from Pr. परिहाण, नाइते 'for bathing' from Pr. न्हा, or नहा and डाइन 'to the right hand,' Pr. दाहिण, the aspirate ह is dropped, so that the Bangâlî has, in a large number of instances, thus weakened the pronunciation of aspirated sounds. In the instances given from Marâṭhî, it will be seen that the letters other than those which are softened are aspirates; hence the weakening consists simply in dropping the heavy breath in one of two aspirated sounds as in the case of the Sindhî बिख and बुख. The aspirates are preserved when occurring singly, which is not the case in Bangâlî. Hence Banglâlî utterance is the weakest, and the Hindî and Panjâbî the strongest.

The Marâṭhî reduces a Sanskrit or Pràkṛit च्छ invariably to स, and in this respect differs from all its cognate dialects. Thus:—

68. Skr. इक्षु sugarcane, Pr. उच्छु, M. ऊस. The H. has ईख or ऊख.
Skr. मत्स्य fish, Pr. मच्छ, H. माछ, M. मासा.
Skr. वत्स a calf, Pr. वच्छ, H. बाछ, M. वास in वासरूं.
Skr. क्षुरिका a knife, Pr. छुरिआ, H. छुरी, M. सुरी.
Skr. मक्षिका a fly, Pr. मच्छिआ, H. माछी, M. माशी.
Skr. पृच्छ to ask, Pr. पुच्छ, H. पुछना, M. पुसणें.
Skr. कच्छप a tortoise, Pr. कच्छव, H. कछुआ, M. कासव.
Skr. कुक्षि a side of the abdomen, Pr. कुच्छि, M. कूस. The H. has कोख.
Skr. क्षेत्र a field, Pr. छेत्त, M. शेत. But H. has खेत.
Skr. छुप् to touch, Pr. छुव, H. छू-[ना], M. शिव-[णें].
Skr. छाया shade, Pr. छाआ, H. छांव, M. सांव-[ली].
Skr. गुच्छ a bunch, Pr. गोच्छ, H. गोच्छा, M. घोंस.
Skr. उत्सङ्ग lap, Pr. ओच्छङ्ग, M. ओसंग.
Skr. छागली a she-goat, Pr. छाअली or छाली, H. छेरी, M. शेळी.

Skr. क्षिण worn out, wasted, Pr. छीण, M. शीण-[णें].

Skr. क्षण a festival, Pr. छण, M. सण.

According to a general rule in Marâṭhî स् is changed to श् when followed by the palatal vowel इ or ए. This change of छ् to स् in this dialect is to be accounted for by the fact that the vocal organs of the Marâṭhâs have a predilection for the dento-palatals, च, छ, ज, झ to which the Sanskrit palatals are in almost all cases reduced by them except when they are followed by इ, ए, or य्. The Sanskrit छ् therefore becoming the dento-palatal छ् passes into स् which differs from it only in the contact of the vocal organs being somewhat less incomplete. The only instances in the Prâkṛits in which the change appears to be the same as that we have been considering are ऊसवो for उच्छवो and ऊसुओ for उच्छुओ.

I have already given instances of the many words with their uninitial consonants dropped which the vernaculars have inherited from the Prâkṛits, and shown what further changes they have undergone. This process of elision has not been continued by any of the vernaculars unless we consider the disappearance of uninitial व् which is very general in Hindî, Sindhî, and Bangâlî to be an instance of the process.

69. B. H. दिया, S. डिओ lamp, Pr. दीवओ, Skr. दीपकः, M. दिवा.

H. नया, S. नआं new, Pr. नवओ, M. नवा.

H. जी, S. जीउ life, Pr. जीओ, Skr. जीवः, M. जीव.

H. S. नाई, B. नायि a barber, Pr. नाविअ or ण्हाविअ, Skr. नापित, M. न्हावी.

H. कछुआ, S. कछउं a tortoise, pr. कच्छवओ, Skr. कच्छपकः, M. कांसव.

H. छू-[ना], S. छुअ-[णु], B. छो (छोया s.) to touch, Pr. छिव or छुव, Skr. छुप, M. शिव-[णें].

H. पा-[ना], S. पाइ-[णु], Pr. पाव, Skr. प्राप, M. पाव-[णें].

H. कुआ, S. कुहो for कुओ, B. कुया a well, Pr. कुवओ, Skr. कूपकः, G. कुवो.

H. ग्वाल=गोआल, B. गोयाला a cowherd, Pr. गोवालअ, Skr. गोपालक, M. गोवळा.

H. ब्याह=बिआह, S. विहाउ marriage, Skr. विवाह.

H. पठा-[ना], S. पठ-[णु], B. पाठाइ-[वा] to send, Pr. पट्ठाव, Skr. प्रस्थाप, M. पाठव.

H. ता-[ना], S. ताइ-[णु] to heat, Pr. ताव, Skr. ताप, M. ताव-[णें].

H. दुआर, B. दोयार door, Pr. दुवार or दुआर, Skr. द्वार.

B. दुइ two, Pr. दुवे, Skr. द्वौ.

B. नय nine, Skr. नव, M. नव, H. नौ.

B. श्येयाला moss, Skr. शैवाल, H. शेवाल.

This elision of व् appears also in the Hindî causal forms such as उठाना, चलाना, जलाना, in which the आ only of the Prâkṛit or Marâṭhî termination आव or अव is retained. The whole termination appears in the Braj and other dialects and in old books, sometimes in the form of औ. The Sindhî causal termination is आइ as in कराइणु 'to cause to do,' वधाइणु 'to cause to increase.' The इ here as well as in some of the Sindhî words given above represents the य which according to the Prâkṛit rule takes the place of the dropped व, and is, as shown before, changed to ए in the other vernaculars. The Sindhî इ is a shortened form of this ए. The termination आइ appears sometimes in its more original form of आअ as in वठाअणु 'to cause to take.' The Bangâlî too forms its causal by adding आइ as in धराइतेछे 'is causing to be held;' but the इ here seems to be an euphonic addition, which even in their primitive form the verbs take, as in धरितेछे 'is holding,' so that the व् is here dropped and the vowel अ combined with the preceding as in the Hindî. In the speech of the Marâṭhâ lower classes of Southern Konkan व् is very often elided, and the causal termination of the Sâvantvâḍî dialect is अय, as in करय 'cause to do,' which corresponds to the Sindhî कराइ-[णु].

There are instances also in which the व् resulting from म् is elided as in H. कुअंर 'a boy,' 'a prince,' Pr. कुमर, Skr. कुमार; बायां 'left-hand-side,' Pr. वामअ, Skr. वामक; धुआं 'smoke,' Pr. धूमअ, Skr. धूमक; अचाना 'to rinse the mouth,' Pr. Skr. आचम, चिराना or बेराना 'to mock,' Skr. विडम्ब, भुइं 'ground,' Skr. भूमि.

There are traces of this change in other dialects too, as in the Oriyâ बां for वाम 'left,' Gujarâtî भांय=भूइं, S. भुइं, Skr. भूमि, and the Marâṭhî भुइं and the termination ईं of the locative which is to be traced to the Pr. म्मि, Skr. स्मिन्. In all these instances we may regard म् as directly elided, and not the व् resulting from it. Hemachandra notices a few instances of the process in the Prâkṛits.

The vernaculars possess a large number of those Prâkṛit words, in which the mute element of hard and soft aspirates was dropped leaving only the ह्. Thus:—

ख.

70. Skr. मुख face, Pr. मुह, H. मुंह, S. मुहु, G. मोहो; M. मोहरे, P. मुहेरहे (with the suffix र) in front, H. मोहरा; H. सोंही, G. सामुं-मो, M. समोर (with the suffix र) from Skr. संमुख face to face.

Skr. नख nail, Pr. नह, H. नह, S. नहु, P. नहुं.

Skr. शेखरकः a chaplet, Pr. सेहरओ, H. सिहरा or सेहरा, S. सिहिरो, P. सिहरा.

Skr. सखी a female companion, Pr. सही, G. सही, H. S. P. सहेली, M. B. O. सई.

Skr. लिख to write, Pr. लिह, M. लिंह-[णें].

Skr. शिखण्ड a lock of hair or शिखण्डिका, Pr. सिहण्डिआ, M. शेंडी.

Skr. सुखकर agreeable, Pr. सुहअर, H. सोहर.

Skr. आखेट hunt, Pr. आहेड (?), H. अहेर.

घ.

71. Skr. मेघ rain, Pr. मेह, G. H. मेह, S. मेहु.

Skr. श्लाघ् to praise, Pr. सलाह, H. सराह-[ना].

Skr. प्राघुणक a guest, Pr. पाहुणअ, M. पाहुणा, H. पाहुना.

To these must be added the several compounds of the word घर some of which at least are modern, as—

H. नैहर house of a woman's family of birth, Pr. नाइघर or नाइहर, Skr. ज्ञातिगृह.

H. पीहर, G. पीयेर a woman's father's house, Pr. पिइघर or पिइहर, Skr. पितृगृह.

M. माहेर, G. महीरुं a woman's mother's house, Pr. माइघर or माइहर, Skr. मातृगृह.

G. भोंयार, M. भुंयार, H. भूंयारा a cellar, Skr. भूमिगृह.

G. देहरुं, M. देव्हारा, H. देहरा, दिहरा an idol-chamber, Skr. देवगृह.

थ.

72. Skr. नाथ a lord, Pr. नाह, old M. & H. नाह.

Skr. मिथुन a pair, Pr. मिहुण, M. मेहुण.

Skr. मथ to churn, Pr. मह, H. मह-[ना].

Skr. मथनिका a churning vessel, Pr. महणिआ, H. मिहानी.

Skr. पथिक a traveller, Pr. पहिअ, M. G. पही.

Skr. पृथुक flattened rice, Pr. पुहुअ (?), M. पोहे, S. पेहूं.

Skr. पृथुलकम् broad, Pr. पुहुलअं-[Ap. उं], G. पोहळुं.

Skr. कथ to tell, Pr. कह, H. G. S. P. B. O. कह-[ना-वुं-णु, &c.].

Skr. कथानक or कथानिका a story, Pr. कहाणअ or कहाणिआ, H. कहानी, M. G. कहाणी, S. किहाणी, B. काहिनी.

ध.

73. Skr. बधिरकः deaf, Pr. बहिरओ, H. M. O. बहिरा, G. बेहरो.

Skr. दधि curds, Pr. दहि, H. M. G. P. O. दहिं, S. ड़हि.

Skr. मधु honey, Pr. महु, O. B. महु, M. मोंह.

Skr. साधु honest, good, Pr. साहु, H. साहु-साह, M. साव.

Skr. वधू a young lady, daughter-in-law, H. G. S. वहू, O. बोहु or बौ.

Skr. परिधा dressing, Pr. परिहा, H. पहिर-[ना], G. पेहर-[वुं], S. पेहर-[णु], P. पहिर-[णा] by the consonants interchanging places.

भ.

74. Skr. प्रभा or प्रभात light, dawn, Pr. पहा, पहाअ, पहाद, H. पह or पोह, G. पोह, M. पहाट. The S. पिरिह must be a later form. From the same root with the prepositions वि and सु we have H. विहान morning, S. सुहाउ light, &c.

Skr. शुभ to become, to adorn, Pr. सुह, H. सोह-[ना], S. सुह-[णु].

Skr. सौभाग्य prosperity, good fortune, Pr. सोहग्ग, H. सोहाग or सुहाग.

Similary, H. पहिचान 'recognize' is from Skr. प्रत्यभिजाना, the consonants interchanging places; G. वहालो or वाल्हो 'dear' from Skr. वल्लभ; सेहलो 'easy' from सुलभ; वेहच-[वुं] to 'distribute' or 'divide' from विभज्, &c.

The existence of many such words as M. H. P. उपाध 'injury,' H. P. साध 'a good man,' M. G. H. P. मध 'honey,' H. G. लिख, लख 'to write,' M. G. H. नख 'nail,' S. सुभाणे 'in the morning' shows that the popular speech of Northern India has now for a long time ceased to have recourse to this process of dropping the mute element of the aspirates of the Sanskrit words adopted from time to time from the parent language. Still, however, a few later instances, such as S. पिरिह 'dawn,' H. G. माह 'middle' from माध and मध्य, and some of the compounds of घर noticed above show that it has not been entirely absent. The elision of simple mutes and of the mute element of aspirates is a natural phenomenon which one always meets with in the course of lingual development; but its operation is generally slow and it is only in consequence of its systematic occurrence in the Prâkṛits that I have attributed it to an ethnological cause, and supposed that the Prâkṛit speakers belonged to another race than those who spoke Sanskrit, and being unused to Sanskrit sounds caught only the initial consonants from their Sanskrit teachers and dropped the rest or the mute portion of the rest. When, however, in the course of time they became used to those sounds and the Sanskrit and Prâkṛit speaking races became united into one community, they ceased to be so dropped, except through the slow and gradual operation of the usual phonetic laws; and hence it is that in modern times we find Sanskrit words not shorn of their elements in the manner in which they were in ancient times as indicated above.

This elision, though it involves economy and is a natural process, constitutes a peculiarity of the Prâkṛits in so far as it is due to peculiar historical incidents. We will now notice the peculiarities which do not involve economy and must be attributed to vocal predilections. Of the words in which a Sanskrit dental is changed to a cerebral in the Prâkṛits the vernaculars have preserved the following:—

75. Skr. बिभीतक myrobalan, Pr. बहेडओ, M. बेहडा, &c. as in table 8.

Skr. पत to fall, Pr. पड, M. G. H. पड-[णें-वुं-ना].

Skr. दंश to bite, Pr. डस, M. H. P. G. डस-[णें-ना-णा-वुं]. From this H. M. G. डांस, O. डाआंश a mosquito, Skr. दंश.

Skr. दंश to stick, Pr. डक्क (*past part.*), M. G. डक-[णें-वुं]..

Skr. शद to decay, Pr. सड, M. H. G. सड-[णें-ना-वुं].

Skr. दोला a swing, Pr. डोला, H. डोला *masc.* From this are derived M. डुलणें, H. डोलना, G. डोलवुं to swing, M. डुलकी a nap, G. डोळा nodding, M. G. H. P. O. डोली a litter or Sedan chair.

Skr. दण्ड a stick, Pr. डण्ड, H. डांड or डांडा, P. डंडा, G. M. (*dial.*) डांडो, H. G. डांडी. M. has दांडा and दांडी.

Skr. दह to burn, Pr. डह, H. डाहना to be spiteful, malicious, H, P. डाह malice.

Skr. शिथिल, Pr. सिढिल, M. सढळ, &c., as in Table 29.

Skr. दम्भ hypocrisy, deceptive appearance, Pr. डम्भ, M. डंभ.

Skr. दोहद longing, Pr. डोहल, M. डोहाळा.

There are many later instances of this change:—

76. M. S. टाण-[णें-णु], H. टानना, B. टानिवा, O. टाणिवा to stretch, Skr. तन; M. टिळा, G. टिळो a mark on the forehead, Skr. तिलक; H. M. टिकली, G. टिकडी, S. टिकिडो a small mark on the forehead, a spangle, Skr. तिलक: by consonants interchanging places; M. G. टाळ, H. टाली a kind of cymbal, from Skr. ताल measured or beaten time. M. टाळा, G. टाळुं the roof of the mouth, Skr. तालु; H. P. डाल-डाला-डाली, S. डारी-डारो, G. डाळी, B. O. डाल, M. डाहळी a branch or bough, Skr. दल; M. कढणें. &c. as in P. 174.

The Sindhî has the largest number of instances, and the Hindî and the Panjâbi come next. The Marâṭhî and Gujarâtî have the smallest number.

77. S. ढुंढो satisfied, Skr. तुष्ट-[कः]; S. ड़ेडो crooked, H. P. टेढा. M. तेडा, M. (*dial.*) तिडो, Skr. तिर्यंक्; S. ठूंठो, H. ठूंठ handless, M. थोटा,

Skr. स्थगु with the suffix ट, Pr. थड्टो (?); S. डखिणु the south, H. दखिन, Skr. दक्षिण; S. इंदु a tooth, H. M. दांत, Skr. दन्त; S. इया pity, M. H. Skr. दया; S. इसणु to show, H. दसना, Skr. दर्शन; S. इह ten, H. दस, M. दहा, Skr. दश; S. डाठ or डाड्ह a grinder, H. डाढ, M. दाढ, Skr. दंष्ट्रा; S. डिओ a lamp, H. दिया, M. दिवा, Skr. दीप·[कः]; S. डिअणु to give, H. देना, M. देणें, Skr. दान; S. डीठो, H. P. ढीठ impudent, M. धीट, Skr. धृष्ट; S. डिसणु see, H. दिसना, M. दिसणें to appear, Skr. दृश्य; S. डिठो seen, H. P. डीठ, G. दिठो, Skr. दृष्ट.

O. डाहांण, B. डाइन to the right hand, H. दहिना.

Thus then the Pâli and Prâkṛit tendency to pronounce dentals as cerebrals is seen in a much more exaggerated form in the Sindhî and next to it in the Hindî and the Panjâbî, while the other modern dialects seem to have kept it quite within the bounds in which we find it in the ancient dialects, though they have changed more words in that way than they.

In the following instances the cerebral mute in the place of the dental is to be considered as due to the influence of an adjoining र्.

78. पड for Pr. पंडि, Skr. प्रति, in the words given in list 52, and हरडा, पुढें, and मढें in the same.

M. G. H. S. P. डर·[णें·वुं·ना·णु·ना], B. O. डरिवा, Pr. डर, Skr. दर fear.

H. डाभ or डाब, G. डाभ or डाभो, S. डभु, Skr. दर्भ a kind of grass, but P. दब्भ.

H. मट्टी or माटी, &c., as in list 4.

H. बुड्ढा, बडा, M. S. वड, &c., as in list 4.

H. केवट, Skr. कैवर्त a pilot.

H. उबटन, M. उटणें, G. उटणु. S. उबटणु a cosmetic, Skr. उद्वर्तन.

H. टाकना or ताकना, M. टकणें, O. टाकिवा, Skr. तर्क to watch, to look out for. G. B. S. have त for ट.

M. H. पवाडा, S. G. पवाडो a narrative, Skr. प्रवाद·[कः].

Even here the Sindhî has more instances than the others:—

79. पुटु a son, Skr. पुत्र, M. पूत.
टिह thirst, Skr. तृषा, P. तिहा.
निंड sleep, Skr. निद्रा, H. नींद.
टामो copper, Skr. ताम्र, M. तांबें, &c.

Uninitial न् is changed to ण् in the Prâkṛits invariably, but when it is at the beginning of a word it undergoes that change optionally.

In the vernaculars the initial न् remains unchanged, but when medial it becomes mostly ण् in the Marâṭhî, Gujarâtî, Sindhî, and Panjâbî.

Initial न्.

80. M. नाव, &c., as in list 64.
H. S. नाईं, &c., as in list 69.
M. नवा, H, नया, S. नओं, as in list 69.
H. P. नेरे as in p. 166.
H. नह, &c., as in list 70.
P. नैण, as in list 16.
H. नौनी as in list 17.
P. नेउल as in list 24.
M. नीज, H. नींद, S. निंड sleep, Skr. निद्रा.
P. नेउंदा, H. नेवता, G. नोतरुं an invitation, Skr. निमन्त्र.
M. नणंद, P. नणान, S. निणुन, H. ननद or ननदी, B. ननद or ननंदा, Skr. ननान्दृ husband's sister, &c.

Medial ण्.

81. M. माणूस, G. माणस, S. माण्हूं, P. माणुस, Skr. मनुष्य a man.

M. दिसणें, S. ड्सिणु, P. दिसणा, Skr. दर्शन or दर्शनक appearing; and all other infinitives in णें-णु-णा.

M. जण, G. जण, S. जणो, P. जणा, Skr. जन-[कः] a person.

M. G. कहाणी, S. किहाणी, Skr. कथानिका a story.

M. G. S. P. पाणी, Skr. पानीय water.

M. G. S. P. जाण-[णें-वुं-णु-णा], Skr. ज्ञाना to know.

M. G. कोण, P. कौण, Skr. कः पुनः who?

M. बहिण, G. बेन, S. भेणु, P. भैण, Skr. भगिनी sister.

M. कठिण, G. कठण, S. कठन, P. कटण-न, Skr. कठिन hard.

P. S. G. जण-[णा-णु-वुं], Skr. जन (*causal*) to give birth to, to produce.

G. लुण, S. लूणु, P. लूण, M. लोण (in सैंधेलोण), Skr. लवण salt.

P. M. G. आपण, S. पाण, Pr. अप्पाण, Skr. आत्मान one's self.

M. G. S. P. ताण-[णें-वुं-णु-णा], Skr. तन to stretch or pull.

M. नणंद, &c., as above.

There are a few instances in which we have the original न् in the body of a word, as in M. G. P. मन, S. मनु, Skr. मनः 'mind,' G. वानुं 'promise' for Skr. वचन, and G. बेन as above. But the general rule seems to be that these four dialects have a medial न् in the place of the double ण् of the Prâkṛits, resulting from a Sanskrit conjunct of which न् is a member. Thus :—

82. Skr. अरण्य, Pr. रण्ण, M. G. रान wilderness.
Skr. कर्ण, Pr. कण्ण, M. G. कान, P. कन्न, S. कनु ear.
Skr. पर्ण, P. पण्ण, M. G. पान, P. पत्ता, S. पनु a leaf.
Skr. जीर्ण (जूर्णकः), Pr. जुण्ण, M. जुनें, G. जुनुं, S. झूनो old.

Skr. विज्ञप, Pr. विण्णव, M. G. विनव-(णें-वुं) to solicit; Skr. विज्ञप्ति, M. G. बिनंती, S. विनती, P. मिनत solicitation.

Skr. संज्ञा, Pr. सण्णा, G. सान, P. सन mark, sign.

Skr. जन्ययात्रा, Pr. जण्णयत्ता, P. जनेत a bridal procession; also, S. जञ, Skr. जन्य, Pr. जञ्ञ.

Skr. यज्ञोपवीत, Pr. जण्णोवईअ, G. जनोई, P. जनेऊ, M. जानवें, S. जण्यो the Brahmanic sacred thread.

Skr. मन्य्, Pr. मण्ण, M. G. मान-[णें-वुं], S. मनणु, P. मन्नणा to think, to regard, to obey.

But even here in Marâṭhî the purely Deśastha Brahmans living in the eastern part of the Deccan or Mahârâshṭra pronounce the न् as ण्; and the ordinary रान, कान, पान, विनंति, &c. of that dialect become in their mouths राण, काण, पाण, विणंति, &c. They have, therefore, preserved in its integrity the old habit of the Prâkṛit speakers to pronounce the Sanskrit न् as ण् throughout. On the other hand, the lower classes of the Konkaṇî population preserve the Paiśâchî peculiarity of reducing ण् in all cases to न् and pronounce पाणी, वाणी, कोण, &c., as पानी, वानी, कोन, &c., and this peculiarity we find in its fulness in the Hindî, and next to it in the Bangâlî. Thus the words with a ण् in them in the Marâṭhî, Gujarâtî, Sindhî, and Panjâbî, given above, have the following forms in Hindî :—

मानस, दिसना, जन, कहानी, पानी, जानना, कौन, बहिन or बैन, कठिन, जनना, लून or नून, अपना, टानना or तानना, ननद or ननदी.

And such of these words as are in use in the Bangâlî have the following :—

मानश, जन, किहानी, जानन, कोन, बहिन or बोन, कठिन, जनन, लोण, आपना, टानना, ननद.

Other words in some of which even in Sanskrit a ण् appears are in the Hindî and Bangâlî thus :—

83. Skr. ब्राह्मण, H. बम्हन or बामन, B. बामुन, but S. बाभणु a Brahman.

Skr. शृण in शृणोति, H. सुन-[ना], B. शुन-[न], S. सुण-[णु] to hear.

Skr. दक्षिण, H. दहिना, B. डाइन, right hand.

Skr. ग्रहण (?), H. B. गहना, S. गहणो, an ornament worn on the person.

Skr. काण-[कः], H. कान or काना, B. काना, S. काणो blind of one eye.

Still ण् does appear in Bangâlî books in a few words such as काण 'ear,' लोण 'salt,' &c. In the Hindî it seems to be entirely absent.

In the principal Prâkṛit and the Śaurasenî all the Sanskrit sibilants are reduced to स्. Sanskrit words, therefore, containing the palatal श् and the cerebral ष् which in the Prâkṛits came to have the dental स्

instead, have the last in the Hindî, Panjâbî, Sindhî, Gujarâtî, and Marâṭhî. But according to a law of Marâṭhî pronunciation, this स्, when followed by the palatal vowel or semi-vowel इ, ए, or य्, is transformed into the palatal श्. The foregoing lists of words contain many instances that prove these points.

84. List 2. M. H. P. दिस, S. ड्रिस, Skr. दृश्य; H. सियार, Skr. शृगाल; G. H. सींग, P. सिंग, S. सिङ्ग, Skr. शृङ्ग; H. P. किस, Skr. कृषिः; M. पाउस, H. पावस, Skr. प्रावृष्.

List 5. M. G. H., &c. सोंड, सूंड, &c., Skr. शुण्डा.

Lists 11 & 8. G. माणस, M. माणूस, H. मानस, P. मानुस, Skr. मनुष्य.

List 14. M. H. बैस, Skr. उपविश; M. हैस, H. भैंस, G. भेंस, Skr महिषी.

List 24. H. सेमल, M. सांवरी, Skr. शाल्मली; list 34. H. S. साध, Skr. श्रद्धा.

List 47. H. P. परोस, G. पीरस, Skr. परिवेष; list 46. H. सलाई, M. P. सळई, Skr. शलाका.

List 36. H. साला, P. M. साळा, Skr. श्यालक; list 63. M. सांवळा, H. P. सांवला, &c., Skr. श्यामलक; M. विसावा, &c., Skr. विश्राम.

List 69. H. सिहरा or सेहरा, &c., Skr. शेखर; list 73. H. सोह, S. सुह, Skr.शुभ; list 74. P. H. M. G. डांस, Skr. दंश; H. सुन, S. सुण, Skr. शृण as above, &c.

H. सीसो, M. शिसवा, G. शिसम, Skr. शिंशप, list 65.

Other instances are M. साळ, H. साल, Skr. शाला 'a school' or 'an establishment;' M. सल, H. साल, Skr. शल्य 'a dart;' M. G. साकळी, H. सांकली, सिकली 'a chain,' Skr. शृङ्खला; M. सुक, H. सूख, Skr. शुष्क 'dry;' H. सीख, Skr. शिक्ष 'to learn;' H. पीस, Skr. पिष् 'to grind;' H. M. G. नास, Skr. नाश 'destruction;' S. वस, Skr. वर्ष 'to rain;' H. P. S. सेज 'a bed,' Skr. शय्या, &c. Even in words adopted later and consequently treated somewhat differently from the way in which they were treated in the Prâkṛits, the Sanskrit श् and ष् are reduced to स्, as in the H. तसेना 'to thirst,' Skr. तृष्; परवेस 'entrance,' Skr. प्रवेश; परसु 'a hatchet,' Skr. पर्शु; निसपति 'lord of the night,' 'the moon,' Skr. निशापति; S. वंसु 'race,' 'descent,' Skr. वंश; वर्सणु 'to rain,' Skr. वर्ष; वसिकरणु to 'subdue,' Skr. वशीकरण; P. सोग 'sorrow,' Skr. शोक; सांत 'quietness,' Skr. शान्ति; परमेसुर 'God,' Skr. परमेश्वर; M. वरिस, G. वरस 'a year,' Skr. वर्ष; G. वरसवुं 'to rain,' Skr. वर्ष, &c. The present speakers of the Hindî, the Panjâbî, and the Sindhî retain therefore the vocal peculiarity of their Prâkṛit ancestors of pronouncing Sanskrit ष् and श् as स्. Of the words given above the सींग, सेमल, सीख and सेज of the Hindî become शिंग, शेवरी, शिक, and शेज in Marâṭhî, because they are followed by a palatal vowel. Similarly, we have शेण 'cowdung,' Skr. शकन्; शेंगट 'a tree,' Skr. शिग्रु; शेवाळ 'moss,' Skr. शैवाल; शिडी 'a ladder', Skr. श्रेढी, &c. Even the original स् of Sanskrit words is pronounced by the Marâṭhâs as श् under those conditions, as शेंदूर 'red lead,' Skr. सिन्दूरः; शिवणें 'to sew,' Skr. सिव्; माउशी 'mother's sister,' Skr. मातृष्वसृ, &c. Gujarâtî too shows the same tendency though it is not so decided; and we have thus शिंग 'a horn,' शिखवुं 'to learn,' शिववुं 'to sew,' शिसम 'blackwood,' Skr. शिंशप, शेज, Skr. शय्या, &c. But we have also such words as सिंचवुं 'sprinkling,' Skr. सिंच, सिजववुं 'to boil,' सिडी 'ladder,' &c. So that the Marâṭhî rule does not seem to be strictly applicable to the Gujarâṭî. Still the sound श् is as natural to the Gujarâtîs as to the Marâṭhâs, as is shown by such forms as शुं for सुं 'what?', करशो 'do,' &c., and in some provinces it is freely used for स् in many words.

The Bangâli forms of such of the above words as are used in the language have श् for the Hindi स्, as:—

	B.	H.	B.	H.
85.	शुकिवा	सूखना to dry.	शियाल	सियार a jackal.
	शुनिवा	सूनना to hear.	शिमुल	सेमल the silk cotton tree.
	शुइवा	सोना to sleep.	शुंड	सोंड, सूंड trunk of an elephant.
	पाशे	पास near.		
	शिंगा	सींग a horn.	शिशु	सीसो blackwood.
	डांश	डांस a mosquito.	शेल	साल a dart.
	भइंश	भैंस a buffalo.	दिवाशलाई	दियासलाई a fire-match.

Bangâlî books and dictionaries contain a good may words derived from the old Prâkṛits or recently adopted from Sanskrit which contain स् in them. The object of the authors in these cases is to give the correct Prâkṛit or Sanskrit forms, and not to represent the correct Bangâlî pronunciation. But it is not necessary to hear a Bangâlî speak or read his language or even Sanskrit for a long time to arrive at the clear conviction that his vocal habits do not admit of the pronunciation of स् or ष् but only of श्. Sanskrit and Prâkṛit स् becomes श् in his mouth. Thus the Bangâlis of the present day possess the same vocal characteristic that is attributed to their ancestors, the speakers of the Mâgadhî, by the Prâkṛit grammarians.

श् has a tendency to pass off into छ् as we observed in going over the Pâlî. Instead of the Pâlî छक for the Skr. शकृत् 'cowdung,' we have छेणु in S., छाण in G., &c., from शकन् another form of the word, and for the Pâli छाप, Skr. शाव 'the young of an elephant,' we have छावा in H. M. &c., the Pr. form being छाव. For the Skr. शेष the G. has छेवट, छेडो, and छेल्लो 'last,' 'end,' with the suffixes ट, ड and ल, for

Skr. छल्ल 'rind,' H. has छल्ली, for Skr. शण 'hemp,' O. has छण, for सूत्रधार 'carpenter,' which is सुतार in the other dialects and must have been pronounced छुतार by the Bangâlîs, the B. has छुतार, and O. also. Other instances may be found. In Hindî Skr. ष् is often pronounced as ख् as in भाख for भाष, 'spoken dialect,' पुरुख for पुरुष, भेख for वेष, विखम for विषम, &c. This is to be identified with the practice of the followers of the Mâdhyam̐ dina recension of the White Yajurveda who read the ष occurring in their books throughout as ख. But other dialects also have a few instances of this change, as विख P. M. G., विखु S. for Skr. विष.

Of the Prâkṛit words in which a vowel or a mute is aspirated through the influence of an adjoining aspirate or an aspirated mute, the vernaculars have preserved the following:—

86. Pr. फनस, M. G. फणस, Skr. पनस a Jacktree. The H. has also फनस but more commonly पनस.

Pr. भिस, M. भिसें, H. भिस, P. भेह, Skr. बिस edible lotus root. S. has बिहु.

Pr. खासिअ, G. H. P. खांसी, Skr. कासित cough.

There are a good many more modern instances:—

87. M. फरशी, G. फरसी, H. फरसा, Skr. परशु an axe.

M. G. फांस, H. फांस-फांसा-फांसी, P. फाहा-फाही-फांसी, S. फासी-फाही, B. फांस-फांसी, Skr. पाश a noose.

M. निभावणें, G. निभाववुं, H. निभाना, S. निभाइणु, P. निभाउणा, Skr. निर्वाह accomplishing. H. S. P. have also the forms with निबाह.

G. खसवुं, H. खिसना, Skr. कृष्यते to dorp away, to be drawn.

G. घऊं, H. घेऊं or गोहूं, P. घेंऊं, Skr. गोधूम wheat. M. has गहूं.

M. G. O. हाड, P. हड्ड-हड्डी, S. हडु-हड्डी, H. B. हाड-हड्डी, Pr. अट्ठी, Skr. अस्थि bone.

B. हांटु knee, H. ठिहुन, by interchange of places, Skr. अष्ठिवत्, Pr. अट्ठीव?

P. भाफ, B. O. भाप, Pr. बप्फ, Skr. बाष्प vapour.

M. घोंस a bunch, Skr. गुच्छ.

P. सभ, S. सभु all, Pr. सव्व, Skr. सर्व.

M. खुशाल safe, well, Skr. कुशल.

H. P. M. भेस garb, Pr. वेस, Skr. वेश.

M. भूस-भुसा chaff, H. भूस-भूसा, P. भुस-भुस्सी, G. भुसो-भुसुं, B. भूषि, Skr. बुस; S. has बुहु-बुहो.

In some cases the aspirate sound is absorbed in the adjoining mute, and it ceases to exist as a separate component of a word. Thus, from the Pr. पहुडि, Skr. प्रभृति, we have the M. पुढें in which the ह् combines with ड्, and the M. *dial.* फुडें in which it combines with प्. In the same manner the Skr. मेष 'sheep' becomes, with the usual Apabhraṁs'a suffix ड or डअ, मेसडड or मेहडड, which in M. and G. assumes the form of मेंढा and मेंढो, the ह् combining with ड, and in H. and P. of भेडा in which the ह् being combined with the preceding मे destroys the nasal character of the sound. P. has मेढा also, and G. भेडा, and B. and O. मेड़ा as well as भेड़ा. By a similar absorption of the ह् sound and the reduction of the nasal to a mere Anusvâra we have H. P. भैंस (*masc.* भैंसा), G. भेंस, B. भंईश, from Skr. महिषी 'a female buffalo,' and G. M. भेळ from Pr. मिस्स, Skr. मिश्र with the suffix ल, through an intermediate form मिहल or मेहल. We have a more ancient instance of the process in the Pr. संभर for Skr. संस्मर, through the intermediate form संम्हर, which has been preserved by the G. in सांभरवुं 'to remember' or 'remind.'

Sometimes a mute is aspirated without any apparent reason in the Prâkṛits, and these instances have come down to some of the vernaculars:—

88. Skr. कुब्ज humpbacked, Pr. खुज्जो, M. खुजा; but P. कोझा, H. कुंजा, B. कुंजो, O. कुंजा, S. कुब्रो; M. कुबडा also.

Skr. कीलकः a nail, Pr. खीलओ, M. खिळा, G. खिळो, B. O. खील or खिला; the rest कील.

Skr. कर्पर potsherd, an earthen cup, Pr. खप्पर, M. खापर, H. P. खप्पर, O. खपरा, B. खाबरा.

Later instances are P. खूहा, S. खूहा a well, Skr. कूपकः; P. छुहणा to touch, H. छूना, Skr. छुप; M. घागर, P. H. गागर, Skr. गर्गरिका; G. खोळो lap, Skr. क्रोड.

Of the instances in the Prâkṛits in which the consonants contained in a word interchange places we have हळू 'slow' in M., Pr. हलुअ and Skr. लघुक, हौला in H. and P. and हळू and हळवे in G.; M. सून 'daughter-in-law,' Pr. सुण्हा, Skr. स्नुषा; M. निढाल 'forehead,' Pr. णडाल, Skr. ललाट, &c. There are a good many more modern instances :—

89. H. पहिचानना to recognize, Pr. पच्चहिआण, Skr. प्रत्यभिज्ञा-(जा) न, P. पछाणना.

H. पहिरना to dress, Pr. परिहाण, Skr. परिधान ; P. पहिराउणा to cause to dress. In both the last two syllables are assimilated and we have पहिन्ना also ; G. पेरवुं by the loss of ह्.

G. वहालुं beloved, Pr. वल्लह, Skr. वल्लभ ; सेहलुं easy, Pr. सुलह, Skr. सुलभ ; बिलाडी a cat, Skr. बिडाल ; उथलपाथल topsy-turvy, the M. form being उलटापालट, Pr. उवल्लत्थ-ड पल्लत्थ-ड, Skr. उपर्यस्त पर्यस्त.

M. शेपूट or शेपटी tail, G. having पूछडुं or पूछडी, Skr. पुच्छ, with the suffix ट, the छ् being changed to श् by the usual M. rule and the palatal vowel being brought in by the palatal श्; थोडकें little, Pr. थोक, Skr. स्तोक, with the suffix ड.

S. छुगो a bunch of flowers, Skr. गुच्छ; ढिलिडो loose, Pr. सिढिल, Skr. शिथिल.

H. M. टिकली, &c., from Skr. तिलक as in list 75.

We will now trace in the vernaculars the Sanrkrit conjunct consonants assimilated in the Pâli and the Prâkṛits, in the order I have observed in treating of them in the lecture on the Pâli. And first I will give a few instances of those in which the second member being strong prevails over the first and is doubled.

90. Skr. कर्म act, business, Pr. कम्म, P. कम्म, S. कमु, H. G. M. O. काम.

Skr. घर्म heat of the sun, Pr. घम्म, H. घाम; M. G. B. O. घाम in the sense of 'sweat.'

Skr. चर्म skin, leather, Pr. चम्म, P. चम्म, S. चमु, H. G. B. चाम, O. चम, M. चाम in चामडें.

Skr. कार्य, Pr. कज्जं, S. काजु, M. G. H. P. काज. The M. has, however, the dento-palatal ज here.

Skr. कर्ण ear, Pr. कण्ण, P. कन्न, S. कनु, H. G. M. B. O. कान.

Skr. पर्ण a leaf, Pr. पण्ण, P. पन्ना (of a book), S. पनु, H. G. M. पान, G. पानुं (of a book), P. S. O. पान in the sense of 'betel leaf.'

Skr. विज्ञप to solicit, supplicate, Pr. विण्णव, H. G. M. विनव-[ना-वुं-णें]; H. also विनौना.

Skr राज्ञी a queen, Pr. रण्णी (?), G. P. S. M. B. O. राणी, H. रानी.

Skr. संज्ञा a signal, Pr. सण्णा, P. सन, H. G. सान; H. सैन also.

Skr. यज्ञोपवीत the sacred thread, Pr. जण्णोवईअ(?), H. P. जनेऊ, S. जण्यो, G. जनोइ, M. जानवें.

Skr. अर्प to make over, Pr. अप्प, G. आप-[वुं].

Skr. समर्प to consign, deliver, Pr. समप्प, H. P. S. सौंप-[ना-णा-णु], M. G. सोंप-[णें-वुं].

Skr. सर्प a serpent, Pr. सप्प, P. सप्प, S. सपु, H. G. M. B. O. साप.

Skr. दर्भ sacred grass, Pr. दब्भ, P. दब्भ, S. डभु, H. डाभ or डाब, G. डाभ or डाभो.

Skr. शब्द sound, call, Pr. सद्द, P. सद्द (*subs. & verb*), H. M. G. साद.

Skr. दर्दुर a frog, Pr. दद्दुर, P. H. G. दादुर, S. डेडरु.

Skr. भक्त boiled rice, Pr. भत्त, P. भत्त, S. भतु, H. M. G. B. O. भात.

Skr. रक्त red, Pr. रत्त, P. रत्ता, S. रतो, H. G. रातो, M. रात in रातांम्बा a red sour fruit of a certain tree.

Skr. सुप्त slept, Pr. सुत्त, P. सुत्ता, S. G. सुतो.

Skr. कर्दम mud, Pr. कद्दम, H. कादो or कादा, G. कादव.

Skr. तर्क to look out for, gaze wistfully, Pr. तक्क, P. तकना, S. तकणु, M. टकणें, O. टाकिबा, H. G. ताक-[ना-वुं].

The following are instances in which though the second member of a conjunct prevails, some of the elements of the first sound are added to it :—

(a) Conjuncts of a sibilant and a mute.

91. Skr. हस्त hand, Pr. हत्थ, P. हत्थ, S. हथु, H. G. हाथ, M. B. O. हात.

Skr. मुष्टि fist, Pr. मुट्ठि, P. मुट्ठ, S. मुठि, H. G. मूठ-मुट्ठी, M. मूठ, O. मूठि, B. मूट.

Skr. प्रस्तर stone, Pr. पत्थर, P. पत्थर, S. पथरु, H. G. पत्थर or पाथर, M. पाथर, B. पाथर or पातर, O. पथर.

Skr. पृष्ठ back, Pr. पुट्ठ-पिट्ठ-पट्ठ, vernaculars as in Table 4.

Skr. प्रस्थापन sending, Pr. पट्ठावण, S. पठणु, H. पठाना, Braj पठैबौ, M. पाठवणें, B पाठाइबा.

Skr. मुस्ता a kind of grass, Pr. मोत्था, vernaculars as in Table 5.

Skr. मस्तक head, Pr. मत्थअ, P. मथ्था, S. मथो, H. M. B. माथा, G. माथुं, M. माथें, O. मथा.

Skr. पुस्तक a book, Pr. पोत्थअ, P. H. M., &c. as in Table 5.

Skr. उपविष्ट sat, Pr. उवइट्ठ, vernaculars as in Table 43.

Skr. दृष्टि or दृष्ट sight or seen, Pr. दिट्ठि or दिट्ठ, P. डिट्ठा-डिट्ठ, and the rest as in Table 2.

Skr. उष्ण hot, Pr. उण्ह, G. उन्हुं, M. ऊन; M. G. S. उन्ह as in उन्हाळा-ळो-रो for उष्णकाळ the hot season.

Skr. स्ना to bathe, Pr. ण्हा or नहा, P. H. M. G. न्हा-[उणा-ना-णें-वुं]; P.H. नहा also.

Skr. अङ्गुष्ठ thumb, Pr. अंगुट्ठ, P. अंगूठ, S. आङूठो, H. अंगूठा, G. अंगूठो, M. आंगठा.

Skr. विष्किर to spread, Pr. विक्खिर, P. विखरना, S. विखेरणु, H. G. M. विखर-[ना-वुं-णें] to be scattered.

Skr. शुष्क dry, Pr. सुक्ख, P. सुख्खा, S. सुको, H. सूखा, G. सूखो, M. सुका, B. O. शुका.

Skr. बाष्प vapour, Pr. बप्फ, S. H. G. बाफ, M. वाफ, P. भाफ, B. O. भाप.

Skr. स्कन्ध shoulder, Pr. खन्ध, H. M. खांदा, G. खांदो; but H. mostly has कंधा and कांधा, P. कन्धा, B. O. कांध.

Skr. पश्चात् behind, Pr. पच्छा, P. पिच्छे, H. पीछे, पाछे, G. पाछुं.

Skr. ग्रीष्म hot season, Pr. गिह्म, M. *dial.* गीम.

Skr. कृष्ण proper name, Pr. कण्ह, vernaculars as in Table 1.

(b) Conjuncts of a dental and a heavy य़.

92. Skr. सत्य true, Pr. सच्च, P. H. सच्च, S. सचु, H. M. साच, G. साचुं, B. सांचा.

Skr. नृत्य of नृत्यति to dance, Pr. नच्च, P. नच्च or नच्च-[णा], S. नच-[णु], H. M. G. नाच-[ना-णें-वुं.], B. O. नाचिवा.

Skr. नृत्य a dance, Pr. नच्च, P. नाच, S. नाचु, H. M. G. B. O. नाच.

Skr. मृत्यु death, Pr. मिच्चु, H. मीच.

Skr. प्रत्यभिजान of प्रत्यभिजानाति to recognize, Pr. पच्चहिआण, H. पहिचान, P. पछाण, B. चिन or चिनिवा, by dropping the first two consonants.

Skr. उत्पद्य of उत्पद्यते to be produced, Pr. उप्पज्ज, P. S. H. M. G. पज -[णा-णु-ना-णें-वुं].

Skr. माद्य of माद्यति to be intoxicated, Pr. मज्ज, M. माजणें.

Skr. विद्युत् lightning, Pr. विज्जु, M. G. वीज, P. विज्ज, S. विजु.

Skr. अद्य to-day, Pr. अज्ज, P. अज्ज, S. अजु, H. M. G. B. आज, B. O. आजि.

Skr. स्विद्य of स्विद्यति to sweat, *also* to boil, Pr. सिज्ज, P. सिज्जणा to be soaked, S. सिझणु, H. सिझना-सिजाना (causal), M. शिजणें, G. सिजवुं, O. सिजिवा.

Skr. वन्ध्या a barren woman, Pr. वंज्झा or वंज्झा, P. वंझा, S. वांझ, H. O. बांझ, G. वांझ-[णी], M. वांझ or वांज, B. बांझा.

Skr. संध्या evening, Pr. संज्झा, P. S. संझा, S. सांझी, H. सांझ, M. G. H. B. सांज, O. संज.

Skr. बुध्य of बुध्यते to know, Pr. बुज्झ, P. बुज्झणा, H. S. बुझ-[ना-णु]; B. O. बुझिवा, M. G. बुज-[णें-वुं].

Skr. मध्य middle, Pr. मज्झ, P. मंज्झ or माज्झ, S. मंझु, H. मांझ or माझ, M. माजीं, B. माझ.

Skr. युद्ध battle, Pr. जुज्झ of जुज्झइ for युध्यति, P. जुज्झ, H. जूझा, B. झुंज (in झुंजार), M. झूज.

When व़, as the latter member of a conjunct, is heavily pronounced the double consonant that takes the place of the conjunct is प्प, ब्ब, and ब्भ according as the preceding member is a surd, a sonant, or an aspirated sonant. Sometimes when the preceding member is a dental the substitutes are च्च, ज्ज, and ज्झ. The following are instances of these changes in the vernaculars :—

93. Skr. त्व abstract termination, Apabhr. प्प, H. पा as in बुढ़ापा old age, मोटापा fatness, S. पो as in माण्हिपो humanity, from माण्हु man.

Skr. त्वन abstract termination, Pr. त्तण, Apabhr. प्पण, H. पन or पना as in कुआरपन celibacy; S. पणु or पणो as in जालपणु womanhood, माण्हुअपणु humanity; M. पण or पणा as in माणुसपण or माणुसपणा humanity; P. पुण as in निआणपुण childhood, &c.

Skr. उद्वेग feeling of repulsion, Pr. उव्वेग, M. उबग.

Skr. द्वार door, Pr. दार or बार, P. H. G. बार, P. दर, S. दरु, M. दार.

Skr. सर्व all, Pr. सव्व, H. सब, P. सभ, S. सभु, G. सहु for सब.

Skr. ज्वल to burn, Pr. जल or बल, S. बरणु, P. जळना-बळणा, H. जलना-बलना, G. जळवुं-बळवुं, M. जळणें and पोळणें where ब seems to be hardened, B. O. पोड़ in पोड़िवा.

Skr. ऊर्ध्व above, erect, Pr. उब्भ, S. उभो, M. O. उभा, B. उबु.

Skr. जिह्वा tongue, Pr. जिब्भा, M. H. P. G. जीभ, B. O. S. जिभ.

Skr. ध्वज banner, Pr. झअ; with the suffix डा or डो, S. झंडो, P. H. झंडा, M. झेंडा.

Similarly आत्मन्, with the loss of the nasal sound of त्म, becomes अप्पण in the Prâkṛits and आपण in M. O. G., आपन in B., पाण in S. and आप in H. P.

Dentals have a tendency to become palatals even when not followed by य् or व्, probably because they do so become when followed by those semi-vowels. Thus, from the Skr. वादयति 'to sound' or 'play on a musical instrument,' we have P. बजाउणा, H. बजाना, M. वाजविणें, &c. from Skr. निद्रा 'sleep,' M. नीज; P. H. ओछा 'trifling,' 'vain,' S. ओछा, from, very probably, Skr. तुच्छ; M. सावज, H. साजा from Skr. श्वापद which appears even in the Prâkṛits to have assumed the form of सावज, though सावय is usually given; M. H. G. छी छी, M. छे छे, Pr. छि छि from Skr. धिक् धिक्, &c.

(c) The conjunct क्ष् when the sibilant is pronounced like ख्, and त्स, and त्स्य.

94. Skr. क्षण ... { a moment, Pr. खण, P. छिण, S. खिण, H. छिन, G. खण, M. (*dial.*) खिण. a festival, Pr. छण, H. छिन, M. सण for छण. }

Skr. क्षुरक-रिका a knife, a razor, Pr. छुरअ-रिआ, P. छुरा-री, S. छुरी, H. छुरा-री, B. O. छोरा-छुरी, M. सुरी.

Skr. मक्षिका a fly, Pr. { मक्खिआ, P. मक्खी, S. मखी, H. G. माखी. मच्छिआ, H. B. O. माछी, M. माशी. }

Skr. कुक्षि a side of the abdomen, Pr. कुच्छि or कुक्खि, M. कूस; the rest कूख or कोख as in Table 5.

Skr. ऋक्ष a bear, Pr. रिच्छ, P. रिच्छ, S. रिछु, H. G. रीछ, M. रीस.

Skr. तक्ष to shave, hew, Pr. तच्छ, P. तच्छणा, M. तासणें, G. तासवुं.

Skr. क्षेत्र a field, M. शेत from Pr. छेत्त; the rest खेत.

Skr. वत्स a calf, Pr. वच्छ, P. बच्छा, S. वछ, H. बाछा, बछा, बछ, G. वछ, वाछ-[रडुं], B. बाछु-[र], O. बाछु-[री], M. वास-[रुं]; P. H. बचा, S. बचो, B. बाचा, M. बच-[डें], &c., in the sense of 'the young one of any animal,' from the same.

Skr. मत्स्य a fish, Pr. मच्छ, P. मच्छ, S. मछु, H. मछ or माछ, B. O. माछ, M. मासा.

Skr. उत्सङ्ग lap, Pr. उच्छङ्ग, H. उछंग, M. ओसंग.

The conjunct क्ष sometimes appears in the Prâkṛits and perhaps even in Sanskrit in the form of झ. The Sanskrit क्षर is ज्झर in the Prâkṛits, and this we have in the H. झरना, M. झरणें and पाझरणें in which last पा stands for the preposition प्र. क्षि is Pr. झिज्झ from which we have M. झिजणें 'to waste away,' and from क्षीण we have S. झीणो, H. झीन, &c.

(d) Instances in which a dental is changed to a cerebral through the influence of a previous र्.

95. Skr. वर्ध to increase, Pr. वड्ढ, H. बढना or बाढना, M. वाढणें, B. बाडिवा, O. बढिवा. But P. S. G. वध or वध-(णा-णु-वुं).

Skr. वर्ध to cut, Pr. वड्ढ, P. बड्ढणा, or वड्ढणा, S. वढणु.

Skr. वर्धक-कि a carpenter, Pr. वड्ढइ, P. वड्ढि, H. बढई, O. बढाइ, B. बाडइ, S. G. वाढो.

Skr. छर्द to let off, leave, Pr. छड्ड, P. छड्डणा, S. छडणु, H. छाडना, B. O. छाडिवा. H. छांडना, M. सांडणें, perhaps from the same, as also H. छोडना, M. सोडणें.

Skr. कर्त to cut, Pr. कट्ट, P. कट्टणा, S. कटणु, H. काटना, B. काटिवा, G. काटवुं, M. काटणें.

Skr. उद्वर्तन a cosmetic, Pr. उव्वट्टन, S. उबटणु, H. उबटन, M. उटणें, G. उटणु.

Skr. कैवर्त a boatman, Pr. केवट्ट, H. केवट.

Skr. सार्ध a half more, Pr. सड्ढ, H. P. B. O. साढे, S. साढा-ढ़, H. M. साडे, G. साडा.

We will now proceed to instances in which the first member of a conjunct prevails over the second and is doubled:—

96. Skr. भग्न-[कः] fled away, Pr. भग्ग-[ओ], H. भागा, S. भगो.

Skr. लग्न adhered to, connected, Pr. लग्ग, P. लग्गा or लग्ग in लग्गणा, S. लग in लगणु, H. M. G. लाग-[ना-णें-वुं,] B. लागा, O. लागिवा.

Skr. नग्न-[कः] naked, Pr. नग्ग-[ओ], P. H. नंगा, S. नंगो, G. नागो, M. नाग-[डा], O. नागा.

Skr. रश्मि a cord, a rope, Pr. रस्सि, P. H. रस्सी, S. B. G. O. रसी, H. G. रास in the sense of 'reins.'

Skr. योग्य fit, Pr. जोग्ग, P. जोग or जोग्गा, S. जोगु, H. G. जोग, H. M. जोगा.

Skr. शून्य void, empty, Pr. सुण्ण, P. सुन्न or सुन्ना, S. सुंन, H. सून or सूना, M. सुना. सुंन has acquired the sense of 'insensibility' also.

Skr. मन्य of मन्यते to regard, Pr. मण्ण, P. मन्नणा, S. मनणु, M. G. H. मान-[णें-वुं-ना].

Skr. व्याख्यान to explain, Pr. वक्खाण, P. व-वखाणना, H. वखानना explain or praise, S. वखाणणु praise, G. वखाणवुं, M. वाखाणणें.

Skr. अरण्य desert, Pr. रण्ण, M. G. रान, H. रन, S. रिणु.

Skr. व्याघ्र a tiger, Pr. वग्घ, P. H. B. O. बाघ, S. बाघु, M. G. वाघ.

Skr. अग्र front part, Pr. अग्ग, S. अगो, H. आगा; P. आग्गु before, G. आगो, G. आगल before, B. आगे, O. आगु first of all.

Skr. चक्र a wheel, Pr. चक्क, P. चक्क, S. चकु (both) a potter's wheel, H. चाक, चक्की in the sense of a 'mill-stone,' G. M. चाक, B. चाका.

Skr. पत्र a leaf, Pr. पत्त, P. पत्त, S. पतो a playing card, H. पात, पाता पत्ता, G. पातरुं, M. पातें blade of a knife, M. पातेरा a collection of dry leaves.

Skr. चन्द्र moon, Pr. चन्द, P. चंद, S. चंडु, H. G. M. B. O. चांद, H. चंद also.

Skr. श्मश्रू as in list 34.

Skr. अभ्र a cloud, Pr. अब्भ, H. अभाल, M. अभाळ or आभाळ, (from अभालि), G. आभ.

Skr. ज्वल, Pr. and other forms with ज as in list 93.

Skr. पार्श्व a side, Pr. पास, S. पासो, P. पास्सा, H. पास, G. पासे, M. पाशीं near, *i. e.*, by one's side.

When र् followed by य् is changed to ल् this last sound prevails over the य् and the conjunct becomes ल्ल् in the Prâkṛits. The following instances of this change have come down to the vernaculars:—

97. Skr. पर्याय rotation, turn, Pr. पल्लाअ, H. पाला, M. G. O. पाळी.

Skr. पर्यस्त changed, Pr. पल्लट्ठ or पल्लत्थ, P. H. पलटा, P. पळटा, M. G. पालट.

Skr पर्यङ्क a bedstead, Pr. पल्लङ्क, P. पलंघ, S. पलंगु, H. M. G. पलंग, B. पालंक or पालंग, O. पलंक.

The following are instances of other cases of the same change:—

Skr. मर्द to squeeze, rub, knead, Pr. मल, P. M. G. मळ-[ना-णें-वुं], H. S. मल-[ना-णु].

Skr. आर्द्रक ginger, Pr. अल्लअ, M. आलें. H. P. B. have आदा, G. आदुं, from Pr. अद्दअ.

Skr. आर्द्रक wet, Pr. अल्लअ, उल्लअ, ओल्लअ, M. ओलें, S. आलो, H. आला, H. has आदा also from Pr. अद्दअ.

P. H. M. भला, G. S. भलो, B. भाल, from Skr. भद्र, through the change of द् to ल् and of the conjunct to ल्ल्.

When क् the first sound of क्ष् prevails and adds to itself the heavy aspiration of ष्, the conjunct becomes क्ख्. Of this change there are many instances in the vernaculars:—

98. Skr. वृक्ष a tree, Pr. रुक्ख, P. रुक्ख, H. रूख.

Skr. रक्ष to keep, to protect, Pr. रक्ख, P. रक्खणा, S. रखणु, H. रखना also राखना, M. G. राख-[णें-वुं], B. O. राखिवा.

Skr. उपलक्ष to mark, Pr. उवलक्ख, M. G. ओळख acquaintance.

Skr. शिक्ष to learn, Pr. सिक्ख, P. सिखणा, S. सिखणु, H. सीखना, G. शिखवुं, M. शिकणें, B. O. शिखिवा.

Skr. क्षेत्र a field, Pr. खेत, P. खेत, S. खेतु or खेटु, H. B. O. खेत, G. खेत in खेती agriculture.

Skr. कुक्षि a side of the abdomen, Pr. कुक्खि, P. कुक्ख or कोख, S. कखि, H. कोख, G. कुख.

Skr. बुभुक्षा hunger, Pr. बुहुक्खा, P. भुक्ख, S. बुख, H. G. B. भूख, M. B. भूक, O. भोक.

Skr. म्रक्षण to anoint, an unguent, Pr. मक्खण, P. मक्खण butter, S. मखणु anoint, butter, H. मक्खन or माखन butter, B. O. माखन butter, माखिवा to anoint, M. माखणें to anoint, G. माखण butter.

Skr. परीक्षा examination, Pr. परिक्खा, H. P. B. O. परख, M. G. S. पारख.

Skr. अक्षि the eye, Pr. अक्खि, P. अक्ख, S. अखि, H. G. आंख, B. O. आखि.

Skr. क्षीर milk, Pr. खीर, S. खीरु, P. H. M. G. खीर a dish of rice and milk, O. खीरि.

Skr. मक्षिका and क्षण as in list 93.

Skr. इक्षु sugar-cane, Pr. उक्खु or इक्खु, H. ऊख or ईख, P. इक्ख.

Though according to Hemachandra and Vararuchi the क्ष् of क्षेत्र, कुक्षि, अक्षि, क्षीर, मक्षिका, and इक्षु is changed to च्छ् in the Mahârâshṭrî or principal Prâkṛit, still we see that most of the vernaculars derive their forms of these words from such Prâkṛit forms as had क्ख् for the

Sanskrit क्ष्. But with the exception of इक्खु and खीर which are mentioned as occurring in the Jaina sacred books, these forms are not given as existing in any of the dialects. This and other similar omissions show that the observation of the Prâkṛit grammarians was by no means perfect. The Marâṭhî forms of these words, however, with the exception of अक्षि which is unknown to the language and of क्षीर which is खीर, have ख् or छ् which is the representative of the Prâkṛit छ्, and hence they are the same as those given by Hemachandra and Vararuchi. Here we have one of several indications that the modern Marâṭhî is the direct daughter of the old Mahârâshṭrî of the grammarians.

It will be seen from the lists given above that the Hindî, Gujarâti, Marâṭhî and Bangâlî mostly drop one component of the doubled consonants and to make up for the quantity thus lost lengthen the preceding vowel. In other words, the speakers of those dialects take the same time to pronounce two syllables the latter of which contains a double consonant which the speakers of the Prâkṛit did; but the preceding forcible vowel utterance and the subsequent strong contact and pressure being avoided, the effect is that one of the two consonants is dropped and the previous vowel lengthened. This then is essentially a case of softening. The Sindhî drops one of the two consonants, but does not engthen the preceding vowel; while the Panjâbî generally preserves the doubled consonants handed down to it by the old Prâkṛits. The Hindî contains more instances in which the original Prâkṛit pronunciation is preserved than the other three dialects. Hemachandra notices in the Prâkṛits the softened pronunciation we have been considering in the case of स्स् only, one स् of which is according to him dropped and the preceding vowel is lengthened, as in पासइ for पस्सइ, Skr. पश्यति, मीसं for मिस्सं, Skr. मिश्रम्, &c. This lengthening of the previous vowel is in the four dialects prevented as observed before* by the accent falling on a subsequent syllable.

In the Pâli and the Prâkṛits, you will remember, the components of some conjuncts such as र्य्, र्ह्, र्श्, र्ष्, श्ल्, क्ल्, ग्ल्, म्ल्, &c., are not assimilated but separated by the interposition of a vowel. The vernaculars have preserved some instances of this process:—

99. H. सराहना to praise, Pr. सलाह, Skr. श्लाघ.

H. अगनी, P. अगन, B. आगुन fire, Pr. अगणी, Skr. अग्नि.

H. बरस, बरिस, M. वरीस a year, Pr. वरिस, Skr. वर्ष. So also H. P. वरस-[ना-णा], G. वरसवुं, Skr. वर्ष.

H. गिलान tired, Pr. गिलाण, Skr. ग्लान.

* See pp. 162-3.

M. किळस disgust, Pr. किलेस, Skr. क्लेश distress.

M. शिलोक stanza, Skr. श्लोक; G. हरख joy, Skr. हर्ष; G. सळेखम, P. सिलेइम, Skr. श्लेष्म, are later instances of the same nature.

In modern times other conjuncts also are similarly dissolved, and we have पतांप S. M., &c., 'exploit' for प्रताप, खेतर, P. G., &c., 'a field' for क्षेत्र, पदम S. 'a lotus' for पद्म, तियाग P. for त्याग, तसं S., others तरास 'vexation' for त्रास, धरम 'virtue,' H. M. G., &c., for धर्म, &c. But the books and dictionaries of some of these languages contain a good many Sanskrit words the conjuncts in which are not changed in any way. This is due to the fact that those languages are now the spoken languages of the educated as well as the uneducated portions of the different communities, and the former pronounce the words correctly and the forms given to them by the latter are not taken into account by the authors of those books. Again, even the latter, though they interpose a vowel between the components of some conjuncts as shown above, have to a certain extent become used to Sanskrit sounds and can pronounce others correctly. But in some of the provinces the old disability of the Prâkṛit speakers has been inherited in certain cases by their modern descendants, whether educated or uneducated, and it is very much to be regretted that the writers of books should in such cases write words in their Sanskrit forms which, when they are read by themselves or others, are read in quite a different way. The people of Sindh,* whether belonging to the higher or lower classes, and the Bangâlîs pronounce the conjunct क्ष् invariably as क्ख्. Thus Sanskrit नक्षत्र is pronounced नक्खत्र, साक्षी as साखी, मोक्ष as मोक्ख or मोख, &c. The speakers of the Hindî more often pronounce क्ष् as च्छ् than as क्ख्, नक्षत्र becoming नच्छंतर with them; साक्षी, साच्छी; मोक्ष, मोच्छ; लक्ष्मण, लच्छमन; लक्षणा, लच्छना; क्षत्रिय, खत्री or छत्री; क्षय, छय; क्षम, छम; &c. The Panjâbîs pronounce the first three words as नच्छत्र, साखी, and मोच्छ, लक्षण as लच्छण, क्षत्रिय as खत्री, &c., so that they also agree with the Hindî people, but seem more inclined towards

*While I was Head Master of the High School at Hyderabad in Sindh I introduced about the beginning of 1865 the study of Sanskrit, and the first thing I had to do was to teach correct pronunciation to my pupils. I had no great difficulty, so far as I can now remember, in making them pronounce the other conjuncts; but when I came to क्ष् all my endeavours to teach its correct pronunciation failed. I got the most intelligent of my boys to pronounce first क् and then ष्. This he did very well, whereupon I told him to utter both the sounds one after another immediately; but instead of making क्ष् of them he invariably gave them the form of क्ख्. I then gave up the attempt in despair.

making क्ख् of the conjunct. The Marâṭhâs, however, pronounce the ष् properly, though ordinarily they make क्श् of it rather than क्ष् as remarked on a former occasion. Similarly, the Bangâlî assimilates conjuncts the latter member of which is व् or य्, ईश्वर becoming इस्सर and व्याख्यान, बाक्खान in his mouth. Similarly he pronounces Skr. आत्मा as अत्ता just as his Prâkṛit ancestors did though it is written correctly.

Some of the vernaculars assimilate the components of a conjunct made up of a nasal and a mute. Thus the Panjâbî has डन्न for दण्ड 'penalty,' मुन्नणा for मुण्डना 'to shave,' सुन्न for सुण्ड, Skr. शुण्डा 'the trunk of an elephant,' कन्हा for कन्धा, Skr. स्कन्ध 'shoulder,' बन्ह for बन्ध 'binding,' खन्न for खण्ड 'a piece,' भन्नणा 'to break' for भञ्जना or भन्जना, थम्म for स्तम्भ 'a pillar,' &c. In the Bangâlî खान 'a piece' one of the two न् sounds of खन्न is dropped, and the preceding vowel lengthened. Similarly, we have थाम 'to stop' from स्तम्भ. In Sindhî we have भञु 'interruption' for भङ्ग; चङो 'good' for चङ्गो, M. चांगला; मञुठ 'madder' for मञ्जिष्ठ; पिनु 'a ball' for पिण्ड; खनु 'a piece of bread' for खण्ड; चुमणु 'to kiss' for चुम्ब, &c. Here the Sindhî, as is usual with him, drops one component of the doubled consonants. With this exception, the modern dialects have got no cases of the assimilation of the members of a conjunct unknown to the Prâkṛits, while as shown above the speakers of those dialects tenaciously retain the vocal habit of assimilation of their Prâkṛit ancestors in a few cases.

And now I close this part of my inquiry. The results at which we have arrived are these:—The vernaculars of Northern India contain the instances and, in some cases, a large number of them, given by the Prâkṛit grammarians or occurring in Prâkṛit literature, of every one of the rules or processes of change grouped by me under the heads of softening, assimilation, dissimilation, interchange of places, accentuation, and peculiarities by which Sanskrit words become Prâkṛit. Most of these processes have been continued and their range widened, to such an extent in some of the dialects as to render them distinctive characteristics of those dialects. Other processes scarcely or rarely observable in the Prâkṛits have come into operation, such as the original accent on the penultimate syllable and the final accent derived from it, the avoiding of the hiatus caused by the elision of consonants in the Prâkṛits in different ways, the change of म् to वँ, and the dropping of one component of a double consonant and the lengthening of a previous vowel; and these have further transformed the Prâkṛit vocables and changed also those Sanskṛit words that have been adopted in later times. Some of the vocal tendencies and habits of the Prâkṛit speakers are exhibited by the speakers of the vernaculars. Thus, like the former, the ordinary Gujarâtî pronounces ऐ and औ as ए and ओ, the Deśastha Brahmans and other people of Eastern Mahârâshṭra have a predilection for ण् to which they reduce न् in most cases,* the Sindhîs make क्ख् of क्ष्, the Bangâlîs do the same and also pronounce क्ष्, ह्य् and त्म as ज्झ्, क्ख् and त्त and the Hindî people reduce क्ष् to छ्. These again and the Konkan lower classes pronounce ण as न् like the speakers of the Paiśâchî, and the Bangâlî reduces all the sibilants to श like the speakers of the Mâgadhî; while the speakers of the Hindî, Sindhî and the Panjâbî exhibit the old Mahârâshṭrî and Śaurasenî characteristic of reducing them to स्. The tendency to pronounce dentals as cerebrals is common to all, though it appears in a very strong form in the mouth of the Sindhîs, and next to them in that of the Panjâbîs and the Hindî people. The general or almost universal elision of certain uninitial consonants, which was a characteristic of the Prâkṛits, has disappeared except in isolated cases, and the assimilation of the components of a conjunct which was also very general has become restricted to the few cases I have mentioned, though the words changed in the Prâkṛits in accordance with these two processes have come down to us in large numbers. While, therefore, this fact shows that the speakers of the Prâkṛits were in a condition which rendered the two phenomena very general in their speech, and that we are now free from it, the fact that we exhibit some of the same vocal peculiarities which they possessed leads to the conclusion that we are their successors or lineal descendants. And the fact that the vocables in ordinary use in our modern dialects are the same as those in the old Prâkṛits, whether of a Deśya or Sanskrit origin, and in the latter case whether derived by the transformation of Sanskrit words in accordance with processes which have ceased or which have continued to operate in the vernaculars, affords strong evidence in favour of the hypothesis that these dialects are but a more developed form of the Prâkṛits. But to place this hypothesis beyond the reach of cavil we must examine the grammar of our vernaculars; and this I propose doing in the next two lectures.

---

* I feel it necessary, for the present, thus to modify the assertion made in p. 186.

LECTURE V.

Remnants of the Older Grammatical Forms in the Northern Vernaculars.

I have already directed your attention to the accent on the penultimate syllable of words in the vernaculars of Northern India and the effect it has had in mutilating and transforming the Sanskrit and Prâkṛit words existing in their vocabularies. Through its influence, you will remember, the final vowel or the vowel of the last syllable is shortened in some cases and often entirely dropped and the word ends in a consonant or silent अ. When the consonant of the last syllable is dropped in consequence of the Prâkṛit law of the elision of uninitial consonants the final vowel and the vowel of the penultimate syllable are brought together and when they are in this condition it is possible for them to unite into one sound and thus the final vowel is dropped in some cases and combined with the preceding in others. The Sindhî, however, oftentimes resists the influence of this accent as I have already mentioned. Now on account of these processes the nominative singular termination ओ of masculine Prâkṛit nouns ending in अ is sometimes shortened to उ and in this form we have it in the Sindhî and in old Marâṭhî and Hindî literature. In the other dialects including the modern Marâṭhî and Hindî it is dropped except in rare instances such as वाटसरू M. and आयसु 'command' H. The Prâkṛit plural terminations आ and ए of this case are also dropped everywhere for the same reason and we have such forms as हाथ S., हाथ H., हात M. G. &c. for the nom. pl. and these are the sing. forms also except in the case of the Sindhî, which has हथु. In the Prâkṛit the plurals of the nominative and accusative cases of all nouns are alike and so are they alike in the vernaculars. The analogy came to be extended to the singulars also in the Apabhraṁśa and accordingly the singulars of the two cases are the same in the vernaculars. An independent accusative case made up by affixing a termination to a noun is given in ordinary grammars; but it has the sense of the dative, or rather of the Sanskrit genitive which expresses relation in general. Thus we say मी काम करितों M. 'I do a work', हुं काम करूं छूं G., आंव कमु थो कयाँ S., मै कम करदा P., मै काम करता हूं H., आमि or मुइ काम करि or करिते छि B., मु कर्म करु आछि O., in which instances काम etc. are really accusatives and we do not use कामास, कामने, कमखे, कमतु, कामको, कामके, and कर्मकु, which forms are generally referred to the accusative. The masculine nom. and acc.

sing. form in उ was in the Apabhraṁśa extended by analogy to the neuter singular also and, though the peculiar neuter plural termination was preserved, the fact shows that in the vernacular speech of the times there was a tendency to forget the distinction between the two genders. Accordingly we now find that in the Sindhî, the Panjâbî, the Hindi, Bangâlî and Oriya the distinction is entirely lost. In Gujarâtî also nouns ending in अ have retained none of the two neuter terminations but the Prâkṛit and Apabhraṁśa इं plural of that gender exists in the Marâṭhî combined with the preceding अ into एं as फळ 'a fruit' sing., फळें 'fruits' pl. This neuter pl. termination is applied in Hindî, Sindhî, and Panjâbî to the pl. of fem. nouns ending in अ as in रातें 'nights' H., जालां 'women' S. and गल्लां 'words' P., though the इ is changed to आ in the last two cases. The change of the final syllables अओ of Prâkṛit words resulting from such Sanskrit words as आम्रातकः-को, पारदः-दो, दीपकः-को etc. to आ by the dropping of the final and lengthening of the penultimate through the force of the general accent on the penultimate in some of the modern dialects such as the Marâṭhî and the Hindî and to ओ into which the two vowels are combined in consequence of the weakness of the accent in such languages as the Gujarâtî and the Sindhî and in some of the minor dialects of the Marâṭhi, has already been noticed in the last lecture. Similarly the change of the Prâkṛit final syllables of neuter nouns अअं or अयं arising from such Sanskrit words as कदलकम्, मस्तकम् have been changed to एं in the Marâṭhî and to उं in Gujarâtî and to आं in some of the dialects of the Marâṭhî. This also has been explained. The pl. of such neuter nouns, most of which are formed by the addition of क and may be called augmented nouns, is formed by the addition of the Apabhraṁśa इं, which being rendered emphatic by the nasal sound absorbs the previous अ or light य and thus we have केळीं for Ap. कअलअ+इं=Skr. कदलक+आनि. Fem. nouns in इ or ई add आं as घोडी-घोडियां H., घोडिआं P. This यां or आं represents the combination of य or अ with इं; such nouns as घोडी being derived from घोटिका=घोडिआ. In Panjâbî after fem. nouns in आ the इं appears distinct, as बला a calamity, बलाइं nom. pl. In Sindhî the neuter termination is added to the original Prâkṛit fem. pl. उ, shortened from ओ, as घोड्यूं 'mares' nom. pl.; हचा 'murder,' हचाऊं 'murders;' जाल a 'woman,' जालूं 'women' nom. pl. This last has जालां also like the P. रातां. In Marâṭhi also it is not very unusual to speak of women in the neuter pl. when respect is intended as राणीसाहेब आलीं. This transference of neuter termination to the fem. must have taken place when genders began to be confused in the Apabhraṁśa period. The nom. pl. termination of masc. nouns, which in the Prâkṛit was आ, is preserved by the class of nouns we have been considering, *i. e.* augmented nouns, in Sindhî and Gujarâtî; while the ए of the Prâkṛit acc. pl. is used for those nouns in the Marâṭhî and its dialects and the Hindî and the Panjâbî. When the two cases were thoroughly confounded one can easily see how this came to pass. Other or unaugmented nouns have dropped both the terminations in all the languages as has been already noticed.

The Marâṭhî has preserved the Apabhraṁśa instr. sing. एं which is used after nouns in अ and the plural हिं reduced to इं. In all the modern languages the इ of the Apabhraṁśa forms is dropped. These terminations are appended to the old instrumental termination न and we have नें and नीं which are now ordinarily used. These you will see are double forms and of such we have many in the various languages. Goan., Mâl. and Chit. have न् for the sing. and the last has इं for the pl. The loc. Apabhraṁśa हिं from the Pâli म्हि and the Skr. स्मिन् is also used as घरीं गेला; this is peculiar to nouns in अ, and in old Marâṭhî it is reduced to आं after the augmented nouns in आ; as गळां, माथां etc. There are instances of the other locative in ए such as मध्ये and मते (माझ्या मते तुम्ही जावे 'you should go in my opinion,' where मते is hardly an instrumental); but here evidently the termination ए is confounded with the एं of the instrumental and we have माझ्या मतें, lit. "by my opinion." The dative स is generally considered a remnant of the Skr. स्य and Pr. स्स. But I have not found it in the Jñâneśvarî and in its place we have शीं in the old poets, which is connected with a similar post-position in other languages which will be considered hereafter. None of the minor dialects of the language have anything like it, but still the derivation may be correct.

Gujarâtî has the old instrumental in एं but it is confounded with the corresponding ए of the fem. and with the locative ए and we have one termination for both, with the nasal dropped. The shortened Apabhraṁśa form in इ is found in old Gujarâtî. It is confounded with that in इं the anusvârâ being dropped.

(1) कान्हतणइ संपत्ति इसी जिसी इंद्रह घरि रिद्धि .... राजभवनि नवनिधि,
'The wealth or affluence of Kanha was as great as that of Indra.'

From the chronicle of Kanhadade-prabandha given in the Gujarati School-paper.

(2) पछि हुं माहरी गामि आव्यो। पाछिं बीजे दिनि.

Panchopâkhyân, the story of Hiraṇyaka.

In this latter, however, there occurs an anusvâra, should which be correct, the termination is a remnant of हिं. The Gujarâtî has also the double instrumental णें in pronouns, as तेणें, जेणें, etc.

The Sindhî has got the ablative terminations आं, ऑं, ऊं, अउ and आउ. The first is from the pronominal instrumental हां of the Apabhraṁśa and म्हा of the Prâkṛit, ऑं and ऊं from the हुं of the former and अउ and आउ from the corresponding Prâkṛit. The locative ए and its shortened form इ are also preserved, but they are used after nouns in अ as in the older dialects, as खुहि or खुहे पिओ 'he fell into a well.'

The Panjâbî possesses the old abl. in हुं with the ह dropped and the उं amalgamated with the preceding अ into ऑं as घरों 'from a house', the locative pl. हिं as घरीं 'in the house', the instrumental pl. हिं as उसदे हथीं 'by the hands' and the locative sing. in ए as उसदो दरगाहे 'in his court.' The instr. in नें is also ordinarily used in the form of नैं.

The Hindî has scattered instances of the loc. in एं, but the instrumental ने is common. The Bangâlî has preserved the former. The instrumental also has ए, though the grammarians do not give it, as—

सरोवर मध्ये हंस देखि रूपवती।
धरिवार मानसे चलिल शीघ्र गति॥
शुनिया भैमीर मन अनङ्गे पीडिल।

'The beautiful one having seen the swan in the lake went in haste with a desire to catch it.'

'Having heard (this) the heart of Bhaimî was oppressed by love.'

गगनथाले केमन दीपरूपे अनुक्षण
शोभि छे शशीतपन.

'How do the moon and the sun in the form of lamps shine in the plate of the sky!'

The Oriyâ also possesses the loc. in ए and as in the B. and G. it is confounded with the instr. in एं, the nasal being lost, as हातें 'in or by the hand.' This dialect has the Pr. abl. in उ also as हातु 'from the hand.'

The nom. pl. ओ or उ of fem. nouns in ओ or ई is preserved in the Mâl., Goan. and Chit. as जीभ, जिभो; साडी, साड्यो; and घोडी, घोड्यो; but the two latter are derived from the Skr. शाटिका and घोटिका which are nouns ending in आ. The final आ, which alone remains after the elision of the consonant क्, is dropped in consequence of the penultimate accent and we have साडी and घोडी. The ओ or उ of the plural of the original Prâkṛit साडिआओ-उ is also dropped like the ओ or उ of घोडओ-उ in the ordinary Marâṭhî साडी and घोडी and, just as the previous vowel in this last is lengthened in consequence of the accent and the resulting form is घोडा, so the previous आ of साडिआओ-उ and घोडिआओ-उ being accented remains and we have साड्या and घोड्या for साडिआ and घोडिआ, but in the dialects of the Marâṭhî in which the ओ or उ of Masc. nouns in the sing. is preserved we have घोडो, कांटो etc.; so also is the ओ-उ of the fem. preserved and we have साड्यो, घोड्यो etc. As to unaugmented fem. nouns in इ or ई the final is, of course, dropped by the penultimate accent, but in the plural it is preserved being accented and the termination of the plural ओ-उ which is unaccented is dropped as वेल sing., वेली pl., Skr. वल्लि, 'creeper'; बहिण sing., बहिणी pl., Skr. भगिनी, 'sister'; कूस sing., कुसी-शी pl. 'sides'; केळ sing., केळी pl., Skr. कदली etc. As in the dialects of the Marâṭhî the pl. ओ is preserved in Gujarâtî; but there it is transferred to the pl. of all nouns whatever and the process is going on even in our times, being extended to the masc. nouns ending in ओ also, which formed their nom. and acc. pl. formerly by adding आ, as घोडो sing., घोडा pl., but now often घोडाओ. The Sindhî also has preserved the fem. ऊ, as I have already observed, but the nasal of the neuter is combined with it to form the nom. and acc. pl.

The nom. sing. of the relative pronoun is जो in M. H. P. S. and जे in G. O. and B. O. has जेउं also. The ए of the latter is another form of the nom. ओ to be traced perhaps to the old Mâgadhî nom. sing. as in एसे पुलिसे for Skr. एष पुरुष: The correlative is तो in M. and H. and ते in G. and सो in P. S. and से in B. and O. The Hindî has सो also. The सो is the old Pr. nom. sing.; but the oblique base in P. S. B. & O. is the old त. The base of the interrogative pronoun is क as in the older languages. The nom. sing. is कौन H., कौण P. and कोण G. M. and के O. and B.—also केउं O. The कोण and its varieties are to be traced to the Pr. कउण which stands for the Skr. कः पुनः. The near demonstrative is इह or एह in H. P. nom. sing. which is also pronounced in other ways; and the nom. pl. is ये. The first is to be referred to the Ap. एहो, Pr. एसो, Skr. एषः; and the latter to आये Ap. The अय of the Skr. अयम् is generalised in this language and is to be found in all the cases of the pronoun. Hence आये is the nom. pl. The G. has ए, M. हा m., ही fem., हें n.,—*dial.* हो-ही-खां for the nom. sing., and the regular हे m. ह्या fem. हीं n. for the pl.; O has ए, एहि, इहि nom. sing., and B. ए all of which are from the Ap. एहो-एह or एहु. The general obl. base is य or इ in M., ए G., इ or हि S., and इ in the rest, the origin of which is the same, M. य, however, being referred to the Ap. आय which is the generalised form of इदम्. The distant demonstrative has उ for its base. The nom. sing. in H. is उ, ओ, वह, pl. वे; in P. उह, S. हू and हो and B. ओ for both. The S. has ऊ also for the sing., G. has आ for the sing. and its usual आओ for the pl. All these are to be derived from the Ap. ओ nom. and acc. pl., ओइ traced to अस of the Skr. pronoun अदस्. The M. and O. have lost this pronoun.

The nom. sing. of the first personal pronoun in M. is मी and Chit. मे both of which are to be traced to the Ap. acc. instr. and loc. मइं, Pr. मइ, Skr. मया and मयि. The Goan. has हांव, the G. हुं, old H. dialects हौ, हु, the Dogar dialect of the P. हउं, which are all from the Ap. हउं to be traced to the Skr. अहकम्,* the उ of which is, you will remember, that of the nom. sing. which in that dialect was freely used as the G. ओ is at present. The Sindhî आंउ and आं are further corruptions of these. H. P. have also मैं like the Chit. मे, the origin of both being the same. The B. & O. have मुइ and मु which may be traced to the Ap. abl. and gen. sing. महु, but I should prefer considering the इ of the Ap. and M. forms to be changed to उ in consequence of the usual fondness of the B. and O. for the उ sound as noticed in the last lecture.

The pl. of this pronoun in M. is आह्मी, dial. आमी, B. आमि, which is the same as the Ap. अह्मइ traced by me to the Skr. अस्मके. The G. अमे and the O. अम्भे are from the usual Ap. and Pr. form अह्मे from अस्मे generalised from the usual Skr. base अस्म by false analogy. In अम्भे ह्म is changed to म्भ as it often is. The H. हम is this अह्म but the aspiration is transferred to the initial अ and the म to which it is attached in the older and the other dialect is left free. The termination ए is also dropped. The S. and P. have असीं. Skr. स्म is sometimes changed in the Pr. to स्स as in the Mâgadhî and Mah. from locative; but in the written Prâkṛits that have been handed down to us the अस्म of अस्मद् is not found corrupted to स्स. It may, however, have been so in some part of the country. The second person sing. is तूं in all the languages except B. which has तुइ. The H. has तैं also. Of these तूं is the same as the Ap. तुहं, the ह of this dialect being as you know dropped throughout; and तुइ and तैं are transferred from the instrumental. The pl. is तुह्मी in M. from the Ap. तुह्मइ similar to अह्मइ and the B. तुमि is softened from this. The G. has तमे softened from तुह्मे the उ being changed to अ by a peculiarity of the Gujarâtî, which has been fully noticed in the last lecture. In the O. तुह्म the

* Mr. Beames traces them to हउ Ap., अहमम् Skr., but such forms do not exist. Prof. Lassen to whom he refers only conjectures अहमं to account for अहअं, but अहअं is clearly derived from अहकम् which exists even in Skr. The reading हउ in the passage from Kramadisvara given by Lassen is questionable. Hemachandra has हउं distinctly and the form occurs in many verses.

final ए is dropped and a softened form of this is the Hindi तुम. The P. has तुसीं to be derived from तुष्म or युष्म in the same way as असीं from अस्म. The S. has तव्हीं, तवीं, तहीं, तइं, अव्हीं, अवी, अहीं, आईं and अंई. In तव्हीं we have the अ to which उ is reduced as in G. and the म् of ह्मी analysed into its labial and nasal elements. The other three are softened forms of this same, and in the rest the initial त is dropped as we have seen it dropped in the Pr. in the bases उह्म for तुह्म, उज्झ for तुज्झ, उब्भ for तुब्भ and उव्ह for तुह्म both of which exist in that dialect.

The Skr. conjugational distinction is, you will remember, lost in the Prâkṛits; but the increments that roots undergo in the several classes are preserved and made parts of the roots themselves. Now these roots so augmented have descended to the vernaculars. Thus we have बिह old M. G. 'to fear' from the Skr. बिभी of the 3rd class; बुझ M. G. ' to understand', सिज M. 'to be cooked,' खिझ S. 'to throw,' नाच M. G. H.,etc. 'to dance,' उपज M. G. 'to be born', निपज M. G. 'to issue forth', जुझ M. 'to fight,' माज M. G. 'to be maddened' and खिज old M. G. 'to be sad' from the Skr. बुध्य, स्विद्य, क्षिप्य, नृत्य, उत्पद्य, निष्पद्य, युध्य, माद्य & खिद्य, all belonging to the 4th class; सुन or सुण H. S. B. P. O. from Skr. शृण of the 5th; जाण M. G. H. P. etc. 'to know', किण B. O. 'to buy' and गिण्ह S. 'to take' from the Skr. जाना, क्रीणा and गृह्णा of the 9th class. We have roots also in the forms which they have in the second and sixth classes, as न्हा and जा from स्ना and या of the 2nd and लिख, लिह, तुट, फुट, लिंप M. लिंब S., कांत, (Skr. कृन्त) also काट ' to cut,' सिंच from the 6th.

Of the three Pr. tenses and moods the Marâṭhî has preserved two, the Present and the Imperative. The third, viz. the Future, is not lost, but the form became by phonetic corruption similar to those of the Present and you will remember, that the difference between the two tenses consisted in the intercalatory स्य, afterwards dissolved into सि, and thence softened to हि, which having dropped its इ in the vernaculars melted away and another sign had to be added to the Present forms to indicate the Future. The Present was used in old Marâṭhî and is used even at present in poetry, but in ordinary speech it has acquired a past habitual sense. It has a potential signification in some cases as मी येईं तेथपर्यंत तेथें थांब. In the Gujarâtî it has acquired a potential sense in addition to the old and, to indicate present time distinctly, the forms of the present tense of the substantive verb are used in conjunction with it as हुं करुं छुं. The Brajbhâshâ agrees with the G. in this respect and adds its हौं as मै करौं हौं. In the H. P. and S. it signifies potentiality only; and in the last थो masc., थी fem. are added to the forms to denote present time. थो is the past part. of the root थिअणु from

Skr. स्थित, Pr. थिअ, which means 'become' in Sindhî. The old Hindî or Braj poets use this tense in the present also. In all these languages, however, the old Present tense of the auxiliary अस् or आस् indicates present time alone.

B. O. preserve this tense in the old sense throughout. M. has two forms of this old Present:—

1st	करीं	करूं	हसें	हसूं
2nd	करीस	करा	हसस	हसा
3rd	करी	करीत	हसे	हसत

In poetry we have ति and सि for त and स as—

आसाचिया काजाचे निपाडें। देखती आपुलें जीवित्व थोकडें ॥

Jñân. I. 112.

ऐशी सामग्री माझ्या आंगीं जाणसी तूं

Jñân. III. 162.

The termination ईं of the first person sing. is derived from the Pr. मि, म् being simply converted into an anusvâra, *i. e.*, मि when pronounced without closing the lips becomes ईं. In the same way the Pr. मु of the pl. becomes उं. The 2nd per. sing. सि remains unaltered, but in ordinary usage the final इ is dropped in consequence of the usual accent on the penultimate. The ह of the Pr. pl. loses its aspiration as we have found it to have done in the cases and thus we have कर+अ=करा. The 3rd per. sing. termination is the same as in Pr. *viz.* इ. The pl. has lost its nasal and in current Marâṭhî the इ also on account of the penultimate accent. In the other set the 3rd per. sing. termination is ए, the same as in Pr., and to be traced to the Skr. ते of the Âtm. In the Prâkṛit there is no Âtmanepada termination for the 1st pers. sing., but still we have एं here. This vowel is inserted before all the consonantal terminations of the present tense of the verb आहे. We have also ई in करीस and करीत, though it has no place in the Pr. This is probably due to the transference of the final इ in करसी and करती to the penultimate syllable. The first of the two, *i. e.*, the Parasm. set of forms, is used for transitive verbs and the second or Âtmanepada for those that are intransitive and some that are transitive but denote a sort of reflexive action as पढ 'to read', शिक 'to learn', बोल 'to speak', सांग 'to tell', etc. The Chit. has both the padas and the ए of the Âtm. is confined to the 3rd pers. sing. in the root अस as तो से but मैं सां or सईं. In the Mâl. we have आ and in the Goan. अ long for ए as आसा, धावा and असा the final अ being long. In these dialects the 2nd pers. pl. termination is त which is transferred from the corresponding 3rd or is a remnant of the Pr. इत्था and the vowels of the first pers. form vṛiddhi dipthongs with the preceding base in both the padas as मी करैं 'I do', or 'I used to do', आम्ही करौं 'we do' or 'used to do.'* The Goan. and Chit, however, have the first pers. sing. Âtm. in आं also. The Âtm. is not used for roots ending in other vowels than अ, though they may be intransitive as न्हा, जा, हो, दे, etc., and in this particular the Marâṭhî remarkably agrees with the old Pr.

O. & B. have the following forms for the present.

O.		B.	
मु करइं	अम्भे करु	मुइ करि	आमि करि
तु करु	तुम्भे कर	तुइ करिस	तुमि कर
से करइ	से करन्ति	से करे	तिनि करेन

These also are from the Pr. forms. O. has lost the nasal of the 1st pers. pl. and B. of the sing. also, i. e., it has one same form for both. O. has lost the स of the 2nd pers. sing. and has उ in its place. The pl. कर of both is pronounced करो; ओ being broad like that to which अ even of Skr. words is reduced in ordinary utterance by the speakers of these languages. This form करो is the same as the M. करा from the Pr. करह. O. has preserved the 3rd pers. pl. न्ति intact; B. has lost the त and इ.

The other languages have:—

G.		H.	
हुं करुं	अमे करिये	मै करुं	हम करें
तुं करे	तमे करो	तुं करे	तुम करो
ते करे	तेओ करे	उह करे	वै करें

S. Tr.

आंऊं मारिआं-यां	असीं मारिऊं-यूं
तूं मारिएं-रें-रीं	अहीं मारिओ-यों
हू मारे	हू मारीनि-रिनि

S. Intr.		P.	
हलां	हलूं	मै करां	असीं करये
हलें	हलो	तूं करें	तुसी करो
हले	हलनि	उह करे	उह करण

* These vriddhi forms appear to be due to the penultimate अ being pronounced long through the accent according to the usual rule and by the combination of इ or उ with it; so that the combined sound is अइ and अउ. When the lengthened अ becomes आ it overpowers the final इ and this latter is dropped and we have मे करां Chit. or हांव करां Goan. 'I do or used to do', just as in घोडउ 'a horse' the penultimate is lengthened into आ and the final उ is dropped and we have घोडा.

The Hindî 2nd and 3rd person sing. and pl. are derived directly from those in Ap. The ह of करहि-हु-इ-हिं being dropped as usual; the forms are करइ-उ-इ-इं and when the vowels are combined we have करे-रो-रे-रें. The G. P. and S. forms are exactly similar, the only difference consisting in the nasal of the 3rd. pers. pl. which has been elided in the first as is done in the instrumental singular. The P. and S. ण and नि must be referred to न्ति of the Pr. since the Ap. possessed the Pr. forms as well as the new ones. In old G. Mss. it is usual to write the इ and उ of these forms separately. The G. & H. first pers. sing. करुं is from the Ap. करउं, while the आं of the P. करां and the S. हलां is to be traced rather to the मि of the Pr. than to this उं as that of the सां in the Chit. and Goan. by the elision of इ and the lengthening of the preceding vowel. There are instances of this change given in the Pr. as we have seen. The S. उ of the 1st pers. pl. is the same as that in M. & O. and to be derived from the Ap. हुं and the Pr. मु. The एं of the Hindî 1st per. pl. is brought over from the 3rd person and this transference was facilitated by the nasal of the original termination; or, since in the Ap. both मि and उं exist, when in a later stage of the language the letter was appropriated and fixed for the sing. the former was adopted for the pl. and changed to इं which became एं by amalgamation. The G. and P. further dropped the nasal of this ए and interposed a vowel which is probably of the same nature as that in the S. मायूं. The S. like the M. inserts इ before the terminations in the case of transitive verbs, as in the forms of मार given above and does not when the verbs are intransitive or reflexive as सिक and पद. The forms of the Ap. Present occur in the older Hindî poets. Thus in Tulsîdâs's Râmâyaṇa we have:—

3rd per. sing.

शंभु गिरा पुनि मृषा न होइ। शिव सर्वज्ञ जान सब कोइ ।

Bâla-K.

'But Śambhu's word is not false.
Everybody knows Śiva to be omniscient'.

निशिचर एक सिंधु मह रहई। करि माया नभके खग गहई ॥

Sundar-K.

' An evil spirit dwells in the sea and having recourse to deceit catches hold of the birds in the sky.'

3rd per. pl.

संत हंस गुण गहहिं पै परिहरिं वारि विकार ।

Bâla-K.

'Good men like swans admit merit like milk leaving off the watery pollution'

नारद शिख जु सुनहिं नरनारी। अवश भवन तजि होंहिं भिखारी ॥

Bâla-K.

'Those men and women that listen to the advice of Nârada become beggars having abandoned their homes.'

2nd per. pl.:

करहु कवन कारण तप भारी।

Bâla-K.

'For what reason do you go through excessive austorities?'

विपिन अकेलि फिरहु केहि हेतू।

Bâla-K.

'Why do you wander alone in the forest?'

1st pers. sing.:

नारद वचन न मैं परिहरऊं। बसौ भवन उजरो नहिं डरऊं॥

Bâla-K.

'I shall not neglect the advice of Nârada and shall not be afraid even if thereby the world stands or falls (becomes desolated).'

1st pers. pl.:

तात सुनहु सादर मन लाई। कहहुं रामकी कथा सुहाई॥

Bâla-K.

'Dear one, do hear with an attentive mind; [we] nerrate the pleasing story of Râma.'

Another reading is कहौं which is sing. and the sense is 'I narrate'.

The old 2nd pers. sing. in सि is met with thus:—

भरत सपथ तोहि सत्य कहु परि हरि कपट दुराइ।
हरष समय विस्मय करसि कारण मोहि सुनाइ ॥

Ay.-K.

'I charge thee in the name of Bharata; tell me the truth laying aside all insincerity. On the occasion of joy thou art gloomy; explain to me the reason.'

There are also specimens of the Âtm.:

देखे जहं तहं रघुपति

Bâla.-K.

'Sees Raghupati here and there.'

जो अब करौं सती सन प्रीती। मिटै भक्ति पथ होइ अनीती॥

Bâla.-K.

'If now you are amorous towards the Satî (Pârvatî) the way of devotion will end and immorality (will) result.'

चले बसह चढ़ि।

Bâla.-K.

'He goes having sat on the bull.'

And it appears that the ए of the Present is used after verbs of the same kind as in Marâṭhî. The vowel इ of the 3rd pers. sing. does not become ए as in the modern Hindî and other, where the distinction between the two padas is lost, but retains its original form as in धरि पुछी (गइ समीप महेश तब हंसि पूछी कुशलात 'when she went near Maheśa smiling asked her how she fared'.)

The Marâṭhi, Oriya, and the Bangâlî have preserved the Imperative mood entire; the others, only the second person sing., the rest being taken over from the old present or the modern Potential.

	M.		G.		B.	
1st	करूं	करूं-रों	करि	करुं	करि	करि
2nd	कर-रीं	करा	कर	कर	कर-करीस	कर करह करीओ
3rd	करा	करोत	करु	करन्तु or करन्त	करुक्	करुन्

In the 1st per. sing. the मु of the Pr. is changed to उं in M. *i. e.* म has lost its labial element as in the Present. O. and B. have got the form of the Present for it, the nasal being dropped. The मो of the pl. is similarly changed to ओं and is also shortened or resolved into ऊं. The B. has the same form as the sing. The 2nd pers. sing. in M. has the form without the termination as in the Pr., the other made up by adding ईं corresponds to that in the Ap. ending in that vowel. Intransitive and reflexive roots have एं instead of ईं which form is also found in the Ap. as धावें, शिकें, सांगें. The O. and B. do not possess these terminations but the latter has स which is to be traced to the Pr. सु. The pl. is the same as in the Pr. the ह having left its trace in the lengthening of the vowel. The O. and B. कर is also really करा pronounced broadly करॅा and the latter retains ह unchanged also. The 3rd per. sing. termination उ of the Pr. is amalgamated with the preceding vowel into ओ in M. and उ in O. and B. M. has also sometimes उ for ओ. The क of the B. is a later addition and is probably to be traced to the Interrogative pronoun beginning with क. It is to be compared with such M. expressions as जाऊं दे किं. The O. preserves the 3rd per. pl. न्तु unchanged but in the optional form the final उ is dropped. M. and B. have transferred the characteristic उ to the preceding syllable and the former has dropped the nasal and the latter the त. In M. the उ is as in the sing. changed to ओ but in some cases it is preserved and we have such forms as जाऊत, देऊत etc. We find instances in which the उ preserves its place after त as in the O. Thus in Jñânes'varî:—

हे वरी भलतें करितु । आतांचि एथें मारितु ।
परी आपण मनें घातु । न चिंतावा ॥ I—225.

'These on their part may do an unwelcome thing, just here and now kill us but we should not think of doing injury.'

H. P. and G. have कर for the sing. as in the above; and करो pl. the same as that of the Present which itself is from the Ap. करहु the characteristic Imper उ being attached to the ह of the Pr. and even in the Pr. and M. B. and O. 2nd per. pl. is the same as in the Present. The P. has also the form in ईं. The Sindhî Imperative 2nd per. sing. of intransitive and reflexive verbs ends in उ as हलु and of transitive verbs and a few others in इ as करि. The उ occurs in the Ap. along with the इ and ए already noticed. Though Modern Hindî has lost the Imperative forms for other persons than the second, old Hindi poets use them; and for the second per. sing. also they have the Ap. form in इ preserved in S. and M. Thus Tulsîdâs:—

2nd pers. sing. प्रभु हनुमंतहि कहा बुझाइ ।
in इ धरी बटुरूप अवध पुर जाइ ॥

'The lord said to Hanumanta, "Assume the form of a boy and go to the city of Ayodhyâ."'

The 2nd pers. pl. is the same as that of Present which prevails in all the languages from the Pr. downwards.

पारवती पहं जाइ तुम प्रेमपरीक्षा लेहु ।

"Having gone to Pârvatî examine her devotion."

The 3rd per. sing. ends in ओ or औ as in the M. & O.

मेरी भव बाधा हरौ राधा नागरि सोइ ।

—Beharîlâla.

"May that polished Râdhâ remove my worldly distress."

करो अनुग्रह सोइ ।—Tuls. R.

"May he confer favours."

The 3rd pers. pl. has हु which is an Ap. form found in some of Hemachandra's quotations. The ह has been introduced simply to distinguish it from the sing.

चरणकमल बंदौं सबकेरे । पुरवहु सकल मनोरथ मेरे ॥—Tuls. R.

"I adore the lotus-like feet of all. May they fulfil all my desires."

The 1st per. sing. is the same as that of the Present and it is difficult to distinguish it; but in such a construction as the following the M. would have the imperative.

चली सती शिव आयसुपाई । करहिं विचार करौ का माई ॥

"The Satî having got S'iva's permission went, and was thinking what deception to use."

The pl. also must be the same. Old G. has also the Imper. forms in इ and उ as:—

पूछइ वात पातशाह इसी । गूजरातिते कहीइ किसी ॥

"The emperor asked this matter "how is Gujarât ?" '

गूजरा स्यूं मांडिसि कलहु । माहारइ साथइ कटक मोकलु ॥

"If you will declare war against Gujarât send an army with me."

The G. and S. have another form for the 2nd per. of the Imper.; the terminations of this are इजि S., जे G. for the sing. and इजो and जो for the pl. The H. has जे and जो for roots ending in ई and ऊ and इये and इयो for the rest. The P. and B. have इओ for the pl. and in the former the singular is confounded with the usual इ termination. In M. such form is not now ordinarily used. In addresses on letters, however, such expressions as प्रविष्ट कीजे, दीजे are used and these forms are found in the works of the old Marathî poets. Thus in Jñânes'varî:—

परियासी घात कीजे । मग आपण राज्यसुख भोगिजे ।

हें स्वप्नींहि मन माझें । करूं न शके ॥ I—213

' This my mind can not think of doing even in a dream that I should kill them and enjoy afterwards the pleasures of sovereignty.'

तरिं अवधान येकलें दीजे । मग सर्वे सुखासीं पात्र होइजे ॥ IX—1.

' Give youra. ttention alone and qualify yourself for all happiness.'

मुनि सांगे नृपनाथ । जनमेजया ॥

जे अद्वितीय उत्तम । पवित्रैक निरुपम ।

परम मंगळधाम । अवधारि जो ॥ I-48-49.

"The Muni narrates this story to Janamejaya the king, saying (you should) attend to this which is unique, excellent, the holy thing, the unsurpassed and the highest abode of all auspicious things.'

आतां देइजो अवधान । तुह्मी बोलविला मी बोलेन ॥ I—8.

' Give attention now; I will speak what you make me speak.'

These forms have been traced by Dr. Trump in his Sindhî Grammar to the Pr. base in इज्ज used in the Present, Imperative and Future and derived by Lassen from the Present and by me from the Potential; and so far as the form in the S. and G. is concerned there is no objection. But these forms are in the vernaculars used when respect for the person spoken to is intended and the Potential as distinguished from the Imperative is by no means more respectful in Skr. The H. forms are not assigned each to each number but both of them are used in the sing. or pl. and its य can by no means be derived from ज; for though the contrary process the changing of य to ज is common there is so far as I am aware no single well established instance of the other. In Skr. nothing is more usual than to use the Passive of the 3rd pers. sing. Imperative in respectful solicitation. The second pers. of the active Imper. is the least respectful since there is a direct reference in that voice to the agent and such a reference to great men is regarded as improper or in the case of others not courteous. The 3rd pers. with भवान् as the nom. is more so; because the reference is indirect but the most respectful construction is the Passive as it does not point to the agent at all but to the thing done by him. Thus the ज in these forms is from the य of the passive and the Hindi ईय from ईअ which is the other corruption of that termination in the Pr. The M. देइजो corresponds to Skr. दीयताम्, the Imper. 3rd pers. sing. termination in that language being उ. दीजे corresponds to दीयते of the Present and the potential sense may be attributed to the fact that the whole tense has assumed that sense in the vernaculars. The agent may, if the forms are passive, be any person and any number since it does not agree with the verb; and this explains the Hindi usage. But as generally in solicitation the person addressed is the second pers. though he is referred to indirectly and is, when cases are used, put in the instr. as in the Jñânes'varî:—

द्रोणातें म्हणे पाहिजे तुम्हीं सकल ।

"He said to Droṇa, everything should be looked after by you."

These forms become in the G. & S. identified with the second and easily because one of the terminations ओ happens to be the same as that of the Imper. 2nd pers. pl. in those languages and got confused with the other Pr. Potential forms in ज; wherefore we find in the S. the Imper. 2nd pers. sing. terminations इ and उ applied to the base as थिजि 'become', सुनिजु 'hear.' This confusion extended to the Hindi also since to roots in इ or उ it appends जे and जो; for the Potential increment ज is given in the Pr. to roots ending in आ, इ, ओ etc. *i. e.* any vowel except अ. In the progress of a language confusion is natural and frequently observable. This double etymology explains all the facts of the case; while if we confine ourselves to one some are not accounted for.

We have seen that there are two classes of verbs in M. one of which takes the augment इ in the Present before the consonantal terminations as करीस, करीत and the other takes ए or अ as धावें, धावत. The Imper. 2nd pers. sing. of the former is made up by adding इ in old or poetic Marathî and of the latter by adding ए. The former takes इ in the Future necessarily in the 1st and 3rd pers. sing. as करील, करीन and optionally in some others as करतील or करितील, करशील or करिशील. This option is extended even to the Present करितो or करतो and the past participle धरिलें or धरलें; while in the present participle these verbs necessarily take इ as करित आहे. The latter class takes ए in the Future 1st and 3rd pers. sing. and the option in the last is not allowed, अ being added in all, including the present part., as शिकेल, शिकतील not शिकितील, शिकला not शिकिला, शिकतो and शिकत आहे; so that this class must have ए in some cases and अ in the rest. The Sindhî has a similar distinction. Those roots that take इ before the termination of the Pres. as कयांथो "I do" form their Imper. 2nd pers. sing. in इ and insert this in the present part. as करीन्दो; while the rest do not add this इ, as हलां 1st pers. sing., हलन्दो pres. part., and take उ in the Imper. sing., हलु Imper. 2nd pers. sing. We thus see that we have इ in the one case and opposed to it are the vowels ए, अ and उ in the other. The former is a characteristic of the transitive or the non-reflexive nature of a root while the latter of the opposite. Why should it be so? The vowels इ and ए form the distinctive marks of the Parasm. and Âtm. in Skr. and Pr. A consciousness of this and of the difference between Parasm. roots and Âtm. roots has been preserved in the modern S. and M. and hence there is an attempt to insert those vowels in all possible cases; and the base itself of the roots is made to end in them. But in the Prâkṛits and to a great extent even in Skr. the base of most of the roots (भण, हस, etc.) has an imperative signification. Hence the newly constituted bases करिं and धावें also came to have an imper. sense. Now these are the forms of the Imper. not only in our languages but the old Apabhraṃs'a also; hence the process I mention must have been gone through even then. This is a better explanation of the Ap. forms than deriving them both from हि, especially since this is a dialect so prone to bring in इ even when it can not be had, that it is not likely to reject an already existing one. You will thus see how subtle the operation of the law of analogy is in the development of a language. Now as regards the Ap. form उ we see that we have it in Sindhî where the other languages have अ, so that it is the old inorganic उ which prevails so much in the Ap. And we have seen that ई is used in many more grammatical forms in M. than ए, whilst instead of it in other places and in the Sindhî in all but the Imper. 2nd pers. sing. we have अ; so that इ is made the distinctive mark of the Parasm. character of a root while its absence or the insertion of ए indicates the Atm. character.

The third Skr. tense preserved by the Prâkṛits is the Second Future. It has descended to the Gujaratî. Thus,

हुं	करीस	अमे करिसुं
तुं	करसे	तमे करसो
ते	करसे	तेओ करसे

The स of these forms is the old Skr. स्य corrupted to स्स in the S'aur. and स in the Ap. From the Skr. downwards the terminations of the Present in each of the languages are appended, as formerly observed, to this tense. So in the G. we find in the 2nd and 3rd pers. the terminations ए and ओ of the G. Present attached to स. But the consciousness of the etymology of these forms has been partially lost; wherefore in 1st pers. we have not करसुं for the sing. corresponding to करूं and करसीये corresponding to करीये. But G. has derived its 1st pers. pl. करसुं directly from the Skr. or Ap. pl. करिस्सामु or करिसमु and the sing. करीस from करिस्सं which, you will remember, was an optional S'aur. form in addition to करिस्सामि, the nasal being dropped according to the usual Guj. rule. We have these forms in the Braj-Bhâshâ but the स is corrupted to ह as it very often is. Thus,

करिहौं	करिहैं
करिहै	करिहौ
करिहै	करिहै

Here in the 1st pers. sing. we have the औं of the Pres. Braj as in करौं, unlike the G. and in conformity with the ancient practice. You will also observe that the old augment इ is preserved. It may be suspected that these forms are derived from those in the Pr. which have ह instead of स, but you will have observed that there we have हि as in करिहिइ and here ह which represents the S'aur. and Apbr. स. The old Future occurs in Tulsidâsa's Râmâ.

3rd pers sing. प्रिया सोच परिहरहु सब सुमिरहु श्री भगवान्।
पारवती जिन निर्मयउ सोइ करिहहिं कल्यान ॥

"Dear, leave off all anxiety, remember the great God. He who created Parvati will do her good."

If the dot on हि is a mistake this is 3rd pers. sing.

3rd pers. pl. छमिहहिं सज्जन मोरि ढिटाई ।
सुनिहहिं बालवचन मन लाई ॥

"Good men will pardon my temerity and hear the words of (this) child with attention."

2nd pers. pl. कहत मम मन अतिसंकुचाई । हंसिहहु सुने हमारि जडताई ॥

"I am ashamed in my mind to tell the truth; for, hearing, at my stupidity you will laugh."

In these forms the terminations of the Apbr. Present are appended to the ह derived from स; but the following are three instances of the Braj form occurring in the same work.

1st pers. pl. तब तव वदन पैठिहौं आई ॥ सत्य कहौं मोहि जान दे माई ॥

"Then I will enter thy mouth; I tell you the truth, let me go mother."

3rd pers. pl. मम कृत सेतु जो दरशन करिहैं । सो विनुश्रम भवसागर तरिहैं ॥

"They who will visit this bridge constructed by me will cross the ocean of life without trouble."

In an essay published in the Bengal Asiatic Society's Journal, 1873, Mr. Beames gives the forms of the Future found in the earliest Hindî poet Chand, which are exactly similar to those in the Braj and, misled by the latter parts है, है, हौ etc. which resemble those of अस or आस so greatly, traces them to the Periphrastic Future of the Skr. चलितास्मि-सि etc. But this Future is in the first place rarely used in Skr. and altogether discarded by the Pâli and not a trace of it is to be found in any of the numerous Prâkṛits. Besides if we derive these forms from the Periphrastic Future we must have in the 3rd pers. such forms as चलिआ–चलिया and चलिआर. And the old forms which Tulsidâs uses of the type of चलिहहि, from which evidently the others are derived, will remain unexplained. There can be little doubt that this derivation is wrong. We have seen the several steps by which we gradually rise to चलिहै from चलिष्यति and the chain is so well connected that this etymology must be admitted as correct. The resemblance to that form in Gujaratî also must not be forgotten.

Past time is in all the vernaculars expressed by means of the past participle as in the Pr., all the Skr. past tenses being lost, as you will remember, except in isolated cases. This participle is in the older languages passive in the case of transitive verbs generally and active when the verb is intransitive and also in the cases of some transitive verbs such as शिकलों, प्यालों etc. This rule is strictly observed in most of the modern dialects and hence in the past tense we have generally no active voice when the verb is transitive and the agent is, as in the older languages, put in the instr., thus in H. लेखकनें पोथी लिखी, P. उसने कम कीता, S. हुन फकीरखे धदुडिणो, G. जवेरिलाले मारीपासे माणस मोकल्यो, M. पारध्यानें वाघ मारिला. In all these sentences the last words are past participles and they agree with the object in the Nom. case in number, gender and person. In the O. and B., however, all distinction between gender, number and person being lost the agreement with the object is not perceptible. In these languages and to some extent in Marâṭhî this participle is made the base of the regular verbal forms; wherefore I shall have to discuss this point again,

The Hindi participle ends in अ which of course is the same termination as in Pr., thus Skr. गत, Pr. गअ the consonant being elided, and with the connecting य्, गय. When augmented by the addition of क in the manner I have shown in the last lecture and also in this it is गया the अ alone of the क being left. In the feminine the augmented form is गयी and where this य is not inserted it is गई. By adding this augmented form आ to any root whatever the Hindî past participle is formed as लिखा, पढा etc. An euphonic य intervenes when the root ends in a vowel as दिया, पीया etc. Similar to this is the B. and O. past participle as देखा in देखाजाव B., लेखा, दिया O. The S. termination is इओ and the P. इआ as जागिओ from जागणु 'to be awake,' परिखओ from पखंणु 'to remain,' गइआ 'gone', घलिआ 'sent;' the nom. termination उ and the augment अ for क being left out of consideration it is reduced to इअ. The G. has यो and the Braj यौ as in राख्यो, राख्यौ 'kept' from राख, कह्यो कह्यौ 'told' from कह, where also the ओ being dropped the termination is य *i.e.* इअ hastily pronounced. These languages therefore preserve the old termination with the augment इ prefixed to it as in the Pr., as हसिओ, पढिओ etc. Some of the vernaculars and notably the Sindhî have also inherited from the Pr. readymade Tadbhava forms of the past passive participles as,

S.	Pr.	Skr.
बधो	बद्धो	बद्धः
बुधो	बुद्धो	बुद्धः
भगो	भग्गो	भग्नः
पातो	पत्तो	प्राप्तः
पुणो	पुण्णो	पूर्णः
पीठो	पिट्ठो	पिष्टः
तपो	तत्तो	तप्तः
तुठो	तुट्ठो	तुष्टः
छिनो	छिन्नो	छिन्नः
डुधो	दुद्धो	दुग्धः
दींठो	दिट्ठो	दृष्टः
गठो	घट्ठो	घृष्टः
लधो	लद्धो	लब्धः

G.	Pr.	Skr.
दीठो	दिट्ठो	दृष्टः
लीधो	लद्धो	लब्धः
पेठो	पइट्ठो	प्रविष्टः
कीधो	किदो S'aur.	कृतः

Hindi also possesses a few.

बैठा	उवइट्ठो	उपविष्टः
	[उ being elided.]	
पैठा	पैट्ठा	प्रविष्टः

But these participles are made the bases of verbal forms; the infinitives being बैठना and पैठना.

The Sindhî seems to have made up the forms of a few roots on the analogy of these though they do not exist in the Pr. as झलतो from झल, Skr. धृत, Pr. धरिओ; पीतो drunk, कीतो done; (P. has this also); but some of these may be modern Tadbhavas. Marâṭhî does not possess this form and past tense is expressed in that language by a form ending in ला-ली-लें. This is adjectival in nature and passive in the case of transitive verbs and active in that of intransitive or reflexive verbs. It is in every respect then like the Skr. and Pr. past participle preserved in the other dialects. But here we have ल (ला) for the अ (आ) of those. This ल has been traced to the Skr. त; but since in the Mahârâshṭrî or principal Prâkṛit that termination leaves its अ only it must be derived from the S'aur. द which often becomes ड and ड is frequently confounded with र and ल as we have seen. In Sindhî Skr. द is always ड as डे 'give' from दा, डुधो from दुग्ध and डिठो etc. Similarly even in the Prâkṛit period such a change must have taken place in several words; for instance, the Skr. दश in एकादश and in some of the succeeding numerals becomes in the Pâli दस but is changed to रह in the Pr. which shows that द must have become ड before it assumed the form of र. ड is interchanged with ळ even in Skr. as पुरोडाश or पुरोळाश; and in the Pr. and modern dialects we have कील for क्रीड, पीळ or पील for Skr. पीड, डालिम for दाडिम etc. So that this etymology is possible; but I shall presently show to you that it is not to the S'aur. that we should first look for the origin of M. words and forms; especially in cases when it stands alone. That the Marâṭhî only should exhibit these consonantal changes in the past participle and none of the other sister dialects and that no instance of the intermediate step between the S'aur. द and the M. ल should be found here or elsewhere as we find them in similar cases goes a great way against this derivation. The Marâṭhî past participle in ला, ली, लें is, I think, of the same nature as similar participles in the other cognate languages ending in that termination. We have in G. besides कह्यो, कर्यो, कह्येलो and करेलो and in S. besides विओ and डिठो, विअलु and डिठलु. There is a little difference in the sense but both are promiscuously used in ordinary usage. B. and O. form their Preterite with this participle as the base as गोपाल आमाके कहिल B. 'Gopal told us;' अम्भे कलम देइ लेखिल O. 'I wrote with a pen.' It is also used as an adjective as गलादिन 'the past day', पडिला गछ 'the fallen tree.' Though it does not occur in high Hindî and is not given in the grammars of the languages the lower classes of the Hindî population use this participle very commonly as बेचल H. 'sold', गयल 'gone'; and it is also found in the works of Kabîra though I have not seen it in Tulsidâsa's Râmâyaṇ which is accounted for by the fact that Kabîra was a S'ûdra himself and consequently belonged to those classes which use it at the present day. Thus:—

तब ब्रह्मा पूछल महतारी। को तोर पुरुष का करि तुम नारी॥

—Râmâyaṇ II–4.

"Then Brahmâ asked his mother: 'Who is thy husband and whose wife art thou !' "

चहुजुग भगतन बांधल बाटी। समुझि न परै मोटरी फाटी ॥

—Ramâyaṇ V-7.

"In all the four ages holy men constructed ways but they did not know that the bundle they had tied had given way or was torn !"

Now in the Sindhi participles ल is a termination appended to other or old participles; as विअ and दिठ with the suffix ल become विअल and दिठल. The Gujarâtî ones are of the same nature; in कहेलो, लो is the suffix and कहे is the original participle in इअ or य or कहिअ or कह्य which is changed to ए, as य often is. Even in Marâṭhî in the forms गेला, केला, आला, आयलो in the minor dialects, जाइला, मेला, भ्याला, प्याला etc. गे represents गय (Pr. गअ. Skr. गत); के, कय (Pr. कअ, Skr. कृत); आय, आअ (Pr. आअअ, Skr. आगत); जाइ, जाअ (Pr. जाअ, Skr. जात); मे, मय (Pr. मृत); भ्या–भीआ, प्या–पीआ and so on. In the B. too we have केल, गेल, आइल which are just like the Marâṭhî forms and are to be explained in the same way. In old Marâṭhî we similarly find this ल appended to real past participles. In an old inscription dated S'aka 1128=1206A.D., the latter portion of which is in the Marâṭhî of the time and being so was difficult to decipher; there occurs the expression मढा दिन्हला 'given to a monastery' in which we see that ला is appended to दिन्ह which is the same as the old Pâli and Pr. participle दिण्ण of the root दा. In Skr. a great many roots formed their participles by adding न instead of त and we find several of these and others formed on the analogy of these in old Hindî and Marâṭhî poetry. In the works of Tulsidâs, Kabîra, Chanda and others कीन्ह 'done', लीन्ह 'taken,' चीन्ह 'known', दीन्ह 'given' and such others occur.

नाना विधि मुनि पूजा कीन्ही। अस्तुति करि पुनि आशिष दीन्ही ॥

'The sage worshipped him in several ways, praised him and gave him a blessing."

In the Marâṭhî poets we have ला added to न as Jñân.:

ते दोनी शब्द अचाट। मिनले एकवट

'Both these dreadful noises mingled together.'

सनकादिकांचिया आशा। वादीनल्या बहुवसा।

'The hopes of Sanaka and others increased greatly."

Ekanâtha.

धर्माप्रति धाविन्नला

' Ran towards Dharma or virtue.'

ऐकोनि हासिन्नला गोविंद

'Hearing this, Govinda smiled.'

Rukmiṇi Svayaṃvara.

In the following ला is applied to old Tadbhava participles:—

जैं भांति सेजे सुतला। तै स्वप्नसुख भुतला। मग तो ज्ञानोदयीं चेइला। ह्मणोनियां॥

—Jñân. V–47.

"Because when he slept on the bed of delusion he enjoyed the pleasures of a dream and then awoke when the sun of knowledge rose.'

भीतरीं पातला उठा उठीं। जेथ जगजेठी श्रीकृष्ण॥

'Went in where the lord of the world S'rî Kṛishṇa was.'

Here सुत, भुत and पात are from सुत्त, भुत्त and पत्त Pr., सुप्त, भुक्त and प्राप्त Skr.; and to these ला is added. There are other instances in these works in which ला is added to past Tatsama or later Tadbhava participles such as दग्धला, लुब्धला, ह्मणितला, ह्मणितला; and in the language of the day we have सांगितलें, घेतलें, मागितलें, धुतलें and one or two others. In the Jñanes'varî we have also such forms as विसणैला 'excited', निदैला 'slept,' and आभारैला where the ऐ represents the अय or इअ of the old participle resembling in this respect the Guj. कहेलो. When the अ or आ of the old participle became too weak to be expressive this form with the suffix ल attached was oftener used and gradually supplanted the other; and ल came in the course of time to be regarded as the past participle termination. Hence it is applied to roots directly without the intervention of the old ए that we have in केला and गेला; and in low Hindi also it is applied in the same way. The original participle was mostly used predicatively as it is in classical Skr. also, and this ल was attached to it to form an attributive expression to be used before nouns. But after a time this new form also came to be predicatively used; and it is now so used in M., G., S. and H. In M. however when it was put to this purpose it drove out the old one and its own attributive sense became faint, though even now it is not entirely lost as in such instances as झाल्या गोष्टीस उपाय नाहीं 'There is no remedy against the thing that has already taken place.' Then another ल came to be attached to it to adapt it for attributive use and thus we have now in M. the form केलेला, गेलेला etc. with a double ल. This ल is to be traced to the Pr. इल्ल or उल्ल which according to Hemachandra is applied in the sense of *Bhâva i. e.* being the thing signified by the base as उवरिल्लं, अप्पुल्लं. These two words are in M. वरील or वरला and आपुलें or आपलें in which instances we see that the initial इ or उ of the suffix is optionally dropped. Or according to other writers quoted by our grammarians आल is also used. And in works such as the Gauḍavadha and in the Bhagavatî we find these suffixes frequently used. These are generally applied to all bases; but ल is another termination which is restricted to certain nouns such as विद्युत्, पीत, पत्र, अन्ध from which we have विज्जुल, पीतल etc. In Skr. also this suffix has a pretty wide range as चूडाल Pâṇ. V. 2-96, सिध्मल, कृष्णल, पांसुल, मांसल, स्नेहल etc. V. 2-97. वत्सल V. 2-98, फेनल V. 2-99.

The present participle of the Pr. has lost its न in M. as करित, धावत, in G. करत 'doing,' चढत 'ascending,' in H. as करता and in B. as करित, देखित, while the O. has preserved it as करन्त, देखन्त. The S. and P. have preserved the S'aur. form which has द instead of त and the former has preserved the nasal throughout while the latter has dropped it after roots in अ as S. मारिंदो, हलन्दो, P. लिखदा 'writing' but जांदा 'going,' होंदा 'becoming;' this participle is used as in the Pr. in the sense of Skr. Conditional equivalent to the English Pluperfect Conditional, as M. तो करता तर होतें 'if he had done it, it would have become,' G. ते करत तो थात; B. से यदि तो माके कहित तबे तुमि विश्वास करिता ना; 'if he had told you, you would not have believed;' O. जेबे सूर्य उदय हुअन्त तेबे अन्धकार न रहन्ता 'if the sun had arisen the darkness would not have remained'; H. जो मैं कहता तो मेरी बात न सुनता 'if I had told he would not have listened to my words;' S. जेहू पाणिअमे न तरंदो 'if he had not been swimming,' जे मै घल्लदा 'if I were to send.'

The absolutive in M. is formed by adding the termination ऊन as करून the same as the Mahârâshṭrî ऊण. Vararuchi, you will remember, gives this termination only, but Hemachandra adds more. The G. has इ the same as the Ap. इ and Pr. इअ, Skr. य and इने from the Ap. एविणु or एप्पिणु the Vedic Skr. त्वीन; or the ने of इने may be the same as the particle ने which means 'and' added to इ. The Sindhî has इ for intransitive and reflexive roots and ए for transitive and another इओ or यो for both as सुणी 'having heard,' मारे 'having beaten' and सुण्यो or मार्यो. The first is the same as the G. but in the ए of the transitive roots the अ of the original इअ seems to be preserved and this termination added to the root with the Parasm. sign. इ. Thus we have first मारी and then, इअ or इय being added, we have मारीय whereupon the य with the preceding इ becomes ए and we have मारे. The last यो is the same as the इउ of the Ap. traced to the infinitive which, you will remember, is confounded with the absolutive. The H. drops the इ of this form and the original root as बोल, जा etc. is used in the sense of the Absol. but to make the sense distinct के or कर is added, as बोलके or बोलकर, जाके

or जाकर. Of these के is a real absolutive derived from the S'aur. किअ and कर is the same as कोल *i. e.* the usual form of it. Now when one form is felt to be not distinct enough it is usual in our languages to add another to it of the same nature. You have instances of this process in the Pâli double genitive तेसानं, and in the instr. नें and नीं of some of our vernaculars. P. agrees with the H. In H., however, the इ is pronounced by a great many people. It is also found in the old poets and in the Brajabhâshâ. The absolutive always ends in this vowel as करि, मारि, though often के the same as H. के is added as करिकै, मारिकै, etc. The O. also has इ as करि and the B. has इ or ए or इया as देखि, देखे or देखिया 'having seen'. In the last the अ of the original इअ is preserved and lengthened and the य is euphonic.

The infinitive of purpose is preserved in M. as तो अभ्यास करूं लागला 'he began to study.' The form in the Pr. is करिउं, but the augment इ is lost in M. O. also has it, but its use is somewhat like that of the Absolutive विचार करु कहिले 'considering he spoke,' खाउ खाउ तृप्त होइला 'eating and eating he was satisfied.' But the original sense is somewhat preserved and it is in this sense made the basis of the present tense definite which will be considered hereafter. This infinitive and the absolutive are I have already observed confused in the Pr., and in some of the modern dialects the absolutive is used where we in Marâṭhî use the infinitive as G. हुं करी सकुं छुं 'I am able to do it,' H. मै कर सकता हूं, बानी जाको नहीं कहि सके है 'whom speech can not express,' Br. मै करि सकौं हौं for M. मी करूं शकतों. For this infinitive the modern vernaculars however have got a reconstructed form which will be mentioned in its proper place.

The potential participle in Skr. तव्य, Pr. अव्व is much used in the modern dialects and made the base of various verbal formations. In M. we have करावें 'should be done', G. करवुं, S. पसिबो from पस to see, Braj. करवौं, B. & O. करिवा. The H. has lost it, so also the P.

The Skr. verbal noun in अन appears as करणें in M., करणु S., करनौ Braj., करना H. and P., कहन O. & B., but in these latter it is probably a modern Tatsama. G. does not possess it. These forms are called infinitives by the Vernacular grammarians. Prof. Hornle traces them to the Skr. potential participle in अनीय; but as before remarked the transition from नीयं to नयं and then to नें is taken for granted; regularly नीय ought in the vernaculars to be changed to नी as in पाणी. According to the observations I made before the एं of करणें and औं of करनौं must be due to अकम्—अअं—अयं Pr. and अकम्—अअं

Ap. as in M. केलें and G. केडुं; so that the verbal noun in M. and H. is an augmented form of the corresponding one in Skr., while that of the Sindhî is from the unaugmented form. A great many other verbal derivatives have come down to the vernaculars but I must not go further.

The Pr. passive base in ईअ and इज्ज has been preserved only in P. & S. Thus मारीए 'he may be beaten' and मारीअन 'they may be beaten' are forms of the 3rd pers. sing. and pl. of the passive old Pres. and modern Potential; while मारीदा the present part. is used as a base to form various tenses. This is the Pr. form in इअ, the अ being lost. Sindhî has ज as पीजणु 'to be drunk,' धोइजणु 'to be washed,' धोइजे sing. धोइजनि pl. 3rd pers. Pres. or Pot. The pres. part. is wanting; the potential participle from तव्य being used instead as धोइबो. The augment इ is introduced before this ज where euphony requires it. Old M. possessed these forms and they are very frequently to be met with in our poets as in Jñânes'varî.

आतां आमुचा दळीं नायक। जे रूढ वीर सैनिक। ते प्रसंगें आइक। सांगिजति ॥

'Now incidentally will be mentioned, the leaders, proved warriors and soldiers in our army.'

तयापरी तूं देवा। मज झकऊन न येसि माधवा।
जरी पुण्याचा ओलावा। नाशिजैल ॥

'In that manner, O lord Mâdhava, you will abandon me and will not come to me if the moisture of virtue is dried up (*lit.* will be destroyed).'

विचारीं तूं अर्जुनु। कीं कारण्यें कीजसी दीनु।
सांग पां अंधकारें भानु। ग्रासिला आथी ॥

'Think Arjuna, you are being made contemptible by sorrow; say, is the sun ever swallowed up by darkness.'

Here we have instances of the Present and Future. Old Guj. had the passive.

जिहां पूजिजइ सालिग्राम। जिहां जपिइजे हरितुं नाम।
स्मृति पुराण मानीइं गायइ। जीणि दिसि कराय जाग्य।
जिहां पट्दर्शन दीजइ त्याग। जिहां......वेदपुराण धर्म बुझीइ ॥
नव खंडे अपकीरति रही। माधवि म्लेछ आणियासही ॥

'Where Sâligrâma is worshipped, where the name of Hari is muttered in meditation and Smṛitis, Purâṇas and the cows are respected, in which country sacrifices are performed and alms are given, where Vedas, Purâṇas and duty are understood, there Mâdhava for certain brought the Mlechha and infamy rests (on his name) in the nine divisions (of the world)'.

Here we have instances of the forms in ज as पूजिजइ and in ई (Pr. ईअ) बुझीइ; and also of the modern forms as कराय which will be presently considered. In old H. poets we meet with such forms now and then. Thus Tulsidâs:

महिमा जासु जान गणराऊ । प्रथम पूजियत नामप्रभाऊ ॥

'The greatness of which (Râma's name) the lord of the Gaṇas (Gaṇapati) knows, he is first worshipped; this is the achievement of the name.'

चहियत युगल किशोर लखि । लोचन युगल अनेक ॥ Behârilâla

'Many couples of eyes are wanted to see the couple of young persons (Râdhâ and Krishṇa).

Here पूजियत and चहियत are forms of the passive in ईय. The verb चाहिये in mod. H. is also a passive form as ज्योइये G. and पाहिजे M.

There are also, as in the Pr., Siddha Tadbhava forms of the passive as बुझणु S. 'to be heard,' भजणु S. 'to be broken' H. 'to flee away,' भुजणु S. 'to be fried,' छिजणु S. 'to be plucked' from Pr. बुज्झ, भज्ज, भुज्ज and छिज्ज and Skr. बुध्य, भज्य, भृज्य and छिद्य; पच-णें-वुं-ना-णु-न from पच्च Pr., पच्य Skr. 'to be cooked' in all, though the sense is somewhat altered. लाभणें M., लभणु S. from Pr. लब्भ, Skr. लभ्य 'to be obtained;' बझणु S., बझना H. from Pr. बज्झ, Skr. बध्य 'to be bound;' दिसणें-वुं-ना M. G. H. P. from Pr. दीस, Skr. दृश्य 'to be seen' also दीखना H.; सुजणें-णु M. S., सूजना H. P. from Pr. सुज्ज, Skr. सूय्, root श्वि 'to be increased,' 'to swell;' कळणें M., Pr. कल्ल, Skr. कल्य 'to be known;' सुचणें-वुं M. G. from; सुच्च Pr., Skr. सूच्य 'to occur to one' etc.

The causal is formed in M. by appending ईव or अव as करीवणें or करवणें, घात्रीवणें or घाववणें; you will remember, I have identified the ई that non-reflexive transitive roots take in M. with the Parasm. इ, and ए or अ of the intransitive and reflexive with the Âtm. Now when a root becomes causative its reflexive character is lost, all verbs become transitive and hence we have अ or ई promiscuously used after all roots. For this reason even in Skr. all causal verbs are both Parasm. and Âtm. I do not derive the rule about M. verbs taking अ or इ from that in Skr., but attribute it to the same causes. In the Goan. and Chit. we have अय for अव, the य being pronounced as a consonant and often like the vowel इ as करयणां or करइणां. In the Sâvantvâḍî and

Vengurla districts it is formed in the same way, but in the other portions of the area over which the Mâlvaṇî is spoken it is formed as in the principal Marâṭhî. The य stands for व; for this semi-vowel is often, by the vulgar, dropped leaving the vowel instead, as नआ for नवा like the H. नया for नवा, नाई for नावी etc. In G. the causal termination is आव as कराववुं 'cause to do,' तपाववुं 'make hot;' in S. आइ as वधाइणु 'to cause to increase,' धोआइणु 'to cause to wash;' in P. आउ or वाउ as कराउना or करवाउना; in H. आ as नचाना, पढाना, but नचावना and पढावना are also used; and the termination वा is invariably added to the first causal to form a second or double causal as नचवाना पढवाना from नचाना and पढाना. The आव occurs in first causals in poetry, as Tulsidas: अब प्रभुचरित सुनावहु मोहि 'Narrate (lit. make me hear) to me the history of the lord;' also

यथा अनेक वेष धरि नृत्य करै नट कोइ ।
सोइ सोइ भाव दिखावै आपुन होइ ना सोइ ॥

'As an actor assuming various masks dances; so he (the lord) shows this character and that but is not himself that (what he shows).'

The B. & O. causal is also similarly formed by adding आ as कराइ 'I cause to do,' देखाइ 'I show' etc. Here also as in the H. the व of आव is elided. The इ of the S. आइ must be the इ which we have observed is used after transitive and non-reflexive roots in Pot., the Pres. part. etc. as मारींदो. Thus then the causal termination in all the languages is आव or अव which is the same as one of the three in Pr. For, you will remember, the Pr. has ए, आवे and, the ए of the latter being dropped there is another आव. We have also a good many examples in the vernaculars of the Pr. causals mentioned by Hemachandra as formed by dropping all terminations and preserving the vowel changes, guṇa or vṛiddhi, which roots take before the Skr. अय or Pr. ए. Thus—

M. G. H.	मरणें-वुं-ना	मारणें-वुं-ना.
H.	खुलना	खोलना.
M. G. H. S.	तुटणें-वुं-ना-णु	तोडणें-वुं-ना-णु.
M. G. H.	फुटणें-वुं-ना	फोडणें-वुं-ना.
H.	फटना	फाडनां.
G. H.	छूटवुं-ना	छोडवुं-ना
M.	सुटणें	सोडणें
M. G.	पडणें-वुं	पाडणें-वुं
M.	चरणें	चारणें
S.	चरणु	चारणु
M. S.	गळणें-गरणु	गाळणें-गारणु
S.	पढणु	पाढणु

I have already mentioned that the causal of some roots is formed in H. by inserting ल before the causal termination आ. G. has ड and Sindhî ड़ for ल, खवाडवुं 'to cause to eat' from खा to eat, देवाडवुं 'to cause to give,' देखाडवुं 'to show' from देख 'to see,' धवाडवुं 'to cause to run,' ड़िअणु 'to give,' ड़िआरणु 'to cause to give,' सिखणु-सेखारणु, वेहणु-वेहारणु 'to cause to sit.' In these instances we have वा or आ before ड; but in G. all these forms have आव optionally added to them when the previous आ is dropped as धवडाववुं 'to cause to run,' खवडाववुं 'to cause to eat' etc.; and in S. we have the causal आइ appended to र after roots ending in आ as खाराइणु 'to cause to eat', घाराइणु 'to cause to wound', धाराइणु 'to cause to suck' or 'to suckle;' so that the intervening आ is inter-changeable in both these languages with the causal termination and hence some way conveys the same sense. M. has a trace of these forms as भोंवणें 'to turn,' भोंवडणें 'to cause to turn,' धावणें 'to run,' धावडणें 'to cause to run,' भिणें-भेडावणें 'to threaten.' Hemachandra mentions भमाडो as the causal base of भ्रम and gives धाड in the sense of pushing which is very likely a causal form of धा. We have this धाड in the sense of sending in M. We have seen that द or त is sometimes changed to ड and thence to र or ल in the Pr. and vernaculars; whence it appears that पिलाना is a denominative or nominal root from पिला or पिडा or पीत by the application of the usual denominative termination आप, which is also the causal termination. In Skr. such a denominative has the sense of doing the thing expressed by the base as पीतं करोति-पीतयति S'aur. पीदावेदि. We have a great many denominatives from past participles; first in the sense of *being* the thing expressed by the base, in which case the participle has simply the verbal terminations appended to it as लग्गइ from लग, अब्भिडइ from अभ्येत, कट्टइ from कृष्ट, पल्लट्टइ, पल्लत्थइ from पर्यस्त etc.; and secondly in the sense of *doing* when आव or आवे intervenes between the base and the terminations, as भीदावेदि in Mâlatî-Mâdhava, from which we have in M. भेडावणें. The forms in which we have आ before ड as देवाडवुं, खवाडवुं etc. are denominatives from the past participles of original Pr. causals as दाविद or खाविद, the causal termination आव being changed to औ and आ as in the H. in ordinary causals. In the vernaculars we have also the first class of denominatives expressive of being like the thing denoted by the base, as:

M. G. H.	काढणें-वुं-ना	to draw	from कृष्ट	p. p. p. of कृष्.
H.	सुतना	to sleep	सुप्त	स्वप्
G.	वुठवुं	to rain	वृष्ट	वृष्
H. G.	बैठना-बेठवुं	to sit	उपविष्ट	विश् with उप
H. G.	पैठना-पेठवुं	to enter	प्रविष्ट	विश् with प्र

H.	कुढना	to cry	क्रुष्ट	क्रुश्
G.	रुठवुं	to be angry	रुष्ट	रुश्
G.	तुठवुं	to be pleased	तुष्ट	तुष्
H. G.	घटना-वुं	to be diminished	घृष्ट	घृष्

We have another verbal base in M. which involves the idea of power and ability as करवतें 'can be done,' बसवतें 'can be sat.' These forms are passive when the original verb is transitive, and impersonal when it is intransitive. In old M. प is sometimes seen for व.

जरी वेदें बहुत बोलिलें। विविध भेद सूचिले। तरी आपण हित आपुलें। तेंचि घेपे ॥

'Even if the Veda has told much and indicated a great many distinct things, still one should take that which is beneficial to himself.'

काय म्हणिपे स्थितप्रज्ञ

'Who should be called स्थितप्रज्ञ?'

Here the sense is simply passive and does not involve the notion of power. These forms are to be derived from the pass. of the causal, whence करवे is करव्वइ Pr. for कराप्यते, Skr. कार्यते. Power is implied on account of the forms being derived in this manner; for, गोविन्देन कर्म कार्यते मया in Skr. means the work is caused to be done by me, and by Govinda; when the agent caused is taken to be the same as that who causes, the sense is 'the work is caused to be done by me by myself' *i. e.* 'I am the causer of myself to do it' *i. e.* 'I can do it.' In. G. this causal pass. अव्व is transformed into आ as the causal अव so often is and the sense is simply passive in some cases and passive and causative in others as आं छोकरो मूर्ख जणाय छे 'this boy is known to be a fool;' आ काम माराथी करातुं नथी 'this work cannot be done from me.' There are traces of these forms in the other languages also, though the grammarians do not notice them as H. एकवचन बस्तुर संख्या एक बुझाय 'By the singulars the number of a thing is known to be one,' वह वाक्य कहाता है 'that is called a sentence' etc.*

Thus then you will see that we have nearly the whole of the grammar of the Prâkṛits *i. e.* all their grammatical forms in our vernaculars. The cases in the forms they assumed in the Apabhraṃs'a have been preserved, some in this language and some in that, but not all in one and the same. And along with them there are sometimes newly constructed forms also. The pronouns are the same as in the

---

* Mr. Beames traces the vernacular causal terminations अव, इव, उ, आ etc. to the Skr. अय. But this is evidently a mistake. The Pr. आवे or आव has escaped him somehow. The उ of the Hindi causal forms he also derives from the य of अय. But this य is too weak to be changed to any other letter than the vowel ए, and य is never changed to a semivowel excepting in the doubtful instance लट्ठी from यष्टि.

Pr. and the Apabhraṃs'a. The two Prâkṛit tenses and one mood are preserved. All the vernaculars have the Present, though, except in the O. and B., it has acquired another sense and another word or expression is wanted to restrict it to the signification of the present time. G. S. P. and H. have lost the Imperative but it is preserved by the other three languages. The Future is retained by the G. and the Braj.; while this latter possesses the solitary form of the Aorist that the old Pr. had retained. These are the only really simple or uncompounded verbal forms existing in our languages; the rest are made up by compounding or by using Pres. participles as bases and appending the Pres. verbal terminations as will be hereafter shown. Past time is almost universally expressed by the past participle, and this retains the pass., in some cases the active, character it had in Skr. and Pr. in all those languages that have not thoroughly lost the distinction of gender and number. The several other Prâkṛit participles are preserved and we have no other. The passive forms are seen in Sindhî and Panjâbî; the former having one set and the latter the other. The Pr. causal termination is preserved almost unchanged by the M. and G. while in the other languages it is somewhat transformed. So that, as they are at present, our vernaculars have between them preserved all that the Prâkṛits had and preserved nothing that the Prâkṛits lost. And as we ascend higher up in the history of each of these languages we find in use such forms as it has now lost. All our vernaculars must at one time have been in the condition in which we find the Apabhraṃs'a, but the dialect of that name which is treated of by the grammarians, and specimens of which we find in the scraps of literature I have noticed resemble the G. and the Braj and in a less degree the S. P. and the ordinary H. The old literary dialect of the H. area was the Braj; and the works of Tulsidâs, Bihârilâl, Kabîra and others are in that dialect, though these are called old Hindî poets, instead of old Brâj poets as they should be called and as they are called by natives. In this old Braj literature we find the Apabhraṃs'a forms of the Present tense unchanged; and from these has directly been derived the Present tense of the modern S. G. P. Braj and H. The Apbhr. Future is found in the G. and in modern Braj and in the poets in an older and less corrupt form also, though the स is changed to ह. Such Apbhr. forms as जेम, तेम are preserved in the G.; and the neuter sing. in उं in that dialect as well as the Braj where it occurs especially in the verbal nouns or infinitives. The first pers. sing. हुं exists in G., old H. and a dialect of the Panjâbî. The other dialects also possess, as I have observed, some Ap. peculiarities, but the four above named bear a closer connection to it. And since the Apabhraṃs'a is referred by the grammarians to the S'aurasenî type we may regard these four modern dialects viz. the G. S. P. and H. as the representatives of the old S'aurasenî, which from the name seems to have been the dialect of the country about Mathurâ. The distinction between this and the old Mahârâshṭrî was as we have seen not very great .and some of the peculiarities were such as could not last for many centuries. The change of त and थ to द and ध, for instance, instead of elision and ह is of such a nature. The law of elision which operated in a great many other cases could not long be kept from extending itself to त. But still we do find in the modern G. such forms as किदुं, पिदुं, खादुं etc. for कृतम्. पीतम् and खादितम्. This change was made in some cases in the S'aurasenî as in सउन्दला, for शकुन्तला, and in others not, as अय्यउत्त for आर्यपुत्र. And the change of न्त to न्द and द we find in the S. and P. present participles. The S'aur. Future which had an intercalatory स्स instead of the Mahârâshṭrî हि is, as we have seen, preserved in the G. and the Braj with the slight modification it underwent in the Apabhraṃs'a. Then if we follow Vararuchi the S'aur. Absolutive termination was इअ and in the prose speeches in the dramatic plays it is this alone that we find. The absolutive in these four mod. languages is formed by adding this same termination with the अ dropped. Now all these peculiarities are absent from the M. In the old Mahârâshṭrî verses occurring in the plays as well as according to Vararuchi the absolutive termination was ऊण, which we find in the M. alone. The past passive participle of कृ and मृ in old Mahr. was कअ and मअ and we have these forms in the M. in केला and मेला as we have seen, while किद instead of के, मुद instead of मे occur in the four S'aurasenic dialects and these we find in the plays. The Pres. and Imper. of the M. have been derived from the Pr. and not from the Apbhr. forms. Thus then the M. is the modern representative of the old Mahârâshṭrî; so that it hardly admits of any doubt that the two old languages derived their names from the provinces in which they prevailed. The B. and O. have a few peculiarities of the S'aur.; and they seem to occupy a middle position between M. on the one hand and the four Apbhr. or S'aur. languages on the other; while the consonantal changes, especially the reduction of all the sibilants to the palatal श, point to their being the descendants of the old Mâgadhî.

LECTURE VI.

New Grammatical Formations in the Northern Vernaculars.

We will now proceed to consider those forms in the grammar of our languages which are not derived from corresponding Sanskrit or Prâkṛit forms, but which have been constructed in recent times. Such new forms owe their origin to various causes. The old ones lose their distinctive portions and become confused by phonetic decay; or, having been in long use, lose all freshness of meaning and cease to be as expressive as one would wish them to be or their sense is not exactly that which one desires to convey. Thus the old Present and Future got confused in our vernaculars and a new Future was wanted. The old Present itself acquired a potential sense in some and a past habitual sense in one, whence for the expression of present time another set of forms was required. In Sanskrit itself such a phrase as द्विजाय यवागूः 'gruel for a Brahman' is not so expressive as द्विजार्थां यवागूः 'gruel for a Brahman's purpose'; which again is analysed into its separate elements for greater distinctness into द्विजस्यार्थे यवागूः 'gruel for the purpose of a Brahman.' When different words so brought together are kept distinct and consciously used there is no growth of new forms. But if by frequent use and the oblivion of etymology such an expression as स्यार्थे comes to be looked upon as an independent word meaning "for the sake of" and applied promiscuously to all nouns including such as could not oiginally by the usage of Sanskrit have it, as in भ्रातृस्यार्थे, it becomes a termination and a new case form grows up and the old one often goes out of use. Then again phonetic decay sets in and by reducing this expression to स्सट्ठे and ultimately to साठे (Me. साठीं the original word being सट्ठम्मि) irrevocably stamps it with the character of a case termination having no meaning by itself. Lastly, if one wishes to say of a book that it belongs to *him* and looks upon it as possessing that attribute and subordinates *him* to it, the expression तस्य पुस्तकम् will not serve his purpose but he must have some such as तदीयं पुस्तकम्. And if this way of looking at things becomes general तदीय supersedes तस्य. In this way our new forms have grown up.

The case terminations are in the majority of the languages applied not to the original noun itself but to a certain modified form of it called the oblique form or by the native Marâṭhî grammarians the Sâmânya-rûpa or the common form because it is used in all the cases. There are two Sâmânya-rûpas for the two numbers. In the old languages plurality is expressed by independent terminations but the new terminations of the modern languages being the same for both numbers plurality is denoted by a distinctive oblique form. Some of the modern languages that have no Sâmânya-rûpa have recourse to a novel way of expressing plurality. Of all the vernaculars it is the Marâṭhî that is most particular in the formation of the oblique and has minute rules. Sindhî comes next, then the Hindî and the Panjâbî; after these the Gujarâtî and lastly the Bangâlî and the Oriyâ, which may be said to have no oblique form at all.

The Marâṭhî oblique forms are made up by adding these terminations :—

Sing.		Pl.	
Sing.	आ	Pl.	आं
„	ई	„	ई
„	ई	„	आं
„	ऊ	„	ऊं
„	ए	„	आं

(1) The following classes of nouns take the first—

(*a*) Masc. and Neut. nouns in अ as हात 'hand'. हाता obl., हातास sing. 'to a hand,' हातांस pl. 'to hands.'

(*b*) Masc. nouns in आ and neuter nouns in एं which combine the final and the termination into या, but to ए in the speech of the Konkaṇî Karhâḍâs and in the Chitpâvanî and optionally to या or ए in adjectives, as आंबा 'a mango', आंब्या obl., आंब्यास sing. 'to a mango;' केळें 'a plantain', केळ्या obl., केळ्यास sing. 'to a plantain;' आंबेस 'to a mango' in the Konkaṇî Karhâḍâs, पिवळा 'yellow', पिवळ्या or पिवळे obl., पिवळ्या आंब्यास or पिवळे आंब्यास sing. 'to a yellow mango' respectively.

(*c*) A good many Masc. nouns in ई, the ई of which is changed to या before आ as न्हावी nom., न्हाव्या obl., न्हाव्यास sing., न्हाव्यांस pl.

All neuter nouns in ई as मोतीं—मोत्या—मोत्यास—मोत्यांस.

(*d*) Some masc. and nearly all neuter nouns in ऊ. Some of these change ऊ to वा and others drop it, since it is the ऊ of the nom. sing. Apbhr., as भाऊ 'a brother'—भावा obl., भावास sing. 'to a brother', भावांस pl. 'to brothers'; वाटसरू 'traveller', वाटसरा obl., वाटसरास sing., वाटसरांस pl.; गळूं—गळवा—गळवास sing., गळवांस pl. लेकरूं—लेकरा—लेकरास sing., लेकरांस pl. Some nouns of this class take आ optionally as विंचू—विंच्वा—विंच्वास sing., विंच्वांस pl.

(2) The following nouns take the second form ई, ई.

(*a*) Tatsamas in short इ as कवि—कवी—कवीस.

(*b*) A few masc. nouns in ई as हत्ती 'elephant', हत्ती-हत्तीस sing., हत्तींस pl.

(*c*) A good many feminine nouns in अ as रीत manner, रिती—रितीस. sing., रितींस pl., केळ 'a plantain tree', केळी—केळीस sing., केळींस pl.

(*d*) Some feminine nouns in ई as भुई 'ground', भुई—भुईस sing., भुईंस pl.

(3) A good many feminine nouns take the third form ई—आं, as घोडी 'a mare', घोडी sing., घोड्यां pl., घोडीस sing., घोड्यांस pl.; साडी 'a garment worn by females', साडी sing., साड्या pl., साडीस sing., साड्यांस pl. In the Goan. and Mâl., however, this form does not exist and these nouns take the fifth form ए—आ, as घोड्ये—घोड्येक sing., घोड्यांक pl.; साडी—साड्येक sing., साड्यांक pl.

(4) Some masc. and feminine nouns in ऊ take the fourth form ऊ-ऊं, as खाऊ—खाऊस sing., खाऊंस pl.; बाजू f. 'a side', बाजू—बाजूस sing., बाजूंस pl.

(5) The following classes take the fifth form:—A good many fem. nouns in अ as जीभ 'a tongue', जिभे sing., जिभां pl., जिभेस sing., जिभांस pl. A good many fem. nouns in ई in the Goan. and Mâl. dialects; see instances given above. Some fem. nouns in ऊ, as जळू 'a leech', जळवे sing., जळवां pl., जळवेस sing., जळवांस pl.; जाऊ 'husband's brother's wife', जावे—जावां etc. Some nouns take this form optionally as सासूस or सास्वेस; सासूंस or सास्वांस. The usage in several cases is still unsettled as regards some of these forms. You will observe that there is an anusvâra in the pl. of all forms. Another fact should also be borne in mind that nouns in ई and ऊ often take the आ—आं or ए—आं forms though these properly belong to nouns in अ.

Sindhi :—

(1) The following classes of nouns take अ for the obl. sing. and आं, एं and अनि for the pl.:

(*a*) Masc. nouns, the nom. sing. of which ends in उ, as देहु 'a country', देह-देहनि obl., देहजो sing. 'of a country', देहनिजो pl. 'of countries', also देहां—देहें—जो.

(*b*) Masc. nouns in ओ, which, however, combine the final and the termination into ए as in the Chit. Mar. as वाढो 'a carpenter', obl. वाढे sing., वाढनि, वाढां and वाढें pl.

(2) The following nouns take अ for the obl. sing. and नि, अनि and उनि for the pl. in addition to आं and एं.

(*a*) Masc. nouns in ई as हारी 'a peasant', हारिअ or हारिआं sing., हार्यें, हारिएं, हार्यां, हारिनि, हार्यनि and हार्युनि pl.

(*b*) Fem. nouns in ई as घोडी 'a mare', obl. घोडिअ sing. घोडिआं, घोडिएं, घोडिनि, घोड्यनि and घोड्युनि pl.

(*c*) Masc. nouns in ऊ; as माण्हू 'a man', obl. माण्हुअ sing., माण्हु-नि, माण्हुअनि, माण्हुआं and माण्हुएं pl.

(3) Nouns in short इ have no separate form for the sing. of the obl., the nom. form being used; the pl. they form like the above class, as गाल्हि *f.* 'a story', obl. गाल्हि sing., गाल्हिआं, गाल्हिएं, गाल्हिअनि, गाल्हिउनि and गाल्हिनि pl. Masc. nouns in इ, however, do not take the forms in अनि and उनि; as केहरि 'a lion', obl. केहरि sing., केहरिनि-आं-एं pl.

(4) Fem. nouns in अ, आ and उ have no separate form for the sing. while in the pl. they take उनि as सध 'wish', obl. सध sing., सधुनि pl.; हुचा 'a murder', obl. हुचा sing., हुचाउनि pl.; विजु 'lightening', obl. विजु sing., विजुनि pl. The first has सधां and सधें also for the pl. Here there is one type for one class of nouns and not two, as is the case sometimes in the M. The form in उनि is taken by all feminine nouns in अ, आ and ई and also masc. nouns in ई. Masc. nouns in ऊ and fem. nouns in उ have उ in the original base itself and it does not belong to the termination.

Panjâbî:—

Panjâbî has the termination ए for the sing. obl. of nouns ending in आ. The sing. of all other nouns has no special form while आं is appended to all nouns to form the obl. pl., before which the final आ of nouns preceded by a consonant is changed to इ, as घोडा 'a horse', घोडे obl. sing. and घोडिआं pl. Final उ preceded by a vowel combines with this आं to form वां, as पिउ or पेउ 'father', पेवां obl. pl.; and final अ forms आं as मनुख 'man', मनुखां obl. pl. There are no other changes.

Hindî:—

Hindî like the Panjâbî has an oblique sing. for nouns in आ only. It ends in ए as that of the S. and Chit. M. nouns in ओ, Karh. M. and P. nouns in आ; as घोडे-घोडेका. The pl. obl. of all nouns whatever is formed by adding ओं which amalgamates with the preceding अ of all nouns and the आ of such as are mesculine and combines with इ to form इयों; as गांव 'a village', गांवोंका pl. 'of villages'; घोडा 'a horse', घोडोंका pl. 'of horses'; पति 'a master', पतियोंका pl. 'of masters.' In other cases it is simply added to the noun as भालू 'a jackal',

भालुओंका pl. 'of jackals.' In the Brajbhâshâ and in the old poets the obl. pl. of all nouns has न or नि instead of ओं, as संत 'a good man', संतनका pl. 'of good men.' This termination is also added to the nom. sing. to form the nom. pl. of those nouns that have no distinctive form for it; as लोग 'people' sing., लोगन pl.; भगत 'devotee', भगतन pl. (चहु जुग भगतन बांधल वाटी (Kabîr)).

Gujarâtî:—

In G. the obl. form of masc. and neuter nouns ending in ओ and ई is formed by substituting आ for those vowels. The latter take an anusvâra in the pl., and the forms of the former for both numbers are alike as घोडो—घोडा—घोडाने sing. and pl. 'to a horse or horses'; केळुं 'a plantain', केळा—केळाने sing. 'to a plantain', केळांने pl. 'to plantains'. But the nom. pl. forms of these are घोडा and केळां, whence it appears that in the pl. the obl. cases are formed by simply adding the terminations to the nom. pl. and there is no such thing as a common oblique form. And this is the case with the sing. as well as the pl. of all other nouns; as माणस 'a man' nom. sing., माणसो nom. pl., माणसने sing. माणसाने pl. The plural termination is ओ and is thus used in all cases. It is added in these days even to the final आ and आं of nouns in ओ and ई to distinguish the pl. forms from the sing. as घोडा or घोडाओ nom. pl., घोडाने or घोडाओने dat. pl. But the practice has not yet established itself and mostly the forms without ओ are used. Masc. and neut. nouns not ending in ओ or ई are often used in the pl. without it in such instances as तिहा घणा माणस छे in the nom. and other cases. And this is the usual practice in old G. literature; as—लोकनां पुत्रना विवाह होईछी (Panch.) 'The marriages of the sons of other people are performed;' सर्व शास्त्रनो परिचय छे 'He has a knowledge of all the S'âstras.

कलजुगना ब्राह्मण जेटला
धर्महीन थासे तेटला
तां घर करसे पोता तणां
स्वर्गारोहणनो कीधो ग्रंथ
जेहमा सकल धर्मनो पंथ

Svargârohaṇa by Sundarabhaṭṭa.

'All the Brahmans of Kaliyuga will be without virtue. They will build their homes there. The work Svargârohaṇa was composed in which there is the way of all virtues.'

अनेक पंखी करे पोकार । गिरिजंगल बहु डुंगरा वळी वांदरना ठाठ

Kâvyadohana, Tulasî.

'Many birds raise a noise. There are mountains, forests, many hills; over these is a crowd of monkeys.'

The ओ however is seen in fem. nouns ending in ई,

as—समुद्र गांमनी नदीयो जे हसे । तेमांथी जळ सुकी जसे ॥

Svargârohaṇa.

'The water of the sea and of the rivers on land (in villages) will be dried up.'

मोठा पर्वत नदियो जेह । तेह तणो नहि लाधे छेह ॥

Kâvyad. Tulasî.

'There is no end of great mountains and rivers that exist.'

It therefore appears that in masc. and neut. nouns the ओ is a modern innovation and that there was no distinction between the sing. and pl. cases except the nom. of nouns in ओ and उं. The true explanation therefore of the modern ओ of the pl. is that fem. nouns in आ and ई preserved this termination, since they had it in the Prâkṛits, as the minor M. dialects have done, and, the sing. and pl. forms of masc. nouns being alike, the fem. ओ was transferred to them afterwards to distinguish the pl. as is now being done to nouns in ओ and उं. Thus then the G. noun may be said to have no real Sâmânya-rûpa or oblique form. Adjectives in ओ however have a form ending in ए when they are used to qualify a substantive in the instr. or old loc. case in ए as आ काम सारे माणसे कीधुं 'this thing was done by a good man', तलावने काटे छोकरा गिया 'boys went te the margin of a tank'; but this may be explained as a remnant of the old agreement between the noun and its adjective and सारे may be regardod as an instr. form and तलावने a loc.

The Bangâlî and Oriya apply the case terminations directly to the nom. and there is no oblique form. The new terminations being, as in all the modern languages, the same for both numbers and there being no oblique form to express the distinction between them as in M. S. H. etc., these languages, like the Guj., were under the necessity of deriving some expression for denoting plurality. The G. found its fem. ओ and employed it for this purpose, but the B. and O. had no such distinctively pl. termination left to fall back upon and so they have recourse to the use of a word signifying collection such as दिग originally 'direction, row, line', गण, समूह and सकल etc. after the noun, the plurality of which is to be expressed. Thus राजा 'a king', राजार 'of a king', राजादिगेर

'of kings' lit. 'of the direction row or line of a king.' Sometimes the word दिग is attached to the gen. sing. as राजारदिगेर to express the gen. relation between राजा and दिग, which is understood in the first expression. To nouns denoting inferior animals समूह and such words are appended and such others as सकल to those signifying inanimate creatures as कुक्कुरेर 'of a dog' कुक्कुरसमुहेर 'of dogs.' The Oriya sign of the plural is मान for rational and animate creatures and सकळ, समस्त etc. for irrational or inanimate, as पशु 'a beast', पशुर sing. 'of a beast', पशुमानङ्कर 'of beasts.' The B. adds रा to the nom. sing. of names of rational creatures to form the nom. pl., while समूह, सकल, etc. are applied to the rest. राजा 'a king', राजारा 'kings'; कुक्कुर 'a dog', कुक्कुरसमूह 'dogs.' The O. adds ए to मान to form the nom. pl. as पशुमाने. This ए is the same as that of घोडे in M. and H.

Now the question is what is the nature of this Sâmânya-rûpa or oblique form, why does a noun undergo a certain modification before it becomes fit to receive the termination and what is the signification of the modified form and of the nasal that appears in the plural. Let us see how we at the present day join certain words expressive of relation such as संनिध or पाशीं with a noun. We say त्याच्या संनिध or त्याच्या पाशीं *i. e.* put the noun into the gen. case. Now this त्याच्यापाशीं is convertible with त्याजपाशीं, in which त्याज is the oblique form of तो the demonstrative. Similarly we append even some of the case terminations to the gen. as माझ्यानें काम करवत नाहीं 'I can not do the work;' त्याच्यांत कांहीं पाणी नाहीं 'there is no spirit (lit. water) in him'. May the Sâmânyarûpa then be an original genitive? The gen. is used in the Prâkṛits and even in Pâli not only with independent words but is made the base of some cases also as we have seen and the case terminations attached to it, thus ममं is acc. sing. of अहम् 'I' in the Pâli and the Pr., ममाइं instr., ममाशे, ममाहि abl., ममम्मि loc. in the latter, in which instances the usual terminations of those cases are added to the original gen. form मम. We find everywhere in the history of our languages that after a time the terminations in some cases come to have an independent sense and then they are detached from the original base and used like ordinary post-positions. Thus, before the loc. म्मि was appended to मम it must have acquired some such sense as 'in the interior of' and that the whole expression ममम्मि might mean 'in the interior of me.' Similarly in the Apabhraṁs'a some of the postpositions which came into use and which as I shall hereafter show have grown into our case terminations are used with the gen. of the noun to which they are attached. Thus :—

हउं झिजउं तउ केहिं पिअ तुहुं पुणु अन्नह रेसि 'I pine away for thee, of beloved, but thou for another', in which we have the postpositions केहिं and रेसि having the sense of 'for' used with the genitives तउ 'thy' and अन्नह 'of another'. And if we examine the oblique forms themselves we shall find that they are derived from the Apbhr. and Pr. genitives. Thus the form in आ sing. and आं pl. which nouns in अ, आ etc. take is derived from the Apbhr. ह sing. and हं or अं pl. derived from Pr. स and णं. The grammarians give the Apbhr. sing. termination as हो but ह is also found, as in अन्नह in the above quotation and in the following occurring in an old work:—

कान्ह तणइ संपत्ति इसी। जिसी इंद्रह घरि रिद्धि ॥

'The wealth of Kanha was like the affluence in the house of Indra' where इंद्रह is gen. sing. The ह of हत्थह for instance is reduced to अ, the aspirate being lost, as is often the case in the vernaculars, and we have हत्था or हाता. Similarly अं of the pl. combines with the preceding अ into आं and we have हातां. The second form ई and ईं is derived from the gen. of nouns in इ or ई masc. or fem. Thus केलीइ is the Pr. gen. sing. from which we have केळी the sing. obl., and केलिणं pl. the णं of, which is reduced to अं as in the other case and we have केलीअं–अ as proved in the last lecture generally goes out in the vernaculars after a long vowel even when medial and after a short dissimilar vowel when final and hence we have केळीं the obl. pl.; or the sing. ई may be derived from another fem. gen. termination अ or the masc. अ for ह, which before the preceding short इ goes out since it is final, as कविह-कविअ-कवी. The fourth form उ and ऊं is similarly derived from masc. and fem. nouns in उ or ऊ as साहुस्स–साहुह–साहुअ–साहू obl. M. though we have not this word in this form in M. श्वश्रू-सस्सू-सस्सुअ gen., सासू obl. sing. M.; सस्सूणं-सस्सूअं-सासूं obl. pl. M. The fifth form in ए sing. and आं pl. is from fem. nouns in आ; Pr. जिब्भाइ or जिब्भाए-जिभे M. obl. sing. and जिब्भाणं-जिब्भाअं-जिभां M. obl. pl. The third form ई sing. and आं pl. is a mixture of the second and the fifth and the nouns that take it form their oblique on the type of the fifth in the Goan. and Mâl. The Sindhî in its अ of the sing. of its first and second forms shortens the आ of the M. *i. e.* the two अ form one strong अ; while in its third or fourth it either dispenses with the special oblique or this is the same as the nom., as in the case of the M. हत्ती, सुई, सासू etc. The Sindhî plural oblique has one form आं, like the corresponding M. एं, which appears to be from the Apbhr. हं of the gen. pl. of nouns in short इ or उ given by Kramadîs'vara and the rest present the gen. न in an uncorrupted form. Of these अनि which all fem.

nouns and one set of masc. nouns take appears to be a combination of the fem. nom. pl. उ and the gen. नि; *i. e.* to the nom. pl. of these nouns the obl. नि was added instead of to the original base. The P. pl. आं is the same as the M. and the H. ओं is from the Apbhr. हुं of nouns in इ or उ. Or it may be explained as a combination of the fem. ओं with the nasal of the gen. as the Sindhî उनि is. The Braj न also presents the gen. termination in an unchanged form. This then is the way in which the oblique forms are derived, but as usual the law of false analogy and simplification has been in operation even here and thus while the M. represents them in a pristine condition, the Sindhî has reduced them to fewer types and the P. and H. and perhaps the G. to one and the B. and O. have dropped them altogether.

It now remains to show why nouns with various endings inflect the obl. in M. and S. according to the same type. I have already shown that the oblique terminations आ and आं properly belong to nouns in अ. Sindhî masc. nouns in उ are as observed on a former occasion really nouns in अ, उ being the nom. sing. termination, whence they take in the sing. आ shortened to अ. Nouns in आ Mar. and P. and in ओ S. also form their oblique according to this type. but the sing. base ends in या or ए in M. and ए in others. These nouns, as shown in the last but one lecture, were originally nouns augmented by the addition of क. Thus Skr. घोटक is Pr. घोडअ or घोडय, since अ is pronounced य, and with इ or अ the gen. termination becomes घोडय+अ=घोडया which by hasty pronunciation becomes घोड्या; but in the older M. poets we find घोडया also. Now in the state of घोडय it may become, as I have once stated, घोडे as कयल for कदल becomes केल or केळ and after a long vowel the following अ is elided, whence we have the form of the M. dialects and S. and P. and H. Similarly we have the plural घोड्यां. Neuter nouns in एं are also nouns with a final क, as has been shown, hence their oblique is like that of the Masc. nouns in आ. कदलकम्–कयलअं–केळें and केलय+अ of the gen.=केळया–केळ्या. Similarly सोनें = सुवण्णअ=सुवर्णक etc. Masc. nouns in ई also take this form. If they do so they must be nouns in अ originally and as a matter of fact we do find some of them at least to be so. Thus न्हावी is न्हाविअ Pr., नापित Sk.; wherefore we have न्हाविअ+आ= न्हाव्या; ताम्बोलिक is Pr. तम्बोलिअ and with the gen. इ or अ the obl. ताम्बोळ्या; वाणिज Pr. वाणिअ and with अ for इ वाण्या obl. etc. Similarly मौक्तिक is मोत्तिअ where with gen. अ we have M. मोत्या; पाणी is पानीअ and thence पाण्या. S. हारी is Skr. हालिक, Pr. हालिअ which is the S. obl. form, since the effect of two अ coming together is in this language to prevent the usual elision and form one strong अ. We thus see that most Mar. & S. masc. nouns in ई & M. neuter nouns in इ are derived from Pr. nouns having a final अ representing Skr. क or any other syllable. In the same way Skr. लड्डुक is Pr. लड्डुअ thence लाडुअ and with the gen. अ for इ लाडवा the M. obl.; so also M. भाऊ must be Pr. भाउअ, Skr. भ्रातृक; M. नातु, Pr. नत्तुअ, Skr. नप्तृक, in order that with the gen. अ they may yield भावा or नातवा. Neuter गडूं is गडुअ, Skr. गडुक and hence by the combination of गडुअ+अ we have गडवा or गळवा. S. माण्हू must have been माणुह from माणुष and the aspiration being transferred to अ we have माण्हुअ which is the obl. form. Thus then those M. & S. masc. nouns in उ and M. neuter nouns in ऊं which take this oblique form were Pr. nouns in अ representing a Skr. syllable ending in अ, mostly क. Now these vernacular nouns in इ or ई and उ or ऊ which in Skr. have not a syllable like त or क at the end must have the क attached to them in the Pr. and Apbhr., as we have seen it was, to nouns in अ which on that account have become nouns in ओ or आ in the modern languages. Those fem. nouns in अ that have इ and ई for their sâmânyarûpa terminations must be Skr. & Pr. nouns in ई, as they are as a matter of fact; as केळ is Pr. केली or कयली, Skr. कदली; भिंत is Pr. and Skr. भित्ति; पारध, Skr. पापर्द्धि, Pr. पारधी; बहिण, Skr. भगिनी, Pr. बहिणी; बांव, Skr. वापी, Pr. बावी; and a good many modern Tadbhavas such as रीत, गत, विभूत from रीति, गति, विभूति etc.; others that end in ई and take these terminations were also originally nouns in इ or ई as भुई, Skr. भूमि and others. Some masc. nouns in ई which form their obl. in this way must also be derived from corresponding nouns in ई as हत्ती is from the Skr. and Pr. Nom. sing. हत्थी. And modern Tatsamas in इ or ई of course can only take this form. Similarly those nouns that form their oblique by taking ऊ and ऊं must be originally nouns in उ or ऊ. Modern Tatsamas ending in these vowels also take these forms.

The fifth form has already been traced to the Pr. gen. of fem. nouns in आ whence those nouns that take the form in M. must have been originally nouns ending in that vowel. Thus जीभ, Pr. जिब्भा, Skr. जिह्वा; भाक—Skr. भाषा (mod. Tad.); माळ—माला—माला; भीक—भिक्खा—भिक्षा; नीज or नीद—निद्दा—निद्रा; सांज—संज्झा—संध्या; सेज—सेज्जा—शय्या etc. All modern fem. Tatsamas in आ are inflected in this way. From the fact that fem. nouns in ई take आं for the pl. obl. it would appear that they were originally nouns in आ. घोडी we know must have been Skr. घोटिका since the masc. is घोटक. Its gen. pl. in Pr. therefore was घोडिआअं whence we have घोड्यां but the sing. obl. घोडी which is the same as the nominative is not formed as it should be according to our theory. But, as observed before, the Goan. and Mâl. have faithfully preserved the old tradition here though the ordinary M. has lost it and in this instance applies the case terminations to the Nom. and not to special obl. form as the other languages do to a much greater extent. The Goan. and Mâl. sâmânyarûpa of घोडी is घोड्ये from Pr. gen. घोडिआइ the last two vowels combining into ए and the इ and ए into ये. Other instances are साडी Skr. शाटिका, वाडी–वाटिका, नळी—नलिका, कळी—कलिका, माशी—मक्षिका, माती—मृत्तिका, मुदी—मुद्रिका, the sing. obl. of which in the Goan. and Mâl. are साड्ये, वाड्ये, नळ्ये etc. Similarly those fem. nouns that take this type of the obl. must have been nouns in आ representing such a syllable as का. Thus M. वाळू is Pr. वालुआ, Skr. वालुका, and वालुआ with the इ or ए of the gen. sing. is वाळवे and with आं of the pl. वाळवांस ; also जळू-जलोआ or जलुआ–जलौका; ऊ a louse Skr. यूका, सासू–श्वश्रूका. The last and also वाळू have also the obl. form in ऊ and ऊं. Several other nouns also masc. and fem. ending in ई and ऊ have the ई and ऊ form of the obl. as well as the आ or ए and आं form. This arises from the practice of adding क or का optionally in the Pr., just as there are some nouns which, as we have seen, end both in अ and आ. In this way the several types of the M. sâmânyarûpa arose from different sets of Pr. nouns, but it is not meant that all those nouns that in the present state of the languages take one or other of those types were derived from the corresponding Prâkṛit set. After the forms came into use words from foreign languages for instance were introduced which can not of course be traced to the Prâkṛit and those were assigned to some one form according to the gender in the first place and then to fancy or accident; there is no reason why दौलत should be दौलती for its oblique and not दौलते or फौज फौजे and not फौजी; the tradition with regard to some Pr. nouns also must have been forgotten and then they also have been in the condition of these foreign nouns and must have been treated likewise and to a certain extent oblivion is the reason why we have two forms in the case of some nouns and no other.

This then is clearly the origin of the oblique forms; and all the facts especially in the Marâṭhî language harmonize so completely with it that there can be no doubt whatever as to its truth. And no other case than the gen. would have served the purpose of reconstruction. When a language is in an early stage of growth and case forms such as the loc. sing. are made up by joining two words such as देव 'a shining being' and इ *this* or *here*, imagination is wanted to connect the *here* or *this* with the shining being *i. e.* in the place of the shining being. But when a language has got the means of expressing the relation denoted by *of* it is necessary that it should be used in connection with the new post-position otherwise the sense would be incomplete. And thus in Skr., Pr. and the modern languages all such postpositions are appended to the gen. case. The gen. forms of nouns as they were in the Prâkṛits and the Apabhraṃs'a have descended to the Marâṭhî only somewhat phonetically altered, while the principal change that the nouns or crude forms have undergone is the loss of final अ or आ answering to such a Skr. syllable as त, क or का when preceded by a dissimilar vowel *i. e.* इ or उ; while the other languages have in most instances taken this mutilated crude or nom. form as the base for all oblique cases, the M. confines it to its own place and uses the old gen. everywhere and without exception if we take the minor dialects also into consideration. The other languages have of course, as has been shown, preserved this gen. in some cases and of them all the S. in the largest number of instances. Some such as the H. and P. have generalized the pl. form of one set of nouns and use it for all. The M. cases are thus more difficult to the learner than those of the other languages but that is a matter with which we are not concerned here.

We will now proceed to the consideration of the new terminations. These have not necessarily sprung up from independent words. We have seen that the old terminations such as the न of the instr. have been detached and consititnted into postpositions. But the most common method the vernaculars have resorted to is to attach the case forms of certain words to the gen. of the nouns. The acc. and dat. terminations in the verious dialects are these: H. तई, कों, Braj कौं, B. के-तें, O. कु, S. खे-ते, P. नूं, ताईं, G. ने, M. स—ला and तें is used in poetry. Of these स has been discussed. The Mâl. and Goan. have कां for pronouns and the former क for nouns and the latter कनां. Khândes'î has ले, P. has ताईं also for नू. Old Bengali has also a dative in रे.

वैदर्भीरे हंस कहे मनुष्यवचने

Mah. Nalop. I.

'The swan said to Vaidarbhî with human speech.'

Here we see a good many languages have the termination with an initial क. What is its origin? Dr. Caldwell traces it to the Dravidian कु. But in our whole investigation we have not yet met a Dravidian influence in the grammar of our languages. Dr. Trump derives the S. खे and B. के from कृते. The last may not unlikely have been derived from it but the aspiration of the S. खे is not accounted for. Trump attributes it to the vowel ऋ; but we have seen that in the old Pr. this goes out leaving nothing but अ, इ, or उ *i. e.* the consonantal portion of it which is subordinated to the vowel portion leaves no trace. There is no other instance in which ऋ is known to exert such an influence. The Hindî कों he also derives from कृत and not कृते. But here the anusvâra is not accounted for and is regarded as inorganic. Besides, as Mr. Beames remarks, कृत is not a word likely to yield the sense of a dative. It is never used in Skr. or Pr. as equivalent to कृते. To be able to arrive at the probable or correct etymology of any of these terminations it is necessary to collect and compare any more ancient forms of it that may possibly be found. Now there are such forms in the case of the H. कों and the Braj कौं. The old H. poets often use कहं, कहुं and even काहुं: for instance in Tulsidas's Râmâyaṇ we have

भानु कृशानु सर्व रस खाहीं । तिन कहं मंद कहत कोउ नाहीं ॥

'The sun and fire swallow all liquids. Nobody calls them stupid.'

काम जारि रतिकहं वर दीन्हा । कृपासिंधु यह अतिभल कीन्हा ॥

'He burned Kâma but gave a boon to Rati; this was an excellent act done by the ocean of mercy.'

कपिन्ह सहित विप्रन कहुं दान विविध विधि दीन्हा ॥

'He gave various gifts to the monkeys and the Brahmans'.

आसन उचित दये सब काहु । कहौं कहा मुख एक उच्छाहु ॥

'Proper seats were given to all; my mouth is one, how shall I relate the festivities?'

कैकई कहुं पुनि मिले मनकर छोभ न जाइ ।

'Met Kaikayî again, but the agitation of the heart did not subside!'

Now we have seen that often in the modern languages the ह of older words is dropped; and thus from कहुं we have कउं and then को or कौं by the usual rule that we have noticed in going over the vowel changes. From कहं the Mâlvaṇî and Goan. कां is derived. The कहं and कहुं are also traced to कृत by Dr. Trump. But Mr. Beames derives them from कक्ष 'armpit, side' which becomes काख and then काह and the anusvâra he traces to the accusative and thus supposes कक्षं to be the original of कौं. कक्ष is preserved in the modern languages in the form of काख but the further change of ख to ह in the suffix he accounts for by considering it to be a later Tadbhava. And corresponding to these two forms he says we have the two forms of स्थान in the ordinary word थान H. 'a place' and in the ह of कहां, जहां. I have no hesitation in saying that Mr. Beames is altogether wrong in deriving कहां, जहां etc. and further on तईं or ताईं from किंस्थान, यत्स्थान, तत्स्थान etc. Such new expressions in the face of the many good old words existing in Skr. and Pr. could not have come in ordinary vernacular use. The B. एथाय, ओथाय, कोथाय etc., which have led Mr. Beames to this etymology are manifestly new combinations of ए and थाय, ओ and थाय, को and थाय like the barbarous compounds एखावे, सेखावे of Skr. and foreign words derived by the Bengali in its poverty of the old Tadbhava element. Neither should we derive the M. एथ and later एथें from एतत्स्थान in the face of the Pr. एत्थ from Skr. अत्र or इत्र which we find everywhere in Pr. works. Now as regards काख, in addition to the objection which Mr. Beames has not succeeded in answering, it is to be observed that the word is found nowhere used in that sense in old H., G. or M. literature and, that it might be the original of the dat. case-affix in nearly all the languages, it is necessary that it should have been used extensively in Skr. or Pr. or in old literature of the modern languages.

One chief and important source of the modern case affixes has been overlooked by all those who have written on vernacular philology. The words most fitted to express case relations are the pronouns and the old Aryan case endings have properly been traced by comparative philologists to pronominal roots. Even in the vernacular speech of the day we use pronominal expressions when a simply general sense is wanted as मी गोविंदाचे एथें गेलों होतों 'I went to (lit.) the here of Govinda' *i. e.* to Govind's place. मैनें आपके यहां सेवकको भेजा था 'I sent my servant to your here' *i. e.* your place. हुं मुरलीधरने तहां गयो हतो 'I went to Murlidhar's there' *i. e.* place. These एथें, यहां and तहां are really remnants of the old Pr. locatives of इदम् (in the forms इ or अ) and तत्. If these were more extensively used they would in the course of time become terminations; and तईं for तहिं the Pr. and Apbhr. loc. of तद् has become a termination in H. as मैं शहरके तईं गया 'I went to the *there* of the town'; उसके तईं 'to him or for him.' In the Apabhraṃs'a according to Hemachandra केहिं and तेहिं were used as postpositions in the sense of 'for', 'on account of' as in the verses formerly given हउं झिजउं तउ केहिं पिअ &c. These, as they are, appear like instrumental plurals of the pronouns किम् and तद् and they may be so really. The instr. and abl. may pass into the dat. and this into either. For of the several relations denoted by the first two cases one is that between a cause and its effect or reason and conclusion and a confusion between an antecedent cause or reason and the final cause or purpose is natural. This last is generally indicated by the dat. case. Even the English preposition *for* has these two senses. In the sentence, 'I bought the book for my own use', it signifies the purpose; and in such a one as 'for this, let people beware' it denotes an antecedent reason. In the same way साठीं or करितां are in M. used in both these senses. In त्याच्यासाठीं मी इतका श्रम केला 'I took so much trouble for him' it has a dative sense and in ह्यासाठीं अशी गोष्ट कधीं करूं नये 'for this, such a thing should never be done' it has an ablative sense. This fact must be borne in mind as we go on discussing the origin of the case forms. केहिं and तेहिं therefore may be instrumentals. This explanation is supported by the fact that another Apbhr. postposition in the sense of 'for' or 'on account of' given by Hemachandra is तणेण which is evidently the sing. instr. of तण a possessive suffix to be hereafter mentioned. The pl. case forms may become adverbs or postpositions as the Skr. शनैः 'slowly,' नीचैः and उच्चैः 'low' and 'high' which must originally have been instr. plurals. Another explanation of these forms is that they are derived from the Pr. gen. plurals केसिं and तेसिं the स being changed to ह. The gen. has all along been used in the sense of the dat. In Skr. itself it is often so and in the Pr. it drove out the old dat. altogether and was used instead. In old M. poetry the obl. form, which we have traced to the Pr. gen., is often used for this case or, since in the Apbhr. nouns the termination हिं was used for loc. pl. also, the forms केहिं and तेहिं are not unlikely to be referred to that case. The loc. is another case which can readily be adapted to express a dat. acc. sense. Tulsidasa frequently adds हिं to nouns to form this case. Thus—

रुद्रहिं देखि मदन भयमाना।

'The god of love was afraid when he saw Rudra.'

रामहिं सौंपिय जानकी नाइ कमल पदमाथ।
सुत कहुं राज समर्पि वन जाइ भजिय रघुनाथ॥

'Having restored Jânakî to Râma and bowing your head at his lotus feet and giving the kingdom to your son go to a forest and adore Raghunâtha.'

That these several cases may pass into the dat. acc. is also proved by the fact that the forms of the Apabhraṃs'a gerund or infinitive of purpose, which has essentially a dative sense, are derived from them. Thus Hemachandra gives these terminations of the infinitive: एवम् as in देवम् 'for giving' which is an acc. of the pot. part. देअव्वम्, अण as in करण 'for doing' in which the case termination is dropped., अणहम् as in भंजणहं 'for breaking' which is the gen. pl. of भञ्जन and अणहिं as in भुंजणहिं 'for enjoying' which is loc. sing. or pl. of भुञ्जण Pr. for Skr. भोजन. Thus then in the Apabhrams'a pronominal forms had begun to be used as postpositions for expressing case relations. It is not unreasonable, therefore, to expect that we should find traces of the practice in our modern case forms and the forms themselves that were used in that dialect.

The Apabhrams'a dat. postposition केहिं survives in the S. खे the aspiration is thrown on के so as to make it खे and the following vowel is dropped. We have already seen several instances of this process but I will add one or two more to the point. The Pr. कहिं 'where' is in the Goan. and Mâl. खंय, तहिं 'there' थंय, अहिं 'here' हंय. Often the old इ is dropped in the moderns and thus we have from केहिं the B. के. The old H. termination कहं is the Pr. कहिं 'where,' so that originally the sense of राम कहं was 'Râma's somewhere.' 'Send to Râma's somewhere' and 'give it to Râma's somewhere' came afterwards to mean 'send it *to* Râma' and 'give it *to* Râma.' The इ of the loc. कहिं is here dropped. as is mostly the case in the pronominal locatives which in the modern languages as well as the Prâkṛit have become adverbs of place; such are जहिं relative 'where', तहिं 'there', अहिं 'here', and कहिं 'where' interrogative which have become जहां, तहां, यहां and कहां and in Tulsidas जहं तहं and कहं. Sometimes the इ is preserved in the current speech as in कहां or कहीं H., अही, यहां G. The other dat. termination कहुं, the origin of कौं or कों, is either the ablative or genitive form of किम् since हुं was in Apbhr. the termination of both these cases. The O. कुं is another form of this कहुं. The M. ते is from the Apabhr. तहिं as के from केहिं. The B. has this affix also used principally in the case of inanimate creatures.

धुयां ते गन्ध आछे ओ ताहाते चक्षुते वेदना होय ।

'There is smell to smoke and from that harm to the eye results.'

तहाते सिंह कहिल ।

'The lion said to him.'

The S. has it also.

सोहल्यो शिकारते 'He went for hunting.' विओ मुस फरिअते 'went on a travel.'

The P. ताइ like the H. तई is from तहिं 'there.'

The M. ला is to be connected with similar terminations in its own dialects and the other languages. Khândeshî has ले, H. possesses a postposition लाय or लिये, P. लई, S. लाइ all in the sense of 'for', Braja लौं or लों 'up to.' The old H. poets have also लै or लाई in the sense of the M. लां *i. e.* 'to' or 'at:' बारहिं बार पांवले पढ़हीं 'again and again they fall at her feet;' हरखि उठाय लिये उरलाई 'joyfully he arose and pressed him to his bosom.' Then there are other forms in all the languages from लग. Goan. has लागीं in the sense of 'to' or 'with,' as माझे लागीं उलय 'speak to or with me.' H. लग 'up to'; P. लग 'near, to;' लागों 'from contact with;' S. लगी-लगे 'on account of;' B. लागें–लागिया-लागे 'for, on account of.' In G. and H. poetry लागीं, लगी or लागि are used in these senses and M. has लागून or लागुनि also. All these forms are derived from the old Skr. root लग to adhere or stick. The past pass. part. of this is लग्न, Pr. लग्ग. This, like many similar participles, is made the base of verbal forms in Pr. and we have लग्गइ=लग्नो भवति 'adheres, sticks.' From this we have लागणें–गुं–व M. G. B. by the usual rules, but S. generally and H. sometimes do not lengthen the preceding vowel when one of the two consonants is dropped and we have लगणु and लगना, though लागना is also used in the latter. There is another form लागयति of this root which is made up according to the 10th Conjugation or which is properly the causal and, when the termination is dropped as is often the case, we have लागई and by the elision of ग् the root becomes लाअ and thence, by the usual introduction of य or व, लाय or लाव. Now लायणा exists in the Goan. and लाइणु in the S. while M. has लावणें. These mean 'to make to adhere,' 'apply,' 'bring in contact.' From लागणें and लायणा or लावणें all the forms we have above noticed have originated. लाई, लै, लागी, लागिया are absolutives as also M. लागोनि, while the other M. form लागीं is the loc. sing. of the noun लाग 'contact' or 'nearness.' The Braj. लौं must be from the old Apbhr. absol. लाउं of लाअ. The M. dat. ला must be from such a form as लाउं 'having applied' or 'for applying,' since the final उ of terminations is dropped in this language as in जिभा 'tongues' from जिभाउ. The dative pl. termination नां represents an euphonic change of ला necessitated by the preceding anusvâra. Instances of this change of ल to न have been given in a previous lecture. Chit. has both ना and न्ला. This ना is by some traced to the णं of the Pr. gen. pl. as स to the स्स of the gen. sing. The Chit. however has ना or न्ला in the pl. while ला alone is the sing. termination and the sameness of the sing. and pl. terminations is the great peculiarity of the modern dialect, whence the Chit. णा is a form of ला and if so then it must be so in the standard Marâṭhî also. Mr. Beames thinks the G. ने to be originally ले and thus to belong to the class of terminations we have just examined, the ल being changed to न. I am not satisfied with this derivation as there is no corroborative evidence, though the change of ल to न is not impossible or unexampled. The gen. termination नो—नी—नुं in this language is derived from the old Apabhraṃs'a termination तण, by the elision of the initial त, as will be hereafter shown. In the same manner the नें of the acc. dat. must have been derived from the Apabhr. dat. postposition तणेण, which, as I have already observed, is the instr. of तण. The last ण of this is changed to an anusvâra, as that of देवेण is, and, just as this becomes देवें, तणेण becomes तणें and by the loss of त, नें. Or the process which in the Apabhr. led to the formation of तणेण from तण may have been resorted to when तण became न in the G. and thus नें is the instrumental or locative of the gen. न or its obl. form. But the anusvâra of नें which is lost in the G. instr. would show that it is derived directly from तणेण. P. नुं may likewise be referred to a form तणहुं the obl. of तण. In H. the termination से is applied in a dative sense to nouns governed by verbs denoting speaking राजानें ब्राह्मणसे कहा 'The king spoke to the Brahman.' It is used in the sense of the instr.: तरवारसे सीर काटा 'He cut off his head with a sword,' रुक्मिनीका विवाह श्रीकृष्णचन्दसे हुआ 'Rukmini's marriage with S'rî Krishnachanda took place;' and in that of the abl. इतना वचन ब्राह्मणके मुखसे निकला 'these words fell from the mouth of the Brahman.' In Braja we have सौं for से as कबीरजी आयकै मोसों कह्यौ 'Kabir came and said to me'; गुरुसों पूछि लेइ 'He should get it explained from the guru.' In old H. also it is used in the form of सौं. In old M., as I have already remarked, we have सी in the sense of the modern dat. acc. स as:—

सारथी शार्ङ्गधर। अर्जुनेसी॥

Jñân. 1—141.

'S'ârṅgadhara was charioteer to Arjuna.'

पंवाडा तुवां केला गंधर्वांसी॥

II—10.

'Thou hast made a song for Gandharvas.'

जे नेदी देवकी यशोदेसी।
ते गति दीधली पूतनेसी॥

समान देणें अरिमित्रांसी ।
उदारतेसीं काय वर्णूं ॥

Rukmiṇî Svayaṃvara I—82.

"He gave that salvation to Pûtanâ which he did not give to Yas'odâ and Devakî. His gifts to friends and foes are alike. How shall I describe his bounty?"

परी कवणेसीं म्यां झुंजावें । हे रणीं लागे पाहावें ॥

Jñân. I—171.

'It is necessary in the battlefield to see with whom I should fight.'

अर्जुन असे पाहत । तो दळभार समस्त । संभ्रमेसीं ॥

Jñân. I—176.

'Arjuna was looking at the whole force with an agitated heart.'

आणि परलोकही अंतरेल । ऐहिकेसीं ॥

Jñân. II—27.

'And the interests of the future life will be lost along with those of this!'

In these three examples सीं has the sense of an instrumental. We do not now use it in the sense in which it is used in the last two passages and say संभ्रमानें पाहतो and ऐहिकासहित अंतरेल. In the Salsette dialect, however, सीं has these senses and also that of an abl. as गांवसीं आयलो 'He came from the village.'

Now we see that the old M. poets do not make a distinction between the सीं, which corresponds to our modern स, and that which even now we use in the sense of *with*. They also use it in other senses in which it is used in H., but not in the M. of the day. The Salsette dialect, however, agrees with the H. in its use of this affix. H. uses से in one case उससे कहा in which we use स as त्यास सांगितलें. Some of these circumstances favour the supposition that the origin of the M. dative affix स is the same as that of H. से and M. सीं. G. poetry has this in the form of सुं or स्यूं as गुजरातिस्यूं मांडिसि कलहु 'Declare war with Gujarati.' S. has सें and सां in the sense of *with*.

All these are derived from the word सम. As is usual, म is in the modern vernaculars changed to वं and thus we have सवं and with the instr. affix ए we have the सवें of the M. poets. I have in a former lecture given a great many instances in which व is dissolved into उ,

which combines with the preceding vowel into औ. We thus get the old H. सौं and the Braja सौं when अ and उ form औ, while in G. the resulting vowel is उं in शुं. Another change of म that we have noticed is its loss of the labial element and reduction to a vowel and anusvâra, wherefore the word becomes सअें or सयं. Thence the अय passes off into ए, as we have several times noticed, and so we have सें which with the anusvâra dropped is the H. से. The य is sometimes, as we have seen, changed to ई as in राइ from राअ-राय, and so we have the M. सीं. Sometimes य does not take the place of the elided consonant and the vowels are combined, whence we have the S. सां. Now the original sense of this word is *with*, but this *with* expresses many relations, the differences between which become wider in the course of time and thus the word सम has come to signify '*to, according to, with* (as an instrument) and *from*.'

The instr. termination नें sing. नीं pl. M., ने H., नइ P. have been traced by Mr. Beames to ले or लै, which are forms of लागि or लइ etc. derived from the root लग. One great objection is that this derivation does not account for the anusvâra of नें or नैं. His argument is that the old एन of the instr. having been reduced to एं there was no other instrumental case to furnish the न of the modern instr. नें—नीं, but in the Apabhr. according to Hemachandra both these forms existed and the instance he gives is

जे महु दिण्णा दिअहडा दइएं पवसन्तेण ।
ताण गणन्ति ए अंगुलिउ जजरि आउ नहेण ॥

'By counting (again and again) [the number of] days which were mentioned to me by my beloved when he set out on his travels [the skin of] my fingers has worn away by the nail.' Here दइएं, पवसन्तेण and नहेण are instances of the instrumental. The first two expressive of the agent in the passive construction and the third of the simple instrument; so that the एण or ण of the instrumental must have descended to the vernaculars. Again Mr. Beames says that the old H. poets do not use the instr. in नें; but the oldest M. poet Jñânes'vara does use it in some cases. His agent instrumental is very often that which ends in एं, but instances of the use of नि, which is another form of नें, also occur.

As :—

कीं वारेनि जात आहे ।

Jñân. 13—197.

'Or whether he is going away by the wind.'

दिसे वारेनि जैसे जाइल ।

Jñân. 13—214.

'Appears as if it will go away by the wind.

मुकेनि घेतले मौन जैसे ।

Jñân. 13—280.

'As the dumb may be said to have assumed silence deliberately.

उन्हाळेनि तापे ।
हिमवंती न कांपे ॥
कायसेनिही न वासि ये । पातलेया ॥

Jñân. 13—347.

'He is not oppressed by heat or does not shiver by cold and is not terrified by anything that takes place.'

Here are instances of the instr. both indicative of the agent and of the simple instrument, but the termination is नि instead of नें. Besides these there are instances of the instrumental in णें of pronouns as येणें मानें Jñân. 13—200 'By this standard,' जेणें तोषें 13-244 'By which satisfaction,' तेणें प्रसादें 18—1147 'By that grace.' Now I have stated my view in the last lecture that नें is a double instrumental, the first part being न of the old instrumental in एन or एण and the second part एं, to which that एण is reduced. Now instead of एं, the instr. ई is added here. The instr. ई represents the इण of the Apabhr. instr. in इण, which we have in such forms as पुत्तिण mentioned by Pischel. Hindi poets as a rule indicate the agent instrumental by the oblique form but Sûrdâs uses the form ending in नि or नें also.

कान्ह कह्यो गिरि गोवर्धनतें और देव नहिं दूजा ।
गोपनि सत्य मानि यह लीनो बडो देव गिरिराज ॥

Sursâgar, pada 12, page 252.*

'Kânha said, "There is no other God besides the mountain Govardhan." Taking it to be the truth the king of mountains was regarded by the cowherds as a great God.'

Here गोपनि is agent instrumental in नि.

सबनि देख्यो प्रकट मूरति सहस्रभुजा पसारि ॥
रुचि सहित गिरि सबनि आगे करनि लैलै खाय ॥

Sursâgar, pada 24, page 254.

* Lucknow Edn., 1874.

'The manifested form with the thousand arms stretched out was seen by all; with taste the mountain taking hold of every thing by all his hands etc.'

Here करनि is the simple instrumental.

अहिरनि करी अवज्ञा प्रभुकी सो फल उनकों तुरत दिखावहिं ।

Sursâgar, pada 44, page 257.

'Disrespect of the lord has been shown by the cowherds, show to them the fruit of it.'

एक पुरुषने आजु मोहि सपनान्तर दीनों ।

Sursâgar, pada 29, page 255.

'Today a certain dream was shown me by a Being.'

Here पुरुषने is agent instrumental.

The Ablative termination in M. is हून, Mâl. सून, Chit. ठीं or पाशी (from पास and थीं), Sals. सिं, G. थी, S. खां—खउं—खों तों तां, P. तें—थीं—थों, H. से, Braj. ते, H. dial. थीं, B. होइते तें. The Sindhî खां is the Pr. and Apabhr. abl. कहां of किम्, the aspiration being thrown on क, as in the case of the dat. खे and in the other instances formerly given; so that the S. abl. etymologically means 'from his somewhere.' खउं and खों are from the Ap. कहुं abl. pl. In the same way तां is the old abl. तहां and तों the abl. pl. तहुं of तद्, in both of which the aspirate is elided but in the P. थों it is compounded with the preceding त. The form थी थीं of the G. and P., and H. dial. and the Chit. ठीं are derived from तहिं the loc. sing. Pr. and Ap. of तद् with the aspiration thrown on त. The differences between some of the significations of the different cases are, as I have already observed, so minute that they frequently run into one another and when, on account of this resemblance, one case form becomes identified with another case, it afterwards acquires senses more widely different from its original. Thus तें पुस्तक मला रामापाशीं मिळालें *i. e.* (lit.) 'The book met me in the vicinity of Râmâ,' easily passes into रामापासून मिळालें 'met me from Râmâ' *i. e.* 'got from Râmâ.' And the B. आपने प्रभुर काछे ताहा पाइलाम is generally considered equivalent to ' I got it from the master,' though काछे is like पाशीं a loc. form meaning 'in the vicinity of.' Thus the old loc. तहिं meaning 'in that' was used as a postposition and thence came to mean 'from that.' Or the transition is first from the loc. to the dat., which I have spoken of, and thence to the causal abl. and afterwards to the local abl. The Braj. and P. तें is from the Apabhr. affix तेहिं (= for) mentioned before in which we have an instance of this passage of the dat. into the abl., as illustrated before in the M. post-position साठीं. In M., S. and B. तें has preserved the dative sense. B. has the abl. तें also, though some grammarians do not give it, but its sense is that of causal abl. or instr. as :—

शृङ्गेर दीर्घताते आनंदित हइल ।

'Became glad on account of the length of its horns.'

ताहाते चक्षुते वेदना होय।

'From that there is harm to the eye.'

Of a different origin are the M. हून and मून and the B. हेइते. The first हून Mr. Beames, following Lassen, traces to the हिन्तो and सुन्तो of the Pr. from a fusion, as it is called, of both, out of which arose हुन्तो, and, the तो being lost, the form is हून. In a similar way सून may be traced to सुन्तो, though its independent existence would make the supposed fusion a fiction. M. however has no instance of the loss of final त and the preservation of न; but the chief objection to this derivation is the want of corroborative evidence. It is possible, but there is nothing to make it certain or even probable. Mr. Beames quotes passages from Chanda in which हुन्त and हुन्तो occur in the sense of 'from.' But they may be derived from the present participle. The B. abl. affix होइते is the loc. of the present participle of हो, corresponding to M. होतां, which has the sense of the Skr. loc. absolute as असतां in मी करित असतां तो गेला 'while I was doing he went away.' In B. too this loc. has the same sense as दिन थाकिते कर्म कर 'work while it is day.' In H. also it is used in the same sense: द्वारपर देखते क्या है कि सिंह मरा पडा है 'looking at the door what did he find? he found that a lion was lying dead. (lit. what is there,–a lion lying dead);' भोर होतेही उसने सखीसे कहा 'She told it to her friend immediately after dawn (lit. after it had dawned).'

In this sense as in that of the Skr. loc. absolute the action denoted by the present participle is made the starting point of another action. 'My doing' in the first instance was the starting point of his going. And herein is the germ of an ablative. In H. होते is sometimes used in this sense as मकानसे होते 'outside of the house, from the house.'

In the B. वृक्षहइते फल पडिल the original sense is 'the tree being there a fruit fell.' The M. हून is the absolutive of हो and equivalent to होऊन 'having become' which yields an ablative sense more directly. The ह is sometimes dropped and the termination ऊन itself is attached in this sense to आं 'in', वर 'above' and पास 'side' to signify 'from in', 'from above', 'from the side' as आंतून, वरून and पासून which are the ablative affixes used in cases when हून can not be applied; and ऊन is sometimes affixed to nouns in अ directly and not to the oblique form as घरून आला. Thus गांवाहून आला means lit. 'the village having been he came.' The Mâl. सून is the absolutive of अस instead of हो. The H. से has been, explained.

We have seen that in the course of the development of our modern languages the genitive which even in Skr. expressed relation in general was used for the dative and sometimes for other cases also. The dative thus went out of use and to express the relations which it indicated various new suffixes, given and explained above, were brought into use and the old genitive being attenuated was felt to be too weak to express the usual genitive relation and was adapted to serve as the base of all oblique cases to which the newly constituted terminations were appended. The relation of possession as well as other genitive relations, such as that of a thing and the material of which it is made, had thus no special expression left for them. In Skr. such relations are indicated, besides the genitive case, by adjectives formed from the name of the possessor, material etc. by the addition of specific terminations and from these mostly the genitive terminations in the modern languages are derived and consequently are adjectival in their nature and agree with the gender of the thing possessed or made. The genitive terminations are as follows :—

M. चा—ची—चें
G. नो—नी—नुं
S. जो—जी
H. का—की

P. दा—दी
B. इर or एर
O. र

In the first lecture I have remarked that in the third stage of the development of Sanskrit the nominal style came into use instead of the verbal style or fluent style. When the language was in this condition adjectival forms expressive of possession or other relations came into use instead of the genitive case and such forms, as :

तदीयम् गृहम् 'the house belonging to him,'

मदीयः छात्रः 'the pupil belonging to me,'

त्वदीया सखी 'the female friend belonging to thee,'

came into use instead of तस्य गृहम् 'his home,' मम छात्रः 'my pupil,' तव सखी 'thy female friend.' When the use of such adjectives became general the real genitive case, so far as it expressed possession and such other relations between nouns, was driven out and adapted to express the various other relations mentioned before. Thus then we find that the case forms expressive of possession and other relations mentioned in the vernaculars are of an adjectival character. It is, however, curious to find that in our seven modern languages they are derived from seven different forms in Sanskrit and Prakrit. The M. चा—ची—चें must be traced to the त्य which certain indeclinables take in Sanskrit as इहत्य or अत्रत्य 'of this place,' तत्रत्य 'of that place,' क्रत्य or कुत्रत्य 'of what place.' इहत्य or अत्रत्य must by the usual rules be changed to इहच, एत्थच, तत्रत्य to तत्थच, क्रत्य or कुत्रत्य to कच or कुत्थच or कोत्थच्च. तत्थच्च is तेथचा, एत्थच्च is एथचा, कोत्थच्च is कोठचा. This च्च was generalised and gradually came to be applied to all nouns to indicate possession and other relations. The G. नो—नी—नुं are derived from the Sanskrit termination तन which is applied in the sense of possession to indeclinables expressive of time, such as अद्यतन 'of this day,' इदानींतन 'of the present time,' सायंतन 'of evening time,' चिरंतन 'of the olden time' etc. This was generalised and Hemachandra gives तण as a noun expressive of 'something related to' or 'belonging to' in his grammar of the Apbhr. dialect. In the line of the verse of Premânanda बाधी विरहतणी वेदना 'the agony of separation afflicts' and in the expressions previously given, such as पोतातण, and तेहतणो नहि लाधे छेह etc. this तण remains, it will be seen, unchanged and in this form it is often used in G. poetry. By the dropping of the consonant त it is reduced to अण or अन and thence to न which with masc., fem., neut. terminations ओ—ई—उं becomes नो—नी—नुं. The S. जो—जी are derived from the Sanskrit possessive termination ईय applied to a great many nouns and all pronouns as तदीय belonging to him, शालीय belonging to the house, गोनर्दीय belonging to or living in Gonarda. Dr. Trump assigns a different origin to this Sindhî जो-जी, which, as well as the etymologies of the corresponding possessive terminations existing in other cognate dialects, hardly bears examination. Another way of expressing possession is furnished by derivatives of the root कृ 'to do or make.' The roar of a lion is his कार्य or act. The roar of a lion is a सिंहकार्य or lion act *i. e.* it is something which belongs to the lion. The word कार्य therefore is adapted to express 'something belonging to one.' Now this कार्य is in the Pr. reduced to केर as the पर्य of पर्यन्त to पेर and the श्चर्य of आश्चर्य to छेर. From this केर we have केरको which means 'something belonging to one' or 'his property.' Madayantikâ in the Mâlatîmâdhava calls her body Makaranda's केरअ or केरक, since he had saved it from the mouth of a lion. Hemachandra gives केर as a noun in the Apabhr. dialect expressive of the thing connected with another. The instance he gives is जसुकेरए हुंकारए मुहहुं पडंति तणाइं । 'From whose mouth grass falls down in consequence of the roar which is the केरअ of the lion.' He also gives in his grammar of the principal Prâkṛit केर as a termination having the sense of possession as in तुह्मकेर 'yours' like तण. Thus then केर which was first a noun came to be used as a postposition expressive of possession and was used as such in the principal Prâkṛit and by the G. and H. poets:

अंधाकेरि लाकडी हूं दुबळीतु धन ।

Tulasi.

'I am the stick of the blind [women] and the wealth of a weak [woman].'

हुकुम होय हजोरि केरो शोषी नाखो बाधो सागर ॥

Sâmaladâs.

'If the command of the lord is received I will dry up the whole ocean.'

One of Kabîra's Sâkhî is—

दर्पण केरी जो गुफा सोण्हा पैठा धाय ।
देखत प्रतिमा आपनि भूंखि भूंखि मरि जाय ॥

'A dog enters a room [made up] of mirrors and runs about and, seeing his own image, he barks and barks until he dies.'

There is another instance:

अमृतकेरी मोटरी सिरसे धरी उतारि ।
जाहि कहो मै येक हो मोहिक है द्वैचारि ॥

'I put down from head the parcel containing nectar. To whomsoever I say that I am one, to me he speaks in return two or four.'

Here we have केरी as a possessive postposition. Similarly in Tulasidâs's Râmâyaṇ we have कहु खबर बिभीषण केरी 'give us news about Bibhîshaṇa,' where also we have the same postposition. When the initial क is dropped we have एर which we find in the Hindî तेरा and मेरा as in Kabîr's Sâkhî,

जो तू चाहौ मुझको छोडु सकलकी आस ।
मेरा ऐसा व्है रहै सब किछु तेरे पास ॥

'If you want me give up the desire for everything else; become mine; and you will have everything else with you.' एर is the general postposition in the B. as पापेर 'of sin,' ईश्वरेर 'of God,' घरेर 'of a house.' Prof. Hörnle and Mr. Beames derive the suffix केर from the Skr. past part. कृत which they say is reduced to करिअ and thence to केर. But I have not met with a trace of करिअ as the Pr. form of कृत. The usual form of it is किअ or कअ. Besides, the इ of करिअ is inorganic, being simply an euphonic augment. Such an euphonic augment can not persist throughout centuries as the ए of केर has done until it was perpetuated in the form of एर in the B. Besides, केरक is, as we have seen, used as a noun in the sense of property. There is no indication that a past pass. part. can be so used. It may be used as an abstract noun, as गतम् in the sense of 'going.' So कृतम् may at the best acquire the sense of 'doing,' but the transition of 'doing' to 'property' is hardly possible. Another derivative of the root कृ has also supplied the vernaculars with a termination expressive of the genitive sense; and that is कर. A good many words in Sanskrit have this कर appended to them such as यशस्कर 'bringing fame,' वचनकर 'obedient,' किंकर 'servant,' प्रभाकर 'the sun,' लिपिकर 'a writer' etc. The original sense is 'one who does the thing' expressed by the nouns to which कर is appended, but the derived senses are many, such as cause, habit, obedience and any other relation into which the doing of a thing brings one with another. When the particular nature of this relation is left out of sight the general sense is 'related to' or 'belonging to.' Thus प्रभाकर originally meaning 'the maker of light' comes to denote 'belonging to light;' a certain person who is लिपिकर or the doer of the writing is a person related or belonging to the writing. Thus कर came gradually to signify a genitive relation like the terminations ईय, त्य, तन etc. noticed above. In the Marâṭhî कर is applied in ordinary use to the name of a place to denote 'one residing in it' or generally 'belonging to it' as काशीकर 'belonging to Kâs'î', पुणेकर 'belonging to Poona.' Instances of this कर occur in the old Hindî poets; thus in Tulsidâs's Râmâyaṇ we have—

तजौं न नारदकर उपदेशू ।

Bâlak.

'I will not set aside the advice of Nârada.'

पुनि पुनि हृदय बिचार करि धरि सीताकर रूप ।

(Ditto).

'Again and again reflecting in her mind she (Pârvatî) assumed the form of Sîtâ.'

मैं शंकरकर कहा न माना ।

(Ditto).

'I did not obey the word of Shankar.'

भरद्वाज सुनु अपर अब राम जन्मकर हेतु ।

'Oh Bharadvâja, hear now another reason for the birth of Râma.'

In Kabîr too we meet with this termination as in:—

तब ब्रह्मा (ब्रह्में) पूछल महतारी ।
को तोर पुरुष का (के) करि तुम नारी ।

Kâbîr's Râmayaṇ, 1—4th Chaupai.

'Then the mother was asked by Brahma "who is thy husband and whose wife art thou."'

Here we have काकरि or केकरि in which we have the feminine of the termination कर. In Sanskrit कार is almost as much used as कर after nouns and the signification is similar. This कार is sometimes used in the Bangâlî in a genitive sense as in आपनकार 'of your honour,' आजकार 'of to-day,' कालिकार 'of yesterday.' From कर, when the initial consonant is dropped, we have the Oriya genitive suffix अर as in घरर, while कार gives us the आर of the Hindî तुह्मारा 'yours,' हमारा 'ours' and of the Guj. तारो 'thine,' तमारो 'yours,' मारो 'mine,' अमारो 'ours.'

Another derivative of the root कृ, the past pass. part. कृत, changed to कअ in the Prâkrit, has been appropriated in Hindî to express genitive relations. As the obl. form has been determined to be a remnant of the old genitive the क appended to it must mean 'done of (by) the thing or person' denoted by the obl. form. The idea of 'a thing done by one' passes easily into a thing belonging to one. पण्डितकृत काव्य 'a poem composed by a Pandit' becomes easily पण्डितका काव्य *i. e.* the poem of a Pandit. The terminations का, की exist in old Hindî along with केरा, केरी and कर, करी. The easiest explanation of the Panjabî दा—दी appears to be that, like the Hindî का—की, they are derived from the past pass. part. of दा 'to give' in the form of दअ made up on the analogy of कअ from कृ. Other explanations may also be given. It may be said that the रो—री of Marvari dialect and certain G. and H. pronouns which results from the Sanskrit कार was changed to डो-डी or डा-डी, as these consonants are frequently confounded with each other; and thence डो-डी or डा-डी passed into दो-दी or दा-दी. The Sanskrit suffixes used by the vernaculars to express genitive relations must have a final क added to them, since, like augmented nouns, the masc. nom. sing. ends in ओ or आ and the feminine in ई. Thus for the original of the M. चा-ची-चें we must have त्यक, for the G. नो-नी-नुं तनक, for S. जो-जी ईयक, for H. का-की कृतक and for old H. केरा and केरी केरक and for कर करक and for कार कारक. In the fourth lecture I have given several instances of the addition of क to all sorts of nouns and adjectives.

The new loc. termination in H. are में, Braj. मैं, and पै, P. ते, S. मे, G. मां, M. आंत and B. ते. The forms with an initial म are derived from the Skr. मध्य which has undergone several transformations. In old H. and G. poetry it occurs in the forms of माहीं and महं etc. as:—

शिव संकल्प कीन्ह मनमाहीं ।

Tulsi., Bâla-K.

'S'iva resolved in his mind.'

जे हि राखे रघुवीर ते उबरे तेहि कालमहं ।

(Ditto).

'Those were safe at that time whom Raghuvîra protected.'

एकवार त्रेतायुगमाहीं ।

(Ditto).

'Once in Tretâyuga.'

पुनि मंदिर महं बात जनाई ।

'He announced the intelligence in the palace.'

सुदामा में पृथिवी माहीं । लीधा दश अवतार ॥

Premânand's Sudâmânuṃ Charitra.

'O Sudâma, I have gone through ten incarnations on this earth.'

सोरठ माहिं सहुको नाठ्तूं ।

'Everybody fled to Soraṭha.'

The Braj. मैं is from माहिं, the ह being elided and आ and इ combining into ऐ, while in the S. and H. मे they form ए. In the G. मा the whole हि of माहिं is dropped. माहिं is loc. sing. of माह for मध्य. The P. and B. ते is from तहिं, the loc. of तद्, or तेहिं which we have noticed as an Apbhr. dative post-position. H. पै is from Skr. पार्श्व, which first becomes पस्स, then पास, and then पाह or पह, and the loc. of पाह is पाहीं or पहं which is its shortened form. पास is used as a post-position in H. and पासे and पाशीं, the loc. forms, in G. and M. respectively. The forms पाहिं and पहं occur in the old H. poets as :—

शंभु गये कुंभज ऋषि पाहीं ।

Tulasi, Bâl.-K.

'S'ambhu went to Agastya.'

गयो कपि राम पहं ।

Tulsi.

'The monkey went to Râma.'

The M. आंत is from Skr. अन्त: and its initial आ is dropped after a dissimilar vowel as मातींत etc.

We will now briefly examine the reconstructed verbal forms. We have observed that the materials out of which the case forms are constructed are not only independent words having, as in an earlier stage of a language, specific significations, the combination of which nearly constitutes the idea required to be expressed; but also independent case forms and existing terminations which have acquired a specific sense. Thus when the terminations came into use for both numbers of the cases the B. and the O. have had recourse to the use of independent words such as दिग 'a row' and मान 'a measure or class,' सकल 'all' etc. to express plurality, while the G. employed the already existing plural termination ओ; and such forms as तहिं and कहिं loc. and कहुं abl. were used to express case relations and afterwards grew into terminations when their etymological sense was forgotten. We have also seen that, as in the case of the new words that come into a language, the new forms at first express inadequately the sense they are designed to convey but in the course of time imagination and usage give them a definite signification; or like words the forms come by natural transitions to express different relations from those they did before. Thus it was that the abl. कहुं and the loc. कहिं or तहिं became dat. affixes or the loc. of the present participle होइते came to express an abl. relation. We shall find these principles at work in the reconstruction of the verb also; and there too you will meet with verbal forms made up by applying the old personal and other terminations to new bases which are adjectival in their nature or by adding verbal forms to them or by appending independent words. The M., S., B. and O. make up some of their tenses and moods in the first way; the others do not. We will first examine these. The bases for their formation are as a matter of course the participles that have come down from the Prâkrits and there are no other. These are the present, past and the potential participles which are, as I have just said, adjectival in their nature. Since an adjective must agree with the noun which it qualifies in number and gender our new verbs must express both these and the person of the nominative. The old verbal forms examined in the last lecture express, as Skr. and Pr. verbs do, only the number and person because they have descended to us from those languages. In the modern dialects those adjectives only that end in ओ or आ agree with the noun to which they are referred *i. e.* take the fem. termination ई when the noun is feminine and the plural ones when it is plural as काळा-ला घोडा M. H. 'a black horse,' काळी-ली घोडी 'a black mare,' काळे-ले घोडे 'black horses,' काळ्या घोड्या, काली घोडियां. Similarly G. and S. When the qualified noun is in an obl. case sing. or pl. these adjectives take the obl. sing. form काळ्या घोड्यास M., काले घोडेकों H., काळ्या घोडीस M., काली घोडीकों H. Hindî has no obl. form for other nouns than those which end in आ and hence in काली घोडीकों the adjective remains unchanged. Adjectives with other endings are not thus inflected as खराब घोडा-घोडे-घोडी-घोड्या-घोडियां-घोड्यास-घोडेकों etc. M. H.; while in the B. and O. no adjectives whatever. Here then we see that, like nouns in ओ-आ, adjectives also with those endings have preserved the old terminations. Now the three participles I have mentioned end in आ or ओ arising from the original affix क, wherefore they must be inflected. In M. and G. however under certain circumstances the present participle ends in अ and therefore is not inflected. The old Present has in M. acquired another sense whence a new one came into use, the forms of which are as follows :—

	Sing.	Pl.
1st pers.	करतों—त्यें or तीं—तें	करतों
2nd pers.	करतोस—त्येस, तीस—तेंस	करतां
3rd pers.	करतो—त्ये, ती—तें	करतात

These are made up by adding the terminations expressive of gender and person to the pres. part. which is करत. With the fem. ई this becomes करती, but there is another form in ये which appears to have been arrived at thus करन्तअ (for करन्तक)—करतय—करतय + ई of fem.—करतये—करत्ये. The neuter form is करतें. These three forms are used in the sing. while the gender is neglected in the pl. There is however such a form as करत्यात used for the 3rd pers. pl. in the pure Deccan in which करत्यात is the fem. pl. of करती. To these adjectival bases are appended the personal terminations of the old Pres. for the two numbers, which, you will remember, are 3rd pers.

sing. इ, pl. त; 2nd pers. sing. स, pl. आ; 1st pers. sing. ईं, pl. ऊं. In the 1st pers. sing. of the new Present the ईं of the 1st pers. sing. is represented by the characteristic anusvâra, the vowels expressive of gender necessitating the elision of इ. In the pl. करत and ऊं become by combination करतों. The 2nd pers. sing. has the स of the old Pres. and the pl. the आ which with the त forms ता to which however an inorganic anusvâra is added by some. The 3rd pers. sing. has no personal termination, the adjective in its own form expressing that idea, while in the pl. the त of the old Pres. is added. In these forms we see that the उ of the nom. which is dropped in ordinary nouns and adjectives is retained and we have करतो but not चांगलो. In the Goan. and Mâl. the gender is not attended to and the forms are the same for all. This arises from the use of the unaugmented participle करत and not करतअ which retains the inflections. The forms are:—

	Sing.			
1st pers.	करतैं or तंय	Mâl.	करतां	Goan.
2nd pers.	करतस	Mâl.	करतास	Goan.
3rd pers.	करता	Mâl.	करता	Goan.
	Pl.			
1st pers.	करतौं—तंव	Mâl.	करतांव	Goan.
2nd pers.	करतात	Mâl.	करतात	Goan.
3rd pers.	करतत	Mâl.	करतात	Goan.

The terminations are those of the old Pres. of intransitive roots in these dialects *i. e.* the real Pr. terminations without the transitive or Parasm. augment ई. The 2nd pers. pl. त, which I have traced to the Pr. इत्था, is peculiar to the Goan. and Mâl. and it is not altogether absent from the ordinary M. In the 1st pers. sing. Mal. we have the old ईं from मि distinct and not reduced to an anusvâra as in the standard dialect and also the Goan.

A process the reverse of that observable in M. as regards the change in the sense of verbal forms has taken place in the O. and B. The old Pres. in M. has acquired the sense of the Past Habitual and the forms made up by appending the old terminations to the pres. part. express present time but in the O. and B. this new Present of the M. expresses habitual past action and the old Pres. retains its present significatoin. In H. too the pres. part. used alone has the signification of the past habitual. The reason why forms expressive of present time have come to denote past time is to be sought for in that natural use of the Pres. which is called Historic Present. A man in narrating a story transports himself for the sake of vividness into that time when the actions are supposed to have taken place and speaks of them as if they were present; and when this habit becomes general in a language the fact of such an imaginary transfer is forgotten and the Present Tense becomes Past Tense. We have many instances of this use of the Skr. Pres. in such books as the Pañchatantra. The forms of the O. Past Habitual are these:—

	Sing.	Pl.
1st pers.	करन्ति	करन्तुं
2nd pers.	करन्तु	करन्त
3rd pers.	करन्ता	करन्ते

As in the M., the 3rd pers. sing. has no personal termination; and the pl. is the M. and H. pl. of nouns in आ as घोडे which we find in the O. nom. pl. पशुमाने 'beasts' also. The second person has the same terminations as the corresponding old Present *viz.* अ and उ. The first person sing. has इ and the pl. उं and they are the same as the इं and उ of the Pres., but there is some confusion about the anusvâras. Before proceeding it is necessary to mention that O. and B. use the sing. forms in speaking of, and to, inferiors, while the pl. is used in an honorific sense. This is so in all the languages; but these two use even a singular nominative with the honorific forms or real plurals and a plural one with the inferior forms. This is due to the loss of the original plural of nouns in these languages, which I have before mentioned; so that one same form of the nom. came to be used for both the sing. and pl. verbal forms; but, since the usage common to all our vernaculars did exist, the pl. forms came to be understood in a simply honorific sense and the sing. in the sense of inferiority. There was nothing in the form of the nom. which expressed plurality and hence the verbs also ceased to indicate it, though originally fitted to do so. Similarly the pl. forms of personal pronouns which were not lost came to be restricted to an honorific signification and the sing. to that of inferiority. The words which were brought into use to indicate plurality expressed an aggregate or collection and thus, being themselves sing., the necessity of pl. verbal forms in connection with them was not felt; and hence they take a verb in the real old sing.

But there is this consistency in the use of the verb, that the honorific pers. pronouns take an honorific verb and the inferior an inferior *i. e.* an original pl. nom. takes an original plural verb and an original sing. a singular.

. These same forms that we have been discussing have in the S. acquired a future signification and constitute the regular Future tense of that dialect. The Pres. expresses in all languages an immediate future—a man's intending shortly to do a thing is considered as good as actually doing it. This is the germ of futurity in the signification of forms of the Present tense; and usage may take hold of it and constitute them into a regular Future. The Sindhî forms are—

	Masc. Sing.	Masc. Pl.	Fem. Sing.	Fem. Pl.
1st pers.	हलंदुसि	हलंदासीं	हलंदिअसि—यासि	हलंदिऊं—यूंसीं
2nd pers.	हलंदें	हलंदउन्दौ	हलंदिअं—एं	हलंदिऊं—यूं
3rd pers.	हलंदो	हलंदा	हलंदी	हलंदिऊं—यूं

Here हलंद् is the old pres. part. The 3rd pers., as in the O. and also M., partially has no personal terminations. The sing. and the pl. are like those of corresponding adjectives in ओ. The 2nd pers. has the termination एं and उ of the S. old Pres. In the fem. the first is optionally reduced to अं and the उ combines with the fem. pl. ऊं. The first pers. pl. has the corresponding S. pronoun असीं 'we' attached to it as a termination as in an early stage of a language. The sing. सि or असि is perhaps the same without the nasal and shortened, which changes are made probably to adapt it to the expression of singularity. The adjectival masc. termination appears also in the first pers. sing., as in M., but it is shortened to उ and the fem. sing. ई and the pl. ऊ or ई ऊ optionally combined into यू throughout. In the M. the adjectival gender terminations are not used in the pl. Dr. Trump considers these personal terminations as the remnants of the old Pr. forms of अस्, which, however, are quite different from these.

The old past part. is similarly made the base of verbal forms expressive of past time. In S. they are made up just in the same way as the above, the 3rd pers. having the purely adjectival forms, without the personal terminations, and the gender affixes appearing in the same places as in the above.

Masc.

Singular.	Plural.
हलिउसि—ल्युसि	हलिआसीं—ल्यासीं
हलिएं—ल्यें	हल्यउ—ल्यु
हलिओ—ल्यो	हलिआ—ल्या

Fem.

Singular.	Plural.
हलिअसि—ल्यसि	हलियूंसि
हलिअं—एं	हलियूं—ऊं
हली	हलियूं

When the verb is transitive the participle is passive and the agent, if used, is put in the instr. case. The verb takes the person, gender and number of the object in the nom. case and the forms are just the same as the above; as मार्युसि 'I was beaten,' मार्यें 'thou wert beaten.'

Marâṭhî has—

	Masc.		Fem.		Neut.	
	Sing.	Pl.	Sing.	Pl.	Sing.	Pl.
1st	गेलों	गेलों	गेल्यें-लीं	गेल्यों	गेलें	गेलों
2nd	गेलास	गेलां	गेलीस	गेल्यात	गेलेंस	गेलींत
3rd	गेला	गेले	गेली	गेल्या	गेलें	गेलीं

Here as before we have simply adjectival forms for the 3rd pers.; and the verbal terminations of the old Pres. appear in the first and second united with the nominal affixes indicative of gender and number, which however are dropped where they can not be easily combined with the other, as in the first and second person plural masc. It should be remarked that the old masc. termination उ or ओ is preserved in the 1st pers. sing., as in the new Pres., and the 2nd pers. pl. has in some cases the affix त, which I have already noticed and traced to the Pr. इत्था. The Chit. and Goan. dialects agree with this in the main, but use त for the 2nd pers. pl. of the Masc. also, as गेलेत. Their masc. sing. is गेलो and fem. pl. गेल्यो, since they do not drop the old उ of the fem. nom. pl. The Mâl. discards gender in the first and second persons, when the verbal terminations are appended, and the first pers. sing. termination is the old इं, which before the ओ of the others is reduced to an anusvâra, and we have गेलइं—लें 'I went.' The 2nd pers. pl. termination is त throughout, as in the other dialects

Goan.

हांव गेलों-लीं-लं	आमी गेलों-ल्यों-लीं
तूं गेलो-ली-लंस	तुमी गेले-ल्यो-लींत
तो-ती-तें गेलो-ली-लं	ते-ल्यो-तीं गेले-ल्यो-लीं

Mâl.

मी गेलइं	आमी गेलौं
तूं गेलस	तुमी गेलात-ल्यात
तो-ती-तां गेलो-ली-लां	ते-ल्यो-तीं गेले-ल्यो-लीं

In transitive verbs M. attempts a curious combination. The participle being passive it must agree with the object and take its number and gender and, if made the base of verbal forms, its person also. But, unlike the Sindhî, the M. does not use this passive participle for an object in the first and second persons. Thus मार्यें and मार्युंसि in S. mean 'thou wert beaten' and 'I was beaten;' but we do not use such forms as मारिलास or मारिलो to express this sense, though a solitary line from Moropant containing धरिलास has been often quoted. In these cases we use the impersonal construction putting the agent and the object in the instr. and dat. and using the sing. neuter form of the past part., as त्याणें मला or तुला मारिलें. Thus then this participle can have a nom. object only of the third person. Properly then it ought to take no personal terminations at all; but when the agent which is always in the instr. case is of the 2nd pers. the characteristic sing. स and pl. त of that pers. are appended to the participle, so that it takes the gender and number of the object which is in the nom. case and the pers. and number of the agent which is in the instr. case. Thus we have तूं पोथी लिहिलीस 'thou transcribedst a book,' तूं पोथ्या लिहिल्यास, तूं काम केलेंस 'thou didst a work,' तुह्मीं पोथी लिहिलीत, पोथ्या लिहिल्यात. These forms are condemned by the Translation Department of the Director of Public Instruction, but the Marâṭhî speakers can not dispense with them; त्वां काम केलें, त्वां पोथी लिहिली, the proposed substitutes, are felt to be weak and emasculated. And the Konkaṇîs are not satisfied with second personal forms alone of this nature and have devised a way of affiliating the past part. with the third personal agent also and, as the old terminations इ and त are not expressive enough, they append to that participle the last syllable of the agent forms *i. e.* the ने or न of the instr. sing. and नीं of the pl., as त्या साहेबानें-न मला बक्षिस दिलेंन 'the Saheb gave me a reward,' त्या साहेबांनीं मला बक्षिसें दिलेनीं 'the Sahebs gave me rewards,' where the न and नीं of साहेबान and साहेबांनीं are added to the verbs to connect them with them. These forms are not used in the Deccan except by some Konkaṇî Brahmans settled there; and they are condemned by all good writers.

The O. and the B. do not inflect their adjectives, whether they end in ओ or any other vowel and have no agent case or instrumental. When the languages came to be in this condition there was nothing to mark off the passive nature of the transitive participle. Hence it was forgotten and we have now active verbal forms only, which are constructed as in the other languages.

	O.		B.	
	Sing.	Pl.	Sing.	Pl.
1st pers.	कलि	कलुं	देखिलाम्	देखिलाम्
2nd pers.	कलु	कल	देखिलि	देखिला—ले
3rd pers.	कला	कले	देखिल (or ल्)	देखिलेन्

As in the Pres. the O. like the other languages does not add verbal terminations to the third pers., but the forms are like those in M., namely the nom. sing. and pl. masc., though they do not indicate gender here. The other persons have the terminations of the Present.

The B. has no termination in the third pers. singular, while the pl. has the corresponding एन of the Present in that language. The 2nd pers. sing. has इ and the first person sing. म्, which are not used in the B. Present but are to be traced to the Apabhr. Present preserved in the इ and उं of the H. and others; देखिल+उं is देखिलांव like the Goan. करतांव from करत+उं, and the anusvâra and the व are hardened into म्. The first pers. pl. has the same form as the sing. and such a confusion is easy in a language without distinction of number. The second pers. pl. appears to be the old adjectival pl. like the M. केले and the O. कले; and the other form is देखिला sing., the two being confounded.

The Skr. potential participle in तव्य, Pr. अव्व, which implies duty, has become the base of the O. and B. Future. In Skr. मया कर्तव्यम् means 'it is to be done by me' *i. e.* it is my duty to do it, and the transition from this idea to 'I shall do it' is natural. The very word 'shall' in English, which primarily signifies 'I owe' and has now become the sign of the English Future, is an example of it. This participle in Skr. and Pr. is impersonal when the root is intransitive and passive when it is transitive. Like the past part. this has lost its passive character in these languages for the same reasons. The usual personal terminations are applied to it as—

	O. Sing.	O. Pl.	B. Sing.	B. Pl.
1st	करिवि	करिबु-वा	करिव	करिव
2nd	करिबु	करिव	करिवि	करिवा-वे
3rd	करिव	करिवे	करिवे	करिवेन्

In the O. the third pers. sing. has no terminations and the pl. has the nom. pl. ए, which we have found in so many cases. The others have the usual affixes. The optional वा of the first pers. pl. appears to be the adjectival sing. वा. The B. first pers. has no termination; the second has the same as those we examined in the case of the Past tense and the third has the affixes of the regular Present. This participle is similarly made the base of a Future tense in Sindhî; but since its passive character was not forgotten by the Sindhîs, as by the Bengalis and the Oriyas, the Future tense it forms is the Passive Future. The same terminations as those we have examined before are appended to it as मारिबुसि 'I shall be beaten', मारिबे 'thou shalt be beaten' and मारिबो 'he will be beaten.' The third person has, as before, no personal affixes. When the verb is intransitive this participle is used only impersonally in the masc. sing., the agent being in the instrumental. In M. however the potential participle has preserved its old sense and is passive and impersonal, and, when used as a base for verbal forms, takes only the second pers. sing. affix स and the pl. त. Like the past participle when it is passive it takes the gender and number of the object in the nom. and the person and number of the agent in the instrumental, as तूं ग्रंथ लिहावास, पोथी वाचावीस आणि दुसरें काम करावेंस 'thou shouldst write a work, read a book and do some other work.' When the object is in the pl. we have लिहावेस, वाचाव्यास, करावींस; and when the agent is in the pl. and the object sing. we have लिहावात, वाचावीत, करावेंत; and when both are in the pl. लिहावेत, वाचाव्यात and करावींत. When the verb is intransitive it is impersonal *i. e.* has no Nom. with which it should agree, since the object alone can be Nom.; but it takes the स and त of the agent as तूं जावेंस—तुम्हीं जावेंत. Dr. Trump and Mr. Beames (Jour. R. A. S. Vol. VII), misled by the circumstance that in the B., O. and S. the व is pronounced like ब, have likened these forms to the Latin *bo* and explain them as made up of the principal root and the Skr. भू. But this latter has in none of the vernaculars assumed the form of ब by dropping the vowel and the aspiration, nor are भ or the aspirated consonants generally ever known to become the corresponding unaspirates. The genius of the Prâkṛits and their descendants is to preserve the aspirate element and to drop the mute. In rare cases the former is thrown on an adjoining letter, but never lost. The usual form in which we have भ् is ह्. And this etymology would not account for the fact that the forms with ब are passive in S.

In these verbal forms then we observe fresh instances of the law of generalization or false analogy. For the Present and Future tenses verbal or predicative forms, *i. e.* such as indicate the person of the Nom., were wanted; and so great is the necessity of such forms that we in M. make up such verbs as करावीस and केलीस agreeing with both the agent and the object as noticed above. But the languages being in spite of this want condemned to use participles only, they made the best of what they had and extended the analogy of the old Pres., which they possessed, to the participles, which they could not avoid, and thus applied the personal terminations to the participles and made verbs of them. The B. and O. rather than make the verbs agree with the object, as the passive nature of the participial base of the verb required, dropped the passive character altogether and made the participles take the personal terminations of the agent, while M. reconciles both and makes the verbs based on the passive participles agree with the person and number of the agent and the gender and number of the object.

We have next to examine the forms that are made up by adding independent words. There are not many of this class. The H. and P. Future is constructed by affixing गा sing., गे pl. masc., and गी sing. and गीं pl. fem. to the forms of the Present. This गा appears to be the past participle of गम् and ordinarily it is used in the form of गया. Participles of other roots also are in H. sometimes reduced to monosyllabic forms as दी for दिई, की for किई; these are feminine and the corresponding masc. monosyllabic forms are दा and का. We have seen that these का-की and दा-दी are appended to the obl. case form to make up the genitive in H. and P. Similarly the participle गा-गी is used to form the Future, so that करेगा means 'gone that he may do.' The M. Future is formed by adding इल or ऊ to the old Present, as you will see from the following forms:—

	Sing.	Pl.	Sing.	Pl.
1st	करीन	करूं	धावेन	धावूं
2nd	कर-रिशिल	कराल	धावशील	धावाल
3rd	करील	करितील	धावेल	धावतील

In the first pers. sing. ल and the anusvâra of रीं together form न as they do in several other cases; the pl. is the same as that of the Pres. What is the nature of this ल or इल ? One ल that is appended to the past participle we have already examined. There is another appended in the Goan. and Mâl. to the present part. and the forms thus made up have past habitual and future sense. Thus Goan. करतालो means 'he used to do' and करतलो Goan. and Mâl. 'he will do.' In both cases the base is the present part., but in the first it occurs in the augmented form or the form with the old Skr. क. The pres. part. has in the O., as we have seen, acquired a past and in the S. a future sense, the germs of both of which are, as I have explained, contained in its original signification, while here in the Goan. it has both the senses. Now, as it was the practice, as I observed in the last two lectures, to attach क and ल or इल optionally to a great many words, the same word had often several forms—one without क, another with it, a third with ल, a fourth without it and a fifth with both ल and क. These terminations did not signify much originally but afterwards, when the words such as the pres. part. began more and more to acquire distinct and diverse significations, one of the forms whether with or without ल became identified with one sense and the other with another. Thus करतालो, made up as it is by the addition of क, which has left its अ, and of ल, was appropriated for the Habitual Past and करतलो without क to the Future. But that the new additions themselves originally were not expressive of that sense is shown by the fact that the augmented form करता in तो करता तर बरें होतें expresses past conditional in M. and H., while it is the unaugmented करत in G. in ते करत तो सारुं थात which conveys that sense. Thus then ल was applied in M. to the Present verbal forms also and, when the old Future was lost, these came to be appropriated for the Future, just as the present participle with ल came to have a future signification in the Goan. and Mâl.

The other tenses are made up by adding the verbal forms of auxiliary roots, but their etymological sense has not yet been forgotten and they have suffered no phonetic corruption except in a few cases. Hence they can easily be recognised. But the various ways in which they affect the sense of the principal root in the different languages are not without interest. The auxiliaries are हो from Skr. भू, the Skr. अस् or आस्, more likely the latter, which assumes the forms of आछे B., अछ O., छे G., है H. and P., आहे M. and S., and Skr. स्था from which the H. था and the S. थो are derived.

You will thus see that in this portion of their grammar the vernaculars have only adapted the materials they inherited from the Prâkṛits to their varying necessities according to the ways resorted to by all the languages in the course of their development. They have got nothing new and have simply given new shapes to the old; and the proposition, that they are descended from the Prâkṛits, holds good even here.

LECTURE VII.

Relations between Sanskrit, Pâli, the Prâkṛits and the Modern Vernaculars.

Thus, gentlemen, have we surveyed the whole field of Indian Aryan speech from the Vedic times to our own, and what is it we have found? The Vedic dialect lost a great many of its words and some grammatical forms, its nouns and roots arranged themselves under definite declensions and conjugations, and thus became what I have called Middle Sanskrit. Till then there was no phonetic corruption except in isolated instances. But after that time the process went on rapidly, and words were altered in form principally by the law of the assimilation of conjunct consonants and a few vowel changes. By the law of generalization or false analogy the declensions and conjugations were reduced to the prevailing types; some new words came into use and a few old ones became obsolete, and thus the language arrived at a stage of which the Pâli, the sacred language of the Southern Buddhists, and the inscriptions of As'oka afford us specimens. Then began a general use of attributive expressions for verbal forms, which had its effect on the vernacular or derived languages also, and thus while a good many of these forms went out of use in Sanskrit, the number of tenses and moods in the derived languages was reduced to three. In the meanwhile the processes which formed the Pâli went on, other laws of phonetic change, and principally that of the elision of uninitial consonants and the reduction of aspirated ones to ह, came into operation. The use of analogy in the simplification of grammar proceeded further, a few words of a non-Sanskrit origin were adopted, and thus arose the Prâkṛits. There were several dialects of this class, but the distinction between them was not great. After a while in the Prâkṛits themselves new phonetic processes began, the chief of which were the dropping of one of the assimilated consonants and in most cases lengthening the preceding vowel, and the obviating of the hiatus caused by the vowels brought together by consonantal elision by combining them or inserting light semi-vowels between them. These were carried on further, the declensional and conjugational terminations were corrupted and mutilated, and the forms began to get confused; case relations came to be expressed by connecting independent words or pronominal forms with the genitive of the noun; and new verbal forms were constructed from the participles by appending the personal terminations on the analogy of the existing tenses, or by using the roots indicative of existence as auxiliaries. About this time the Prâkṛit speaking people came to be divided into independent communities, separated from each other by hills and rivers, or communication between them decreased; and therefore these several processes of destruction and construction were carried on at a varying rate and with a difference of detail in each; and thus grew up the modern Hindî, Mârâṭhì, Gujarâtî, Sindhî, &c. This is the whole history. The vernaculars have descended from the Prâkṛits, and the Prâkṛits from Sanskrit; and since a language is transmitted from generation to generation orally, if the modern dialects are spoken languages the Prâkṛits must have been so, and if the Prâkṛits were spoken dialects the Sanskrit must have been so.

But these conclusions have been denied by some scholars. Professor H. H. Wilson says that the Prâkṛit of the plays is an artificial modification of the Sanskrit language devised to adapt it to peculiar branches of literature. And the reason he gives is that even in later plays composed but a few centuries ago the Prâkṛit used is not the vernacular of the day, but that which we find in the very earliest work of the species. But he is by no means certain, and leaves the question undecided. The reason advanced by him is evidently of no weight. If I choose at this day to express my thoughts in Latin and compose a treatise in that language instead of my vernacular, does that prove that that language is artificial? Latin is sometimes still used in Europe for literary purposes, though it is not the vernacular of any country. Sanskrit playwriters of later ages, and even a stray dramatist at the present day use the old Prâkṛits for their inferior characters in orthodox obedience to the rules laid down by the old authorities on the histrionic art; and since the Prâkṛits, like Sanskrit, Latin, and other languages are preserved by means of grammars and literary works, it is possible to write in them as in these languages.

Mr. Beames at one time expressed himself decidedly on this point: "The Prâkṛit of the poets is clearly not a dialect that ever was spoken." So Dr. Pischel, a German scholar: "I agree with Mr. Beames, that none of the Prâkṛits was ever a spoken language, and that in order to learn what was the spoken language of the Aryans we must turn principally to the modern vernaculars." This, gentlemen, we have done; we have examined the vernaculars and found that there is not a rule about the changes of letters in passing from Sanskrit into the Prâkṛit given by Vararuchi or Hemachandra, of which instances are not found in the vernaculars. Of such as are general the examples are abundant; and in a great many cases even the words in which the change is of a special kind are preserved in the vernaculars in their Prâkṛit form, slightly altered according to the processes that afterwards came into operation. A good many of the vocal peculiarities of the Pâli and Prâkṛit speakers are preserved by the speakers of the Gujarâtî, Marâṭhî, Hindî, Sindhî, and Bangâlî. I have already drawn your attention to the fact that the ordinary Gujarâtî cannot pronounce ऐ or औ but makes ए or ओ of it, the Marâṭhî De'sastha ण् of न्, and the Sindhî and the Bangâlî क्ख् of क्ष्, and the Hindî क्ख् or ख् of it and स् of the sibilant. The Bangâlî pronounces a conjunct ending in य् as a double consonant and preserves the old Mâgadhî peculiarity of reducing all the sibilants to श्, while the Hindî still manifests the Pais'âchî peculiarity of making न् of ण्. The case terminations in the forms they assumed in the Apabhraṃs'a have been perserved, some in this dialect, some in that. All the three Prâkṛit tenses do exist and none other; past time is expressed in just the same way as in the Prâkṛits; the participles, the causals, the passives, the denominatives, the nominal and verbal bases, and the remnants of the Sanskrit conjugations are just as they were in the Prâkṛits; and the new verbs and cases are formed out of Prâkṛit materials only. Then again a good many of the Des'ya or non-Sanskrit words that existed in the Prâkṛits are found in the vernaculars.

Now if the Prâkṛits were not spoken dialects, what these scholars probably mean is that they were artificial adaptations, as Professor Wilson calls them. But we have seen that they grew up by such natural laws as guide the development of any language whatever. The development of the Prâkṛit dialects from Sanskrit is paralleled by the development of the Romance languages from Latin. If the Prâkṛit dialects are to be considered artificial, it is difficult to conceive upon what principles they could have been constructed and for what purpose. A conscious manufacture of a language would be conducted upon some general principles and would not admit of such isolated forms, not obeying any general rule, as we have noticed. The analogies would be perfect; but on the contrary we have seen that in the Pâli and the Prâkṛits a good many forms are made up according to a certain rule brought into use by analogy, as for instance making the passive by adding इज्ज or इअ, while there are others which are not thus constructed but have descended by simple phonetic corruption of Sanskrit forms, as दीसइ, लब्भइ and others. In all parts of grammar there are such forms, and these have descended to the modern Vernaculars, as we have seen.

Again, if these had been artificial languages they would not have been called after the names of provinces as we have seen they were. I have given reasons for believing that though the difference between the S'aurasenî and the Mahârâshṭrî was not great, some peculiarities of the former have been preserved by the modern Sindhî Panjâbî, Braja and Hindî, while the Marâṭhî represents the old Mahârâshṭrî, and some of the peculiarities of the Mâgadhî Prâkṛit are distinctly observable, as we have seen, in some of the inscriptions of As'oka, in which it would be absurd to suppose an artificial language was used. And how, if they were not popular dialects, could the idea of using them for women and the inferior characters in dramatic plays have in the first place arisen? That a poet should make certain persons in his work speak their peculiar dialect, especially when that is an inferior dialect and likely to create mirth, is natural, and this device is resorted to by writers in all countries. But it was probably more from considerations of propriety than liveliness that these languages began to be used by Sanskrit dramatists. For they are no less particular about such proprieties, and of even the so-called unities, than other nations. For one of the rules of the Art is that one act should not contain the events of more than a day. Similarly the minute directions about the use of certain Prâkṛit dialects in the case of certain persons are explicable only on the supposition that the original idea was to represent in the drama a state of things actually existing in the world. For these varied reasons it admits of no question whatever that the Prâkṛits of the poets and of the grammarians were really at one time spoken languages. But it is of course not meant that they were spoken just as we find them written, or that they were necessarily spoken at the time when the poets that use them flourished. The Prâkṛits became literary and dead dialects as Sanskrit itself had before them, and, as already remarked, they may be used for literary purposes even now, if one wishes to do so. The distinction between the written Prâkṛits and the corresponding spoken Prâkṛits cannot be greater than the usual distinction between the language of books and that of ordinary life; and probably the Prâkṛits of some of our early plays represent the vernaculars of the time faithfully. I must not omit to mention that Mr. Beames has considerably modified his opinion since he wrote the article from which the above extract is taken, for in the beginning of the Introduction to his Comparative Grammar he speaks of the Prâkṛits as spoken languages, and attempts to account for the use of so many in the dramatic plays instead of setting it down to a mere fancy.

We will next proceed to consider the views that have been put forth, opposed to the conclusions we have arrived at, as regards the relation between Sanskrit and the Prákṛits, and endeavour to determine that relation more definitely than we have done. Professor Weber believes that in the Vedic times there were several dialects, and that by a fusion of these a common language called the Sanskrit was formed, while at the same time the dialects ran on their course and formed the Prâkṛits. He says, "I incline to the opinion of those, who deny that the Sanskrit Bhâshâ, properly so called, was ever the common spoken language of the whole Aryan people, and assign it to the learned alone. Just as our modern High German, arising out of the ancient dialects of the Germans, reduced what was common to all to universal rules and laws, and by the power of analogy obliterated all recollection of varieties; and just as, on the other hand, these dialects while they gradually degenerated often preserved at the same time fuller and more ancient forms; so also the Vedic dialects became partly combined in one stream, in which their individual existence was lost, and so formed the regular Sanskrit Bhâshâ, and partly flowed on individually on their own original (Prâkṛita) irregular force, and continued to be the idioms of different provinces in the corruption of which they participated. The Sanskrit language and the Prâkṛit dialects had, therefore, a common and simultaneous origin; the latter did not spring out of the former." Professor Weber gives a few instances of Prâkṛitised Sanskrit words from the Vedic dialect, as he calls it, to show that the developments of the Prâkṛits began then, but nearly all of these are from such works as the Upanishads, which must be assigned to a very late period when the language was in that confusion which we find in the Buddhistic Gâthâs. Now if the development of Sanskrit and the Prâkṛits was contemporaneous, how comes it that almost all the words and grammatical forms in these latter dialects are manifest corruptions of Sanskrit words and forms? Professor Weber's theory does not account for this fact, but this defect is supplied by Mr. Beames, who holds nearly the same view as the Professor. He says, "The idea of a common language is the creation of modern times, and the effect of the spread of literature." "The most probable hypothesis is, that the Aryans from the earliest times spoke many dialects, all closely akin, all having the same family likeness and tendencies common to all, perhaps in every case mutually intelligible, but still distinct and co-existent." In a note we are told that this is probable but cannot be proved. The dialect of the Vedic hymns was, he says, only one of these. Then "after a time the Brahmans consciously and intentionally set themselves to the task of constructing a sacred language, by preserving and reducing to rule the grammatical elements of this Vedic tongue." "They seized on the salient features of Âryan speech as contained in all dialects, and moulded them into one harmonious whole." They (the popular dialects) were anterior to Sanskrit, contemporary with it, and they finally survived it. Nevertheless, Sanskrit is older than the dialects. This sounds like a paradox, but it is true in two senses; first, that "as ages rolled on, the vulgar dialects went on developing into new forms, while Sanskrit remained fixed and fossilized for ever." The second is, that though Pâṇini, who is credited with this feat of constructing the Sanskrit language, lived when the early dialects were much changed, still among the Brâhmans there was a traditional memory of the ancient and then obsolete forms of many words............In teaching his pupils the true principles of speech, Pâṇini would naturally use these archaic words in preference to the corruptions current around him, and thus the language which he, to a certain extent, created, was in great part a resuscitation of antiquated terms."

To be able to estimate the views of these writers at their true worth, it is necessary that we should try to fix the meaning of the word dialect, which is the source of some confusion, and endeavour to form some idea of the origin and growth of dialects generally. If little differences are to be regarded as sufficient to constitute a dialect there are as many dialects as human beings. For just as no two human faces are exactly alike, no two men speak exactly alike. Every one has his peculiarities of pronunciation, and is fond of particular words or turns of expression. The principle of individuality is strong in human nature, but its effects are counteracted by the principle of community, which guides the development of human life; and the necessity of communication compels a man to drop peculiarities in speech and to conform himself to the prevailing model. Thus then, the individual differences come to be minute and insignificant, and hence the language of a community becomes practically one language. But, constituted as communities generally, but not necessarily, are, they are composed of classes; and there is not as much communication between separate classes as within the limits of a class, and hence there come to be class languages, or varieties of speech in the same community. There may be many such classes; but the smaller ones may be neglected, and we may distinguish between two large ones, generally called the lower and the higher, or the uneducated and educated classes. The languages of these differ, that of the lower class being more subject to those laws of development, growth, or corruption which I traced in the first lecture. Thus an uneducated Englishman uses many such forms as "I knowed," "you says," formed upon the prevailing analogies; and his pronunciation of a good many words is corrupt, as "genlman" for "gentleman," "wot" for "what," "guvner" for "governor," &c. And in the same way the language of the Marâṭhî, Gujarâti or Hindî lower classes is not the same as that of the higher. But still the word dialect is not used in speaking of these two varieties, one principal reason being that the language of the lower classes is not acknowledged to have an independent existence. Again, when a community comes to have a literature, the style that is used, as a rule, differs from the ordinary conversational style. There are certain words, turns of expression, modes of construction, and even solitary forms which, though used in conversation, do not appear in books. Even these two varieties are not called dialects. The dialects of a language therefore or kindred dialects, as they may be called, are the languages of kindred communities, which, while they possess a large body of common words and forms, have also many others which are different, though in most cases the roots from which these are derived are common to all. And according to the proportion in which the similar and dissimilar elements are mixed, the dialects are more or less distant from each other. The causes that divide men into distinct communities are the causes that create dsitinct dialects. The laws of change and development are always in operation in a language, in a changing condition of society, and the processes of destruction or disappearance of old words and forms and the construction or appearance of new ones, are constantly going on. Hence, when after the separation of men into distinct communities, communication between them is lessened, these processes go on in a varied and dissimilar manner. The conditions of life in their new habitations may also be different, and when they are so they bring about a varied linguistic development. But though the processes of destruction and construction are always going on in a language, they suppose that the society, whose language it is, is moving and not stationary. The life of a community may, however, be even and unvaried, in which case there will be little change in its language. Or certain races may be very conservative, and cling to the past with tenacity. Thus the Lithuanian peasants of the present day have through a number of ages, though they possess nothing like a literature, preserved a good many old Aryan words and forms in a purer condition than all their European neighbours. So that even after men are divided into distinct communities it is by no means necessary that distinct dialects should grow up. They may or they may not. But the possibility of slight differences, such as those which exist in the speech of the different classes of a community, even when the dialect is the same, is not denied. Now, if for the various reasons above indicated dialects have come into existence, these continue until by the development of civilisation and by political events kindred communities come to form a nation; and then by increased communication and the growth of a common literature these dialects are fused together, and one harmonious language is formed; though, however, in remote quarters they may continue to have an independent existence. The writers whom I have quoted pay exclusive attention to this fact, of which there are several instances in modern European history, the most notable of which is the development of the modern German; and lay it down as a universal proposition which requires no proof, that in an early condition of society there must be a plurality of dialects, and there could be no such thing as a common language. This seems to be the opinion of Professor Max Müller also. But if there was not one common original dialect, whence are the common portion of the words and forms of kindred dialects, and the common roots derived? And does not comparative philology itself, in its comparisons and classifications, go upon the assumption that there was such a language? Thus then, since the creation of dialects depends on causes and the causes may not exist, it will not do to assume that there were several dialects in Vedic times without positive proof or even positive indications. Several independent Aryan communities or tribes may not have migrated into India, but only one. Or even if more than one tribe came over they may have been, like the Lithuanian peasants, very conservative as regards their language. The circumstances we know about the language of the period do not necessitate the supposition of a plurality of dialects. Besides, if according to Professor Weber these originally existing dialects went on in their own isolated course as the idioms of different provinces, and became the Pâli and the Prâkṛits, we should expect to find much greater divergences between them, produced in the course of the many centuries that elapsed between the Vedic period and that in which they were as we now find them. But the distinction between the dialects of the inscriptions of As'oka and even between the different Prâkṛits is by no means great, and concerns chiefly the pronunciation of individual letters. The plea of linguistic conservatism which I have before used in a certain case, cannot be brought in here, since those early dialects resembling the language of the Vedas, as they must have done if they existed, were already very greatly corrupted in passing into the Pâli or the Prâkṛits. Surely such very extensive changes as from the Vedic to the Prâkṛit form, if carried on in different provinces by different communities, must occasion very great divergences, greater even than we find between the modern vernaculars. For the degree of departure from the old Prâkṛits which these last exhibit is not so great as that which the Prâkṛits do from the Vedic dialect. The divergence ought to be at least as great, but it certainly is not so.

Now the way in which the supposed contemporaneous development of Sanskrit and the Prâkṛits is accounted for by Mr. Beames is, as we have seen, this:— That the Prâkṛits arose by a natural development, while Sanskrit was created by the Brâhmans, and principally by Pâṇini, out of the Vedic dialect, the salient points of Prâkṛit speech, and by a resuscitation of antiquated terms. Hence it contains the old words and forms from which those in the Prâkṛits are derived. And this also accounts for the existence of what Mr. Beames calls an Aryan but non-Sanskritic element in the Prâkṛits, by which he probably means those few forms that are not found in classical Sanskrit, but must be referred to the Vedic dialect, or others that must be Aryan, though not found either in classical or Vedic Sanskrit. Of the latter there are almost no instances which may be regarded as beyond the possibility of doubt. But such a theory is calculated to bring relief to a puzzled philologist who, not knowing to what Sanskrit word to trace any Prâkṛit or Vernacular word, will at once get out of the difficulty by putting it down as an Aryan word not found in Sanskrit. But how is it possible to create such a language as the Sanskrit out of the elements indicated by Mr. Beames? A literary style, as distinguished from a conversational style, is what one can understand, but a language which never had anything to correspond to it in ordinary vernacular speech, but is simply created, is inconceivable. And if the creation of a sacred language was the conscious and deliberate aim of the Brahmans, and Pâṇini resuscitated old or obsolete words, why did they or he not include in the new language all the innumerable old obsolete Vedic words and grammatical forms, which would have, from the very reverence that was paid to the Vedas, rendered their invention more sacred; and why should they, instead of doing so, have distinguished between a Chhândasa or Vedic, and Bhâshâ or popular, speech? And, if the inventors seized all the salient features of the popular dialects, would they have left a few but striking Vedic peculiarities in the popular speech, such as the absolutive in त्वान or तून, unrepresented in their new language? And how could they from the popular dialects, in which the conjugations and declensions were reduced to fewer types, construct the innumerable forms of the Sanskrit noun or verb, the Perfects, the Aorists and the lost tenses or moods? And what must have been the basis of the incalculable Taddhita or nominal, and Kṛit or verbal derivatives, which have left but few traces in the Prâkṛits? Even the Vedic dialect is not calculated to afford much help. For if the grammar of the later Sanskrit had been framed by the conscious inventors upon the model of the Vedic, the declensions, conjugations, and the derivatives would have been like the Vedic; whereas, as a matter of fact, the differences are great, and some of these I pointed out in the first lecture. There remains the third alternative, that there was a traditional memory of these forms. But why should they have been committed to memory when there was no motive? The sacred formulas which Mr. Beames says were orally transmitted do not, if they were the same as those that have come down to us, contain a large number of such forms; and, if they were different, they are simply imaginary. And, though the Vedas were and are committed to memory, the literally incalculable number of case forms, verbal forms, Taddhitas, and Kṛidants, in the absence of any general rules which were laid down afterwards, as the theory supposes, by the grammarian creators of the languages, it is thoroughly impossible to commit to memory,—impossible, as the great author of the Mahâbhâshya says, even for Indra, with Bṛihaspati for his teacher and a thousand celestial years during which to learn them. Of course it is a different thing when they are current in a language which one learns from his childhood, though even in this case very few know all the words and forms which are current in their own country, and nearly all only such as they are immediately concerned with. And what is the evidence for the truth of this theory? Absolutely none is given. It is simply the vague feeling of an individual or individuals, and not a conclusion arrived at after a deliberate weighing of evidence; while it sets at naught the clearest evidence available in the works of the grammarians themselves, which I shall presently adduce. The theory, therefore, is utterly untenable, and the contemporaneous development of Sanskrit and the Prâkṛits derived from it, to account for which it was invented; is an impossibility. Professor Aufrecht, though he does not believe in a plurality of Vedic dialects, derives the Prâkṛits from the Vedic language, and assigns Sanskrit to schools of the learned, but does not explain its genesis. Those who believe the Vernacular dialects to be derived directly from the Vedic must explain the origin of classical Sanskrit in some such way as Mr. Beames has done; there is no other way.

Dismissing feelings which we have been considering so long, we will for a time examine the reason or reasons that are given for doubting the derivation of the Pâli and the Prâkṛits from Sanskrit. Thus Professor Childers, in the preface to his Pâli Dictionary, states the relations between Sanskrit and Pâli in the following lucid manner :—

" If we compare Pâli with classical Sanskrit, we find that about two-fifths of the vocabulary consists of words identical in form with their Sanskrit equivalents, as *Nâga*, *Buddha*, *Nidâna*. Nearly all the remaining words present a more or less late or corrupted form............Words of the above two classes nearly exhaust the Pâli vocabulary; but there remains a small though important residuum of forms distinctly older than Sanskrit, and found only in the oldest known Sanskrit, that of the Vedas. Nay, I do not feel sure that Pâli does not retain a few precious relics older than the most ancient Sanskrit, and only to be explained through the allied Indo-Germanic languages. It results from all this that Pâli cannot be derived from Sanskrit; both, though most intimately connected, being independent corruptions of the lost Aryan speech which is their common parent; but that Pâli is on the whole in a decidedly later stage than Sanskrit, and, to adopt a metaphor popularised by Max Müller, stands to it in the relation of a younger sister." Then in a footnote he gives these Vedic forms in the Pâli: the infinitive in *tave*, as *kátave* "for doing," the absolutive or gerund in *tvâna*, as *katvâna* "having done." These two terminations, however, occur only occasionally, the usual ones are the Sanskrit *tum* and *tvâ*. The next two, *imassa*, genitive singular of *ayaṃ*, and *gonaṃ*, genitive plural of *go* "a cow," I consider as made up by false analogy, as I have already indicated; *tinnam*, genitive plural of *tri*, is similar. Then *vidû* from *vid* to know and meaning "one who knows;" *divo*, which is masculine in the Veda and in the Pâli, while it is feminine in Sanskrit; the Imperative first person plural in *âmase* as in *yamâmase*, "I shall or may restrain" *kasâmase*, "I shall or may plough;" the Imperfect *akâ* of *karoti* from the Vedic *akat*. Pâli has the Vedic *ḷ*, but this is a sound natural under certain circumstances, since we have it in Marâṭhî and Gujarâtî, and *kuham* corresponding to the Vedic *kuha*. The Vedic Instrumental plural termination of nouns in अ is retained in the Pâli and also corrupted to *ehi*. Professor Childers, however, thinks it is corrupted from the Sanskrit ablative *bhyas*. I agree with those who derive it from the Vedic affix. To these may be added the Prâkṛit कुणइ "he does," in which there is a remnant of the fifth conjugation, while the root belongs to the eighth class; and also the affix त्तण of abstract nouns, while it is त्व in ordinary Sanskrit. Prâkṛit possesses तूण or ऊण corresponding to the Pâli त्वान or तून and the instrumental affix एहि.

Then in another note Professor Childers gives the Pâli *garu* "heavy" or "great," while Sanskrit has गुरु, though the गर appears in the Sanskrit comparative and superlative forms गरीयस् and गरिष्ठ. The अ is seen in the Greek word *Barùs* and Latin *gravis*. The Potential अस्स "let him be," is also said not to have anything to correspond to it in Sanskrit; but it may be traced to the Vedic subjunctive or लेट्, असत्, or regarded as a corruption of अस्यात् for Sanskrit स्यात्, the अ though dropped in Sanskrit being brought over by analogy from the singular of the other tenses. He also gives इध, while Sanskrit has इह, which is doubtful, and also सब्बधि "everywhere" the धि in which corresponds to *fi* in some Greek words. The Pâli धि is the locative singular of the root, the instrumental singular of which is preserved in the Sanskrit धा in एकधा, पञ्चधा &c. Of these the Prâkṛits have गर in such words as गरुअ, गारव &c., and इध.

Here the question is reduced to a point. Two-fifths of the words in the Pâli are pure Sanskrit, the rest are corrupt Sanskrit, while there are about six or seven forms which are lost in classical

Sanskrit but exist in Vedic Sanskrit; and there are one or two which exist in neither. The dialect then from which the Pâli was corrupted or immediately sprang, granting for a moment that it was different from the Sanskrit, had two-fifths of its words exactly like those in Sanskrit, and the other three fifths from which the Pâli corruptions were derived were also exactly like Sanskrit, but it contained these eight or nine forms which Sanskrit has lost. In other words, Pâli itself, if we take the original forms of the corrupt three-fifths of its words into consideration, is exactly like Sanskrit but for these nine forms. Is the dialect for this difference to be considered an independent dialect ? Is the distinction enough to entitle the Pâli or its supposed immediate parent to be considered a dialect, that is, a language, elaborated, according to the definition given before, from the ancient speech by a community distinct from that which elaborated the Sanskrit ? If one thinks it is, he may do so, and regard the Pâli as a distinct dialect; but he must for the same reason consider Surat Gujarâtî and Ahmedabad Gujarâtî; Komkaṇî Marâṭhî and Dekkanî Marâṭhî; or the Marâṭhî, Gujarâtî, English and any other language as spoken by the uneducated classes of the population, and as spoken by the educated, to be distinct dialects of the same ancient speech. In the same community, as I have observed, varieties of speech may or do prevail and must prevail, but the distinction between them is not enough to constitute them distinct dialects; wherefore Sanskrit and the immediate parent of the Pâli or the uncorrupt Pâli must be considered as one language, even though the latter contained a few more ancient forms; and if both were one, the Pâli must be regarded as a daughter of Sanskrit and not its sister. Some of its few peculiarities it may have derived from the spoken variety of Sanskrit, and the rest from that in use among the inferior classes. It often happens that the lower classes sometimes retain an old word or form after it has been given up by those above them, whence it is likely that the Pâli was corrupted from the language of those classes. And as a matter of fact it was for a long time the speech of the uneducated, as will be presently shown. These observations apply to the later Prâkṛits also ; wherefore, if these derived languages were spoken, that from which they were derived, *i. e.*, Sanskrit, must have been a spoken language also.

And, independently of this consideration, there is positive evidence that Sanskrit was a spoken language. Yâska in the Nirukta frequently refers to the Vedic dialect and to another called Bhâshâ, the peculiarities of which mentioned by him are observable in classical Sanskrit. Pâṇini in his Grammar gives a good many rules which are exclusively applicable to the dialect of the Vedas, to which he refers by using the words *Chhandas*, *Nigama*, *Mantra*, and *Brâhmaṇa*, and others which are applicable to the Bhâshâ alone, but by far the largest number of his sûtras have reference to both. Now, since Bhâshâ, or the ordinary Sanskrit, is thus distinguished from the dialect of the Vedas, it must be the language in use at the time when these writers lived. "Bhâshâ," as used by them, is a proper name, but in later Sanskrit it acquired a generic signification and meant language generally. The root from which the word is derived, signifies "to speak," wherefore the original sense of the word as a proper noun must have been the "speech" or "the spoken language." And, because this was its signification, it afterwards came to denote "explanation." When we ask for an explanation of something that is obscure and unintelligible, what we mean is that the sense should be expressed to us in the ordinary language of men, a language that we can understand. Thus such a sentence as स्थितप्रज्ञस्य का भाषा, means "what is the Vernacular of स्थितप्रज्ञ," an expression similar to "what is the English of it?"

Pâṇini refers certain points expressly to popular usage. He says that the names of countries are conventional, and no grammatical analysis should be given of them, because it is fictitious; these should be used as we find them used. Similarly he says grammarians should not make rules to teach such things as these:— That the two words of a compound express the thing denoted by the principal word as qualified by the sense of the subordinate word; as for instance, राजपुरुष, a compound of राजन् "a king" and पुरुष "a man", does not denote "a king," but "a man," and not "man" *alone* but *as connected with a king*, *i. e.* a king's man or officer; and that the base and the termination express the sense of the termination as qualified by that of the base; as औपगव signifies not उपगु but a child, and not a child *alone* but a child *as connected with* उपगु *i. e.* Upagu's child. For the significations of words are to be learnt from usage.

In the introduction to the Mahâbhâshya Patañjali tells us that some persons in his or Kâtyâyana's time considered the study of grammar to be unnecessary. For said they, "Vedic words or forms we know from the Veda, and those current in popular usage from that usage; grammar is useless." Now the grammar which is thus declared useless is the grammar both of the Vedic and classical Sanskrit; and the depreciators of the science profess to derive a knowledge of the first dialect from the Vedic books, and of the second not from other books but from popular usage. Hence Sanskrit must have been in the times of those two grammarians a spoken language.

Similarly in the passage from the same work which I placed before you in the first lecture, you will remember that the objector (or *pûrvapakshin*) argues that, since usage is the authority upon which the grammarians go, certain verbal forms which are no longer used by people ought not to be taught by the grammarians, and says that instead of those verbal forms participles are employed. The principal teacher (*Siddhântin*) does not deny the facts, but refers the objector to the vast literature of the language, where he may find them used, though obsolete at the time. It is evident from the whole passage, that Sanskrit was then a spoken language though some of its verbal forms had fallen into desuetude. I have also shown that the language was considerably changed between the times of Pâṇini and Kâtyâyana, and called the Sanskrit that prevailed when Pâṇini and Yâska flourished Middle Sanskrit, and that which was current in the time of Kâtyâyana Classical Sanskrit. Now these changes from the one form to the other could not have taken place if the language had been dead or petrified into a merely literary language.

I am at a loss to see why some scholars should find it so difficult to believe that Sanskrit was a vernacular. If its declensions and conjugations are considered too complicated for the language of everyday life, it must not be forgotten that such a fact did not prevent the ancient languages of Europe from becoming spoken languages. And this objection would do equally well against the Vedic dialect, which, or others like which, are regarded as the vernaculars of their times, and which are richer in inflexions than the later Sanskrit. Then it is held that the artificial regularity of Sanskrit makes it improbable that it should have been a vernacular. Where is this artificial regularity ? On the contrary, it is the absence of regularity that renders its grammar so difficult and complicated. There is a freedom in the choice of words, expressions, and forms. In every department of its grammar there are innumerable optional forms; nouns and verbal roots are often declined and conjugated in several ways. One same root in a good many cases forms its special tenses in more ways than one, and in the nominal derivatives, the verbal derivatives, the formation of the feminine, and the uses of cases and tenses there is a freedom which some may consider a license. The only difference is, that Sanskrit has had the most perfect grammarians in the world, who observed all the facts of their language and laid them down as unchangeable facts, and it is this which gives that language a stiffened appearance. Then the Saṃdhis or euphonic combinations of letters, which are necessary in Sanskrit, are regarded as inconsistent with the character of a spoken language. It is, however, not denied that such combinations are observable in all languages, and paticularly so in Latin and Greek; but it is urged that in Sanskrit there is a regularity or universality about them which is not found anywhere else. It should not, however, be forgotten that Saṃdhi in the same word and the same compound, and of a preposition with a root is alone necessary. Between different words it is optional, which means that it was on occasions neglected. Now Saṃdhi in the same word is necessary by a law of nature. The Sanskrit does not allow a hiatus; and this is a characteristic of most of the modern idioms also. Some languages, such as our Prâkṛits and the old languages of Europe, tolerate it. But the euphonic combination of consonants in the same word is necessary even in Latin; as in rex = reg-s, scriptus = scrib-tus, cinctum=cing-tum, lectum = leg-tum, tractum from traho, though the *h* like the Sanskrit ह stands for an original *gh*; *d* and *t* combine to form an *s*, as defendo, defensum; sedeo, sessum; claudo, clausum; &c. Prepositions are really parts of words, and hence by the same law they also must form one harmonious sound with the initial letter of the word to which they are attached; and modern vernaculars have got corruptions of the combined words, which shows that they must have been used in those forms in the colloquial Sanskrit. Sk. पर्यस्त, Pr. पल्लट्ट, M. पालट; Sk. प्रत्यभिजाना, Pr. पचहिआण, H. पहिचान; Sk. अत्यर्थ, Pr. अचट्ट, M. अचाट, &c. Now, as to compounds, this peculiarity of the Sanskrit has been carried to an extravagant extent by later writers, but Pâṇini allows only certain formations of this nature. These grew up as independent words in the language, and hence in the matter of Saṃdhi were treated like other words. In the spoken language the euphonic combinations we have been considering were not consciously made, but the words themselves acquired those forms by habitual use in the same manner as in other tongues. The grammarians, however, discovered and laid down these rules; and the practice of using them in books even in combining different words gained ground, though, however, many instances in which there is no such Saṃdhi are found in the Itihâsas and the Purâṇas. But if in colloquial speech such a combination was not possible, the grammarians do not enjoin that it should be made; and very probably it was not made.

And traces of many expressions, which only a colloquial use of language can generate, have been preserved, not so much in the literature, as by the grammarians. Such is one expressive of an intensive or excessive action, composed of the Imperative second person form of a root repeated, followed by a verbal form of the same in any tense of the Indicative and in any person or number; as खाद खादेति खादति, lit. "eat, eat, he eats," *i. e.* eats much, कुरु कुर्विति करोति "do, do, he does," *i. e.* does much. This expression exists in Marâṭhî and is considered so colloquial that no Marâṭhî grammarian has noticed it, as खा खा खातो, कर कर करतो, in which, as in Sanskrit, खा and कर are forms of the Imperative second person singular. A similar expression is used when several actions are attributed to the same agent; as ओदनं भुङ्क्ष्व सक्तून् पिब धानाः खादेत्येवायमभ्यवहरति "eat rice, drink barley water, devour fried grain, in this way he fills his stomach"; which in Marâṭhî is भात जेव पेज पी लाह्या खा असें पोट भरतो. In this case the Indicative should signify a general action of which the Imperatives denote the species, and we may have here करोति "does" instead of अभ्यवहरति. Similarly those innumerable expressions consisting of a form made up by adding अम्, technically णमुल्, to a root, preceded by a noun, and of a verbal form of the same root must be colloquial; as हस्तग्राहं गृह्णाति "holds by the hand," जीवनाशं नश्यति "he perishes," उदरपूरं भुङ्क्ते "eats a stomachful," यथाकारमहं भोक्ष्ये तथाकारं भोक्ष्ये किं तवानेन "I will eat as I eat (as I like), what have you to do with it?" &c. Etymologically हस्तग्राहम्, जीवनाशम् &c. are accusatives, and they may in these cases be called cognate accusatives, and the expressions somewhat resemble such ones in English, as "run a race," "walk a walk," "die a death," &c. The compounds दण्डादण्डि, केशाकेशि &c. meaning "a scuffle in which there is a brandishing of sticks and seizing each other by the hair;" and a great many others made up of Imperative forms of verbs, or of a verb and its object, which are used as nouns, are of a nature suited for the purposes of a light conversation; as अत्र खादतमोदता वर्तते "'eat and enjoy' is the rule here," अत्राश्नीतपिबता वर्तते "'eat and drink' is the rule here," उद्धरोत्सृजा तस्य दानशौण्डीरस्य गृहे "'take out and give' is what takes place in the house of that bountiful man," जहिस्तम्बोयम् "he is one who constantly says, 'strike the sheafs of corn'", एहिस्वागता वर्तते "'come, welcome to thee' is the practice", &c.

Sanskrit was not the only language spoken in the times of Kâtyâyana and Patañjali. In the Mahâbhâshya there are several passages which contain allusions to a dialect arising from a corruption of Sanskrit. Thus, in the comment on the Vârtika *Siddhe S'abdârthasaṃbandhe*, we are told, with reference to the question, whether words are created or exist of themselves, that Pâṇini's rules suppose that they are not created but exist of themselves; and so is the relation between them and the things they denote, *i. e.* their power of expression, uncreated and self-existent; and, according to another interpretation of the Vârtika, the things also which words denote are so. How is it known that all these are self-existent? Because in the affairs of the world or in ordinary life men think of certain things and use words to express them; they do not set about producing words before doing so. But this is not the case with those things that are created and not self-existent. If a man wishes to do something with an earthen pot, he goes to the house of a potter and says, "Make a pot for me, I have to do something by its means." Now, if he has to use words, he does not in the same way go to the house of a grammarian and say, "Make words, I want to use them"; but immediately that he thinks of this thing and that he uses words [for expressing them]. Well then, if words are to be taken from ordinary life [and are not made by grammarians], what is it that the Śâstra [grammar] does? "The Śâstra lays down a restriction by observing which a man may attain religious merit. It does what other Śâstras in ordinary life do. Thus, while it is possible to satisfy hunger by eating anything whatever, it is enjoined that one shall not eat a domesticated fowl or pig; and the object is, that he may by regulating his conduct thus attain religious merit. In the same way this Śâstra (grammar) tells us that, while it is possible to express one's meaning by using correct words or incorrect words, correct ones alone which it teaches should be used to secure the religious merit arising therefrom." After this follows the discussion translated in the first lecture; and then we have another of which the following is a portion:—

PÛRV. Does religious merit arise from a knowledge of correct words or from their use?

SID. What is the difference?

PÛRV. If you say religious merit arises from their knowledge, religious demerit also must arise. For he, who knows what words are correct, also knows what words are incorrect. If merit results from the knowledge of those that are correct, demerit must result from the knowledge of those that are incorrect. Or greater demerit must arise [from their knowledge], as the number of incorrect words is larger, and that of correct words smaller. For the corruption of one correct word are manifold; as, for instance, the corruptions of the correct word गो are गावी, गोणी, गोता, गोपोतलिका &c. And the Ṛishi also indicates (in a passage which is quoted) that the restriction as to correct words concerns their use [and not knowledge].

SID. Well, then, let it be that religious merit arises from their use [and not from knowledge].

PÛRV. If from their use the whole world would obtain heavenly felicity.

SID. And now why should you be jealous if the whole world obtain heavenly felicity?

PÛRV. No, certainly, I am not jealous. But what I mean is, that it thus becomes useless to make any effort; such effort only as is fruitful should be made. If you get the fruit without any effort, the effort is useless. [The effort meant is that involved in the study of grammar, *i. e.* of correct words. People use some correct words at least without studying grammar, and, if eternal felicity results from the *use* of such words, they get it without making the effort of studying the subject.]

SID. Why, verily those who make the effort will largely use correct words, and will obtain a large amount of heavenly felicity.

PÛRV. That the fruit does not follow the effort is also an observed fact. For there are persons who though they have made the effort are seen to be incompetent [in the use of correct words], while others, who have not, are competent; wherefore it is possible, the fruit, *i. e.* heavenly felicity, may not follow.

SID. Well then, religious merit arises not from knowledge alone, neither from use alone.

PÛRV. From what then?

SID. Heavenly felicity arises from the use of correct words when it is accompanied by the knowledge, that they are correct, derived from a study of the Śâstra.

And thus it goes on.

Now it is clear from all this that correct words, *i. e.* Sanskrit, was spoken in those days by all, but that incorrect words had got mixed up with it, and the object of grammar was to teach how to avoid incorrect words or corruptions, though there were men who could speak correctly without knowing grammar. And this is the state in which more or less all languages are at all times; and even at the present day the purpose of grammar is considered to be to teach how to speak correctly. By the way, it will be seen how Sanskrit grammarians distinctly declare that they teach nothing that does not exist, they do not create words, but separate the correct ones from such as are incorrect. But what did Patañjali consider to be the standard of correct Sanskrit, who was it that spoke the language correctly, and in whose speech were corruptions observable? This is clear from another passage at the beginning of the third pâda of the first chapter of the Mahâbhâshya. Patañjali interprets the sûtra भूवादयो धातवः (I, iii, 1.) in a manner to yield such a connotative definition of a dhâtu or root as this, that a dhâtu is that which denotes action or being. Then a question is raised, if this is the way to distinguish a root why should a list of roots be given; in other words, if we have got a connotative definition, a definition by enumeration is not wanted. In this case there is a difference of opinion between Kâtyâyana and Patañjali.

PÛRV. If you have given a connotative definition now, enumeration should not be made, *i. e.* a list of roots should not be given.

SID. It should be made.

PÛRV. What for?

SID. The enumeration of [the verbal roots] bhû and others should be made for the purpose of excluding nouns (prâtipadika) and the verbs that begin with आणपयति. [*i. e.* If the roots are not actually enumerated, nouns also which express action or being may come under the connotative definition. In the same way it will extend to roots used in ordinary life, which are not Sanskrit, such as आणपयति and others.]

PÛRV. What verbs are those which begin with आणपयति?

SID. आणपयति, वट्टति and वड्ढति. And enumeration should also be made in order that the anubandhas or indicatory letters and accents of roots may be made known; *i. e.* that one may know what the accents and indicatory letters of roots are. It is not possible to know the accents or indicatory letters unless the roots are enumerated. [Anubandhas are certain letters attached to roots to denote some conjugational or other peculiarity belonging to them.]

PÛRV. Now those roots whose accents are capable of being inferred, *i. e.*, are उदात्त, and which have no anubandhas, but still are inserted in the list, may be omitted from it. [*i. e.* When those roots which have the अनुदात्त accent are enumerated, it may be inferred that the rest have the other or उदात्त accent.]

SID. Even those should be enumerated in order that आणपयति and others [*i. e.*, corrupt Sanskrit roots] may be excluded.

Hereupon Patañjali disagrees with Kâtyâyana and says:—

PAT. No, आणपयति and others will be excluded, because the usage of the educated or Śishṭas is to be followed. This usage of the Śishṭas must be necessarily referred to in other cases even; for instance, in order to exclude the altered forms of those roots that are enumerated. For in ordinary life they use कसि for कृषि and दिसि for दृशि. [The sense is, that since in grammar we follow the usage of the Śishṭas or educated, these verbs आणपयति, वट्टति and वड्ढति, and also कसि for कृषि and दिसि for दृशि which are not used by them will necessarily be excluded from our connotative definition; hence for the purpose of excluding them enumeration is not wanted.]

Now आणपयति is a corruption of the Sanskrit आज्ञापयति, वट्टति of वर्तते, and वड्ढति of वर्धते, ते *Âtm.* being replaced by ति *Parasm.*, and कस् of कृष्, and दिस् of दृश्. These and such other corruptions were in use at the time, but Patañjali clearly lays down that they were not used by the Śishṭas or educated people, and therefore they belonged to the language of the vulgar. Now all these roots are found in the Pâli in these very forms, आणपयति being, however, आणापयति; but the reading in the MSS. and the Benares lithographed edition which I have consulted is faulty. So also of the corruptions of the word गो given by our author, we find गावी in Professor Childers's Pâli Dictionary, and गोण the masculine of गोणी. Thus our grammarians recognise one language only, the Sanskrit, and these words and forms which are found in the Pâli they assign to the speech of the vulgar.

In another passage still we are told more definitely who the Śishṭas were that spoke the Sanskrit language correctly without studying Pâṇini's grammar, and whose usage was the standard of correctness. Pâṇini's Sûtra VI. iii, 109, lays down that such words as पृषोदर should be regarded as correct in the form in which they are *upadishṭa*, *i. e.*, used or uttered; the changes in them such as the elision, or augmentation, of letters or the alteration of their forms do not obey any general rules laid down by him, but still the words exhibiting those changes should be taken as correct, just as they are used. Now the Pûrvapakshin raises the question.

PÛRV. What is meant by *upadishṭa* ?

SID. Uttered (used).

PÛRV. How does it come to mean that?

SID. The root 'dis'' signifies 'uttering.' One utters (uses), letters, and says that they are thus *upadishṭa.*

PÛRV. By whom *upadishṭa* (uttered or used) ?

SID. By the Śishṭas.

PÛRV. Who are the Śishṭas ?

SID. The grammarians.

PÛRV. How so ?

SID. The character of a Śishṭa is conferred upon one by the knowledge of the science (Śâstra) ; and the grammarians know the science [of grammar].

PÛRV. If a man is made Śishṭa by the science, and the science depends upon a man's being Śishṭa, this is reasoning in a circle. An argument in a circle does not hold. [The circle is, one is Śishṭa, and consequently an authority in matters of language if he has studied grammar ; and grammar itself depends on the usage of the Śishṭas.]

SID. Well, then, the character of a Śishṭa is conferred upon one by the country in which he lives and by his conduct. That sort of conduct must be associated with residence in Âryâvarta alone (lit. that sort of conduct must be in Âryâvarta alone).

PÛRV. Which is Âryâvarta ?

SID. The country which is to the east of the Âdarśa, west of Kâlakavana, south of the Himâlaya, and north of the Pâriyâtra. Those Brahmans in this country of the Âryas who do not store up riches (lit. who keep only so much grain as is contained in a jar), who are not greedy, who do good disinterestedly, and who without any effort are conversant with a certain branch of knowledge are the worshipful Śishṭas.

PÛRV. If, then, the Śishṭas are an authority as regards language, what function does the Ashṭâdhyâyî (Pâṇini's grammar) perform?

SID. The purpose of the Ashṭâdhyâyî is to enable us to find out the Śishṭas.

PÛRV. How is it possible to find out the Śishṭas by means of the Ashṭâdhyâyî?

SID. A student of the Ashṭâdhyâyî finds a man who has not studied the book using words just as they are taught in the Ashṭâdhyâyî. He then thinks, "Verily, this man possesses some good luck or innate nature by means of which, though he has not studied the Ashṭâdhyâyî, he uses words just as they are taught in that book. Verily he knows other words also" [not taught in the Ashṭâdhyâyî, such as पृषोदर]. Thus, the purpose of the Ashṭâdhyâyî is to enable one to find out who is a Śishṭa [in order that he may refer to him and learn such words as do not obey the rules laid down by Pâṇini, but still are correct].

Here then we have the clearest possible evidence that Sanskrit was the vernacular of holy or respectable Brahmans of Âryâvarta or Northern India, who could speak the language correctly without the study of grammar. The corrupt language mentioned by Patañjali which was composed of correct and incorrect words, that is, a dialect like the Pâli, must, therefore, have been the vernacular of the other classes. And this is what you may say even with regard to the modern vernaculars. Who is it that speaks good or correct Marâṭhî? Of course, Brahmans of culture. The language of the other classes is not correct Marâṭhî. The word Śishṭa may be translated by "a man of education or culture;" and this education or culture has, since remote times, been almost confined to Brahmans. Thus the dialects of the inscriptions of Aśoka and the Pâli were the vernaculars of the non-Brahmanic classes; but a greater importance must evidently have been attached to them in the times of Aśoka than is now assigned to the Marâṭhî of the non-Brahmanic classes, since they are used by him in the inscriptions. They are, however, not recognized as independent languages by our grammarians who treated them as we treat the Marâṭhî of the lower classes; but they were in use and bore the same relation to Sanskrit that low Marâṭhî does to high Marâṭhî, the English of the lower classes in England to the speech of the higher. And the English of the lower classes contains, as we have seen, a great many such grammatical forms as "I knowed," and "you says," along with others that are correct.

It is on account of the mixture of such correct words and forms with others that were incorrect that the Pâli was not regarded as an independent dialect. The case was different with the Prâkṛits. They assumed a more settled and fixed character, and were used over a larger area, and thus came to be considered and treated as separate languages. But the propagators of Buddhism, who, like all teachers of a new religion, addressed themselves to the lower or uneducated classes, soon raised this speech into importance. They wrote their religious works in it, and in the course of time it became their sacred language; but it is unknown in India as an independent tongue. From these passages in the Mahâbhâshya, therefore, it is clear that it is by no means true, as is generally supposed, that Sanskrit had ceased to be a spoken language when the Pâli arose. The two varieties of speech existed side by side; but as education and culture retrograded the number of Sanskrit speakers gradually decreased, and the lower variety went on spreading itself over a wider area, and developed into the Prâkṛits.

This contemporaneous existence of the Sanskrit and the Pâli and the Prâkṛits as the spoken languages of two classes of the community explains, and is therefore confirmed by, several facts that we noticed before. If when the Pâli arose Sanskrit became a dead language, it could not influence the grammar of the low dialects. Though words from a language that has ceased to be spoken may be adopted into a spoken dialect, the grammar remains intact. Even a living language, if it is foreign, does not affect it. But we have seen that the gradual disappearance of verbal forms is a phenomenon common to both Sanskrit and the Prâkṛits, and that the latter derived some grammatical forms from the former, which they did not possess when they were in the stage represented by the Pâli. This could not have been the case if the two languages, Sanskrit and Pâli, had not existed as two varieties of the varnacular of a homogeneous community. The fact that Sanskrit words are so greatly corrupted as to be difficult of recognition and are set down as Deśyas by the native grammarians, while others can easily be traced to their original forms, also points to the same conclusion. Those that are greatly corrupted were early adopted into the language, and removed from subsequent influence. Most of the others, that exhibit only the ordinary changes, are such as denote elementary notions, and must therefore have been adopted as early as those of the first sort. But, because they were such elementary words, they were heard again and again in their original forms as used by the higher classes; and thus a further corruption was prevented; and they exhibit only such changes as were necessitated by the vocal habits of the Prâkṛit speakers. Another fact is the use of Sanskrit for the higher characters in the plays, and of Prâkṛit for women and the lower ones. This supposes that when the idea first originated, and for a considerable period subseqnent to it, though not afterwards when dramatic plays were written more according to rule than with a view to exhibit any existing state of things, women and persons in a low condition could understand Sanskrit, but not speak it. It was the same with Sanskrit then, as it is with Marâṭhî, for instance, now. A Chitpâvnî or Mâlvaṇî woman speaks in her own dialect when conversing with an educated Marâṭhâ, but understands the standard Marâṭhî that he uses, though she cannot speak it hereself. And this is the case everywhere; a person in a low condition understands what is said to him by one belonging to the higher classes, but cannot himself speak like him, and must use his own variety of the language. Thus then at the time, when the earliest Sanskrit dramatic plays were written, that language must have been in vernacular use to such an extent as to be intelligible to uneducated persons. And that educated dramatic characters do actually speak it shows that those whom they represent used it in real life. Again, the dramas were composed to entertain an audience, and were actually acted. If the audience did not understand Sanskrit, as woll as Prâkṛit, the poet defeated his own purpose by making some of his characters speak in that language.

Sanskrit went on gradually losing ground, the number of those who spoke it grew smaller and smaller, and after a time it ceased to be used by anybody for the ordinary concerns of life, though even now Pandits carry on their disputations in it. But at all times it has been acting the parent to the vernaculars and adorning and enriching them. The ancient Prâkṛits borrowed everything from it when it was in vernacular use; but the moderns mostly adopt such words as express abstract notions. There is, however, an apparent difference in the manner in which the borrowed words were treated by the Prâkṛits, and are treated by the modern dialects. A Sanskrit word when used by a Prâkṛit-speaking person was changed according to his habits of pronunciation; but in modern times it is preserved in a state of purity. This, however, is due to the fact that in modern times the educated classes as well as their uneducated brethren speak the vernaculars, and it is the former that pronounce the word properly. But the latter, and often women belonging to the former, corrupt it. Now the Prâkṛit was, as I have shown, for a long time the language of precisely these persons. It is their pronunciation that is recorded by the Prâkṛit grammarians and poets. In some provinces in modern times even the higher classes mispronounce the Sanskrit words adopted into the vernaculars, and also in reading Sanskrit books. But in the printed books the correct orthography is used. As I have observed in a previous lecture and at the beginning of this, some of the vocal habits of the Prâkṛit speakers have come down to their modern descendants; but not all. The lapse of time and other causes have generated other peculiarities. Hence a Sanskrit word in these days is not corrupted in exactly the same way as in ancient times; and thus we get what are called modern Tadbhavas. Thus, then, as the Sindhî and the Bangâlî cannot but pronounce Sanskrit मोक्ष as मोक्ख, and the Hindustâni as मोछ, or the average Gujarâtî, the Sanskrit word मौन as मोन and जैन as जेन, so did his old Prâkṛit ancestors. It should be borne in mind that the Prâkṛit corruptions of Sanskrit words were not necessarily caused by their continual use for a number of ages, but were due in a good many cases to the vocal peculiarities of the men that used them. Most of those words that represent only the ordinary changes are words of this class, *i. e.* the corruptions simply represent, as I have above observed, the transformation which they underwent in the mouth of a Prâkṛit speaker. At all times Sanskrit words have been coming into the popular languages, but in old times they were pronounced in a manner natural to the men of those times, and thus became Prâkṛit words; and now they are pronounced in some cases in the same manner, but in a great many in another, and thus they become modern Tadbhavas; while the educated classes often, though not always, pronounce them correctly, and thus we have modern Tatsamas. This is the way to account for the fact that there are so many pure Sanskrit words in our vernaculars, while there were but a few in the old Prâkṛits; and we need not connect their introduction with the expulsion of Buddhism and the selfish schemes of the Brâhmans, with which it has nothing to do, as is done by one writer.

We will now try to form some idea of the chronology and historical causes of the several linguistic changes we have noticed.

The later or classical Sanskrit is in the same phonetic condition as the Vedic dialect from which it sprang; and it was for a long succession of centuries spoken by the Indian Aryans. If it was so, the corruptions observable in the other variety of speech or low Sanskrit, as it may be called, must have been due to the vocal peculiarities of another race than that which elaborated the classical from the Vedic Sanskrit. The universal assimilation of conjunct consonants which we observe in the Pâli could not have proceeded from the same community that could speak Sanskrit with purity. And such an extensive assimilation we find in the Italian which was formed out of the Latin spoken by the lower classes of the ancient Roman population by the barbarian races that overran the country. As remarked in the opening lecture, phonetic corruption is rapid and extensive when one race learns and adopts the language of another. The Pâli corruptions, therefore, represent the manner in which a foreign race pronounced the Sanskrit of the Aryans. And from such history as we can glean from Sanskrit literature we know that the Aryan race when it emigrated to India came in contact with other races. After a time some of these were incorporated into the Aryan community, and formed its fourth order, known by the name of Śûdras. As long as these Śûdras were in a thoroughly degraded condition and remained distinct from the other three orders, their speech produced no perceptible effect on that of the latter. But after a time this order began to mingle with the rest, principally by means of intermarriages which must have extensively taken place, since some *Smṛitis* or Indian law-books allow them under certain circumstances and others prohibit them; so that the orthodox belief of learned Pandits at the present day is that the Kshatriya and Vaiśya orders do not exist, and that all those who are not Brahmans are Śûdras. But there are indications that even Brahmanhood did not escape pollution. As this combination proceeded, the Śûdra corruptions of the language came into prominence, and after a time such a language as the Pâli became the ordinary speech of the uneducated. By the time of Aśoka, we may suppose, the so-called Aśishṭa or uneducated people, who spoke the incorrect, or corrupt language, comprehended among them the greater portion of the military, trading, and cultivating classes. Professor Childers is of opinion that there are no Des'ya or non-Aryan words in the Pâli. But the Prâkṛits do possess some at least; and you will remember that they exhibit other phonetic changes of which the chief is the elision of consonants. Up to the time of As'oka and even to that of

Patañjali these phenomena are not observable in the popular speech; though they may have existed in the speech of the very lowest classes. It, therefore, appears that, when this amalgamated community, with Sanskrit and Pâli as the two forms of speech prevailing among the higher and the lower classes, spread over different parts of Northern India from the Himâlayas to the southern confines of the Marâṭhâ country, they came in contact in the provinces with other races which led to the further corruptions we have been speaking of; and thus the Prâkṛits were formed. These new races while they adopted the language of the conquerors gave them a few of their own words.

Patañjali lived in the middle of the second century before Christ and king Aśoka in the middle of the third. Between Patañjali and Kâtyâyana a pretty long time must have elapsed, since in the Mahâbhâshya various readings or emendations in a few cases of the Vârtikas of the latter are noticed and sometimes their interpretations as given by other writers; so that a sort of literature must have grown round the Vârtikas. I am, therefore, inclined to accept the popular tradition which refers Kâtyâyana to the period of the Nandas, *i.e.*, to about the first quarter of the fourth century before Christ. Now we have seen that in the time of this grammarian the Sanskrit language assumed a different form from that it had in that of Pâṇini; and by the time of Patañjali very great reverence had come to be paid to this last author. For in giving the uses of grammar the author of the Mahâbhâshya says that it is the duty of a Brâhman to study the Vedas along with their *aṅgas* or illustrative *S'âstras*; and of the six *aṅgas* grammar is the chief. Patañjali is not likely to yield this honour to any other than Pâṇini's grammar. To account for these and some of the other circumstances noticed by Dr. Goldstücker we must place Pâṇini about four centuries before Kâtyâyana, *i. e.* refer him to about the 8th century before Christ. Yâska must have flourished a short time before him. Though the Pâli or an idiom very close to it was the language of the uneducated classes in the times of Kâtyâyana, Aśoka, and Patañjali, still its formation must be dated some centuries earlier, since in its verb it represents what I have called Middle Sanskrit or Sanskrit of Yâska and Pâṇini. Yâska notices local varieties of Sanskrit words, and gives one or two instances, but makes no allusion to any apabhraṁs'as or corruptions, though from the nature of his work he may be expected to do so; while Kâtyâyana and Patañjali mention them frequently, as we have seen. Even if they existed in his time, therefore, they must have been insignificant and unimportant, and did not enter into the speech of any class of the Aryan society to any appreciable extent. After his time, however, *i. e.* about the seventh or sixth century B. C., the elaboration of the Pâli, or low Sanskrit as it might be called, began in a decided manner; and the language continued to be spoken up to the time of Patañjali. Till then it did not specifically assume a Prâkṛit form, though in the inscriptions of Aśoka some of the characteristics of a later Prâkṛit, the Mâgadhî, were developed, as we have seen, in one province, very likely Magadha itself. The Prâkṛits must have begun to be formed about that time, but they did not then attain any distinctive character; and the vernacular speech probably did not finally leave the Pâli stage till a very long time afterwards. About the time when the inscriptions in the cave-temples were composed, the Pâli was, as I have stated, a sacred and literary language. The longer and more important of the inscriptions are therefore in that language. But in a good many of the shorter inscriptions, especially of private individuals, we have words exhibiting Prâkṛit characteristics.* The growth of the specific Prâkṛits, therefore, must be referred to the early centuries of the Christian era; and we may therefore infer that about the time our first dramatic plays were written they were actually the spoken dialects of those classes of the people whose representatives use them in those works. About the sixth or seventh century the Apabhraṁśa was developed in the country in which the Brajabhâshâ prevails in modern times; or, if the speeches in that dialect contained in the fourth Act of the Vikramorvaśî were really composed by Kâlidâsa, which, as remarked in a former lecture, we have the gravest reasons for doubting, its growth must be assigned to a somewhat earlier period. Daṇḍin mentions the Apabhraṁśa, and a good many verses from his Kâvyâdarśa are found in Vâmana's Alaṁkâravṛitti; and if this be the same Vâmana that lived at the court of Jayâpîḍa, king of Kaśmîr, who reigned from 751 A. C. to 782 A. C., Daṇḍin must have flourished before the eighth century. The modern vernaculars seem to have begun to assume a distinctive character about the tenth century. In the copperplate inscription containing the name of Bhâskarâchârya, dated 1128 Śaka or 1206 A. C., which I once

---

* Such are काणभोअस for काणभांजस्य, पवइतिकाअ for प्रव्रजितिकायाः, महाभोयस for महाभोजस्य, भयंत for भदन्त, वेयिका for वेदिका, पडिक for प्रतिक &c.

mentioned before, Marâṭhî appears in its specific character, and so also does Hindî in the work of Chand, who flourished about the same time.

And now, gentlemen, I close. It was impossible in the course of these lectures to do justice to the subject without entering into matters which are not interesting, except to those who have already paid some attention to it. Besides, the subject was wide, and I was compelled to compress a great many facts into a small space, but in spite of this and though I frequently omitted large portions of what I had written, the lectures were long and tedious. I am, therefore, obliged to you for the honour you have done me by your presence here, notwithstanding these drawbacks, and my thanks are specially due to those who have attended the course throughout.